MANUFACTURING

A Study of Industrial Location

MANUFACTURING

A STUDY OF INDUSTRIAL LOCATION

E. Willard Miller

The Pennsylvania State University Press
University Park and London

Library of Congress Cataloging in Publication Data

Miller, E. Willard, 1915–
   Manufacturing. A study of industrial location.

   Includes index.
   1.   Industries, Location of.   2.   Industries,
Location of—United States.   I.   Title.
HD58.M47   338'.09   76-1849
ISBN 0-271-01224-2

Figures 1.14, 1.15, 1.16, 1.17, 1.18, 1.19, 1.20, and 1.21 redrawn from
Location and Space Economy by Walter Isard by permission of The M.I.T.
Press, Cambridge, Massachusetts.

Tables 2.7, 2.8, 2.9, 2.10, and 2.11 from *The Elements of Input-Output
Analysis*, by William H. Miernyk. Copyright 1965 by Random House, Inc.
Copyright 1957 by Northeastern University. Reprinted by permission of the
publisher.

CONTENTS

PREFACE

This study is devoted to providing the concepts necessary to an understanding of the localization of manufacturing. There is thus an attempt to analyze and interpret from both a theoretical and an empirical viewpoint the diverse forces that shape spatial industrial patterns. A dynamic approach is used to analyze the development of industrial theory through time and the way in which locational patterns change over time. Although theory plays an important part in this book, it is recognized that reality in spatial industrial location is still only vaguely perceived by existing theory. As a consequence emphasis is placed on factors of localization as they directly influence the spatial pattern of manufacturing in the world.

The book is divided into three parts. Part I analyzes industrial location theory beginning with the classical partial equilibrium and general equilibrium theories and follows the evolution to modern-day theoretical approaches. Part II provides the foundation for the development of empirical models through the study of the factors of localization. Because the book is fundamentally concerned with the actual localization of manufacturing, Part III provides a spatial analysis of industrial location for eight selected industries. Thus this book provides a theoretical and empirical foundation for the study of industrial location, which is then applied to the localization of selected industries.

In any work of this nature, the author must rely heavily on material already published; the present work is no exception. For example, the material in Part I has been selected from several thousand pages of writings on location theory extending over nearly a century. An extensive reference section is provided at the end of each part. It is hoped that this book will encourage the reader to penetrate to a greater depth the study of industrial location. There is no claim to completeness or even rigor. The mathematical level of the material is elementary. The tools and techniques utilized in this book have been selected to contribute to the analysis of the spatial pattern of manufacturing.

This book is meant to be useful to such individuals as the industrial geographer, city and regional planner, regional scientist, industrial analyst, management scientist, and economist. The material presented is pertinent to such courses as industrial geography, geography of manufacturing, location theory, economic geography, regional economics, planning techniques, methods of regional analysis, and other related areas.

I wish to make several specific acknowledgments. An invaluable contribution has been made by my students, who were challenging and stimulated me to pursue this study. I am greatly indebted to my colleagues, scattered throughout the world, who have also provided intellectual motivation. To my secretaries, I owe a special debt of gratitude for invaluable assistance and seemingly endless typing and retyping of the manuscript. A special word of appreciation is given to my graduate assistants for their never ending willingness to search for the most elusive wisps of information. Finally, I dedicate this book to my wife, not only for her able assistance but also for her inspiration.

E. Willard Miller

INTRODUCTION

The term *manufacturing* means those activities by which man changes the form or nature of raw materials, converting them into useful products. These transforming activities may be performed as operations in factories or in homes, as handicraft industries. In any case, raw materials are brought from various sources to the place of processing and the finished products go to diverse market regions.

WHAT IS "INDUSTRIAL LOCALIZATION"?

What features of manufacturing are significant from the viewpoint of spatial analysis? The industrial locationist is interested primarily in three aspects of manufacturing: its pattern of distribution, its relationship to other elements within its region of location, and its relationship to other regions.

The relationships both within the region of location and to other regions are observable in terms of the association of manufacturing activities with certain other elements. Some of these are physical, such as raw materials, power resources, surface configurations, and climate. Others are cultural elements resulting from human activities, for example, labor supply, markets, transportation, subsidies, and the ever increasing role of governmental regulations.

Factories that characterize industrial regions may be interrelated: Some may supply semifinished items to other factories; others may be branch plants; and still others may have a service relationship, such as a power plant that supplies electrical energy to other factories. A relationship also exists between factories and manufactural elements. For example, the factory may procure raw materials in the local region, a natural power source may be present, a portion of the factory's sales may be made locally, most of its labor probably resides there, and favorable transportation facilities may be present. On the other hand a factory affects other elements within its region. Thus the relationships existing within the region of location are two-way entities, in which certain elements affect manufacturing and manufacturing in turn affects certain elements. The significance of manufacturing to its region of location is a question of constant concern to the industrial location planner.

The relationship between an industrial region and other regions is expressed in terms of market areas, transportation routes and services, freight rates, raw materials, and power supplies. The bonds of association may tie the industrial region to other manufacturing regions, which may be related through a common market for manufactured goods or because they are source regions sending raw materials or fuels to the factories.

Because the industrial location analyst is concerned with spatial relationships, his main emphasis in studying manufacturing is on industrial location and the factors by which manufacturing is related to other elements that also differ in spatial distribution—whether the elements occur within the immediate industrial region or in other regions and whether they supply factories or factories supply them.

LOCATIONAL STUDIES OF MANUFACTURING

Locational studies of manufacturing may be approached from a number of viewpoints. Basically these studies should describe, analyze, and interpret manufacturing in such terms as pattern, amount, type of production, and locational factors. Such items as these are fundamental characteristics that differentiate regions of manufacturing.

Emphasis must also be placed on the relationships that tie manufacturing to other elements in its region of location. Questions such as the following can be raised: What percentage of the region's labor force is employed by manufacturing? How much labor resides within the area? Is the labor force stable, or does it have characteristics that might cause manufacturing to seek more favorable areas? How significant is the region's market to the region's manufacturing? Does the region supply any raw materials or power? What is the transportation situation? What local forces influence the development of manufacturing?

Relationships between a manufacturing region and other regions are analyzed by such factors as those relating to markets, raw materials, power, labor, and transportation. The study of costs is significant because manufacturing is an economic activity that ceases when costs become too high. In fact the fundamental reason for spatial differentiation in the location of manufacturing is the spatial differentiation in costs of manufactural operations. Moreover, facts on costs enable the drawing of comparisons between different regions of manufacturing.

An understanding of trends as to how manufacturing began in a region, how it has progressed, and what it can be expected to do in the future is essential in evaluating the importance of industry in a region. Studies of such trends also help to distinguish regions where industry is expanding from regions where it is not.

There are other questions that can be raised that are pertinent in identifying a geographic approach to a manufactural study. Factual information is not enough. Only part of the picture is revealed when it is determined that a community has X amount of iron and steel industry which feeds on coal from one source, iron ore from another, and local limestone and water, or that it sells its product in certain market regions. Just as important are such questions as these: What are the problems the industry faces in a particular region? To what degree does it compete successfully with industries in other regions? In what respect is it handicapped by such physical features as terrain and climate? To what extent is it handicapped by such economic and cultural features as public attitudes, transportation services, and available labor?

Other types of problems involve those factors created by the industry's activities. What problems exist in the area because a particular type of industry is located there? How does manufacturing affect the life of a community? An understanding of such problems may enable the location analyst to conclude that some other region would be more desirable for the industry. Applications of geographic analysis are fundamental to all plans in locating branch factories or new plants. For example, geographic analysis has been basic to an understanding of the regional shift of entire industries, such as the decision of cotton textile producers to de-emphasize operations in New England in favor of expansion in the Piedmont. Business executives, research men, and specialists in the field can make more precise proposals for the future location of manufacturing if they apply geographic techniques to the problems of industrial location.

Locational studies focused on manufacturing may be of several types. The *industrial* study centers on a single industry. It may be a broad industry, such as food, leather, or metal fabricated products. Or it may be a specialized industry, such as cane sugar refining, women's gloves, or electronics. Whatever the scope of the industry, study is directed toward the factors that affect its location and the geographic relationships it is involved in.

The *regional* study focuses on a single region of manufacturing. It may be a broad region, such as a nation or a state; it may be more restricted, such as a metropolitan area or a core area within a city. Whatever the extent, attention is directed toward the patterns of manufacturing in the region, the industries that compose the industrial complex, and the associations relating to it.

A geographic study of an *individual factory* explains the relationships between that factory and two types of regions, those that affect the factory and those that the factory affects. The same region may be represented in both instances. The first type of region supplies the factory with such things as demand for its product, raw materials, power, labor, buildings, subsidies, or other necessities. The region may be the local territory in close proximity to the industrial plant, or it may include territories at a considerable distance. The second type of region results from the factory's existence. It rarely exceeds the local territory because it is in the home community that such effects as smoke nuisance, traffic and parking problems, workers' housing, and workers' demands for trade, schools, and other services all give evidence of how that factory is affecting the community.

A *location factor* study is centered on a particular relationship by which manufacturing is tied to its local region or a distant region. The relationship may be with raw materials, markets, labor, freight rates, or various other factors. The purpose is to show how a particular factor operates in the location and development of manufacturing.

A study of *potential manufacturing areas* is a predictive effort to discover regions that would be suitable for the location of manufacturing (or for additional manufacturing if some already exists). It postulates the character of possible relationships in the manufacturing process.

Location theory studies have been undertaken primarily by economists such as Weber, Lösch, Hoover, Isard, and Greenhut. From the practical viewpoint, their studies remain in the formative stage. There is a fundamental need to develop "concepts at a more meaningful level of abstraction so as to make possible the understanding of the whole economic system and to provide a conceptual framework into which to put the microdescriptions."[1]

The manufactural problems pertaining to location theory can best be studied from a hierarchy of elemental and field theories and working hypotheses.[2] At the initial level are theoretical studies that consider the spatial structure of manufacturing.

The second level of studies focuses on linkages between places in which different industrial structural elements fit together in interdependent spatial systems. The gravity model, which attempts to show that the movements between areas are in direct proportion to the products of the masses and inversely proportional to distance separating the areas raised to an exponent, has been a major tool in these studies. This model focuses on the urban center in the organization of spatial systems and attempts to relate the transportation networks to spatial distributions and relationships. Regrettably, an adequate theoretical base has not been provided for this model.

At the third level is the study of the dynamics in industrial spatial systems. The two approaches to this concept involve deterministic analysis and the utilization of stochastic processes. The first of these involves the simple extension of ideas of structure and functional organization. For example, if a system is in equilibrium, what changes will occur if one element is altered? The dynamics of spatial systems offers new dimensions to future locational studies of manufacturing.

[1]William Warntz, "Progress in Economic Geography," in Preston James, ed., *New Viewpoints in Geography*, Washington, D.C.: National Council for the Social Studies, 1959, p. 55.

[2]*The Science of Geography*, Washington, D.C.: National Academy of Sciences-National Research Council, Publication 1277, 1965.

I

INDUSTRIAL LOCATION THEORY

By the last part of the nineteenth century manufacturing was becoming widely dispersed throughout many sections of the world, especially in the United States and western Europe. As a result questions were being raised as to why particular localization patterns were evolving. Thus there was a growing need to provide general models to explain the origin of the evolving industrial patterns. A theoretical foundation was sought to understand the spatial aspects of manufacturing on a regional, or intranational, scale.

The major objective of Part I is to trace the principal threads in industrial location theory from its beginnings late in the nineteenth century to the present. Since its origin, the basic aim of location theory has been to provide the means of weighing the desirability of alternative locations.

The material of Part I begins with the classical location theories of Weber's least cost and Lösch's maximum profit conceptualizations and continues with the evaluations and elaborations of these pioneer studies. These classical theories followed the partial equilibrium approach. Thus they assumed a given set of conditions. Although each provided some intriguing concepts for viewing a locational situation, there was no attempt to approach reality. For example, the assumption in the least cost theory that the location and cost of raw materials were fixed is not justified in the real world.

When the least cost and maximum profit theories and their refinements did not provide a framework for understanding the establishment of alternative locations in the real world, other approaches were developed. Because the Weber approach neglected the market influences, a group of economists began to investigate the importance of the locational interdependence of firms. These concepts were based on the idea that a manufacturer had to recognize the importance of his competitors' markets. The constructs of such men as Palander, Hoover, Lerner, Singer, Smithies, and Ackley, however, although providing some interesting insights into the location of a manufacturing establishment, did not provide a set of locational principles.

The next stage in the evolution of industrial location theory involved the attempt to provide a general equilibrium approach. In the middle of the twentieth century, Isard and a group of fellow economists, regional economists, and geographers attempted to provide a unified theory that would be applied to industrial location. The major contribution of the general equilibrium theory has been the attempt to interrelate all factors in a dynamic setting. However, because of the complexity of the theory, it has been formulated only in abstract and mathematical models. As a result there have been few empirical studies attempting to test the validity of the concepts of general equilibrium theory.

Because the partial equilibrium theories have proved to be too simplistic and the general equilibrium theory too complex to provide models to explain reality, new thrusts have evolved. Whereas the past models were predominantly based on economic considerations, recent viewpoints are wider in concept; they recognize that factors other than economic factors play a role, possibly even a deciding role, in industrial location. Of the recent contributions, the behavioral theories have received the most attention. The assumption of the behavioral theorists is that locational decisions cannot be made from the perspective of complete economic rationality. Thus, because optimal decisions of industrial location are impossible, the best that can be achieved is a location that provides a satisfactory situation. Of these theories, Pred has provided a provocative statement for a geographic location theory based on a behavioral context. However, until his theory is tested by many more empirical studies, it remains an interesting abstraction.

A number of other theories that provide a potential for understanding industrial location problems are reviewed in Part I. The general systems, growth pole and growth center, economic base, stage, cycle, differential growth, concentration, agglomeration, and economic restriction theories have intrinsic appeal. Each adds an additional dimension to the study of industrial location. Although model building from these theories is still in the early stages, these new viewpoints provide additional perspectives.

To illustrate the contrasting theoretical frameworks that have evolved between the capitalist and socialist worlds, the evolution of industrial location theory in the Soviet Union will be reviewed briefly. The Soviets rejected Weber's least cost theory and its implication of immediate profit in favor of constructs that have as their basic goal the development of industry in a region with little or no regard for cost or profit. There is thus a basic philosophical difference between the industrial location theories of the capitalist and socialist worlds. The socialist theories are presented to illustrate a different theoretical approach to the localization of industry. Because the Soviet Union has developed the second largest industrial system in the world, it is important that Western theorists have an understanding of socialist industrial locational concepts.

Although industrial location theory has not evolved to a stage where locational principles or laws exist, theory does provide a basic framework for the investigation of locational problems. Thus theoretical concepts provide the basis for penetrating insights into the operation of the factors of industrial localization in the real world. Further, the theoretical framework may aid in the selection of pertinent factors in empirical analysis and interpretation of spatial patterns. Consequently theory sets the stage for the ultimate understanding of the manifold processes that determine the location of a particular industry.

EARLY LOCATION THEORIES

The earliest industrial location theories were developed in Germany. One of the most important of these was formulated in 1826 by Johann H. von Thunen, who was concerned with the optimum location for agricultural crops in relation to a city. Von Thunen's theory was formulated within a framework postulating an industrial city situated in a homogeneous plain having uniform resources. To formulate the theory, he assumed that the price of all agricultural products is uniform because price is determined within the city, that land rents are highest nearest the city and decrease with distance as land competition lessens, and that transportation costs increase with distance from the city. Thus land rents and transportation costs were the determinants that affect the type of agriculture which could be practiced. Although this theory was formulated to determine the least cost areas for agricultural crops, it provided a theoretical framework for later industrial location theory by utilizing the two variables of land rents and transportation costs.

In 1878 A. Schaffle presented the viewpoint that industry is attracted to particular towns in direct proportion to the ratio of the distances between them. Thus the larger towns attract the greatest amount of industry. This was one of the earliest uses of the gravity model in explaining the concentration of industry in the larger centers.[1] Schaffle suggested that the availability of raw materials or energy could change this type of localization.

Of the early theorists, Wilhelm Launhardt provided the most significant

---

[1]Schaffle's gravity model was expressed as follows:

$$M_{ij} = P_i P_j (dij)$$

where M_{ij} = market attraction of towns i and j
P_i and P_j = population of the two centers
dij = distance separating the two towns

contributions (30).[2] He explained the differences in the location of industry by variables in cost and demand factors at alternative locations. With differences in the cost of production, the market areas are modified in size and shape. Launhardt also developed the concept that the ton-mileage of raw material times the transport costs are of utmost importance in determining the cost of production at a particular location. He then introduced the idea that a manufacturer would locate at the point of least cost.

Launhardt also introduced the idea of the "locational triangle" to locate a factory; two points of the triangle represent raw material sources, and the third point represents the market. The least cost location of the factory was determined as the point within the triangle that was the shortest distance from each of the three points. He thus demonstrated the importance of transportation costs in the location of manufacturing. This was the basis for the theory of industrial location later developed by Alfred Weber.

Launhardt presented other ideas that were developed by later economists. One of the most significant was that a hexagon provided the ideal market area, but in reality the market areas tended to be irregular polygons with curves of the fourth degree as boundaries.

LEAST COST THEORY

Alfred Weber, a German economist, developed a pioneer comprehensive theory in 1909 for the location of manufacturing activities.[3] A number of assumptions were made in the Weberian least cost theory. The initial assumption is that there is an isolated country that is homogeneous as to physical conditions, technological development, political authority, and race of the people. Second, it is recognized that resources may not be evenly distributed; that is, certain resources are ubiquitous whereas others are localized. Third, labor is not uniformly distributed but is fixed at particular localities; thus labor does not possess mobility. Finally, transportation is a function of weight and distance, with rate increases directly proportional to the length of shipment and weight of the freight. Besides the quantifiable factors of cost of raw materials, labor, and transportation, Weber recognized another factor, which he called *agglomeration*. The agglomeration factor results from the social nature of production and cannot be discovered by analyzing an isolated process of production. Thus when social factors cause agglomeration, there is no way of determining what production costs will be at a particular place. Only empirical analysis can ascertain whether production costs will rise or decline.

[2]The numbers in parentheses refer to the Selected References at the end of each part; when a second number is given, it refers to the page in the reference.
[3]This section on the least cost theory has been taken from Alfred Weber, *Theory of the Location of Industries* (Chicago: University of Chicago Press, 1929).

Transport Costs

Because the two fundamental factors of transport costs, weight and distance, can be mathematically defined, Weber indicated that they provide the basis for abstract theory. However, besides weight and distance the cost of transport depends on the type of transportation system and the extent of its use, the nature of the locality, and the nature of the goods themselves (50–42).

LAWS OF TRANSPORT ORIENTATION. Weber postulated that if the weight and distance are the only determining factors, transportation costs will attract industrial production to those places where the fewest ton-miles originate during the entire process of production and distribution because transportation costs will be lowest at those points.

Before the location of processing can be considered, however, the nature of the raw materials and their transformation must be considered. Some raw materials are found everywhere; such materials are called "ubiquitous." Naturally ubiquitous materials can be located at any single place in limited quantities. However, when the local supply does not exceed the limits of the demand, they are termed "absolute ubiquities." If the demand does exceed local limits, they are "relative ubiquities" for the place. Other raw materials not found in the vicinity of consumption are considered to be "localized."

In regard to the nature of the transformation of raw materials into a product, a material enters into a product either with or without a residue. If there is no residue in processing the raw material, it is said to be "pure." If there is a residue, the raw material is said to be "gross." Thus a pure material imparts its total weight to the product whereas a gross material imparts only a part of its weight to the finished product.

Simple Applications. If there is a single raw material and a single market, there are three possible locations depending on the following conditions. If the raw material is ubiquitous, the processing will take place at the market in order to eliminate transport costs of the product. If the raw material is fixed in location but is pure, the processing will occur at either the raw material source or the market because there will be an equal transportation cost for moving either the raw material or the finished product. Finally, if the raw material is fixed and gross, the industry will locate at the source of the raw material to reduce the bulk and consequently the freight costs to the market.

LOCATIONAL TRIANGLE. The problem of location becomes more complex if, for example, there are two sources of raw materials and a single market. This situation is represented by Weber's use of the locational triangle. One corner of the triangle is the market, and the other two corners are the two most advantageous sources of raw materials. Assuming that only the transport cost influences the selection of the location, this locational figure gives the only possible mathematical basis of orientation. Consequently, the location of manufacturing, given two raw materials and a market, will depend on the transport costs of the raw material and the finished product.

A number of examples can demonstrate the simple application of the locational triangle. If the raw materials are fixed and pure, manufacturing will occur at the market. If the processing occurred at one of the raw material sources, there would be an additional transport cost to move the one raw material to the other raw material and then on to the market. But transportation costs dictate that both raw materials are moved directly to the market. The only exception to a market orientation would be if one raw material passed through another raw material source on its way to the market. In this situation, the processing of the raw material could occur with equal cost advantage at either the market or the raw material source nearest the market. In the situation in which one raw material is ubiquitous and a second raw material is fixed, the manufacturing will occur at the market. In this type of location, transport costs must be paid only on the movement of one raw material.

The problem becomes more complex if both raw materials are fixed and gross. In this situation, Weber utilized his locational triangle to its greatest advantage. To illustrate, let us suppose that to produce 1 ton of the product two raw material sources are required, each of which produces 1 ton of material (Fig. 1.1). "These weights represent the force with which the corners of the locational figures draw the location toward themselves, it being assumed that only weight and distance determine transportation cost. . . . It follows as a general principle that the location will be near the individual corners or far from them according to the relative weight of their locational components" (50–54).

To determine the exact location, a mechanical solution is possible by using the Varignon frame. The corners of the frame become the corners of the locational triangle. Over each of the corners, threads are extended bearing determinate weights of the components. Connect the threads in the inner part of the triangle. Wherever the connecting point of the three threads comes to rest, that is the point of least transportation costs for processing the raw materials and reaching the market.

Three locations can result if the locational figure is a triangle. First, if the weight at one corner is equal to or larger than the sum of the other weight, the processing lies at that corner; second, if the weight at one corner is not equal to or larger than the sum of the other weights, but predominates, the orientation is to that corner; third, if the weight at no corner predominates, the processing point will lie somewhere within the triangle according to the weights of the components. This method can be adapted to a wider range of choices. For example, it can determine any desired number of production sites.

Labor Costs

Labor costs are the second factor that Weber considered vital in the localization of manufacturing. After minimum transport costs have been determined, a vital question arises: Will manufacturing occur at other points in a region where labor costs dominate and create a least cost point? Thus it becomes clear that labor costs become a factor in industrial location only when they vary from place to

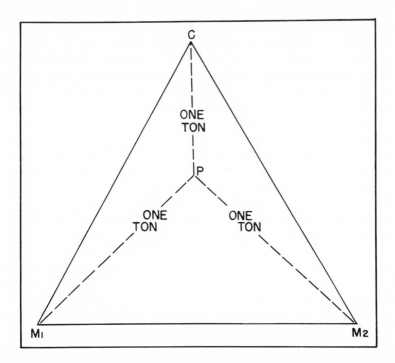

Figure 1.1. Weber's locational triangle. M_1 and M_2 represent raw material sources, and *C* represents the point of consumption. *P* represents the point of processing where neither the weight of the raw materials nor consumption dominates at the corners. Thus the processing point lies within the triangle according to the weights of the components. (Source: E. Willard Miller, *A Geography of Industrial Location,* William C. Brown, Dubuque, Iowa, 1970, Fig. 1.1.)

place. Further, labor costs are important in specific locations only if they occur at a geographically defined point.

Weber recognized that labor costs differ depending on two sets of causes: (1) different levels of efficiency and (2) differences in the efficiency of the organization and equipment. From the viewpoint of influencing location, it is important to recognize the geographic "form" of the differences in labor costs. The labor differences may be "according to area," that is, an entire region may have the same labor cost; or differences may be "according to place," that is, they may relate to a particular place, such as an urban center. In treating these basic ideas, the theoretical discussion differs greatly. In the first case the discussion deals with the mathematical concept of the "plane" and, in the second, with that of a "point."

LAW OF LABOR ORIENTATION.   The basis of the law of labor orientation is related to the idea that every point of lower labor costs constitutes a center of attraction which tends to draw industry from the point of minimal transport cost. Thus this raises a fundamental question: When will industry be attracted to one or the other point? Weber states, "a location can be moved from the point of minimum transportation costs to a labor orientation only if the savings in the cost of labor which this new place makes possible are larger than the additional costs of transportation which it involves" (50–103).

THE ISODAPANE.   Whether an industry should be attracted to a minimum transport point or an advantageous labor cost point is thus the basic question. To answer this question, Weber developed the concept of the isodapane. This is a method for connecting points of equal transfer costs. In this theoretical system, a series of isodapanes are drawn around the minimum transfer cost points. For each production point with a labor supply there is a "critical isodapane," or the isodapane where additional transport costs are equal to the nontransfer or labor cost economies obtainable at that point. If the alternative production point lies within the critical isodapane, the nontransfer or labor cost savings exceed the extra transfer costs and industry is therefore attracted to this point. If it lies outside the critical isodapane, the economy in the nontransfer or labor costs is less than the extra transfer costs.

To illustrate this procedure, the following simple example is given (Fig. 1.2): Suppose there is a single market and a single raw material for a product to be produced. When freight rates increase uniformly from the market and raw material points, the transfer costs can be represented by connective circles known as *isovectures*. Further, assume that the raw material is pure and will not lose weight in processing. If the factory were located at the raw material source, there would be nine units of freight costs to reach the market. If the factory were at the market, the freight rate would also be nine units to move the raw material units.

However, if the factory is at neither the raw material nor the market source, it is necessary to determine transfer costs at an intermediate point for the shipment of raw materials to the point of manufacture and the shipment of the finished products from the factory to the market. To determine these transfer costs, isovectures were used to construct isodapanes. The simplest isodapane is derived from two families of isovectures. If the factory is located at any point on the isodapane represented, it will have a transfer cost of 12 monetary units for the assembly of the raw materials and the shipment of the finished product to the market. If other isodapanes are drawn, additional points of lowest transfer costs can be determined. The isodapanes aid in revealing the advantages or disadvantages of transfer costs in relation to nontransfer costs, such as labor, in the location of an industry at neither the raw material nor the market sources.

MEASUREMENTS OF LABOR ORIENTATION.   The importance of labor in industrial location can be measured by an index of labor costs, the locational weight, and the labor coefficient.

Index of Labor Costs.   The index of labor costs provides a measure of labor orientation. According to Weber, the formula reveals that "with a high index of labor costs, a large quantity of labor costs will be available for compression, with correspondingly large potential indices of economy of the labor locations, and

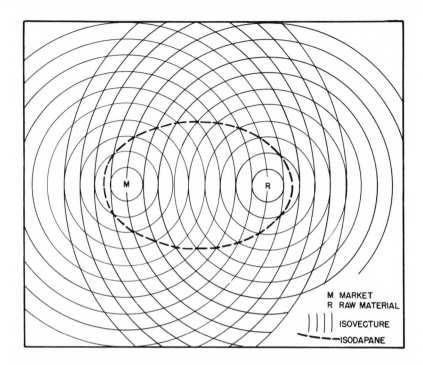

M MARKET
R RAW MATERIAL
‖‖‖‖ ISOVECTURE
– – – – ISODAPANE

Figure 1.2. The isodapane and isovectures. The isodapane is a line connecting points of equal total cost. By using this technique, transport costs can be evaluated at a given point in relation to other costs. (Source: E. Willard Miller, *A Geography of Industrial Location,* William C. Brown, Dubuque, Iowa, 1970, Fig. 1.2.)

correspondingly high critical isodapanes; therefore we shall find a high potential attracting power of the labor locations. And vice versa: low index of labor costs, small quantity of labor cost available for compression" (50–107). This indicates that the potential attraction to labor parallels the indices of labor costs of the industries. The index of labor costs thus indicates the attraction that labor exerts on locating an industry. For example, when labor costs are extremely low, they may be the dominating influence.

The Locational Weight. The locational weight influences the extent to which an industry may change its location through its effect on the distance and form of isodapanes. To illustrate, the locational weight affects the spacing of the isodapanes as follows: "Low locational weight, small mass of material per ton or product to be transported, great distances of the isodapanes from each other, wide extension of the critical isodapane; consequently the industry may be deviated to a large extent. And vice versa" (50–108).

The locational weight will affect not only the spacing of the isodapanes but also their form. It does so through the size and composition of the material index. It also shows that the tendency of a given industry to deviate from the minimum point is not likely to be of equal force in all directions. Thus the following are general rules of the influence that locational weights have on location:

> Industries which have components of equal strength determining their location have a tolerably equal tendency to deviate their location from the minimum point in all directions. An industry having components of varying strength, and hence an eccentric minimum point, will more easily deviate in the direction of the strongest corners of the location, and the stronger its components are, the more it will do so. In essence industries having a high and a small material index will deviate unevenly, while industries with a medium index of materials, will deviate more or less evenly in all directions. (50–109)

Coefficient of Labor.   The amount of labor costs associated with the locational weight of a given industry is the coefficient of labor. If the form of the isodapanes is disregarded, it is the locational weight that has to be changed to affect location. The locational weight is the only factor that alters the influence of the labor costs as they are compressed. Thus locational weight costs may be compared with labor costs in determining the least cost sites.

The coefficient of labor is the labor cost in each industry per ton of locational weight to be transported. Thus the labor orientation of industries is determined by their labor coefficient. To illustrate, if the manufacture of agricultural machinery has a labor coefficient of $1,500 per ton, primary metals $500, and production of wood products $100, then, according to these coefficients, a 10 percent saving in labor costs at any place means respectively $150, $50, and $10 saved per locational ton. If there is a 10-mile rate of 50 cents, we find that the manufacture of agricultural machinery might deviate 3,000 miles, the primary metals industry 1,000 miles, and the wood products industry 200 miles. The orientation of these industries is explained by these figures.

Agglomeration

Besides the costs of transportation and labor that affect the regional location of industry, there are other factors, known as *agglomeration factors*, which contribute to the local distribution of industry.

Weber defines an agglomeration factor as an "advantage" in production or marketing costs at a specific place. In contrast, a *deglomerative factor* is one that lowers production costs because of the decentralization of production. When an interaction of agglomerative and deglomerative factors occurs, certain indices of cost per unit of output result. When the indices of cost are smaller in large concentrations than in smaller concentrations, they become indices of economy for the industry considered.

AGGLOMERATIVE FACTORS.   The agglomerative factors distinguish between two stages of agglomeration. The first and simplest way that industry is concentrated is by the enlargement of the plant. Each large plant with a complete organization represents a local concentration compared with production scattered in small neighborhood plants. The economies of scale provided by large-scale production as compared with small-scale production are effective local factors of production. As the size of the plant increases, technical applications that result in lower costs are possible.

The second stage of concentration occurs when a close association is developed between several related plants. The local aggregation of several plants carries forward the advantages of the large plant; thus the factors of agglomeration that create their advanced stage of social agglomeration will be the same as those which created the large-scale plant. Weber recognized three factors essential to the development of the association of several plants. These are the increased use of technical equipment, the creation of a labor organization, and the development of a more effective market organization.

The state of advancement of technical equipment influences the concentration of industry. When equipment becomes so specialized and costly that it cannot be fully utilized in a single plant, other factories must be developed, which become the basis of independent auxiliary enterprises. In reality these new plants may be physically separated from the parent plant. However, they form a single technical unit and usually function best when locally concentrated. The development of specialized and related auxiliary machines establishes a technical minimum of agglomeration. This leads to a second factor in that the agglomeration of machines provides better opportunities for replacement and repair of equipment. This specialized development is best performed when the amount of technical equipment exceeds that of a single plant.

Weber further stated that a fully developed, differentiated, and integrated labor organization is an essential feature for agglomeration. Specialized labor makes the application of a given technical innovation possible in a plant, which results in lower cost output. Thus the division of labor leads to social agglomeration.

Weber stressed that the most effective marketing organization exists at the stage of social agglomeration. The large-scale plant is more effective in marketing its products because it can buy and sell on a larger scale. Further, being a safer investment, it can get cheaper credit. Grouped large-scale plants can obtain other economies. The concentrated industry develops its own market for purchasing its raw materials. In contrast, the isolated enterprise is forced to buy its materials in advance and store them. This means an increase in money outlay and a wasteful temporary tying up of capital. Finally, social concentration permits economies in marketing the product because the concentrated industry produces in itself a large unified market for its product.

With agglomeration there is a reduction in general overhead costs. As Weber illustrated, water mains, streets, and other facilities become cheaper for the individual enterprise having a high level of technical development and effective utilization.

DEGLOMERATIVE FACTORS.   As agglomeration increases, deglomerative forces gradually become active. These factors result from the size of the agglomeration. All deglomerative factors are fundamentally the result of the rise of land values due to a rise in the demand for land.

Weber evaluated this situation only theoretically and was not directly concerned with reality. A number of situations may arise as the economic rent increases. For example, if the rent makes land for industry more expensive, general overheads will rise; or if economic rent increases the cost of labor, it means that the lowering of labor costs due to better management will be absorbed. Two conclusions can be drawn: the deglomerative factors are forces that weaken the agglomerative factors, and the deglomerative forces are directly associated only with the size of the agglomeration.

Elaboration of Least Cost Theory

Since Weber presented his least cost theory in 1909, several writers have developed the original concepts. Of these Edgar M. Hoover has provided significant contributions.[4] Hoover, using the Weberian approaches, states:

> The question of the location of manufacturers may be resolved . . . into a balancing of the transport advantages of nearness to materials and nearness to markets. For each contribution of material sources and markets there must be a point or points at which the total transportation costs involved in assembling the materials and delivering the product to the market are less than they would be anywhere else. In the absence of production–cost differentials, the best location for the production process is at the point of minimum transport costs. (22–35)

Hoover thus stressed transportation costs but also evaluated labor and production cost differentials and the importance of economies of concentration.

TRANSPORTATION COSTS.   The importance of transportation costs was recognized by Hoover in that the conceivable combinations of material and market points for the localization of industry are quasi-astronomical in numbers. It is therefore the influence of transport costs on location that reveals which of these combinations is best. Thus the theory of market areas and the theory of orientation are complementary.

In the location of production, Hoover used the Weberian term *orientation*. Orientation may be determined by the construction of *isotims*, which are lines of equal transport costs around material and market points. These lines will depend on several factors. The first factor concerns the weight of material per ton of

---

[4]This section relies on Edgar M. Hoover, Jr., *Location Theory and the Shoe and Leather Industries* (Cambridge, Mass.: Harvard University Press, 1937), pp. 34–111.

product produced. Second is the relation between the ton-mile transport rates on material and product. The finished product usually has a higher transportation rate than raw material because of its greater bulk, higher fragility, and less elastic demand. Finally, an important element influencing orientation is that transport costs vary with distance. This factor represents a major deviation from Weber.

Hoover analyzed the *material index* of Weber. He believed that although Weber exaggerated the importance of the index, it does aid in indicating tendencies of orientation. For example, if the material index is two, the isotims around the material source will be two times as close together as those around the market. In Weber's approach the material will "pull" production two times as strongly as the market will. Hoover recognizes that the ideal weights and the material index are constant only when the ton-mile transfer costs for each commodity are uniform for all distances in every direction (22–41). When transfer costs are less than proportional to distance, the relation between the ideal weights of two materials will vary.

Hoover assumed that in the determination of orientation, the market is a given point. He extended this concept by indicating the basic question: How will the various material and market points be associated? This association can occur by having market areas defined from production points or by delimiting "production areas" for given markets (22–42).

Two of Hoover's illustrations are utilized to determine the market areas using only transfer costs. In Fig. 1.3 there are two primary sources of materials, M_1 and M_1'; there are secondary sources of material at M_2 and M_3. If there is a market-oriented production process, the only transfer costs involved are for the assembly of the raw materials. Thus the market area for each production point will be the point itself; but it is possible to mark off zones, within each of which the market-oriented production points will be supplied by a combination of material sources.

Figure 1.4 shows the variation of bringing the desired combination of two materials to various points from different combinations of sources: M_1 and M_2, M_1 and M_2', M_1' and M_2, and M_1' and M_2'. The figures illustrate that there are certain areas that provide the cheapest combined delivered price. The shadings in each zone of the figure are parallel to a line between the two material-sources supplying that zone.

LABOR COST DIFFERENTIALS.   Hoover also attempted to analyze how labor cost differentials arise. This is approached from "two sets of materials: The industrial materials in the ordinary sense, and the *budget materials*, the prices of which determine the workman's cost of living. . . . To the extent that the two categories of materials fail to coincide, the location of a factory must choose between good transfer relations with sources of industrial materials and good transfer relations with sources of budget materials" (22–62). The importance of the two will depend on the relative ideal weights of the two types of material. This relation varies approximately, as does the Weberian labor coefficient. Hoover advanced the concept by recognizing that Weber's labor coefficient is not

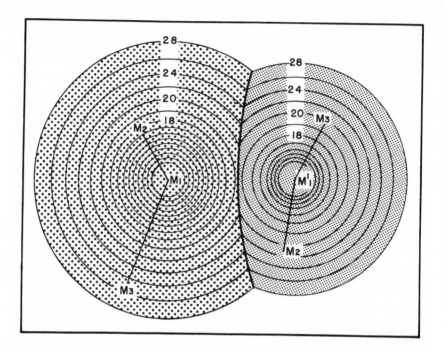

Figure 1.3. Two material-oriented production points with market area boundaries. If the market is localized at the point of the raw material, production will also be localized. However, it is also possible to delimit production zones, within each of which the market-orientation production points will be supplied by a combination of material sources. (Source: Edgar M. Hoover, *Location Theory and the Shoe and Leather Industries,* Harvard University Press, Cambridge, 1937, Fig. 17.)

a pure number but varies according to the units in which it is expressed. For example, it might be expressed as so many dollars per short tons; and

> unless this is supplemented by some information on rates of transportation, it gives no clue to the importance of labor costs relative to other locational factors. But if we can resolve equalizing differences in labor costs into ordinary transfer costs of materials and products, the importance of labor relative to materials and product may be expressed as a pure number; the ratio of the ideal weight of all the budget commodities to the ideal weights of the industrial materials and the product together. (22–63)

Hoover showed that when labor is mobile, its locational effect can be stated in terms of transfer costs. For example, it is assumed that labor-oriented industries will seek locations having good transfer relations with agricultural districts because of the low cost of living and therefore low labor costs. Thus if all

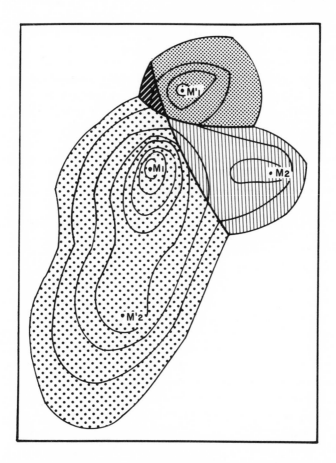

Figure 1.4. Two materials from different source combinations. This figure represents the variations in costs of assembling a combination of two materials from a variety of sources. (Source: Edgar M. Hoover, *Location Theory and the Shoe and Leather Industries,* Harvard University Press, Cambridge, 1937, Fig. 18.)

industries were oriented to low labor cost, labor would migrate to districts of more advantageous agricultural production, so that the price of labor (i.e., the cost of living) would in the long run be equalized. However, other factors that affect location besides labor costs are frequently decisive.

When labor is immobile because of such factors as the expense of migration, political and linguistic obstacles, and preferences for certain economic, cultural, and natural environments, an interregional inequality of real wages results. Such an inequality may be permanent or temporary (frictional). The most important cause of differentials in labor costs is temporary immobility. Any time there are differences in real wage levels, which are really differences in psychic income (intangible satisfactions such as sunshine), the wage levels are in the process of being adjusted by migration. Labor cost differentials due to immobility are often accurately indicated by comparison of wage rates between regions. The advantages of favored locations are frequently due to the special skill of the labor, a large body of labor providing an elastic supply, and relative freedom from artificial restrictions imposed by unions or legislation.

PRODUCTION COST DIFFERENTIALS. Because a large segment of labor cost differentials are not explainable in terms of transfer costs, Hoover considered it necessary to investigate the locational effect of production cost differentials. In his analysis, he assumed that the costs of production vary from place to place but are constant at each place. The basic difference between the locational effects of transfer costs and production costs must also be clearly understood. For example, coal supply and climate both influence the location of industry, but the former is a matter of transfer costs and the latter is a matter of production costs.

Hoover followed Weber closely in his analysis of the importance of production costs as an influence on industrial location. He believes that production will move from the point of minimum transfer costs only if greater economies can be obtained by offsetting the additional transfer charges.

Whereas Weber utilized the isodapane to explain the influences of production costs, Hoover concluded that the fundamental defect in this approach is that it is based solely on terms of orientation; that is, it applies solely to situations in which the sources of materials and market are given. As soon as the scope is widened to factors besides raw materials and markets, the analysis becomes ineffective because it is not stated in terms of market areas.

Weber recognized this in his discussion of the replacement of material deposits. In the extreme case, for example, when the material is ubiquitous, each possible production location involves a different source. Hoover recognized that this part of the location theory needed development in terms of market areas. He states:

> The effect of production-cost differentials is to enlarge the market areas of certain low-cost production points by making it possible for them to serve some markets for which they are not points of minimum transfer costs. By virtue of their lower costs of production, they can deliver the product more cheaply to those points than could production points located where transfer costs are a minimum. (22–79)

Let us illutrate this concept by using Hoover's example, which involves

> a production process in which the ideal weight of one of the materials is so preponderant that under the influence of transfer costs alone production would always take place at one of the sources (M_1, M_1') of the material. Two sources of the lesser material (M_2, M_2') are also available, and under

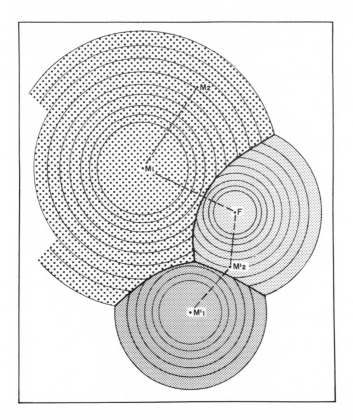

Figure 1.5. Production at the point of raw materials. When the weight of one of the raw materials is so predominant that it cannot be transported, production will occur at the source M_1 or M_1' of the material. If secondary sources of material M_2 or M_2' plus transportation costs to market are added, costs become lower at F than at M_1 or M_1'. Other production points can be determined in the same manner. (Source: Edgar M. Hoover, *Location Theory and the Shoe and Leather Industries,* Harvard University Press, Cambridge, 1937, Fig. 24.)

the influence of transfer costs alone the whole market would be shared between M_1 and M_1', each using the most convenient source of the other material. But at a point F, production costs are lower than at M_1 or M_1'. For certain market points, the product can be delivered at equal cost from M_1 and from F, since the saving in transfer costs involved in production at M_1 is just balanced by the saving in production costs involved in production at F. Similarly, for certain other points the product can be delivered at equal cost from M_1' and from F. These two series of points constitute the market-area boundaries between M_1 and F and between M_1' and F.

It is plain that F will have no market area unless it offers economies at least equal to the difference between the costs of shipping the material from its source to F and those of shipping the product the same distance. This minimum depends on the distance between M_1 (or M_1') and F, and also upon the relative ideal weights of material and product. If, for instance, the material is very bulky and difficult to transport, while the product is relatively compact, then production costs must be very much lower at F to make it feasible to carry the bulky material that much farther. If on the other hand, the economies offered at F are greater than the sum of the costs of shipping the material from, say, M_1 to F plus those of shipping the product from F back to M_1, thus no production will take place at M_1, and F can ship even to markets beyond that point. (22–79)

ECONOMIES OF CONCENTRATION.   Hoover concluded his locational analysis with a discussion of differences in production costs that depend on local concentration. Here the Weberian assumption is altered in that it is assumed that manufacturing is carried on at costs which are constant regardless of volume of production, other industry in the vicinity, or the size of the city. In the Weberian theory,

> the force of agglomeration which manifests itself in the economies of concentration would be resolved into a reënforcing of the attraction of cheap labor locations, but none the less he developed a separate theoretical mechanism to weigh the influence of agglomeration against that of transport costs. . . . Two or more locational figures will emerge, according to Weber, if the economies attainable by pooling their production at a common location more than compensate for the extra transport costs occasioned by the distortion of the patterns of transport orientation. (22–90)

Hoover considered this one of the least satisfactory aspects of Weber's theory. He showed that a concentration of industry is not limited to locations of cheap labor but can also occur at a source of materials, at a strategic distributional point, or at a site of advantageous product costs. The concept of a single agglomerative or single deglomerative force is simply not realistic. Hoover stated that the greatest deficiency of the Weberian theory of agglomeration combines three quite distinct influences on local production costs: large-scale economies, localization economies, and urbanization economies. In these there may be diseconomies as well as economies. These are intermingled in Weber's theory, and further analysis is impossible until they are separated.

Industrial location cannot be analyzed without understanding large-scale economies and localization economies. In Weberian theory, these concepts cannot possibly be resolved by any of the theoretical constructions. Hoover de-

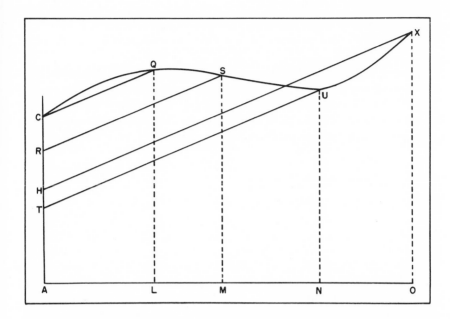

Figure 1.6. Market area and economies of localization. This figure illustrates that production costs vary with the size of the market area. For example, if production is at *A* and the market extends to *L*, the cost at *A* will be *AC*, and at *L*, *LQ*; but if the market extends to *M*, the cost at *A* will be *AR*, and at *MS*, *M*. (Source: Edgar M. Hoover, *Location Theory and the Shoe and Leather Industries*, Harvard University Press, Cambridge, 1937, Fig. 29.)

veloped these viewpoints in the following manner. Because he assumed that each production location is occupied by a considerable number of firms in a given industry, the analysis is restricted to economies of localization. The basic issue is whether a plant with a market area can continue to produce if it lacks economies of localization.

The market area under these conditions is illustrated by Fig. 1.6. Let A represent a production center and AC the costs of production. Distance is represented to the right of A. The transport gradient CQ shows what the delivered price of the product will be at various distances from A, where the price at A is AC. Economies of localization mean that the cost of production will vary according to the size of the market area. Figure 1.6 shows that if A's market area extends to L, the cost at A will be AC. When the market extends to M, a new, lower transport gradient will exist and costs will range from AR at A to MS at M. This technique can be extended to all sizes of market areas.

MAXIMUM PROFIT THEORY

The maximum profit theory of industrial location is based on conditions of monopolistic competition, as opposed to the perfect competition as advocated by Weber's least cost theory. Thus this theory, developed by August Lösch in Germany in the 1930s and early 1940s, recognizes that if the market is dispersed, producers of manufactured goods will also be dispersed.[5]

Orientation of Industry

The market theory of industrial location recognizes that the site of an industrial enterprise rests not only on objective facts but also on subjective considerations. Consequently, two entrepreneurs may choose two different locations under exactly identical external conditions. The range of sites depends on the size of the possible profit. Whether a satisfactory site has been chosen can be determined only by experience. It is extremely difficult to determine the best site at a single moment in time and virtually impossible to foresee how future conditions will affect locational decisions.

Lösch suggests that

> with complete orientation, production necessarily takes place at a favored point only when it requires an irreplaceable or immobile production factor or consumer, or a still rarer combination of such factors as consumers (technically conditional special location) whether at one place (definite special location) or several (indefinite special locations). In the latter instance the location will be determined by the simultaneous consideration of all the other location factors, including proceeds, in contradiction to one-sided orientation by total costs. Definite technically conditioned special locations will necessarily be confirmed by profit calculations; others, which depended on one-sided orientation, may be so confirmed. (33–31)

In reality there may be more locations that are one-sided than locations which have a complete orientation.

In the maximum profit theory, the costs of production cannot be isolated from the costs of freight, raw materials, or the finished product. As a result differences in total costs may attract an industry to a particular location even though neither production nor transportation costs are lowest at that point, provided that the sum of the two costs is lowest. Moreover, in situations that remain indeterminate in respect to production orientation, total costs provide the basis for a locational decision. For example, it may be found that a factor of production is immobile but not irreplaceable, or that it is located at several sites.

[5]See August Lösch,*The Economics of Location* (New Haven, Conn.: Yale University Press, 1954), pp. 16–35, 103–108.

The conditions of production require only that in the case of replaceable factors some particular location may be selected. Only total costs can decide the solution of a site among the various locational possibilities. In addition, when production is technically restricted to a unique location, or when excessive costs lead to a special location, this location will also be determined by the influences of total cost. Finally, if present lower transport costs lead to a particular location, this location may lose its cost advantages if other factors result in greater profits at another location.

A factory may also be established at a place where revenue is greatest rather than where cost is smallest. Lösch refined this concept: The plant may not be established at the place of largest sales, but where one of the sales' components, such as quantity or price, prevails. Orientation to quantity reflects the number of buyers, whereas orientation to price recognizes the importance of purchasing power. The former favors populous areas while the latter favors prosperous areas. Both locations have monopolistic characteristics.

If gross receipts are most important in locating a plant, production will be oriented to the consumer—if the market is technically tied to the buyer and if the purchasers cannot or will not change their location. If such areas of consumption exist everywhere, there is no need for a special location; but if several possible locations exist, a particular location is a necessary condition in order to secure the greatest profit. As a result the market will govern the location of a plant. A unique location is technically feasible only when all, or nearly all, buyers are in one place.

When gross receipts are utilized to determine the location of a factory, a one-sided orientation to production costs is avoided. Demand for the product varies not only with price, but also with the site of production chosen and the ultimate market area. The relation between price, demand, and location is such that for each factory price of a product the greatest total demand will be achieved with a different location of each plant because with every change in price the market area also changes in size. The factory location achieving the greatest total demand would thus be more strongly affected by the location of neighboring markets when prices are higher than when they are low. The optimum location changes with each price change, which directly affects demand. Thus when variability in market demand is considered, as Lösch indicated, the least cost theory—which is based on cost of production—loses validity. It then becomes meaningless to attempt to locate the point of lowest cost. As a result there must be an attempt to find the largest market area that will then provide the greatest profit. This is the central theme of the maximum profit theory.

Theoretical Market Area

Lösch provided a number of basic assumptions regarding the theoretical evolution of market areas (32). It is assumed that there is a vast plain with an equal distribution of raw materials and a complete absence of inequalities in other

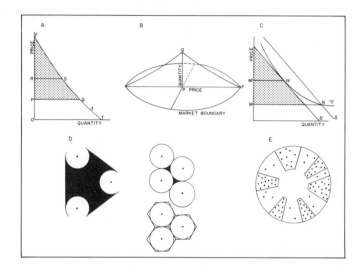

Figure 1.7. The evolution of market areas. This figure illustrates the development of market areas beginning with a single producer and evolving into a multiple pattern of factories. The design develops the concept of the hexagon region as the ideal market area for a plant. (Source: August Lösch, *The Economics of Location,* Yale University Press, New Haven, 1954, Figs. 21, 22, and 23.)

factors. It is further assumed that the only economic activity takes places at self-sufficient farms distributed equally over the area. The basic question that Lösch raised is how spatial differences can evolve under such conditions.

To understand the evolution of the market area, let us assume that one farmer begins to manufacture a product (Lösch uses beer in his illustration) that is a superior quality and can be sold in the area. This is illustrated in Fig. 1.7A. Let d be the assumed demand curve for the product; OP will be the price at the center of production P; and the demand for the people living there will be PQ. PR is the cost of transportation from P to R, and at this point, the demand for the product is RS. At point F the increased cost of transportation becomes so great that the demand falls to zero. Thus PF is the maximum radius for the product produced at O. The total demand for the product is equal to the volume of the cone, which is determined by rotating the triangle PQF around the PQ axis.[6] (See Fig. 1.7B.)

[6] This can be expressed algebraically (33–107):

$$D = b \times \pi \int_0^R f(p + t) \times t \times dt$$

where D = total demand as a function of f.o.b. price p

b = twice the population of a square in which it cost one unit price to transport one unit along one side

Once a single factory is established in a region, there is the incentive to begin manufacturing the product at other locations. Because these centers will have different costs, the demand curve will also change. Lösch illustrated this idea in Fig. 1.7C. Curve Δ represents the total demand as a function of the factory price. π is the so-called planning curve indicating the minimum costs at which a given output could be produced if a new factory were built. Only if the planning curve π intersects or is to the left of the total demand curve Δ, is it possible for a factory to exist. Otherwise it would operate at a loss.

The market areas of the isolated factories then begin as circles (Fig. 1.7D). However, as factories develop there will be markets that cannot be reached if the market regions remain circular. All the blank areas between the markets are left unused, and the size of the individual firms will be reduced from MN to M'N' without rendering them unprofitable. In order to have no space outside a market area, its shape must be changed to a hexagon. This will shift the curve Δ slightly to the left because a hexagon is smaller than a circle that circumscribes the market area. Moreover, the hexagon area will continue to be reduced in size until the corresponding demand curve Δ' just touches the offer curve in N'. At this time the market is saturated, and apparently no new factories can develop because MN is the longest possible shipping radius and M'N' is the minimum radius.

A separate net of hexagons will be developed for each product manufactured. If the individual nets are thrown over the region at random, every place on the plain will have access to every product in spite of the apparent disorder. In reality the nets are so set in order to provide a more economical arrangement. The first step is to set each net so that all of them have one center of production in common. This point has the advantage of a large local demand. The second step is to rotate the nets around the center to develop six sectors where centers of production are frequent and six where they are scarce (Fig. 1.7E). This arrangement makes it possible for every place to have access to every product and at the same time minimize transportation costs. An orderly system of market areas was visualized by Lösch in this manner. Further, by this procedure numerous market areas can evolve on what was originally a plain with no inequalities. In conclusion, the theoretical evolution advances through three stages: the development of (1) a single hexagonal market surrounding each center of production, (2) a set of nets of market areas for each commodity, and (3) a systematic arrangement of the nets of market areas for the various products manufactured.

$\pi = 3.14$

$d = f(p + t)$, individual demand as a function of price at the place of consumption

p = price at point of production

t = shipping costs per unit from plant to consumer

R = greatest possible transfer cost (PF)

Deviations in Reality

There are several deviations in reality from the perfect theoretical market situation. When the basic assumptions of a uniform plain are relaxed, the size and shape of the market areas lose their hexagonal shape and become irregular. Lösch recognized that as a consequence, the individual market areas for the same line of production will overlap and gaps in the market will occur on the periphery of the area.

A second deviation reveals that the concept of a net does not always prevail. Market areas may overlap in reality. As a result the shape of the regions may more closely resemble irregular ovals or slabs. The results may be belts and ultimately districts when the nets are compressed. Because of the irregular shapes, it may be difficult to determine the size of areas by measuring the minimum distances from the centers of each one.

A third divergence concerns a deviation from the theoretical distribution of the nets and the distribution of the centers of production. Only the distribution of the nets had to be coped with in the theoretical markets, while the distribution of the centers of production were conspicuous for their regularity. However, when the centers of production are irregularly spaced a new and difficult problem evolves. Traditional locational theory cannot solve this problem, for the theory of location proper is applicable only to a single establishment, not to a whole industry, and the theory of comparative costs is applicable only to trade between individuals, not to trade between regions or nations. The only adequate solution of the location of all the interdependent centers of production is a system of locational equations.

The system of nets is difficult, if not impossible to achieve in the real world. It is impossible to arrange all irregular nets so they have a single common point. No city or region can be found where there is a complete set of industries. In reality even small cities that produce a specialty product may have huge market areas. In contrast to such specialty cities, a regional center that produces a variety of products may be linked to the immediate area and have a relatively small market. Although these centers differ from the ideal in that they are not self-sufficient, they correspond to the ideal in that they have a large concentration of production and have the most economic arrangement of transportation. Thus many places of this type are found in reality.

Equilibrium of Location

The market area of a firm is determined by two fundamental tendencies: the maximization of the advantages of the individual firm and the maximization for the economy as a whole. In the latter situation, the firm is affected by competition from without; in the former, by competition from within. Because the individual firm is located at the place of highest profit as a producer, or at the least costly market as a consumer, an increase in the number of firms is encouraged. There is thus a continuous competition for market space. As a consequence an equilibrium is ultimately achieved.

Lösch presented the stages for the development of general equilibrium. The first condition is that the location of the individual firm must be as advantageous as possible in that the profit is maximized. As soon as this occurs, opposing tendencies begin to develop. Thus the second condition is fulfilled when the locations become so numerous that the entire space is occupied. Consequently, the third condition results when entry is so open that abnormal profits disappear. Prices will thus correspond to cost. Under these conditions there is still room for more competitors without detriment to the profitability of the industry. Thus conditions force the areas of supply, production, and sales to be as small as possible because only then can the maximum number of firms that can survive be established. With the addition of any new firms, all enterprises would become unprofitable. Thus condition four results: At the boundaries of economic areas it must be a matter of indifference to which of two neighboring locations they belong. These four conditions are necessary if the spatial order of the economy is to have meaning and permanence.

THEORIES OF LOCATIONAL INTERDEPENDENCE

As concepts developed, the early theories of industrial location based on competitive situations were considered inadequate to explain certain locations. A school of economists began to investigate the importance of the market area as it influenced industrial location. The basis of this approach is that the size of a manufacturing plant depends on the consumers that can be monopolized within an area. The goal of each firm is to control the largest number of purchasers at prices yielding the largest returns. This is achieved by the locational interdependence of firms.

Establishment of the Theory

Hotelling provided one of the pioneer papers that established the foundation of locational interdependence (24). The basic viewpoint

> is the existence with reference to each seller or groups of buyers who will deal with him instead of with his competitors in spite of a difference in price. If a seller increases his price too far he will gradually lose business to his rivals, but he does not lose all his trade instantly when he raises his price only a trifle. Many customers will still prefer to trade with him because they live nearer to his store than to the others, or because they have less freight to pay from his warehouse to their own, or because his mode of doing business is more to their liking, or because he sells other articles which they desire, or because he is a relative or a fellow Elk or

Baptist, or on account of some difference in service or quality, or for a combination of reasons. Such circles of customers may be said to make every entrepreneur a monopolist within a limited class and region—and there is no monopoly which is not confined to a limited class and region. The difference between the Standard Oil Company in its prime and the little corner grocery is quantitative rather than qualitative. Between the perfect competition and monopoly of the theory lie the actual cases. (24–44)

To develop this concept Hotelling assumed the following: (1) the consumers are evenly distributed along the market; (2) the f.o.b. mill price is the same for all producers; (3) the cost of transport of a unit of the product per unit of distance is constant; (4) the seller's procurement and production costs are equal throughout the region; (5) all sellers and buyers have identical qualities; (6) the different sources of supply are owned by different entrepreneurs, who are completely indifferent to each other's gains and losses; (7) costs are independent of location; (8) each producer is capable of supplying the entire market; (9) the transport costs are paid by the purchaser so that no seller is able to charge discriminatory prices at the plant to different buyers; (10) each manufacturer has complete freedom of movement without cost; and (11) costs are independent of location.

Hotelling's concept is illustrated by Fig. 1.8. Let us assume the buyers of a commodity are distributed along a line of a length l. At distances a and b from the two ends of this line are two manufacturers, A and B. To reach each purchaser, there is a cost of c per unit distance. It is also assumed that there is complete inelasticity of demand. Each customer has no preference for either manufacturer except that of differences in transportation costs.

To illustrate the concept, suppose that B's production price is no higher than A's. Thus, if B is to share the market with A, his price cannot exceed A's by more than the cost of transportation from A's location to his own. Let p_1 denote A's price, and p_2, B's price. Thus B's price, p_2, must be lower than $p_1 - c (l - a - b)$ at which A's goods can be brought to the buyer. The market area for B will be the total segment of b and the y segment, depending on the difference in prices between A and B. Likewise A will have the entire market of a and the x segment, where x decreases as $p_1 - p_2$ increases. The point of division between the market areas of A and B is that location where it is a matter of indifference as to whether the purchaser buys from either A or B. This was illustrated by Hotelling (24–44) as follows:

$$p_1 + cx = p_2 + cy$$

Another equation between x and $y\sigma$ is

$$a + x + y + b = l$$

Solving we find

$$x = \frac{1}{2}\left(l - a - b + \frac{p_2 - p_1}{c}\right)$$

$$y = \frac{1}{2}\left(l - a - b + \frac{p_1 - p_2}{c}\right)$$

So that the profits Π are

$$\Pi_1 = p_1 q_1 = p_1(a + x) = \frac{1}{2}\left(l + a - b\right)p_1 - \frac{p_1{}^2}{2c} + \frac{p_1 p_2}{2c}$$

and

$$\Pi_2 = p_2 q_2 = p_2(b + y) = \frac{1}{2}\left(l - a + b\right)p_2 - \frac{p_2{}^2}{2c} + \frac{p_1 p_2}{2c}$$

As each competitor adjusts his price to maximize profits, the following equation results:

$$\frac{\partial \Pi_1}{\partial p_1} = \frac{1}{2}\left(l + a - b\right) - \frac{p_1}{c} + \frac{p_2}{2c} = 0$$

$$\frac{\partial \Pi_2}{\partial p_2} = \frac{1}{2}\left(l - a + b\right) + \frac{p_1}{2c} - \frac{p_2}{c} = 0$$

from which is obtained

$$p_1 = c\left(l + \frac{a - b}{3}\right)$$

$$p_2 = c\left(l - \frac{a - b}{3}\right)$$

and

$$q_1 = a + x = \frac{1}{2}\left(l + \frac{a - b}{3}\right)$$

$$q_2 = b + y = \frac{1}{2}\left(l - \frac{a - b}{3}\right)$$

Hotelling recognized that in reality the manufacturers are not strung in a line but are distributed over an area in varying densities. Nevertheless, the principles of determining the market area remain the same. If there are two factories, A and B, the market boundary between the two factories is

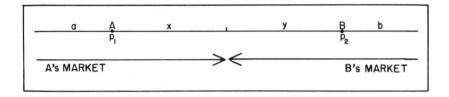

Figure 1.8. Spatial distribution of markets. The market area of two manufacturers, A and B, will depend on the cost of production at the point of production plus the transportation costs between the two factories. (Source: Harold Hotelling, "Stability in Competition," *Economic Journal,* 1929, Fig. 1.)

the locus of points for which the difference of prices, i.e. for which the delivered price is the same whether the goods are bought from A or from B. If transportation is in straight lines (perhaps by airplane) at a cost proportional to the distance, the boundary will be a hyperbola, since a hyperbola is the locus of points such that the difference of distances from the foci is constant. If there are three or more sellers, their regions will be separated from each other by arcs of hyperbolas. (24–54)

Elaboration of the Theory

TORD PALANDER.　Palander develops the concept of the market area by questioning a number of the earlier works, particularly those of Hotelling (35–245). First, he showed that Hotelling's solution for the preceding example is inaccurate; in this situation there is a constant changing of prices in order to be competitive. In the extreme situation, a firm may reduce the price to the cost level to gain a temporary advantage. This creates a continuously unstable condition. Palander stated that a stable equilibrium will result only when the two firms are distant and have small hinterlands.

Palander elaborated policies of operation that firm B can assume in selecting a location in relation to a competitor A. B can choose to establish a policy of pricing to eliminate his competitors, to share the market with A, or to raise prices and thus limit sales to his own hinterland. This last practice is known as "hinterland defense." If B adopts the first procedure in the hope of eliminating competition, he will locate as near to A as possible and reduce his price below A's. If, however, he pursues a policy of hinterland defense, he has a choice of locations either near or far from A depending on A's price. If B's policy is to share the market with A, it would be to his advantage to locate at a distance from A. This situation encourages decentralization of industry.

EDGAR M. HOOVER.　Hoover demonstrated the importance of transfer costs as applied to the market of two competitors (22–15). The extractive industry is utilized for his example, but the model can be applied directly to manufactur-

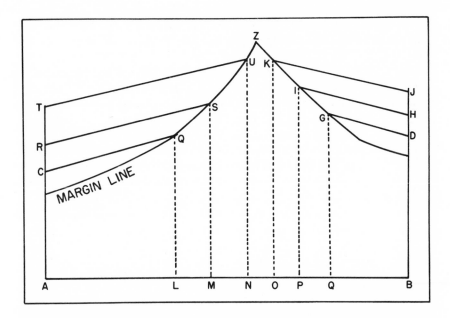

Figure 1.9. Market areas and transport costs. When there are two manufacturers, A and B, the size of the market will depend on the initial cost plus the freight rate. The height of the transport gradient depends on the cost of the commodity at the production point, and, under the influence of diminishing returns, the price will rise as the market area increases. (Source: Edgar M. Hoover, *Location Theory and the Shoe and Leather Industries,* Harvard University Press, Cambridge, 1937, Fig. 7.)

ing (Fig. 1.9). It is assumed that there are two producers, A and B. The price of the product will be the initial cost plus the freight rate. Thus the height of a transport gradient depends on the price of the commodity at the point of production, and, under the influence of diminishing returns, the price will rise as the market area increases. For each rate of output, there is a different cost level of the transport gradient.

To illustrate, if A's market area extends to L, the cost at A will be AC, and transport costs will make the delivered price grade up to LQ at L. If A's market area extends to M, delivered price will range from AR at A to MS at M. There will be similar gradients for B. Of these transport gradients, the significant points are those indicating the price at the edge of the market area. When all such points are connected, they show how the delivered price at the edge of the market area varies as the extent of the market area itself changes. Hoover designated this line as the *margin line.* When the producer controls his local market and price competition is restricted to intermediate zones, the outcome of this competition is determined by the intersections of the respective margin lines. Equilibrium is thus achieved with the market boundary at Z.

A.P. LERNER AND H.W. SINGER.   Lerner and Singer also based their
study on Hotelling, but disputed the belief that producers will always tend to
cluster together (31). In Hotelling's approach, it is assumed that "B will come just
as close to A as other conditions permit. Naturally, if A is not exactly in the
center of the line, B will choose the side of A toward the more extensive section
of the markets to get, so to speak, between one's competitor and a mass of
customers" (31–147). In disagreement, Lerner and Singer state, "it is only possible for each buyer to purchase one unit, irrespective of price, if there is no upper
limit of his expenditures. In such a case the location of a single seller is indeterminate, for in any location a unit can be sold at an infinite price. It is necessary,
therefore, to assume an upper limit to the price each buyer is willing to pay for
his unit of the commodity if we are going to be at all realistic" (31–148). This
assumption rests on three factors: the size of the market, the cost of transport, and
the price buyers are willing to pay for a delivered commodity.

Lerner and Singer illustrated this problem by using one producer, A. It is
assumed that the upper limit to each consumer's absolutely inelastic demand is
the same, called the "demand price." With the demand price and the length of
the market as unity, this relationship can be expressed in terms of C, the cost of
transport. Thus if the cost of transporting one unit of the commodity across the
total length of the market is equal to the demand price, C will equal 1. Transport
costs can also be expressed as $d = 1/C$, where d is the distance. With increase in
the demand price, while market distance and transport costs are constant, there
will be proportional decreases in C or increases in d. Likewise an increase in the
cost of transport per unit product per unit distance will result in an increase in C
or a decrease in d.

This concept is seen in Fig. 1.10. OG is the length of the market. OP is the
demand curve. The slope of FN or FM or PQ results from a rise in the cost of
transportation, so that the slope of the lines (OP/OQ) equals C, the cost of the
transportation. Thus the location of any producer, his price, the number of
customers he supplies, and the cost to each of them is shown by $MNFA$. F
shows the location and the price charged, the abscissa measuring the location in
terms of distance from OP, and the ordinate measuring the price charged. MN is
the length of market served, and any point on FM or FN indicates the location of
consumers, the abscissa measuring his location and the ordinate measuring the
cost to him. The producer wishes to maximize the profit, which will be equal to
AF (price) multiplied by MN (quantity sold). This is maximized when $AF = 1/2$.
"The demand curve is represented by PV, which will be a straight line with a
slope of $C/2$, a reduction in price will increase the length of the market that is
supplied on either side by a distance over which the transport cost is equal to the
reduction in price. His output will be $OV/2 = OQ = MN = d$; his price will be
$OP/2 = AF = 1/2$; and profit will be $d/2$" (31–150).

Lerner and Singer illustrated this situation as it becomes more complex:
They started with two producers, then showed the repercussions when the producers react with each other; when competitors change positions; when the
locations are fixed but prices are free to vary; and, finally, when both location

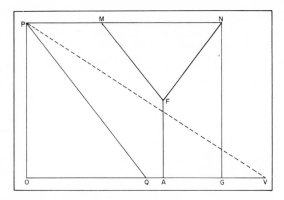

Figure 1.10. Market areas and profits. Lerner and Singer, by using a single producer, A, illustrate the concept of profit and market area. (Source: A.P. Lerner and H.W. Singer, "Some Notes on Duopoly and Spatial Competition," *Journal of Political Economy,* 1937, Fig. 1.)

and price are adjustable in that each competitor will react, but not to the point where either is eliminated for fear of retaliation.

A major section of Lerner and Singer's article (31) considers the location of competitors when they vary in number. The authors dispute the earlier works of Hotelling and Chamberlin. Chamberlin accepted Hotelling's viewpoint of two competitors, but suggested it will not apply to more than two. Chamberlin indicated that when there are more than two competitors, they will disperse. He stated that for "three sellers the outcome seems to be that two of them would be located at the quartile points and the third at any point between them. . . . There is no reason for sellers grouping by two's for their dispersing" (10–194). The sellers may then be "distributed at equal intervals along the line. . ., the result being but little different from the ideal" (10–194). Lerner and Singer considered this interpretation incorrect.

They suggested that a different spatial pattern will evolve with the increase in the number of producers (Fig. 1.11), as follows. A single producer will locate at the center of the market. Two producers will also locate together at the market center. With the arrival of a third producer, the spatial pattern is complicated. The assumption is that the third producer will locate as close to the other two as possible in the central position. As a result the middle producer will find himself surrounded and thus cut off from the market on either side. At this point, the movements of the producers begin. The producer in the middle position will move past one of his competitors, imprisoning him in turn. If, when the middle producer moves, the producers on the outside fill the gap, they remain in the center regardless of the number of moves.

If, however, as movement occurs, the prisoner in the middle leaves the group entirely for an outside position, the group is broken into two parts. The

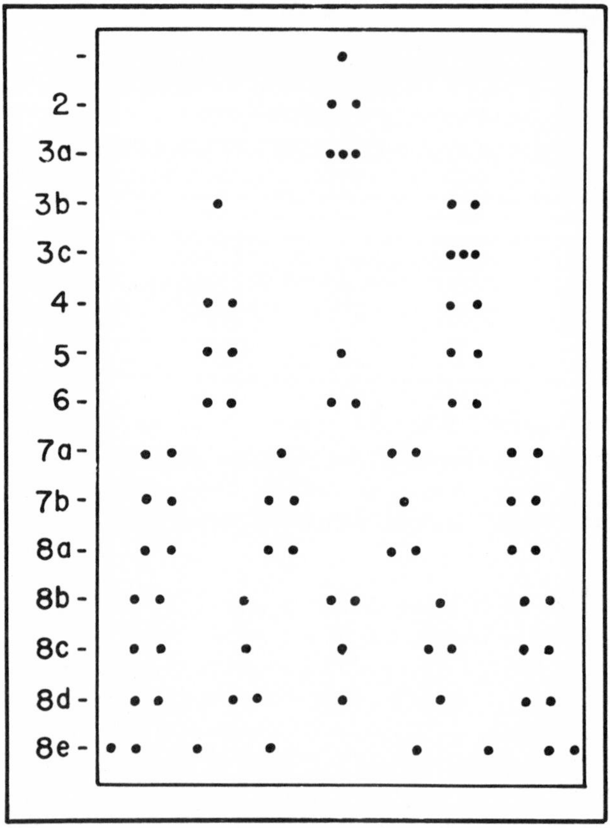

Figure 1.11. Location of competitors when they vary in number. Spatial patterns evolve as the number of producers increases. As competition increases, the pattern is in constant change in order for each producer to gain a more favorable position. (Source: A.P. Lerner and H.W. Singer, "Some Notes on Duopoly and Spatial Competition," *Journal of Political Economy,* 1937, Fig. 10.)

movement continues until it is no longer profitable for the middle competitor to go outside because the market in the middle has grown while the producers were moving away from each other, and the market outside has diminished. This point will be reached when the producers are at the quartiles of the market (two at one quartile, the third at the other). The single producer who has a quartile to himself will make twice as much profit as either of the others. Stability remains until the single competitor moves toward the other two. If he moves so as to achieve the position 3*b*, he will supply 3/4 of the market. However, at this point the middle competitor will move and the process will begin once again after the whole group has moved to the center of the market. (Each escaping competitor will always choose the larger market on either side of the center.) Thus 3*a*, 3*b*, and 3*c* illustrate the extreme positions in an unstable cycle. Given the assumption stated in the preceding paragraph, three is the only number of competitors that does not give any position of stable equilibrium.

A stable equilibrium is achieved when a fourth producer enters the scene. He will immediately locate next to the single producer, as shown in 3*b*. Every producer supplies 1/4 of the market, and no one can gain by moving. A fifth producer would be able to supply 1/4 of the market by locating on either side of the quartiles or anywhere between the quartiles. If he locates in the median position, the pairs at the quartiles will move away from him until their distance from him is twice their distance from the edge of the market. This creates an equilibrium, with the central producer supplying 1/3 and each of the other four 1/6 of the market. If the producer chooses an inside position but not the center, his competitors on the side farthest from him will have a larger market area. Movement of the competitors will begin as a result. One of the competitors on the farther side will be tempted to go over to the other side, imprisoning one of the pair already there. The partner left alone will move to the single newcomer to form a pair with him. The pairs again move to positions 1/3 of the distance from the edge toward their nearest competitors, and the movement continues until a lone producer occupies the center. If the newcomer locates on the outside of one of the pairs, the trio thus formed will break up in the manner described above, except that the steps of the escaping prisoners will not be alternatively right and left.

> For each that goes toward the edge of the market, three will go toward the center. This is because each movement of one unit to the edge diminishes the market there by a whole unit, but a movement of one unit toward the center diminishes the market by 1/2 because part of the burden falls on the seller at the other end and there is then a gain of 1/6 due to the other pair moving 1/3 of a unit away where their competitor moves one unit toward them (as they wish to keep 1/3 of his distance from the edge). The movement of three steps to the center for each step to the edge will finally take one section of the trio to the center and the other to a point 1/6 of the market from the edge. If the center section is an individual producer, we have the equilibrium. If the center section is the pair, the end one moves up to it, so that a new trio is formed, which splits, with a pair going off to 1/6 from the edge and leaving an individual in the center; and so there is final equilibrium. (31–181)

The same procedure can be applied to other numbers.

ARTHUR F. SMITHIES.   Smithies developed a number of further considerations in generalizing the theory of spatial competition (41). He agreed with Hotelling that competitors tend to cluster, but he felt it is also important to analyze why the competitors remain together. Further, Smithies assumed there is an elastic demand at every point of the market and that competitors expect a

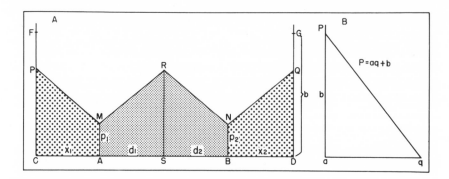

Figure 1.12. Optimum location in spatial competition. In this diagram Smithies analyzes the market area of two competitors. (Source: Arthur F. Smithies, "Optimum Location in Spatial Competition," *Journal of Political Economy,* 1941, Fig. 1.)

reaction from rivals with each adjustment. Finally, Smithies was concerned with the effect of the magnitude of the freight rates and the changes in marginal costs for one or both producers.

To establish a model, the following conditions were assumed: (1) there is a linear market bounded at both ends; (2) there is a single price throughout the market; (3) there are two competitors, A and B, having single locations; (4) the competitors are subject to constant marginal costs; (5) there is a uniform freight rate per unit of distance for each competitor; (6) each competitor sells on an f.o.b. mill basis; (7) each competitor is free to move instantaneously and without cost; (8) each competitor will attempt to establish his mill price in order to maximize profits in respect to total sales; and (9) there are sales at every point in the market.

Smithies described these assumptions by using Fig. 1.12. CD represents the length of the linear market. A and B are the two producers, and AM and BN are the respective mill prices, denoted by p_1 and p_2. The lines MP and MR show the delivered prices for A, while NR and NQ are the delivered prices for B. The freight rate determines the slope of these lines. The market regions are thus determined with A not being able to sell to the right of S and B to the left of S. The vertical lines CF and DG are drawn for reference, with the height of b being the price intercept of the demand curve, which is assumed to be in the form of $P = aq + b$, where P denotes the delivered price charged at any point in the market and q denotes the quantity sold at that point. The distances AC and BD are denoted x_1 and x_2, while the distances from AS and BS are denoted as d_1 and d_2. The areas of x_1 and x_2 are completely within the control of A and B, respectively, but the control of d_1 and d_2 depends on the mutual interaction of their price and location policy. Thus AB is designated the "competitive" region, and AC and BD the "hinterlands" of A and B.

Smithies's next step was to establish hypotheses as to the behavior of the competitors. Three types of equilibrium situations were analyzed under conditions of monopoly, full quasi-cooperation, and full competition. In a monopoly situation, a firm has the total market area and, if freight costs are not considered, it could locate anywhere. If there are freight costs, the situation of the firm's location is altered. As freight rates are added, the uniform price throughout the region disappears. As a result the optimum location for the plant becomes the center of the market. If the manufacturer increases the number of plants, the market will be divided equally among them, each maintaining a monopoly over a given portion of the market area.

With quasi-cooperation, the essential difference between two competitors and a two-plant monopolist is that each competitor attempts to secure more than half of the market area. As each firm moves to increase its market area, it is accompanied by less successful exploitation of the original hinterland. However, it is postulated that there are no profits to be gained by invasion of new territory because, as each firm changes its price or location, the rival firm will meet the identical situation. Thus neither firm can hope to control more than half of the market area.

With full competition, each producer believes that he can increase his selling territory by moving toward the center and by price cutting; these are interdependent. With equal prices and territories, equilibrium will thus be achieved closer to the market center than to the quartiles. This means that by altering his position, a producer does not affect his position in the hinterland because freight charges are always passed on to the consumer. As a result there are no restraints to territorial advance so that the competitors, if both are free to move, will inevitably move to the center of the market.

GARDNER ACKLEY. Ackley approached the problems of spatial competition from the viewpoint that the demand is not evenly spaced but is concentrated at particular locations (1). It is assumed that consumer demand is generally spaced approximately according to the distribution of population. The discussion shows "that even if each of two f.o.b. sellers does assume that his rival's price is given, the fact of discrete markets instead of a continuous market may give exactly the same level of prices as would have ensued if each seller had made the monopolistic assumptions that the other would immediately duplicate any price change, up or down" (1–212).

Ackley used the same assumptions as Hotelling except that all buyers are evenly spread along the market line—all having identical and completely inelastic demand for the product—and the sellers take each others' prices as given. Thus locations are fixed and the prices are the only variables.

To illustrate the model, Ackley assumed two producers A and B and five markets at specified distances between them (Fig. 1.13). The following is also assumed:

$$X_1 = 400 - 4p_1$$
$$X_2 = 100 - p_2$$

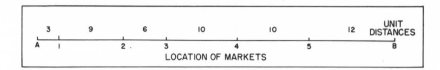

Figure 1.13. Location of markets. Ackley approached the problem of locational interdependence by assuming that demand is not evenly spaced, but rather is concentrated at particular locations. This figure is used to illustrate a dispersed market. (Source: F. Ackley, "Spatial Competition in a Discontinuous Market," *Quarterly Journal of Economics,* 1942, Fig. 1.)

$$X_3 = 700 - 5p_3$$
$$X_4 = 300 - p_4$$
$$X_5 = 400 - 3p_5$$

where X is the amount sold, p is the delivered price, and the subscripts designate the markets. It is also assumed that the freight rate is one unit per mile, the same in either direction and for any distance. The important aspect of this model is that the quantity sold by either seller is not a simple continuous function of his or his rival's price, but is a discontinuous function of the prices. To illustrate, when both sellers have the same price, $p_a = p_b = 50$, buyers in markets 1, 2, and 3 have lower delivered prices by purchasing from A, and seller B has the advantage in markets 4 and 5.

A basic question investigated is the effect on the market of a change in prices. Ackley showed that when one seller lowers his price, he increases sales within present market boundaries, but his market is not enlarged until he reaches the price of the competitor in the new area. As soon as the price cutter sells at the price level of his rival, his sales will increase rapidly. If, however, the price cutter is able to sell at a lower price, his rival will be driven out of the market, and the price cutter's sales will rise substantially. Again, price cutting will increase the market only slightly until the price is lowered below the original competition within the region, when again a major change occurs in the market area of the two competitors. Ackley, however, stated that it is highly questionable whether an equilibrium of the market area will ever be achieved. As soon as seller A changes a price, seller B will reciprocate so that the battle for market areas will continue indefinitely. Thus no generalized solution to the size of the market area emerges. The solution to each specific case must be considered individually under the various assumptions regarding the competitors' situations.

INTEGRATION OF LEAST COST AND LOCATIONAL INTERDEPENDENCE

Melvin Greenhut has provided the most logical theory in attempting to integrate the least cost and locational interdependence theories.[7] His theory is broader in scope than earlier works in the field and thus permits consideration of numerous factors that influence the locational pattern of industry.

Location Factors

Fundamental to Greenhut's approach is that the location of any manufacturing establishment depends on several factors. Generally one factor is basic while others are secondary. Locational factors may also be classified as general or specific. The general factors relate to regional considerations, while specific factors influence location within a city or district.

TRANSPORTATION COSTS. Transportation costs become the most important factor in the localization of manufacturing when the processing costs, market demand, and personal factors are held constant. When transportation costs dominate, they become an important influence in the decentralization of an industry. In general, transfer costs draw firms producing consumer goods to the market and pull the earlier stages of processing to raw materials. When the raw material sources and markets are separated, locational dispersion occurs. Greenhut stated that decentralization occurs best when the market is scattered over a wide area and to those industries that produce nonhomogeneous products (18–107).

Freight rates are important in localizing industry only when they vary over space. Thus the ratio of transport costs to total costs and the differences at alternative sites are the critical issues. Variations in transport costs influence the locational patterns in a number of ways. For example, the higher transfer costs encourage dispersion of industry in order to reduce total costs at a given place. In effect, high transfer costs operate as a protective tariff for local industries. Lower transfer costs act in a reverse fashion. When transfer costs are low, the production units are large, tend to concentrate, and can serve large areas.

The freight costs for an individual firm are determined by the means that raw materials and the finished product may be moved. Firms that process raw materials are thus concerned with the source of raw materials and the market they serve, while finished goods manufacturers are concerned with the source of the partially manufactured items they require and the market they ultimately serve. Greenhut states, "The governing elements in the respective locations are (1) the transportability of various goods, (2) the location of raw material produc-

[7]Melvin L. Greenhut, *Plant Location in Theory and Practice: The Economics of Space* (Chapel Hill: University of North Carolina Press, 1956), pp. 103–176, 273–286.

ing industries, and (3) the situs of the buying markets" (18–108). There is thus an interdependence in the stages of manufacturing. Each industry seeks to lower the transfer costs to increase profits. Thus the importance of transfer costs depends on their proportion and variability over space.

PROCESSING COSTS. Processing costs may dominate in localizing industry when neither transport costs nor market conditions demand a location at the market center. The raw materials source appears to have little or no locational influence on an industry when the cost of transport is negligible, or when the freight cost is substantially the same for raw materials as the finished products. Thus some other factor must explain the localization of an industry. Greenhut concludes that when transportation costs are small and are less variable than processing costs, the processing costs become the significant locating cost factor. This is particularly the situation when the product process is complex (18–124).

The variations in processing costs are primarily due to the immobility of different factors that affect the costs in processing. Theoretically, if the processing costs were completely mobile, there would be no spatial differences and thus they would play no role in the localization of industry. In reality, the factors that make up processing costs are highly immobile. For example, land is completely fixed and human resources are relatively immobile. Real wages, however, vary from place to place depending on available labor. For example, when labor is scarce, wages will be high. The cost of interest and capital equipment also usually varies from area to area.

Greenhut discussed the relationship between industrial concentration or dispersion and processing costs. The lowering of processing costs as a result of agglomeration will take many forms. The particular characteristic of an industry may favor concentration or dispersion. A major factor of concentration is the economies of scale possible in large factories. Plants also concentrate to obtain cheaper and quicker repairs. Finally, such items as insurance rates, capital, and police and fire protection are generally more favorable in concentrated areas. Factors favoring dispersion are also numerous. The economies of scale obtainable at a given place may not compensate for higher transportation costs. When raw materials are scattered, industries tend to be dispersed. Other dispersal factors include scarcity of building sites, increasing cost of travel to work, and increasing cost of auxiliary items.

In discussing the processing costs Greenhut devotes sections to labor, capital, and taxation. It is stressed that the influence of labor on location is determined by five conditions: wage level, productivity, turnover and attitudes of the workers, labor supply, and labor laws. Although capital rarely, if ever, is a dominant force in localizing industry, it influences industrial locations in three ways. First, the availability of capital at a particular location affects location. Second, funds are required to insure a successful industry. And third, the interest on funds varies from place to place and thus influences competition. There is little evidence that the tax structure of a region either attracts or repels industry.

DEMAND FACTOR.   The market is important in locating an industry because of the variability of demand for products. Two types of locational data affect total demand: demand varies with the price, and demand varies with distance. Thus the objective is to locate the lowest delivered price over the largest possible market area.

Greenhut considered several types of market situation. The first example discusses locational interdependence and market area under a nondiscriminatory f.o.b. price system. Under such conditions, it is concluded, demand affects industrial agglomeration by

> (1) the shape of the demand curve (*ceteris paribus,* an infinitely inelastic demand curve promotes localization, a negatively sloping straight line demand curve induces distant locations, an infinitely elastic demand curve causes perfect dispersion with consumer scattering), (2) the shape of the marginal cost curves (*ceteris paribus,* if the marginal cost curves are negatively sloping, freight absorption is small, price tends to be high, and sales to buyers located at the fringe of the market are unprofitable; this factor encourages dispersion, and vice versa, if marginal costs are rising), (3) the height of the freight rates (the higher the freight rates, the greater the dispersion, and vice versa), and (4) the degree and type of competition in the industry, which itself is largely influenced by these other factors. (18–147)

These factors are always related in some manner.

COST-REDUCING AND REVENUE-INCREASING FACTORS. There are special characteristics that influence costs of production and thus affect plant location. For example, the sale of women's clothing depends to a great extent on the mood of the final purchaser and the speed of service, and direct contact with buyers may determine the quantity of a product sold. Personal factors may influence the location of a factory by indirectly affecting cost, partially determining demand, and/or providing nonpecuniary awards.

Greenhut believes that a variety of localizing forces have been disregarded. These are considered from the viewpoint of such cost-reducing factors as the establishment of branch plants to reach scattered markets and the establishment of a plant near a banker because the entrepreneur believes friendship influences the availability of materials or funds.

General Theory of Plant Location

The theories of plant location developed along two approaches. The first approach emphasized the search for the least cost location. The second was oriented to an analysis of market area monopolistic competition. In Greenhut's theory, consumers are assumed to be scattered rather than confined to a point. The cost of procuring and processing raw materials is assumed to be the same everywhere. Each manufacturer charges the same mill price, and the price to the consumer varies with transfer charges. Manufacturers, by dispersing, gain control of markets near the plant. Demand will then be controlled by the location of competitors. The market area approach emphasizes the control over specific buyers.

Greenhut's theory attempted to correlate the demand and market approach. There is thus an integration of cost and demand influences that are considered codeterminants of location. This theory must include, then:

1. Cost factors of location (transportation, labor, processing costs).
2. Demand factors of location (locational interdependence of firms or attempts to monopolize certain market segments).
3. Cost-reducing factors.
4. Revenue-increasing factors.
5. Personal cost-reducing factors.
6. Personal revenue-increasing factors.
7. Purely personal considerations, perhaps.

Only when all of these factors are considered on determining the location of an industry can an understanding of the forces for determining location be acquired.

In the appraisal of his general theory, Greenhut outlined the following steps toward a spatial equilibrium:

> If we imagine first a well developed economy and, subsequently, the innovation of a new product, it would follow (under the simplifying assumptions of zero costs everywhere and identical demands everywhere) that the innovating firm would locate in the center of the market area. Further, it is obvious that under the profit-maximizing nondiscriminatory f.o.b. mill price system, the innovator will deliberately limit his sales radius. Over this restricted sales area, his net-mill price will be something greater than zero, if economic profits are possible, its exact value depending upon the ratio of the freight rate per unit of distance to the highest price that the homogeneous consumers will pay. Later rivals then would locate either in the non-supplied regions, next door to the innovator, or at some place distant from him, depending upon the demand factors. If the stringent postulate of zero costs is discarded, cost differentials would exert their force directly and indirectly (through locational interdependence), thereby influencing the ultimate locations. (18–284).

The basis of the theory is that each firm will seek a site so that it can operate at the lowest total cost. It is further recognized that when competition develops not only will costs change but demands also will be altered. As more and more competitors locate at the profit maximizing site the demands will be reduced and profits shrink. When the ultimate of new firms are established a state of locational equilibrium will exist. Such an equilibrium will exist when marginal revenues are equal to marginal costs, average revenues equal average costs, and when a new plant distributional pattern would cause losses.

The theory recognizes that as change occurs in such factors as the demand curve and cost of a product, a new relationship which affects the location of plants develops. As a consequence of such changes, the equilibrium at any moment in time is upset. This situation encourages relocation and the establishment of new plants in different regions.

SPATIAL GENERAL EQUILIBRIUM

There has long been an interest in the study of general economic equilibrium. In 1889 Leon Walras published the first fully designated general equilibrium analysis. In more recent years John Hicks, Paul Samuelson, and Walter Isard have produced mathematical equilibrium models, which can be proved conceptually but not empirically. Nevertheless, each provides penetrating insights into economic situations under which a stable economic condition could develop.

As Bramhall states, "in the economic context a general equilibrium model is a set of statements about an entire economic system which specifies the motivating principles of economic actors, the physical-technological conditions of economic activity, and the nature of markets in which participants interact."[8] To elaborate, Kuenne states that general equilibrium is "a specific solution to an economic model describing a state of rest and resulting from the opposition between identifiable desires of men and obstacles to their fulfillment, including among the latter the desires of actors other than any one of the specific firms or consumers under consideration" (28–18).

General equilibrium theory developed largely outside a spatial framework. In general, a spatial equilibrium model must consider the number and type of economic components, the set of relevant commodities, the economic sectors included, the motivating forces, and the dimensions of distance and direction.

One of the earliest statements relating to spatial equilibrium was made by Lösch in 1939. In the same year, J.R. Hicks developed a number of implications. He states, "It turns out, on investigation, that most of the problems of several variables, with which economic theory has to concern itself, are problems of interrelations of markets" (21–2). The first comprehensive theory of general equilibrium using a spatial concept was developed by Walter Isard, in *Location and Space Economy* (25), and the following discussion is based on that work.

Isard conceived

the general theory of location and space-economy to be one which com-

---

[8]David F. Bramhall, "An Introduction to Spatial General Equilibrium," in G.J. Karaska and D.F. Bramhall, eds., *Locational Analysis for Manufacturing* (Cambridge, Mass.: MIT Press, 1969), p. 468.

prehends the economy in its totality. Not only are the mutual relations and interdependence of all economic elements, both in the aggregate and atomistically, of fundamental importance; but the spatial as well as the temporal (dynamic) character of the interrelated economic pressure must enter the picture. (25–26–27)

Isard further states,

The general theory of location and space-economy is conceived as embracing the total spatial array of economic activities, with attention paid to the geographic distribution of inputs and outputs and the geographic variations in prices and costs. Modern general equilibrium theory is a special case of this theory, in which transport costs are taken as zero and all inputs and outputs are viewed as perfectly mobile. (25–53)

Isard considered the substitution principle as one of the best analytical tools for developing this general theory. The substitution principle must include the relation between transport inputs and other types of costs and revenues. This formulation thus begins with transportation and, later, adds other factors.

Transport Orientation

Isard's analysis of the locational equilibrium of a firm using transport orientation illustrates the application of his substitution principle. The Weberian locational triangle is utilized as the basic framework, with one corner, C, representing the market and the other two corners, M_1 and M_2, representing raw material sources (Fig. 1.14). When the raw material at M_2 is mobile, "for each possible (realistic) distance from M_2, there exists a transformation line between the variables, distance from C and distance from M_1; and for each possible (realistic) distance from M_1 there exists a transformation line between the variables, distance from C and distance from M_2; and finally for each possible (realistic) distance from C there exists a transformation line between the variables, distance from M_1 and distance from M_2" (25–97). The transformation function embraces the numerous technical substitution relations between any pair of outputs, any input and any output, and any pair of inputs.

The initial problem is to find the optimum location for production. This will depend on the relative position of C, M_1, and M_2. To illustrate, assume that the distances between C and M_2, C and M_1, and M_2 and M_1 are 8, 5, and 7 units, respectively. Further, assume there are 3 distance units from C to obtain a transformation line representing the different possible sets of variables, distance from M_1 and distance from M_2, represented by arc TS. TS thus represents a locus of possible points.

The next procedure is to transpose the TS arc into a transformation line on a graph in which distance from M_1 is plotted against distance on M_2 (Fig. 1.15). As

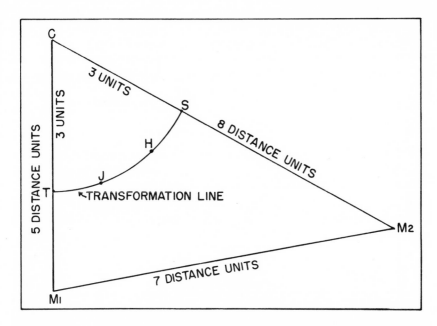

Figure 1.14. Isard's locational triangle. The transformation line *TS* represents a locus of possible production points. (Source: Walter Isard, *Location and Space Economy,* MIT Press, Cambridge, 1956, Fig. 17.)

there is movement from S to T, distance from M_1 decreases and distance from M_2 increases. In this way transport inputs from one source are being substituted for transport inputs from another source. To illustrate, assume 1 unit of cost per unit of distance. If a factory is located 4 miles from M_1 and 5 miles from M_2, it would have a cost of 4 transport units from M_1 and 5 from M_2. If the production point were at T, the expenditure would be 7 units at T but only 2 units from M_1, transport inputs from M_2 having been substituted for those from M_1.

This follows to the next question, Where is the least cost location on arc ST? To find this location, equal outlay lines must be added to Fig. 1.15. To accomplish this, assume that production requires 1 ton of material from M_1 and 1 ton from M_2. Thus the transportation charge per unit of distance for each distance variable is identical. As a result of these assumptions, the price ratio lines for these two distance variables must be straight and have a negative slope of 1. These equal outlay lines are EF and BD. The transformation line and the desired price-ratio lines yield point J as a partial equilibrium position. This results because J is that realistic point on the arc TS which lies on the lowest possible price-ratio line (Fig. 1.16).

If, however, the distance from C varies and the distance from M_2 is consistent with location at point J, a transformation line can be constructed for the variables, distance from M_1 and distance from C. The construction of partial

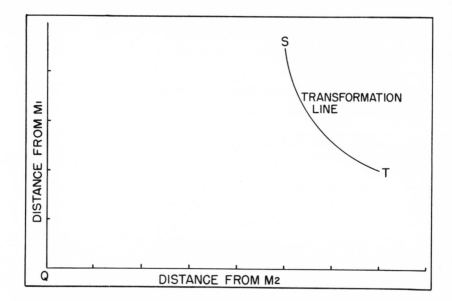

Figure 1.15. A transformation line for a locational triangle. The transformation line *TS* transposed on the figure indicates how transport inputs from one source can be substituted for transport inputs from another source. (Source: Walter Isard, *Location and Space Economy,* MIT Press, Cambridge, 1956, Fig. 18.)

equilibrium positions continues until a full equilibrium position evolves. This occurs when the distances from C and M_1, C and M_2, and M_1 and M_2 coincide. Isard recognized that this procedure can be applicable to a polygon as well as a triangle. In the four- or more-sided polygon, the distance variables are not held constant except two, but only the total transport expenditure on these other distance variables.

Labor Orientation

After a consideration of transportation orientation, Isard introduced differentials in factor costs and revenue potentials. Again, it is necessary to consider the problem in terms of substitution—this time between outlays and revenues. The location of production is influenced by the variations from site to site in the prices of inputs and outputs.

For each transport cost point on the transformation line as given by the iso-outlay (transport plus labor outlay) line, there is also a labor outlay point. This can be illustrated by Fig. 1.17. In this diagram, E, F, G, H, J, L, M, N, and R represent cheap labor sites. Other points could be plotted. If F, J, L, M, N, and R are connected according to transport outlay, an "outlay substitution"

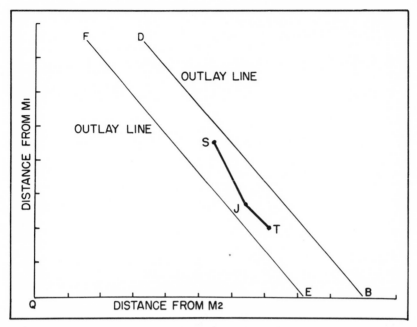

Figure 1.16. Locational equilibrium by using discontinuous transformation line. This diagram demonstrates the determination of the least cost location on arc *ST*. (Source: Walter Isard, *Location and Space Economy*, MIT Press, Cambridge, 1956, Fig. 21.)

line is obtained. This line represents the substitution possibilities between transport outlays and labor outlays, just as the transformation line does for two inputs. A new set of iso-outlay lines (transport plus labor outlay) are constructed. These have a negative slope of unity. *TU* and *CD* are two such lines, representing combined outlays of $56.00 and $50.00, respectively. Of all the points, *J* lies on the lowest iso-outlay line. This point has a lower labor cost than that at *F*, the minimum transport cost point, and thus there can be a substitution of transport outlays for labor outlays if location were initially at *F*.

Substitution Framework for Spatial Analysis

Isard classified location factors into three groups. The first group includes transport and certain other transfer costs. Because these costs vary regularly with distance, they provide a relevant set of reference points—whether raw materials, service, or market points—which establish systematic variations of these costs over space.

A second group of factors comprises costs associated with labor, power, taxes, water, insurance, climate, and a number of other items. Although these

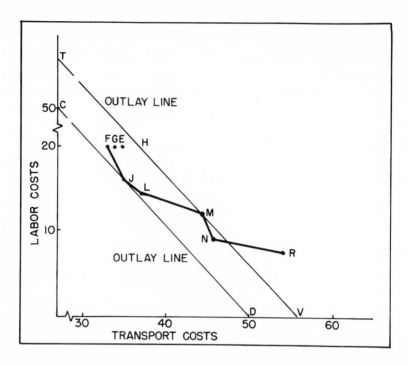

Figure 1.17. Outlay substitution line using labor orientation. For each transport cost point on the transformation line as given by the iso-outlay line, there is also a labor outlay point. (Source: Walter Isard, *Location and Space Economy,* MIT Press, Cambridge, 1956, Fig. 25.)

items possess a relatively stable geographic cost pattern, they do not vary systematically with distance as do transport costs. By contrast, these costs vary independently of distance and direction.

The third group includes those elements that cause agglomeration and deglomeration economies. The agglomeration forces include economies of scale, localization economies, and urbanization economies. The deglomerative forces include diseconomies within a firm, the rise of rents and costs of urban services, and the rise in the cost of food as the rise in the size of population settlement compels the importation of foods from greater distances. The agglomerative and deglomerative forces operate independently of geographical position.

Isard concluded that of the three groups only transport costs, which are functionally related to distance, impart regularity to the spatial pattern of activities. Substitution analysis among various transport inputs provides an understanding of the geographic pattern of production and the impact of the friction of distance.

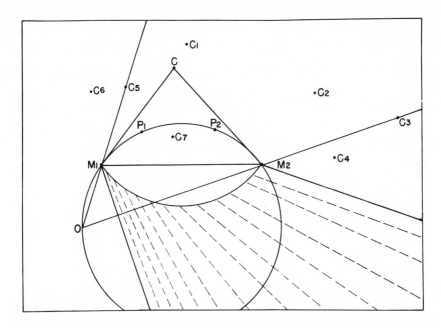

Figure 1.18. Launhardt-Palander localization of industry. Assuming two raw material sources and one consumer, a locational and corresponding weight triangle can be drawn. The point of intersection P of the pole line OC with the circle is the transport optimal point for serving the customer at C. (Source: Walter Isard, *Location and Space Economy,* MIT Press, Cambridge, 1956, Fig. 44.)

Partial Graphic Synthesis

Isard presented a number of illustrations to demonstrate the general form of the space economy under different assumptions. Using the concepts developed by Launhardt and Palander in presenting the problem of transport orientation, Isard postulated a situation in which there is (1) the absence of various agglomeration economies and geographic variations in the prices of various inputs and outputs, except change in prices due to transport costs and raw materials, and (2) uniform transport facilities that radiate in all directions from all points.

In Fig. 1.18, M_1 and M_2 are the sources of two raw materials, and C is the location of the initial consumer. From this distribution, the locational triangle CM_1M_2 can be drawn, and the corresponding weight triangle OM_1M_2 can be constructed. A circle is circumscribed around the weight triangle, and O and C are connected. The point of intersection, P_1, of the pole line OC with the circle is the transport optimal point for serving the customer at C.

Other production locations can be determined using similar procedures for

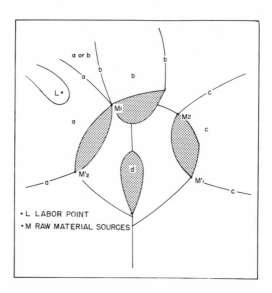

Figure 1.19. Spatial production patterns: two sources of each of two raw materials, and one labor location. This diagram emphasizes a market area problem when there are different sources of raw materials and one labor source. (Source: Walter Isard, *Location and Space Economy,* MIT Press, Cambridge, 1956, Fig. 47.)

customers located anywhere from C_1 to C_7. For example, for a customer located at C_3 when C_3 is connected with O, the line intersects M_2, a raw material source; thus M_2 becomes the logical production point for C_3. M_2 is also the transport optimal point for C_4. This occurs even though the pole line OC_4 does not intersect the circumscribed circle at M_2, but lies outside the locational triangle $C_4M_1M_2$. At M_2, the external angle of the locational triangle is less than the corresponding angle of the weight triangle. Customers C_5 and C_6 should be served from producers at M_1. When a customer is located at C_7, the pole line OC_7 does not intersect the circumscribed circle at a point within the locational triangle $C_7M_1M_2$. Angle conditions indicate that C_7 should be the production point for customers at C_7.

Isard extended this approach by the incorporation of a cheap labor location into the Launhardt-Palander construction. This can lead to a market area problem. Isard developed this concept with an illustration that was taken from Palander (Fig. 1.19). It is assumed that there are four sources of raw materials, M_1, M_2, M_1', and M_2', and aside from a district of consumers served from a cheap labor source L, there are four groupings of consumers indicated by the heavy solid lines. It is also assumed that production in these districts need not be market oriented.

In this situation production occurs at raw material sources, at market points,

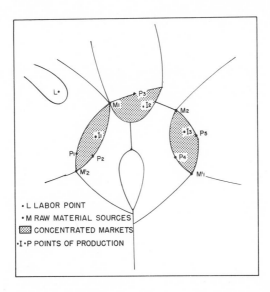

Figure 1.20. Spatial production patterns with scale economies introduced. As the economies of scale increase, output will be concentrated at single points in each of the three large market-oriented areas. (Source: Walter Isard, *Location and Space Economy,* MIT Press, Cambridge, 1956, Fig. 48.)

and at points where relevant pole lines intersect with an arc of a circle circumscribed about the relevant weight triangle. In district a and the cheap labor area L, producers utilize raw materials from M_1 and M_2'. In district c, producers at raw material sources, market points, and intersection points procure their raw materials from M_1' and M_2. In district d, all producers are market oriented and obtain raw materials from M_1' and M_2'. Finally, since M_2 and M_2' are at an equal distance from M_1, and also supply the second raw material at the same price, it makes no difference whether production at M_1 secures its raw material from M_2' or M_2. Therefore the subdistrict served by M_1 can be part of either a or b.

Isard then introduced scale economies. In Fig. 1.20, the smallest scale of output is associated with market-oriented producers. As economies of scale increase, output will be concentrated at a single point in each of the three largest market-oriented areas—I_1, I_2, and I_3. Production points along a single pole line also operate at a small scale. With economies of scale, production will be concentrated at single points P_1, P_2, P_3, P_4, and P_5. This illustrates the impact of variability in scales.

Economies of localization and urbanization are introduced in the final stage (Fig. 1.21). The assumption is that, for many firms, there are advantages to locating in an urban center. The decision to settle in an urban area thereby involves substitutions among various outlays and revenues. A variety of firms

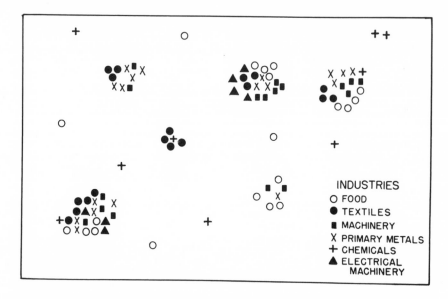

Figure 1.21. Spatial production patterns with urbanization, localization, and scale economies introduced. When these three factors are introduced, there is a tendency for agglomeration to occur for most industries. However, as the diagram illustrates, certain industries are not influenced in their localization by these factors. (Source: Walter Isard, *Location and Space Economy,* MIT Press, Cambridge, 1956, Fig. 50.)

tend to concentrate at urban centers. Some firms, however, do not relocate in urban agglomerations and remain dispersed. These firms are not attracted by localization economies.

RECENT CONTRIBUTIONS

There has been little progress in the last two decades in the elaboration of classical location theory. Locational analysis has continued its development, with new perspectives evolving. Although many of these contributions do not involve new conceptual frameworks, they provide generalizations based on observations of the real industrial world. They are thus concepts useful for the understanding of the industrial locational process.

Behavioral Theory

Within recent times, there has been increasing criticism of the relevancy of classical industrial location theory as applied to real-world situations. Some of these criticisms are based on the following arguments. Under the least cost approach of Alfred Weber, which depends on the input mix and cost structure of the industry considered, the optimum location is either one where total transport costs per unit of output are minimized or one where the agglomeration and/or labor economies per unit of output are sufficient to offset the transport diseconomies as a result of not operating at the point of lowest transport costs. With August Lösch's approach of profit maximization, the optimal location is at the place where the largest possible market is secured. For either of these approaches to be practical in securing an optimal location, the decision maker not only must possess all possible information but he must also apply it with the characteristics of rational economic man. Thus the value of classical theory, predicated on the existence of an omniscient rational being—economic man—is questioned.

The concept of economic man is a normative one; that is, decisions are made under the assumption of complete economic rationality. Thus economic man does not have the limitations of imperfect knowledge, but has omniscient powers of perception, reasoning, and prediction. In reality, however, the decision maker does not have the full range of information, and even if he did he would not have the ability to use the information. Consequently a rational optimal industrial location decision becomes impossible. Thus if there is no methodology capable of determining optimal locations, the actual spatial patterns of manufacturing must deviate from the prescribed distributions suggested by classical location theory. As a result normative economic models have not been adequate in exploring actual locations and locational patterns for industry. They attempt to indicate what the location should be, rather than what it is. As Wolpert indicates, "The presence of uncertainty eliminates the possibility of profit maximization" (52–549). Even Lösch, who was the foremost advocate of profit maximization, states, "There is no scientific and unequivocal solution for the location of the individual firm, but only a practical one; the test of trial and error. Hence Weber's and all other attempts at a systematic and valid location theory for the individual firm were doomed to failure" (33–29).

BEHAVIORAL CONTEXT. Concepts began to evolve in the 1950s in an attempt to relate theory more closely to reality. During this period Simon developed the concept of the "principle of bounded rationality" as an alternative to the normative approach of economic man. This concept stated that "the capacity of the human mind for formulating and solving complex problems is very small compared with the size of the problems whose solution is required for objectively rational behavior in the real world—or even for a reasonable approximation of such objective rationality" (39–198). This viewpoint was elaborated by March and Simon in the development of the "satisficier" concept. This concept

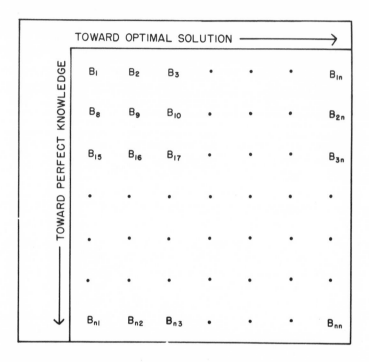

Figure 1.22. Behavioral matrix. The behavioral matrix is based on the two concepts of the availability of information and the ability to use that information. This is a device to assist in understanding reality as it deviates from location patterns as produced by deterministic models based on the assumption of economic man. (Source: Allan Pred, *Behavior and Location: Foundations for a Geographic and Dynamic Location Theory,* Lund Studies in Geography, Uppsala, Part I, 1967, Fig. 1.)

rests on the contention that most human decision making, whether individual or organizational, is concerned with the discovery and selection of satisfactory alternatives (34–141). Thus the search for an industrial location is not for one that is optimal, but for one that will simply satisfy the needs of the decision maker. For example, the decision maker will not know whether he has achieved an industrial location at the site of least cost or maximum profit, but he will be satisfied if he has selected a site that brings to him what he considers a reasonable profit.

BEHAVIORAL MATRIX.   Allen Pred prepared an interesting statement for a geographical location theory based on a behavioral context (37). He conceived the location theory in the form of a behavioral matrix. This is based on the belief that "any economic-geographic distribution is an aggregate manifestation of individual decision arts made at the personal, group and/or firm level. Once the premise that each constituent element of an economic geographic aggregate

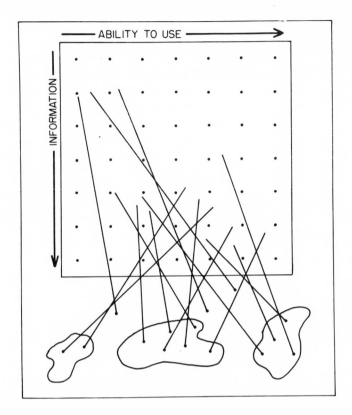

Figure 1.23. The behavioral matrix and industrial location choice. This diagram demonstrates how plants may locate within or without the spatial profitability margins using the information available to them. (Source: Allan Pred, *Behavior and Location: Foundations for a Geographic and Dynamic Location Theory,* Lund Studies in Geography, Uppsala, Part I, 1967, Fig. 11.)

reflects a discrete locational decision is accepted, then the rejection of the economic man hypothesis assumes great relevance" (37–21).

Pred's matrix is based on the simultaneous operation of Alchian's adaptive and adoptive categories translated into a spatial context. Thus diverse locational decisions can always be classified according to two polar viewpoints: One maintains that economic activities adapt themselves to the conditions of the society in which they exist; the other assumes that activities react to their environment in relative ignorance, with the "lucky ones" being adopted by the system (2).

In the behavioral matrix, the quantity and quality of information, which theoretically ranges from no information to complete information, is given on the vertical axis (Fig. 1.22). The ability to use information, which ranges from no ability to ability to make optimal solutions, is shown on the horizontal axis.

Thus each decision has a spatial attribute and behavioral qualities that can be located on the behavioral matrix.

SPATIAL ELABORATION.   Let us suppose that there is a region having a total of 15 plants. Area one contains 2 plants; area two, 6 plants, and area three, 4 plants. It is now possible to relate plant location to the behavioral matrix (Fig. 1.23). This diagram shows that 12 of the plants lie within the bounded rational, satisficier spatial limits of profitability; 3 of the firms are located outside the spatial limits of profitability.

As to the use of the behavioral matrix, many of the plants have a great deal of information and have been able to use it in achieving a satisfactory location. However, there is at least one location where the decision maker had little information and was not able to utilize it effectively and still secured a profitable location. Further, there are 3 plants located where little information is available, and they have not been able to utilize effectively what little information they had. These plants are located outside the profitable area and are operating at a loss. This situation can reflect a number of factors. For example, one of the plants may have located in what is now an unprofitable area at a time when the factors of production were different. With changing factors of production, the plant was not able to cope with the new situation. The other two plants may have been attracted to the unprofitable area because of the presence of the first. Thus these plants may exist because of industrial inertia. However, in the long run these plants will cease to exist because continuing economic losses will not justify their existence.

LIMITATIONS.   Behavioral theory has been little developed to date and has not as yet found the basis for model construction. Pred's behavioral matrix is only a conceptual device that requires testing. The present state of knowledge in the behavioral sciences does not permit precise measurement of the varied phenomena that make up the myriad information necessary for the decision-making process. Initial studies, however, give sufficient promise that the behavioral approach will yield fruitful results (44).

General Systems Theory

There was growing concern in the late 1940s about increasing specialization and the general inability to view problems in their totality. At the same time, it was recognized that problems of an organismic nature were everywhere. Although it was considered necessary to continue the study of isolated problems, it was also felt that a more important approach would be to study the problems of organization, of wholeness and dynamic interactions. Out of these views have evolved the concepts of general systems theory. The notion of a systems approach, initially elaborated by Ludwig von Bertalanffy, has come to be defined as "a set of objects together with the relationship between the objects and between their attributes" (19–18).

BASIC CONCEPTS.   General systems theory has developed a common language and viewpoint to express its concepts. Of fundamental importance is the notion of *open* and *closed systems*. Open systems are those in which there is a continuous import and export of energy and materials. By contrast, a closed system is defined precisely by boundaries across which there can be no imports or exports of energy (ideas) and materials. Thus in reality closed systems are extremely rare, while open systems are common. Change is affected in closed systems only through innate or given differences within the system.

Another basic concept is that of *information*. To receive information and then act on that information is the essential function of every system. Thus related to information is the notion of *entropy*, which can be defined as a tendency toward disorder or randomness. Negative entropy is maximum order or organization while positive entropy is maximum randomness. Thus the tendencies toward negative entropy are measures of the effectiveness of the decision-making process.

Another central concept in systems theory is *feedback*. This implies that certain systems have the property by which a part of their output, or behavior, is fed back to the input to affect succeeding output. Feedback must occur in all systems to achieve *homeostasis*, or the maintenance of balance within the system. The following terms have also become a part of systems analysis: *Adaptation* refers to the ability to react to an environment in a way that is favorable to the continued operation of the system. *Compatibility* refers to the construction of a system to match a given environment. *Optimization* means adapting the system to its environment to secure the best possible performance. There are situations where a general structure bears an intimate resemblance to similar techniques and structures in other areas. A one-to-one correspondence between objects that preserves the relationships between the objects is called *isomorphism*.

It is clear from the basic definition that a system can be further divided into subsystems. Objects belonging to one subsystem may well be considered as part of the environment of another subsystem. Further, the behavior of a subsystem may not be completely analogous with that of the original system. Some authors have referred to this concept as the "hierarchical order of systems."

APPLICATIONS. There appear to be many opportunities for the use of systems analysis in manufacturing. Traditionally, the systems approach has been utilized in the understanding of manufacturing processes. However, a much wider application seems possible.

To illustrate, in all manufacturing there are firms or industries—aggregates with similar functions—to which firms are added and subtracted, and in which the factors of production are identifiable variables. These firms exhibit dynamic trends that can frequently be described by fairly simple systems of equations. The firms of different kinds also exhibit dynamic interactions among themselves. These interactions can be discussed in such terms as "competition" and "complementary" or "parasitic" relationships. Another phenomenon of almost universal significance for all firms is that of the interaction of a firm with its "environment." Each of the firms exhibits "behavior" actions that are in some way related

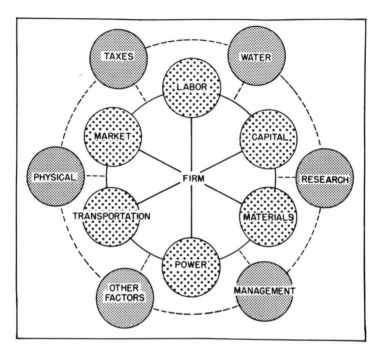

Figure 1.24. The systems approach to industrial location. A diagrammatic sketch of a system of factors that influence the localization of a firm.

to the environment of the firm. Thus a firm or industry functions within the totality of the manufactural system.

The systems approach could also be utilized in analyzing the relationship of the factors of production to the localization of a firm (Fig. 1.24). For a firm to exist at a given site, the primary factors of production must be satisfied. These are represented by the initial ring around the location of the firm. Each of these primary factors plays a role, but at the same time their individual importance may vary from site to site. Around the primary factors are the secondary factors of production that influence the localization of an industry at a given site. Because these are the permissive factors, they are connected by broken lines. Thus specific secondary factors may or may not be a locational influence for a firm. The systems approach recognizes that the totality of the factors of production must be considered by a firm to secure a satisfactory location. Thus there must be steady flows of information in order to understand the links and relationships between the factors. In the systems approach, there is the continuous attempt to reduce the randomness of location. It is also recognized that in the open system, as a result of the continually changing importance of the factors, locational advantages of a particular site are always in a state of modification.

PRESENT USE OF SYSTEMS ANALYSIS. Modern general systems theory as formulated by Bertalanffy had its initial applications in the biological and physical sciences. The concepts have been applied gradually in the social sciences. However, in a survey of industrial location literature, no study was found that applied the concepts directly to the localization of manufacturing. This is somewhat surprising because the history of industrial location has been related directly to the functional approach, that is, an understanding of the relationships of complex wholes. So far geographers and regional economists have developed few conceptionalizations in systems terms. A few authors have pleaded that geographers and economists think in terms of systems, but little has been done beyond this stage. Thus systems analysis has not achieved a strong operational status in industrial location. This may be attributed to the complexity of systems analysis, which invokes advanced mathematical techniques. More importantly, to develop an operational procedure there are many intriguing judgments, such as the definition of the factors, the identification of the linkages and relationships, and the closure of the system. The lack of experience with systems in industrial location prevents an effective evaluation of the potential of the systems approach. In present attempts to apply the concepts to industrial localization, the use of systems analysis is at the stage of an a priori model.

ADVANTAGES AND LIMITATIONS. Possibly the major advantage of systems analysis is its ability to study complex interacting phenomena. It thus encompasses classical theory while extending the analytical framework to areas where interactions are so complex that they are not analyzable with traditional techniques. The theory of general systems thus provides an inductive and analytic approach to the study of complex problems. By this procedure it is possible to operationalize systems concepts. A major notion in systems analysis is the belief in the usefulness of a synthetic approach by combining contributions from numerous fields to achieve greater understanding of a specific problem.

Criticism has developed because general system theory has not been able to formulate a precise model of approach. One of the most penetrating criticisms has been offered by Chisholm (11). He indicates that a major problem is defining the systems to be investigated. If the system can be defined, the next obstacle is the search for analogies in the behavior of systems. While this technique is important to obtain hypotheses that can be tested, analysis exists independently of general systems theory. Thus the only contribution is the search for analogies that are related directly to systems instead of single phenomena. Chisholm also criticizes the inductive approach to systems theory. Inductive reasoning does not possess the strength of deductive logic. "This basis in inductive reasoning means that there is a fundamental weakness to general systems theory that cannot be disguised by the use of symbolic logic or by phrasing systems theory in terms of set theory" (11–49). Chisholm concludes that "if we view our phenomena as open systems, and concentrate our analysis upon the processes and relationships that exist within and between the systems, then this is nothing but plain common sense. General systems theory seems to be an irrelevant distraction" (11–51).

Growth Pole and Growth Center Theory

The concept of the *pole de croissance* ("growth pole") was introduced by François Perroux in the 1940s. Today the growth pole concept, along with the related concept of the growth center, is widely considered.

GROWTH POLE.   Perroux's original concept was not related to physical space but rather to *abstract space*. This was defined as sets of relations which respond to responses without involving directly the location of a point or an area. Therefore "by pure and simple transposition of this distinction between Euclidean and abstract space, we may distinguish . . . as many economic spaces as there are constituent structures of abstract relations which define each object of economic space" (36–91). Thus abstract space is expressed only by a constituent structure or by a mathematical system of relations. Further, Perroux conceptualized that economic activities cannot be localized.

Perroux indicated that economic spaces are defined by the economic relations which exist between economic elements. As a result economic space is reduced to three types: space defined by a plan; space defined by a field of forces; and space as a homogeneous aggregate.

In the first place, a firm has a space defined by a plan; this is known as *banal space*. Thus the banal space of a firm is that in which the factors of production localize a firm. This establishes a set of relations that exist between the firm and, on the one hand, the suppliers of inputs and, on the other hand, the market. The economic distance, measured by costs, is determined by factors outside the plan.

The economic space of a firm is also determined by a *field of forces*. As a field of forces, economic space consists of centers (or poles or foci) from which centrifugal forces emanate and to which centripetal forces are attracted. Thus each center of attraction and repulsion has its proper field, which in turn is set in the field of other centers. The economic zone of influence is delimited by this process. Perroux states, "the topographical zone of influence of Michelin in France is described in a region, but its economic zone of influence, like that of all large firms, defies cartography" (36–96). Thus growth poles are likely to be firms or industries or groups of firms and industries. It is within these "poles" that growth and change are generated, while the connections between the poles, in terms of inputs and outputs, transmit the forces generated. It has been suggested that the poles are best regarded as sectors of an economy which can be represented by an input-output matrix in which changes can be transmitted across the rows and columns.

In its third aspect the economic space of a firm is defined as a *homogeneous aggregate*. The relations of homogeneity are relative to the units and their structure, or relative to the relations between these units. Thus a firm has, or has not, a structure more or less homogeneous with the structures of other firms that are its neighbors topographically or economically.

The concept of the growth pole is associated with the notion of the "propulsive industry." A propulsive industry must possess three characteristics. First, and of fundamental importance, is the dominance of the firm. Dominance occurs when the flow of goods from industry A to industry B is a greater proportion of A's output than is the flow from B to A of B's output. Thus firm A is called "dominant" and firm B "dependent." A second consideration concerns the size of the pole. There must be an oligopolistic concentration of industry, with price leadership and a keen sense of anticipation regarding changes in its own sector. Finally, there must be a high interaction with other firms.

GROWTH CENTER.   The development of abstract space left a void for the study of reality. As Darwent states, "Since all units must have a location, and since in regional economic development the question of 'where' looms large, then despite the facts that poles are independent of geographic space, their existence within it poses complex problems unexplained by growth pole 'theory'" (14–5). As a result another group of concepts, based on *growth centers*, has arisen. The growth center concept specifically considers the distribution of change and the allocation of investments in geographic space. However, there are few studies that connect the conditions for the existence of a "pole" defined in abstract space, and the conditions of its appearance in geographic space as a "center."

Along with the concept of a growth center, the notion of *polarization* has also evolved. Polarization implies a collection of geographic studies in which connections and flows of, for example, raw materials to an industry, are predominantly in one direction: in essence, toward a central point that dominates the region. The boundary of a polarized industrial region is therefore the line beyond which flows and connections are predominantly in another direction to another pole. The polarized industrial region can exist at any scale. For example, smaller centers will tend to nest within larger ones. The concept of a polarized industrial region is similar to that of central place theory of a hierarchy of cities.

USE OF THE CONCEPTS.   Because neither the growth pole nor the growth center is well defined theoretically, they do not provide a normative base for understanding the localization of industry. Neither the growth pole nor center notion give much information on what factors transmit growth or how industrial change is initiated.

Despite the limited theoretical foundation and general lack of empirical verification, there is a great deal of intuitive appeal in the growth center concept for understanding industrial localization and growth. From the growth center concepts such issues as regional industrial development and the allocation of resources in both space and time have evolved. Thus the notion has developed that industrial investment is best concentrated in growth centers rather than being widely distributed in a vague hope for a balance of distribution. The growth center concept gives promise of becoming a dynamic theory for industrial growth and development. In this way development models may be given a spatial dimension. From the geographic viewpoint, a major contribution of the growth center concept has been the removal of reliance on the growth pole concept, which maintains that growth lies in the development of the big firm or industry.

Economic Base Theory

The economic base theory is predicated on the concept of "basic" and "nonbasic" activities. As applied to manufacturing, a basic industry is one that produces for more than the local market and thus has goods for export. By contrast, a nonbasic manufacturing activity is one that produces only for the local market. The concept is that a manufacturing industry has the greatest potential for growth if it produces for the largest possible market. Manufacturing that serves a local market can grow only in response to the demands of that limited market.

TECHNIQUES FOR DETERMINING THE BASIC-NONBASIC RATIO. A number of techniques have been devised for determining the basic-nonbasic ratios in manufacturing. Thus the industrial base study generally seeks to identify the areas of export activity and then evaluate the impact of that additional amount of export on the nonbasic output. Hence the goal is not only to achieve a projection of the region's potential growth and structural changes, but also to produce a model that can be used in evaluating the effects of alternative types of development.

The techniques to measure the basic-nonbasic ratio of manufacturing in an area can be applied with various degrees of precision. The simplest, and no doubt least effective, is to assign total industries to the basic or nonbasic category on the basis of general information. For example, the electronics industry of an area may be considered basic, while a baking industry in that area may be considered nonbasic.

A more logical approach is to recognize that all manufacturing in a region produces for both the local and the outside market. It thus becomes necessary to determine what portion of the output is basic and what portion is nonbasic. The simplest procedure for making estimates is to use the location quotient. For example, in 1973 Pennsylvania produced 22.48 percent of the national total of pig iron while the state's total population was about 5.80 percent of the national total. The location quotient is 22.48/5.80 = 3.87. From this it can be assumed that about 60 percent of the pig iron output is for export and about 40 percent is for consumption within the state. Thus 60 percent of the pig iron production is assigned to the basic, and 40 percent to the nonbasic, category. This conclusion is based on the assumption that the population figure is a good measure of the consumption of pig iron. Other variables, such as personal income or value added in manufacture, may be more indicative of the demand. However, as Tiebout indicated, the location quotient does have the advantage of taking account of "indirect" as well as direct exports. He states, for example, "A community with a large number of packing plants is also likely to have a large number of tin can manufacturers. Even though the cans are locally sold, they are indirectly tied to exports. Location quotients will show them as exports..." (45–48). Within any industrial classification, there are specific subproducts, some of which will be imported and some of which will be exported by the region. Because the location quotient gives an indication of net surpluses only, it may underestimate the total export of that industry's product (23–223).

Another technique to measure basic-nonbasic proportions is the minimum requirement approach. This model is based on the concept that a minimum employment (or some other measure) in an industry is required to maintain the viability of the area. The minimum requirement closely approximates the nonbasic needs of the area, and the excess employment is essentially the basic portion. For example, one could base such a study on, say, 100 Standard Metropolitan Statistical Areas (SMSA's). Suppose that the range of employment in the food processing industry is from 3.4 to 18.8 percent of the total manufacturing. According to the minimum requirement technique, the presumption is that 3.4 percent of the employment in food processing is the minimum required by any SMSA to satisfy its own needs and that all employment in food processing in excess of this percentage in other SMSA's is basic, or export, employment. Repeating this process would yield a basic total for each industry for each SMSA, and, by addition, the total basic employment in industry for any SMSA could be determined. This approach is likely to provide only an estimate. Its major difficulty is that it is based on the lowest figure, which may be atypical for some reason or another. It has been suggested that if there are, say, 100 communities in the study, it might be desirable to drop a number of communities at the bottom of the list in each industry considered. This could avoid some spurious cases. The major problem is to determine what this number should be. Obviously, the higher the cutoff the lower the basic employment will be.

The most precise, but also most difficult, procedure is to survey shipment from individual industrial firms. The U.S. Census of Manufactures has begun to collect some information of shipments between large regions. On smaller regions, such as SMSA's, information from governmental sources remains meager. If data are collected by individual surveyors, the "significant enterprise" approach facilitates the procedure. In using this technique, it is considered unnecessary to survey the complete base; but a few significant enterprises will reveal the basic-nonbasic component of the total industrial structure of an area. This method was used by Alexander for his studies of Oshkosh and Madison, Wisconsin (4–258). Three-fourths of each city's basic-nonbasic employment was tabulated firm by firm. As estimate was then made for the fourth of the economy not contacted directly in the survey.

EMPLOYMENT MULTIPLIER.   A major concept of the basic-nonbasic model is that when a basic industry grows, it will, in the long run, increase the nonbasic employment. The size of the increase will depend on the ratio between the basic and nonbasic portions. For example, if the initial basic-nonbasic ratio is 100:60 and the basic employment is increased to 200, the number employed in nonbasic industrial jobs will rise to 120. This multiplier effect is fundamental to the economic base concept. It is the addition to the basic employment that acts as a catalyst to increase the nonbasic employment. Thus, if growth is to occur, the basic component of employment is the critical one. Unfortunately, to date this concept has had little empirical testing as to its validity.

QUALITIES OF THE ECONOMIC BASE CONCEPT.   The economic base concept is important as a tool for industrial studies because it attempts to classify manufacturing endeavors in terms of market location. Four aspects may be considered: (1) The concept provides a perspective of the manufacturing linkage of a city with other regions. (2) It permits classification of how important different types of manufacturing are in the industrial structure of a city. Cities are more accurately distinguished by their basic manufacturing than by their total manufacturing because the basic manufacturing defines a city's relationship to its region. For such a purpose, the nonbasic manufacturing should be subtracted from the total manufacturing. Although empirical testing is incomplete, it is generally believed that nonbasic manufacturing is quite similar for all areas. (3) The basic-nonbasic technique provides a ratio that may have significance in differentiating types of manufacturing. For example, if a city has a total of 50,000 employees in manufacturing, with 25,000 engaged in basic and 25,000 in nonbasic manufacturing, the ratio then is 50:50. However, if another city also has 50,000 manufactural employees but has 30,000 in basic and 20,000 in nonbasic manufacturing, the ratio is 60:40. It may be assumed that this city has the greater manufactural growth potential because of the dominance of basic manufacturing. The differences in the basic-nonbasic ratios of manufacturing in cities need a great deal more study to determine their significance. (4) The basic-nonbasic ratio can be utilized to prepare a classification of individual manufacturing endeavors. For example, a manufacturing industry that produces entirely for a local market may have factors of localization that are distinctly different from one that produces for outside markets. Specifically, one is tied to a local market and the other to surrounding regions.

Locational Constructs

Much of the theory discussed to this point has concerned itself primarily with the concepts of least cost or maximum profit. A number of authors have, however, approached the study of industrial location from a different perspective by attempting to show how the spatial structure of manufacturing has evolved and what its regional impact has been (43). Although these constructs of industrial location are usually deficient in precise model-building techniques, they are presented here as potential theories that may contribute to an understanding of the spatial patterns of manufacturing. To the present, little attention has been given to these generalizations. They deserve greater consideration in future studies.

THEORY OF ECONOMIC RESTRICTIONS. This concept was stated as a principle by Rawstron as a guide to the analysis of industrial location (38). Further, it was not presented to contribute to classical locational equilibrium theory, but rather to provide an understanding of the spatial limits to the economic viability of plants.

Rawstron's principle is that "restrictions will tend to be greater where the cost of at least one of the components in the cost structure of an industry varies markedly from place to place, if this variation is likely to form a large and/or clearly discernible proportion of costs as a whole" (38–136). In this concept,

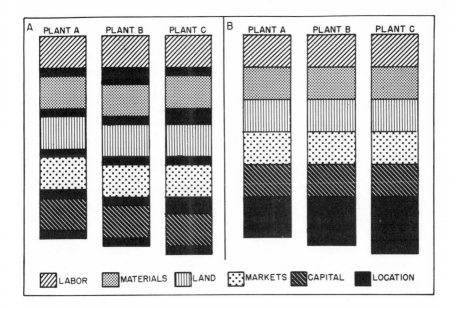

Figure 1.25. Profit margins of a plant. These diagrams demonstrate the effects of location on three imaginary plants. (Source: E.M. Rawstron, "Three Principles of Industrial Location," *Transactions and Papers, Institute of British Geographers,* 1958, Fig. 1.)

costs—such as raw materials, labor, capital, and others—are not the only economic restrictions; they are only under perfect competition. Therefore the concepts of imperfect competition become essential to explain the locational pattern of industry. It thus becomes necessary to postulate the constancy of all costs except those related to location. As Rawstron indicates, location is the key to locational costs. It is demonstrated in its simplest form in Fig. 1.25A. Plant A has the lowest locational cost and is assumed to be profitable. Plant B has a higher locational cost and is assumed to have a marginal profitability. Plant C has the highest locational cost and lies outside the cost margin. These three hypothetical situations illustrate how locational costs can influence the profit margin.

In a somewhat more practical example, Rawstron allocated a portion of the locational cost to each of the other factors of production (Fig. 1.25B). The profitability of Plant A may be related to the even distribution of the locational costs among the factors of production. By contrast, the high cost of labor due to locational costs at Plant B makes this plant marginal and, in Plant C, the high locational costs related to materials and marketing gives it an unprofitable location.

Rawstron concludes that

the economically determined margin bounds the area or areas within which viability can be attained and that the margin may be deemed to apply to locational costs as a whole or, with certain provisos, to one component or part of a component in the cost structure. Since in many industries one or two components are the dominant factors locationally, the application of the marginal concept cartographically may be simpler than appears at first sight. (38–138)

STAGES THEORY.   The stages theory indicates that over time different sectors of the economy will assume lesser or greater importance. A historical sequence of events is hypothesized. The economy of an area develops initially around a primary activity—agriculture, forestry, mining—that provides an exportable surplus over local needs. The proceeds from these sales provide the means for importing items not produced locally, typically manufactured items. Thus during the early stage, employment in the primary industries dominates.

As the economy advances, the market grows sufficiently to make it feasible to produce locally some of the goods formerly imported. As a response, the importance of the primary industries declines and the manufacturing industries grow. As more sophisticated capital goods are produced internally, the secondary industries assume a dominant position in the employment structure. During this period, the number of urban centers grows and the great manufacturing regions can come into existence.

By this time in the stage of economic growth, the area has embarked on a process of self-generative growth that ultimately takes it to a stage of tertiary industry dominance. As a result the importance of manufacturing stabilizes and ultimately declines. Thus as the tertiary stage advances, it becomes increasingly difficult for a region to attract new manufacturing plants. To complicate the situation, the mechanization and automation of factories permit the rise of productivity at a given place so that new factories are not built. Now services are of major relative importance because manufactural sources of employment play a lesser and lesser role in the area's economic life.

The stages theory of development has an intuitive and historical appeal. The theory seems to fit the type of growth that has appeared in numerous regions over time. Probably, if the stages theory had an easily applicable quantitative counterpart, it would challenge the basic-nonbasic theory in the frequency of empirical applications.

However, for all of its intellectual appeal, the stages theory is more descriptive than analytical and its approach is suspect. In fact, not all areas pass through the series of stages hypothesized. Some begin the sequence as visualized, make progress, then stagnate. Others make progress and then return to an earlier stage; these are cases of retrograde development. Still others skip stages and never experience the sequential development.

The basic strength of the stages theory lies in its emphasis on the evolutionary character of an industrial region. However, it provides meager insight into the conditions that are necessary and sufficient for the completion of the entire process. More studies need to be made on such aspects as economies of large-scale production, the size of the market, and import substitution. These are concepts useful for an understanding of the growth process, even though they are not precisely quantifiable at present.

CYCLE THEORY. The cycle theory of industrial growth maintains that an industry or a manufacturing region, once established, will advance through a predictable sequence of changes, each with particular characteristics. Each industry or region will thus change with time at varying rates of growth or decline. Nevertheless, they will all demonstrate a common pattern in their course of development. All pass through a period of experimentation, a period of rapid growth, a period of diminished rate of growth, and a period of stability or even decline. This growth cycle has been called the *law of industrial growth* (3–13).

The development of the cotton textile industry in the New England region can well illustrate this "law." The modern textile industry began in the region in the early nineteenth century, and the period of experimentation lasted about 20 years. It was during this first period that new techniques were introduced and tested. The cost of the product was high and the quality relatively low. The demand for the product increased at a moderate rate. It was also a period when failures in the industry were high.

Because of initial technical efforts, however, the quality of the textiles improved. The marketing organization expanded at the same time. As a result the period of rapid growth in the New England cotton textile industry began about 1830 and lasted until about 1900. The price of textiles declined due to technical improvements, and new markets were secured because of a consequent increase in production. The industry was able to secure economies of scale and reduce prices even further.

The third period was characterized by diminished growth, which lasted until about 1925. Technical progress was no longer as rapid as in other regions. Problems were created by antiquated methods. Costs could not be reduced at the same rate as before. Demand grew, but at a lower rate than in the preceding period. New markets were difficult to achieve because all who desired textiles were already customers. Even improvements in quality reduced the market because the life of the product had been extended.

The final period of stability and decline began for the cotton textile industry in New England about 1925. The region had become a high-cost producer and could no longer compete economically with other areas. Markets decreased as a result. This led to a decline in capital for investment in new plants and in research to secure greater efficiencies. As the profit margins declined, transportation costs could not be absorbed and the friction of distance increased. Consequently New England, which had possessed the largest cotton textile industry in the late nineteenth century, had essentially no cotton textile industry remaining by the 1970s.

Manufacturing regions commonly exhibit a cycle of existence similar to that of an industry.

DIFFERENTIAL GROWTH THEORY. The differential growth theory maintains that, as an industrial society progresses, the demand for certain types of manufactured products changes. This is essentially a concept that conforms directly to the idea of what the economists call "transformation."

The changes in the structure of the industrial economy well illustrate this theory. The early industries, such as textiles, food, and primary metals, were developed to serve fundamental needs of the society. In the early stages of industrial development, there were very limited amounts of money with which to purchase luxury items. As the industrial economy advanced and income increased, there was not a proportionate increase in the consumption of the basic items; rather, more was spent on such items as automobiles, refrigerators, and TV sets.

Differential growth has had a major influence on the pattern and growth of industries in the United States. The areas with fast-growing industries are in general likely to experience greater prosperity than areas that possess slow-growth industries. For example, the textile industry brought prosperity to numerous towns in the nineteenth century when the industry was expanding. However, as demand reached a point of relative stability for textiles and as industrial progress continued, the demand for other products rose much more rapidly. As a result many areas specializing in textiles were adversely affected. In contrast, other areas producing other items (e.g., automobiles) expanded greatly. As a consequence industrial areas have been continually striving to produce a higher-value-added product.

Differential growth of industrial regions will continue as long as industrial progress occurs. The factors that established an industry in a region may not be favorable to the establishment of a different type of industry. As a result industry in certain regions will decline while that in other regions grows. In many instances, if older regions are to survive, they must realign their industrial economy. The theory of differential growth recognizes that with progress there will be a transformation of regions over time.

CONCENTRATION THEORY. The concentration theory is based on the concept that, because of strong locational affinities, manufacturing activities group together to form a hierarchy of concentrations. Thompson recognizes at least six classes of concentrations differentiated in terms of amount, density, and, probably, linkage (43–360). In order of ascending importance, the six classes are the plant or individual factory, district, central place, urban system, zone, and belt.

The plant, which consists of buildings and the surrounding grounds, is the primary unit of the classification system. The entire area occupied is used for manufacturing. The plant's importance in the total pattern of manufacturing may be small or large, depending entirely on the industry considered.

A number of plants will comprise a district, usually associated with an urban area. Besides the factory buildings and grounds, there are such associated features as transportation facilities and loading zones. Manufacturing may occupy from 25 to 100 percent of the land area in the district.

A number of districts will form a central-place concentration. Because these districts are not contiguous in the urban area, manufacturing is likely not to utilize more than from 5 to 20 percent of the total area. The industrial districts within the urban area may vary in many respects. Some may have arisen with the initial growth of the area while others may be very recent in origin. Some districts may have high specialization while others are diversified. The linkages between the districts will vary considerably depending on the type of industries developed.

An urban system will include two or more central places. These central places may be urban areas that are in close proximity, such as Gary, Whiting, and South Chicago in northwestern Indiana. The manufactural employment of such an urban system will be in the tens of thousands. There is generally considerable diversity in output as well as a strong linkage between the central places. Manufacturing activities will, however, occupy only about 1 percent of the total land area. Employment continues to increase as the size of the urban system increases.

A number of urban systems will comprise a zone. For example, the urban systems of the Pittsburgh-Johnstown-Youngstown area comprise a zone. The zone approximates areas of manufacturing that are found within the American Manufacturing Belt. The zones will contain hundreds of thousands of manufactural employees, but manufacturing itself will occupy an infinitesimal portion of the area.

The belt is the largest of the areal units in the classification; it will comprise at least two zones. A typical belt of manufacturing extends from Portland, Maine, to Washington, D.C., on the Atlantic Coast; another is the belt from Buffalo to Milwaukee along the lower Great Lakes. These are the great cores, or manufacturing axes, of a nation.

It is of importance to note that whereas the individual plants are widely dispersed, the great belts are highly restricted in their areal distribution. It is also important to note that at the individual plant level, a plant may disappear and not be replaced; by contrast, once a great belt has evolved not one has disappeared since the beginning of the Industrial Revolution.

AGGLOMERATION THEORY. The agglomeration theory was developed in the 1920s by Robert Murray Haig, when he adapted location analysis to the general theory of urbanization (29). In his conception, urban industrial concentration became the first premise of spatial logic. Thus agglomeration theory visualizes that as manufacturing expands it has greater attraction to the largest urban centers. This theory is related to the concentration theory but advances the concept further in recognizing the perspective of economic development.

It is generally agreed that to secure a higher standard of living, there must be an increase in output per man-hour of work. Further, there must not only be higher productivity, but there must also be a larger consumption. Although economic development may be partly attributable to increases in the size of the labor force and capital accumulation, the major reason stems from productive efficiency. Of all the factors affecting productivity, the improvement in technology and management are most important because they reduce the real costs of increased production. The basic question is whether there are features common to both technical and locational change that will cause an agglomeration of industry in cities. If so, how will an urban situation differ from a nonurban situation?

In the development of this concept, Lampard presented the viewpoint that specialization provides the essential link between the technical and spatial conditions of economic progress. It is generally agreed that the degree of specialization is related directly to the size of the markets. Because specialization provides a greater economy of time, effort, and resources, it is most effective where it is most advanced. The process is thus cumulative and dynamic.

Most significantly, specialization alters the preindustrial spatial order as economic progress occurs. In preindustrial society, industry was relatively unspecialized, organization was simple, and the activities were widely dispersed. The urban nuclei in such a culture are essentially service centers. The spatial pattern of industry is altered as specialization develops. For example, to reduce operational imperfections and the friction of space, interdependent specialisms are linked into a more integrated structure. Differential and complementary productive requirements concentrate the geographic distribution because greater advantages occur with local specialization.

If only economic considerations prevail, agglomeration of manufacturing is limited by the physical availability of resources and the friction of distance. This type of operational efficiency becomes the basis of industrial agglomeration. According to the agglomeration theory, the great concentrations of manufacturing through time are thus the product of a single thrust—specialization. The fundamental theme of this viewpoint is that the specialization of functions results in the specialization of areas. It makes possible a distinction in function between town and country and further differentiates one area from another. Areal specialization becomes the corollary of functional specialization. Thus the concentration of differentiated but functionally integrated specialisms simply represents the advantages of a particular locality.

A major goal of specialization is to reduce distance inputs to a minimum. There is a continuing effort to surmount the effects of spatial friction. The indiscriminate location of industrial activity may result in increasing costs equal to or more than the utilization of inefficient production methods. Thus the ideal would be to locate all production and all consumption at a single point. However, this is impossible in reality, so production remains dispersed. This is not irrational because it indicates that transfer costs to scattered markets cannot be offset completely by economies of concentration.

The agglomerations of population have increased greatly since about 1800. At that time there were only 20 cities in the world having more than 100,000 people. Today there are over 100. Thompson suggests that in the northeastern United States the threshold size for a city to acquire substantial manufacturing is 100,000 persons as a minimum. Cities below this level do not appear to be able to attract manufacturing in significant quantities. It is even suggested that the threshold may be as high as 300,000 population.

SOVIET INDUSTRIAL LOCATION THEORY

The industrial location theory that has evolved under the socialist system of the Soviet Union in the past half century differs sharply from that of the capitalist world. The Soviet theory reflects the establishment of goals to develop an industrial society within a particular governmental framework. The following brief analysis is provided to present a contrasting viewpoint to capitalist industrial location theory.

Rejection of Capitalist Industrial Location Theory

Before the Communist Revolution, Western industrial location theory had received scant attention in Russia (27). Only Weber's theories were widely known, but they had little influence on industrial location policies. In the early 1920s a few Soviet economists expressed the viewpoint that Western location theories could be useful for Soviet planning. For example, the economist S.V. Bernshtein-Kogan stated, "In choosing the location of these new enterprises, we can utilize the basic approach to the Weberian scheme and not waste time on new methodological approaches. . . . As a basis for our work on the geographical distribution of industry, the method worked out by German economists and systemically presented by A. Weber may be used." The geographer N.N. Baransky wrote, "the location theory of A. Weber enjoys quite a general recognition, particularly by use in the USSR, and research based on it is carried on in industrial branches" (27–July 1967, 4).

A number of other Soviet economists in the early 1920s recognized the importance of Weberian theory, but did not refer directly to it. For example, A.M. Ginzburg and E.A. Preobrazhensky advocated that weight-losing industries locate near raw materials to reduce transportation costs of gross raw materials. Ya. Dimanshtein argued that the iron and steel industry should be expanded in the Donets Basin rather than the Urals and the Kuznetsk Basin because transportation costs for tying the iron ore of the Urals with the coal of the Kuznetsk would be excessive.

However, in the development of the Soviet industrial location theory, the official party policy quickly rejected Weber's and other capitalist theory on the grounds of its inapplicability. The basic Soviet viewpoint was that other factors were more important than the principle of lowest-cost location. After official rejection no Soviet economist could advocate the use of capitalist location theory, and only writings condemning the Weberian theory appeared. The Soviet planners criticized Weber on a number of counts. It was argued that Weber's theory analyzed only the relationships between the sources of raw materials, fuel, transportation, and like items with the location of industry. The Soviet critics argued that these material conditions exerted their influence only indirectly through social conditions. Thus such important locational determinants as labor relations, ownership of production, technological stage, and others were disregarded by Weber. The Weberian theory was also criticized for not taking into account changes over time.

The Soviet economists also indicated that Weber's theory was not adequate in explaining the location of industry in the capitalist countries. Weber assumed that price was established in the individual firm and that demand was infinite, relative to what the firm could supply. Thus profit can be maximized if the cost of production is kept at the lowest point. Soviet critics argued that this was completely unrealistic for capitalist markets, particularly when monopolies exist. In this situation, the variables that affect a producer are not only cost but also demand and price. Thus a manufacturer should not locate his plant where costs are lowest but where profits are greatest.

Weber's theory was also criticized as being too abstract and therefore impractical because the variables were restricted to three, although in reality there are many variables. Further, Weber did not include all relevant factors, and the analysis of those he did include was not satisfactory. The methodological approach based on a partial equilibrium was therefore inadequate.

The Soviet economists also criticized Weberian theory for being concerned with the location of the individual firm. Under the Soviet system it was assumed that social costs and returns accruing to the national economy as a whole were much more important than the welfare of a single firm. Thus the decisive factor is not the lowest cost for a single plant but the lowest cost to the national economy as a whole.

Another adverse consideration elaborated by the Soviets was that Weber's theory was of a short-term character. They felt that capitalists were unwilling to build plants at locations where profits could be realized only in the long run. Consequently, the long-term growth was handicapped and would result in the decline in the economy.

Soviet Location Theory

As the Soviets rejected Western location theory, a new set of theories based on the concepts of a socialist economy evolved. Soviet location theory was based on the concept of "laws" relating to "socialist production." Because of the particular Soviet spatial situation, the theories that evolved were related to the linkages between widely distributed enterprises in a very large nation, to the differences in the availability of labor, and to the specialization and comprehensiveness in the development of individual regions.

The Soviet industrial location theory was founded on the works of Marx, Engels, and particularly Lenin. In the *Communist Manifesto*, Marx visualized that after the proletarian revolution there would occur a "combination of agriculture with manufacturing industries; a gradual abolition of the distinction between country and town, and a more equable distribution of population over the country." Engels also recognized that there should be no distinction between manufacturing and agriculture and that the growth of large cities could be prevented with the even distribution of industry throughout the nation.

In 1918 Lenin laid the foundation for modern Soviet location theory in his "Draft Plan of Scientific and Technical Works":

> The Supreme Economic Council should immediately give its instructions to the Academy of Sciences, which has launched a systematic study and investigation of the natural productive forces of Russia, to set up a number of expert commissions for the speediest possible compilation of a plan for the reorganization of industry and the economic progress of Russia.
>
> The plan should include:
>
> the rational distribution of industry in Russia from the standpoint of proximity to raw materials and the lowest consumption of labor-power in the transition from the processing of the raw materials to all subsequent stages in the processing of semimanufactured goods, up to and including the output of the finished product;
>
> the rational merging and concentration of industry in a few big enterprises from the standpoint of the most up-to-date large-scale industry, especially trusts;
>
> special attention to the electrification of industry and transport and the application of electricity to farming, and the use of lower grades of fuel (peat, low-grade coal) for the production of electricity, with the lowest possible expenditure on extraction and transport.

Lenin thus provided basic locational objectives that have remained the foundation of locational theory to the present day. For example, Premier Aleksei Kosygin, at the Twenty-Third Communist Party Congress in 1965, referred to Lenin in the establishment of industrial goals for the 1966–1970 plans.

Soviet Locational Objectives

The major objectives of modern Soviet industrial location policy are:

1. To develop industry at sources of raw materials and markets in order to reduce transport costs.
2. To plan the location of industry on a national scale so that regions can specialize in industries that utilize local raw materials most efficiently. This regional specialization will facilitate territorial division of labor.
3. To distribute industrial production throughout the country in order to utilize all human and natural resources of a region. Thus each region should strive for economic self-sufficiency.
4. To abolish the economic differences between rural and city areas,

which traditionally have been based on differences between industrial and agricultural production.

5. To establish industry in all regions inhabited by national minorities.
6. To create industries that will strengthen the defense capacity of the nation.

Most of these objectives do not need further explanation, with the possible exception of numbers 1 and 2. As to the first objective, there are many problems of locating industry close to both raw materials and markets. In reality the close proximity of raw materials and markets is the exception rather than the normal situation. In practice the Soviets have oriented heavy industry to raw materials and fuel and have established the lighter and frequently the higher-valued industries, such as machinery and electronics, near the largest markets. Recent publications have usually stated this objective: Industry will locate close to raw materials *or* markets.

One interpretation of the second objective is that all regions of the country are to be industrialized. This is based on the ideological concept that an industrial society is the only kind that can make progress. The objective recognizes that not all types of industry can develop in every region, but that factors favor the growth of one industry over another. The emphasis on particular industries will give the region a specialized character within the framework of the total national economy.

Communist Party Congress Implementation of Soviet Industrial Location

The Communist party congresses have, from the 1920s, presented resolutions directing the location and development of industry. Socialist theoretical concepts of localization appear to have been followed in all instances. A few examples will illustrate the practical applications of the theoretical policies.

At the Communist Party Congress in 1921, it was recognized that industrial differences existed between the Russian peoples and other nationalities. A major resolution stated that these differences were to be abolished as rapidly as possible. The first efforts to abolish economic inequality of the minority groups were through the planned distribution of industry in all areas and the development of plants near sources of raw materials. In reality progress toward achieving this goal was extremely slow.

The fourteenth congress (1925), in its resolutions, advocated a requirement for proportional distribution of industry throughout the nation. The fifteenth congress, in 1927, recognized the possibility of foreign attack on the nation and recommended that industry be developed in those regions that were the least subject to invasion. At the Sixteenth Party Congress, in 1930, Stalin stated "that the industrialization of the country cannot be based in the future on a single southern coal-metallurgical base. In order to facilitate the speedy industrialization of the country, it is imperative to establish in the east the second basic coal-metallurgical center of the USSR, utilizing the rich coal and iron ore deposits of the Urals and Siberia." This statement conformed precisely to Lenin's industrial location theory and provided the foundation for the establishment of the Urals-Kuznetsk Combine. To reinforce this decision, the seventeenth congress (1934) directed that a large share of the industrial investment of the second Five-Year Plan be utilized in the east. The congress also directed that emphasis be placed on the development of light industry which would be oriented to raw materials.

By the end of the second Five-Year Plan, problems in the directed location of industry were becoming evident. Transportation bottlenecks were impeding the development of industry, and the philosophy of "giantism" in the construction of large and highly specialized plants had caused technical and economic difficulties. In 1939 the eighteenth congress recognized these problems and sought to adjust locational planning. The congress directed that (1) the construction of new plants be close not only to raw materials but also to market areas, (2) stress be placed on the development of regional self-sufficiency, and (3) the construction of giant plants be de-emphasized and medium and small establishments be built instead in an attempt to disperse industry. Because of the imminent war dangers, the development of the east continued to be stressed.

The Communists have continued to use the party congresses as vehicles to outline their industrial goals. There is, however, strong evidence that Soviet theory has not been able to develop principles or laws that depict the real world. In 1976 when the tenth Five-Year Plan was implemented by the Twenty-Fifth Party Congress planning continued to be based on instruments for forecasting and the attempts to manage the most complex economic processes. It was recognized that among the most difficult of the complex tasks was the application of new scientific and technological findings. Further, the planning process reflected continuous changes to improve the organization of economic management. This indicates that theory is still in a stage of formulation, and that empirical applications prevail. Thus the Soviets are still striving to attain a real-world theoretical model.

LOCATION THEORY VERSUS REALITY

Although location theory has experienced a notable evolution in the past century, it still lacks a conceptual framework to explain reality. Each of the three basic theoretical approaches—partial equilibrium, general equilibrium, and behavioral theory—remains deficient in conceptualizing general principles for explaining alternative locations of industry.

Partial Equilibrium Theory

Partial equilibrium theory, illustrated by the least cost, maximum profit, and locational interdependence concepts, is based on the selection of a few critical factors but ignores a wide range of considerations. An analysis of the limitations of Alfred Weber's least cost theory illustrates the problems of understanding the real world using the partial equilibrium approach. The least cost theory is based on a number of assumptions to which there are numerous exceptions.

The following illustrate the fallacy of assuming set conditions. Transportation costs were a basic theme of the least cost theory in determining industrial location. However, Weber assumed that transportation costs were directly proportional to distance. In reality rates are not a direct function of distance. Weber also assumed that raw materials and markets were fixed points. But this does not conform to the real-world spatial distribution of raw materials and/or markets. As a response to the false assumption that raw materials and markets are established points, Weber also assumed that these points would coincide with maximum profit points. It was further assumed that production costs were firm and therefore transportation costs, which varied, were the single factor determining the market area. But it is easy to establish, from empirical analysis, that production costs are not fixed. Weber's theory provides a static model in that it does not provide for either spatial or temporal changes in raw materials or markets. Many precise details of the theory can also be criticized. For example, Weber confused the use of coal as a raw material and as a fuel in his weight index. It has also been demonstrated that the material index has little relation to real locations, particularly when the weight loss of materials in manufacturing is less than 75 percent.

Other examples could be given to show that Weber's least cost theory does not achieve reality. The essence of the total model has been undermined through this piecemeal process of undermining the individual aspects of the theory. Nevertheless, this approach has not led critics to a new and better model that has economic integrity.

Although the maximum profit theory was outlined by Achille Loria, an Italian economist, between 1888 and 1898, it was not until Weber's least cost model was strongly cricitized that Lösch provided a maximum profit model that received wide attention. Unfortunately, Lösch also assumed conditions that do not conform to reality. His basic assumption of a homogeneous economic surface with negligible variations in cost of raw materials and production at alternative locations does not approach objectivity. With this as the basic assumption, the development of optimum market areas—which Lösch showed to be hexagonal to minimize freight rates and thus maximize profit—does not conform to modern complex market areas.

As with the least cost theory, critics have reconstituted Lösch's original concepts in the attempt to achieve more realistic conditions. It has been suggested that the hexagonal system be enlarged to emphasize agglomerations around nodes of development. The theory has also been further elaborated to evaluate alternative locations existing under varying costs in our present oligopolistic economic system. This viewpoint visualizes that, as a firm seeks the least cost–maximum profit location, the number of localizing variables increases and the market area increases. Although game theory offers an approach to the study of this situation, analytical tools are still not adequate to evaluate all alternative location situations. Thus, although there have been refinements to the original maxim profit theory, as with the least cost theory, a workable model approaching reality for all situations has not been achieved.

The partial equilibrium theories of locational interdependence have attempted to visualize the market position of firms. The basic idea is to present a model of how a firm can control the largest market area in order to obtain the greatest profit. These viewpoints are, however, for the most part simplistic. For example, it is frequently assumed that two firms will locate near the center of the market if the demand is inelastic; that they will locate further apart if elastic; or that they will locate to divide markets so that each plant can gain a dominant position. However, there is still no general aggreement that a firm will occupy a precise position in a given situation. Further, there is no model that provides for a locational decision when the number of plants becomes large in a market area.

General Equilibrium Theory

In contrast to the partial equilibrium theory, with its selectivity of factors, general equilibrium theory attempts to provide a model for evaluating the total complexity of factors affecting the localization of an industry. Although this conceptual framework attempts to be comprehensive, there are some serious limitations. The theory assumes static conditions. However, the conditions that influence the localization of manufacturing are dynamic, and the development processes must be viewed in a time perspective. A more possibly fundamental problem is that the economic sciences are not developed to the point where general equilibrium theory can be tested in real-world situations. To the present there have been few attempts to develop empirical studies based on the general equilibrium model. The model thus remains an intriguing abstraction for future consideration.

Modern Developments

Because the partial equilibrium and general equilibrium theories have not provided a means of evaluating alternative industrial locations in the real world, there have been efforts in recent years to approach the subject from different viewpoints. The behavioral theory appears most intriguing among the new perspectives. However, behavioral theory also remains an abstraction and real-world models have not evolved to date. General systems, growth pole and growth center, and economic base theories have likewise not provided normative models for evaluating alternative industrial locations. These concepts need more empirical studies to develop general models of real-world situations.

Future Considerations

Although industrial location theory has experienced significant evolution in the past 100 years, it remains for the future to devise workable real-world models. There are many areas that appear to be fruitful for future study. Of fundamental importance will be the ability to define more precisely the various factors that relate not only to economic but also to noneconomic considerations in industrial location. There is a need for determining explicitly, through more precise empirical studies, how the factors are interrelated. Procedures for evaluating preference statements, together with a presentation of preference functions, must be developed to secure a deeper understanding of noneconomic factors. Thus the link between economic and noneconomic factors affecting industrial location also offers an area for fruitful development.

As the list of unrealistic assumptions has expanded, the reformulations and restatements of theory have become increasingly remote from reality. Thus a reevaluation of present theory from the viewpoint of reality must become a part of the future decision processes. A classification system that is more effective in providing more insight into a larger set of examples is needed. At present, the categorization of this type of knowledge is clearly inadequate.

There is also a need to evaluate other basic variables that are now explicit in general postulates and assumptions. For example, in theory it is frequently assumed that the factors of localization for a plant are similar in all respects except the preference for a particular site, or that the factors influencing growth are identical for plants located at two different places. It is thus suggested that plants have similar situations and, from these situations, guiding principles of localization may be deduced. But to date proof of such assumptions is lacking.

Another fruitful area of investigation involves the assumption that the factors of localization of a plant remain constant independent of the changes in information over time. There is a basic need for a theory that can provide an understanding of the changes of spatial preferences of a plant—particularly for situations when the information is incomplete. A basic question then arises: How can spatial preferences of a plant be predicted? The need to develop a model that will analyze the interdependent locational decision processes is of the essence.

To the present little is known about the profit aspirations of a plant or industry and their effect on location. This variable needs a great deal more attention. There is little doubt that the decision process in locating a plant is affected by the expected rate of return. This raises another basic question: What is the lowest possible profit that will justify the existence of a plant at a given place? Further, if the profit of an industry falls short of the expectations, what decision processes will affect the spatial stability of the industry? Models should be developed to test aspirations, both economic and noneconomic, of industry as these decision processes affect spatial aspects.

Fundamental to future considerations is the need to present theory in a modern industrial context. Many of the foundations of present-day locational theory evolved at a time when the industrial patterns of the world were relatively simple. As a consequence the complex of factors that localized early industry was relatively simple. This is possibly reflected in the simplicity of the early theories. As the industrial pattern has evolved, the factors localizing industry have become increasingly complex. Consequently, the rigid assumptions of classical theory should be relaxed. Further, more elements should be introduced into the comparatively static framework of existing theory. In essence, new approaches are needed in the future for the construction of theoretical models.

The preceding material suggests only a few of the possible studies that might prove fruitful in furthering existing theory. Progress in extending the concepts of industrial location theory in the past 20 years has been relatively slight. Thus the basic question remains, *Can* an industrial location theory be devised that can have real-world practicality?

SELECTED REFERENCES

1. Ackley, G., "Spatial Competition in a Discontinuous Market," *Quarterly Journal of Economics*, 56 (1942), 212–230.
2. Alchian, A.A., "Uncertainty, Evolution, and Economic Theory," *Journal of Political Economy*, 58 (1950), 211–221.
3. Alderfer, E.B. and H.E. Michl, *Economics of American Industry*. New York: McGraw-Hill, 1957.
4. Alexander, John W., "The Basic-Nonbasic Concept of Urban Economic Functions," *Economic Geography*, 30 (1954), 246–261.
5. Beckmann, Martin J., *Location Theory*. New York: Random House, 1968.
6. Bertalanffy, L. von, "An Outline of General System Theory," *British Journal for the Philosophy of Science*, 1 (1950), 134–165.
7. Beyers, William B., "Growth Centers and Interindustry Linkages," *Proceedings of the Association of American Geographers*, 5 (1973), 18–21.
8. Campbell, J., "Growth Pole Theory, Digraph Analysis and Interindustry Relationships," *Tijdschrift voor Economische en Sociale Geografie*, 63 (1972), 79–87.
9. Casetti, E., L.J. King, and J. Odland, "The Formalization and Testing of Concepts of Growth Poles in a Spatial Context," *Environment and Planning*, 3 (1971), 337–382.
10. Chamberlin, Edward H., *The Theory of Monopolistic Competition*. Cambridge: Harvard University Press, 1933.
11. Chisholm, M., "General Systems Theory and Geography," *Transactions and Papers of the Institute of British Geographers*, 42 (December 1967), 45–52.
12. Claus, R.J. and Karen E. Claus, "Behavioral Location Theory," *Australian Geographer*, 11 (1971), 522–530.
13. Cooper, L., "An Extension of the Generalized Weber Problem," *Journal of Regional Science*, 8 (1968), 181–197.
14. Darwent, David F., "Growth Poles and Growth Centers in Regional Planning—A Review," *Environment and Planning*, 1 (1969), 5–31.
15. Faden, Arnold M., "Inefficiency of the Regular Hexagon in Industrial Location," *Geographical Analysis*, 1 (1969), 321–328.
16. Garrison, William L., "Spatial Structure of the Economy," *Annals of the Association of American Geographers*, 49 (1959), 232–239, 471–482; 50 (1960), 357–373.
17. Greenhut, Melvin L., "Integrating the Leading Theories of Plant Location," *Southern Economic Journal*, 18 (1952), 526–538.
18. ———. *Plant Location in Theory and Practice: The Economics of Space*. Chapel Hill: University of North Carolina Press, 1956.
19. Hall, A.D. and R.E. Fagen, "Definitions of Systems," *General Systems Yearbook*, 1 (1956).
20. Hamilton, F.E. Ian, "Models of Industrial Location," in *Models in Geography*, edited by Richard J. Chorley and Peter Haggett. London: Methuen, 1967.
21. Hicks, J.R., *Value and Capital*. Oxford: Oxford University Press, 1939.
22. Hoover, Edgar M., *Location Theory and the Shoe and Leather Industries*. Cambridge: Harvard University Press, 1937.
23. ———, *An Introduction to Regional Economics*. New York: Knopf, 1971.
24. Hotelling, Harold, "Stability in Competition," *Economic Journal*, 39 (March 1929), 41–57.
25. Isard, Walter, *Location and Space Economy*. Cambridge: The M.I.T. Press, 1956.
26. Karaska, G.J. and D.F. Bramhall, editors, *Locational Analysis for Manufacturing*. Cambridge: The M.I.T. Press, 1969.

27. Koropeckyj, Iwan S., "The Development of Soviet Location Theory Before the Second World War," *Soviet Studies*, 19 (July 1967), 1–28, and (October 1967), 232–244.
28. Kuenne, Robert E., *The Theory of General Economic Equilibrium*. Princeton: Princeton University Press, 1963.
29. Lampard, Eric E., "History of Cities in the Economically Advanced Areas," *Economic Development and Cultural Change*, 3 (1954), 81–93.
30. Launhardt, W., *Mathematische Begrundung der Volkswirthschaftslehre*. Leipzig, 1885.
31. Lerner, A.P. and H.W. Singer, "Some Notes on Duopoly and Spatial Competition," *Journal of Political Economy*, 45 (1937), 145–186.
32. Lösch, August, "The Nature of Economic Regions," *Southern Economic Journal*, 5 (July 1938), 71–78.
33. ————. *The Economics of Location*. New Haven: Yale University Press, 1954.
34. March, J.G. and H.A. Simon, *Organizations*. New York: Wiley, 1958.
35. Palander, Tord, *Beitrage zur Standortstheorie*. Uppsala: Almqvist och Wiksells Boktryckeri, 1935.
36. Perroux, François, "Economic Space, Theory and Applications," *Quarterly Journal of Economics*, 64 (1950), 89–104.
37. Pred, A., *Behavior and Location: Foundations for a Geographic and Dynamic Location Theory*. Uppsala, Sweden: Lund Studies in Geography, Part I, Series B,27, 1967; Part II, Series B, 28, 1969.
38. Rawstron, E.M., "Three Principles of Industrial Location," *Transactions and Papers of the Institute of British Geographers*, 25 (1958), 135–142.
39. Simon, H.A., *Models of Man: Social and Rational*. New York: Wiley, 1957.
40. Smith, D.M., "A Theoretical Framework for Geographical Studies of Industrial Location," *Economic Geography*, 42 (April 1966), 95–113.
41. Smithies, Arthur F., "Optimum Location in Spatial Competition," *Journal of Political Economy*, 49 (June 1941), 423–439.
42. Stafford, Howard A., "An Industrial Location Decision Model," *Proceedings of the Association of American Geographers*, 1 (1969), 141–145.
43. Thompson, John H., "Some Theoretical Considerations for Manufacturing Geography," *Economic Geography*, 42 (1966), 356–365.
44. Tiebout, C.M., "Location Theory, Empirical Evidence and Economic Evolution," *Papers and Proceedings of the Regional Science Association*, 3 (1957), 74–86.
45. ————. *The Community Base Study*. Supplementary Paper No. 16. New York: Committee for Economic Development, 1962.
46. Törnqvist, G., *Transport Costs as a Location Factor for Manufacturing Industry*. Uppsala, Sweden: Lund Studies in Geography, Series B, 23, 1962.
47. Townroe, P.M., "Locational Choice and the Individual Firm," *Regional Studies*, 3 (1969), 15–24.
48. Turner, Robert G., "General Theories of Plant Location: A Survey," *American Industrial Development Council Journal*, 6 (1971), 21–36.
49. Valavanis, S., "Lösch on Location: A Review Article," *American Economic Review*, 45 (1955), 637–644.
50. Weber, Alfred, *Theory of the Location of Industries*. Chicago: University of Chicago Press, 1929.
51. Webster, F.A., Model of Vertical Integration Strategy," *California Management Review*, 10 (Winter 1967), 49–58.
52. Wolpert, Julian, "The Decision Process in a Spatial Context," *Annals of the Association of American Geographers*, 54 (1964), 537–558.

II

FACTORS OF INDUSTRIAL LOCALIZATION

If the objectives of industrial location theorists in providing spatial models that could be applied to explain real-world locations had been achieved, the need for building empirical models based on the factors of industrial location would have been lessened. However, empirical models are needed—not only to test theory, but also to advance the understanding of real-world situations. Because practical industrial locationists are fundamentally concerned with the actual or future spatial distribution of manufacturing facilities, an empirical analysis and interpretation of industrial location require an examination of the factors that determine the location of manufacturing.

Thus the major purpose of Part II is to examine the factors of localization that play a role in determining industrial locational patterns. Only when the interplay of these forces is understood can a valid understanding of why industry is localized at a particular place be perceived. There are two fundamental questions: What are the factors that play a role in the world's industrial spatial patterns and how are they interrelated? Part II thus provides an empirical framework for the study of these basic questions. The discussion begins with the factors of localization that must be considered in the initial localization of industry; then it proceeds to factors that affect the growth or decline of industry in a region; it concludes with examples of empirical models for the analysis and interpretation of the spatial patterns.

The first portion of Part II is devoted to a discussion of the primary and secondary factors that influence the initial location of manufacturing. In the selection of a site for the location of manufacturing, six primary factors—raw materials, energy resources, capital, labor, transportation and transfer costs, and market—must be present in some combination. If one of these factors is absent at a place, manufacturing cannot occur. However, the importance of these localizing factors varies depending on the industry and its spatial relationships. Further, the requirements may change from one location to another within a single industry. For example, labor conditions and market potential may differ from region to region, or the general economic and social conditions may require a different type of combination of the factors of localization.

Besides the primary factors of production there are many secondary factors—physical, political, economic, and cultural—that influence industrial location. Although secondary factors are not fundamental, as are primary factors, they can become critical for a particular location. For example, if raw materials are the critical locational primary factor, and they are widely distributed, there are many alternative locations that would initially appear feasible for establishing a plant. Under these conditions, the secondary factors may tip the balance toward a particular location for the raw-material-oriented plant. The secondary factors discussed in this section are physical environment, governmental policies, taxes, research, management, regional perception, and personal considerations.

Although the primary and secondary factors are determinants in the initial location decision, they do not explain existing locations or why industries flourish or decline in a new area. It is thus the purpose of the second part of this section to analyze and interpret the processes that help explain the growth or decline of an industry in its spatial setting. These factors are economies of scale, technological innovation, geographic concentration, linkage, industrial splintering, geographic inertia, and development controls.

The concluding section provides a number of techniques that have been developed to analyze industrial location. The models selected have been found to be generally useful and practical. The techniques analyzed are comparative cost analysis, industrial complex analysis, input-output techniques, and correlation and regression analysis.

PRIMARY FACTORS

The location of manufacturing is determined by a complex of factors. An area usually possesses both favorable and unfavorable conditions. However, as previously stated, the six primary factors of production must be available in the area in some combination. In essence, the problem of locating an industry becomes a question of finding a site where the favorable factors outweigh the unfavorable factors. Because there are many places where an industry can be located, locating an industry does not normally entail finding a unique place; rather, it entails finding a region or regions that contain many potential sites where a plant can exist in a sound economic environment.

Raw Materials

The availability of raw materials is frequently a major locational factor. All manufacturing requires a supply of raw materials. Furthermore, raw materials are not equally distributed over the earth but are localized in certain regions. The availability of raw materials was frequently the dominating factor in locating an industry in the early period of American manufacturing. For example, the early shoe industry in Massachusetts was concentrated there because of the presence of local leather supplies. The early woolen mills were localized in New England, where wool from the local sheep industry was available. The early iron industry sought sources of iron ore. The development of Cincinnati as an early soap center was primarily due to the availability of fats from local stockyards.

However, the influence of raw materials as a location factor has declined in the twentieth century for a number of reasons. The development of a network of transportation systems has facilitated the movement of raw materials. Further, as manufacturing becomes more complex, there is relatively less processing of basic raw materials by individual manufacturers. At the present time only one out of five manufacturers in the United States directly processes basic raw materials. Most industrial firms purchase partially manufactured commodities from widely distributed sources. Thus no one raw material dominates in localizing the industry in a particular locality.

Technological improvements, which have resulted in a more intensive utilization of raw materials, have also lessened their importance in localizing manufacturing. Moreover, as labor and market exert greater locational influences, raw material orientation diminishes. Finally, the general decentralization of manufacturing, combined with competitive sales equalization practices, has encouraged manufacturers to increase the distance between the producing plant and the raw material source.

A basic question was posed in a study by Wilfred Smith (101): "Is it possible to devise tests of the location of industry on the site of its materials in addition to loss of weight during the course of manufacture, and in particular, is it possible to sort out industries in the middle ranges of the loss-in-weight classification?" Because industries may have the same percentage loss of weight during manufacture but may employ different aggregate weights of materials, and because the weight of materials processed by each industry varies with the size of the industry, there is a need for a common denominator.

The relation of the weight of raw materials to the size of the labor force was found to provide this common base. Smith's study revealed that those industries with high raw material weights in relation to number of workers were located at raw material sources, and those with low raw material weights per worker were divorced from materials. Further, certain categories of industries are oriented or not oriented to raw materials depending on the value of the finished product. For example, earthenware and refractories are usually oriented to raw materials, but the production of china may not be. Smith concluded that the weight of materials per worker is a more significant factor in determining the influence of raw materials on the location of industry than loss of weight during the manufacturing process. Loss of weight becomes significant only when it is combined with large weight per worker because variations in transport costs are significant only if the weights handled are large. A combination of large loss of weight and large amount of materials per worker orients an industry to raw materials. By contrast, a combination of gain in weight and small utilization of material per worker releases the industry from locating near its raw materials.

Many industries are still closely tied to their raw material source. Excellent examples of industries that lose considerable weight and bulk and also have a relatively low employment are those involved in the drying of fruits and the dehydration or evaporation of milk. Other typical industries in this group are the extractive industries that involve the smelting or concentrating of low-grade ores (e.g., copper smelting). The sawing of lumber at the timber source is another example of reducing the raw material (timber) at its source; this is done by the removal of slabs, the loss of sawdust, and the culling of knotty, splintered, and decayed boards. This initial processing reduces the bulk from 25 to 40 percent, resulting in substantial savings in freight costs. There is also a great reduction in bulk in the production of turpentine. As a result, naval stores plants, comprising nearly 1,000 small factories, blanket southeastern United States where the trees are tapped.

A second group of raw-material-oriented industries is made up of industries that convert perishable raw materials into nonperishable—or at least less perishable—products. The relative weight of materials and products is about equal in these industries, but procurement costs are considerably greater than distribution costs. Sugar beets are refined near the field; vegetables are canned near the field; butter and cheese are produced near the dairies that contribute the milk; salmon canneries are located near the salmon fisheries; and berries are made into preserves near the producing tracts.

When the raw material is not perishable and there is not a substantial loss in processing, the number of workers in relation to weight and the relative transportational rates between the raw material and the finished article will determine the best location for the plant. In general, the number of workers and freight rates increase with value added in manufacture. Raw materials normally receive lower freight rates than finished products. However, when the manufactured goods are of relatively low value and at the same time enjoy transportational advantages, the freight rates are about the same as for raw materials. Consequently, the influence of a market is minimized. For example, the cost of shipping raw cotton and some finished goods is about equal, so mills have a choice of either a raw material or a market location.

When either the market or the raw material is dominant in localizing an industry, it is usually situated at one or the other place and not at an intermediate site. Generally, intermediate points between raw materials and markets are costly centers of manufacturing because increased transportation costs for freight rates are normally composed of terminal costs plus a line-haul cost. As the distance between terminals increases, the terminal charges become relatively lower; when the average hauls are shortened by intermediate terminals, both the inbound and outbound rates must reflect terminal charges. Accordingly, the total freight cost at an intermediate location may be higher than would result from location at either the raw material source or the market.

In selected industries, the disadvantages of an intermediate location are overcome by the establishment of in-transit privileges. Under such an arrangement the through rate from origin to final destination is instituted. Such industries as grain milling and cotton compressing have had this arrangement developed for their benefit.

Energy Resources

Historically, the site of power resources was one of the major factors in determining the location of manufacturing. Until the Industrial Revolution, power in industry was primarily supplied by human and animal muscle. With mechanization, power was required in greater amounts. There are basically two types of power available to industry: power that must be used directly, such as water and wind power, and indirect power from coal, oil, natural gas, and nuclear sources, which is used to generate heat, which in time provides a motive force. Thus modern industry has a choice of the type of primary energy source to use and the form in which to use it. For direct use of energy by an industry, the industry must be located on the site of the power source. Used indirectly, the primary energy is converted into another form of energy and may be transported to the user.

The principal uses of energy are to generate heat and provide a motive force. It is thus frequently necessary to distinguish between fuel requirements for heat and power requirements for moving an object (30–52). The fossil fuels are used to provide both heat and motion by numerous methods. In contrast, waterpower is used in great amounts only in the production of electricity. It is used as a source of heat only in specialized industries. Consequently, while the fossil fuels provide power sources for almost the whole range of modern industry, waterpower as an energy source is limited to a restricted group of industries.

The uses of power have evolved with advances in technology. In the early stages of the Industrial Revolution, numerous manufacturing regions developed where waterpower was directly available. In southern New England, an initial area of concentration of American manufacturing, early industry was oriented to waterpower sites. Although this source of power is no longer utilized, there are many plants strung along the small streams that reflect the influence of an earlier period. In the Middle Atlantic and Southeast states, much of the early industry was attracted to cities situated along the Fall Line—that line where rivers left the higher Piedmont Upland and entered the lower Atlantic Coastal Plain. At these points, where rapids and falls exist, waterpower was available to operate the factories, and the small ocean-going vessels could navigate to wharves immediately below the factory sites. This attributed to the growth of such Fall Line cities as Trenton, Philadelphia, Wilmington, Baltimore, Richmond, Raleigh, Columbia, Augusta, Macon, and Columbus. The localizing influence of waterpower was also evident in the textile centers of Lancashire, England; the industry was situated in the foothills of the Pennine Range where waterpower was most readily available.

With the development of technology enabling the use of fossil fuels to provide motive power, manufacturing was no longer restricted to power sites. For most industries, an adequate supply of coal could be secured at any place served by railroads or water routes. Still later the mobility of power was further enhanced by the development of electrical transmission. Before 1900 electricity could be transported only a few miles; but better transmittal facilities have been developed, and now electricity can be transported over 1,000 miles.

Nevertheless, cost is involved in the transportation of energy. Consequently, for those industries using huge quantities of power or where power input costs are large in comparison with other manufacturing costs (e.g., raw materials, labor, or transportation), nearness to a source of power is essential (111). This is illustrated effectively by the electrometallurgical and electrochemical industries. Niagara Falls was the first major hydroelectric power center in the United States. From the beginning, power-oriented industries were attracted to this region. Because of competition for the power, only high-value-added electrochemical industries remain today. Those industries that produce a lower-valued product have sought power sources for which there is less competition for available energy and therefore lower costs.

The enormous hydroelectrical potentialities of the northwestern United States have attracted industries of the electrometallurgical group. The Tacoma, Washington, copper refinery has long drawn copper from not only western United States but also from such foreign countries as Chile. In the 1940s, when the demands for aluminum rose greatly because of the war emergency, the aluminum industry located plants in both Oregon and Washington to take advantage of the available hydroelectric power.

As a locational factor in manufacturing, energy varies greatly in importance from industry to industry. From a fundamental viewpoint, energy should attract manufacturing to it. In those industries that use large quantities of energy as a basic raw material, the manufacturing processes are frequently oriented to the fuel source. There are numerous examples of this situation. In the beehive process of producing coke, in which about 40 percent of the raw material is lost, the industry is invariably located at the source of the coal supply. The orientation of the petrochemical industry to such Gulf Coast cities as Houston, Galveston, Texas City, Beaumont, and Lake Charles reflects the availability of natural gas and crude oil used as raw materials.

In many of the heavy industries, fuel—when considered along with assembly costs of raw materials and freight rates to markets—becomes an important consideration in locating plants. Manufacturing processes that require large quantities of energy and involve a high proportion of weight loss are likely to be localized near energy sources because the weight of the energy does not enter into the resulting product. Most of the industries using large amounts of energy use it in the initial stages of processing. The metallurgical industries and the making of cement, glass, calcium carbide, and the synthetic nitrates are examples. Orientation to coal sources has been a principal factor in the development of many of the iron and steel regions of the world. The heavy metallurgical centers of Pittsburgh–Cleveland–Steubenville; Birmingham, Alabama; the Midlands and East Pennine areas of England; the Scottish Lowlands; the Ruhr; the Sambre-Meuse Lowland; Silesia; and the Donetz and Kuznetsk basins are oriented to coal areas. However, not all metallurgical centers are situated at coalfields. Changes in pricing policies, freight rates, and shifting markets are reducing the influence of a fuel supply on the location of blast furnaces.

The declining influence of a fuel source as a location factor is also reflected in the glass industry. Until the beginning of the twentieth century, most glass plants were situated close to fuel sources, first charcoal and later natural gas. In the manufacture of glass containers, fuel represents as much as 33 percent of the total production cost. However, modern glass plants are being established closer to market areas, indicating a lessening influence of the locational attraction of natural gas supplies. It is cheaper to transport the natural gas to the glass market area than it is to transport a fragile glass product.

Capital

In the past the availability of capital within a region was a major factor in the growth of manufacturing. Local capital was necessary for industrial progress at the beginning of the Industrial Revolution in Europe and America. This situation prevails today only in the few isolated areas such as Borneo and Papua where local economies persist (85). The availability of local capital applies only to early stages of industrial development and only when capital does not enter the area from the outside.

The growth of corporate finance has greatly reduced the importance of local capital. As economic maturity progresses, capital becomes mobile. Nevertheless, there are variations in the availability of capital from one area to another. The quantity of money available in an area depends on the area's earning power. There are usually many possible forms of investments, and each must compete as to the rate of interest and security of the investment. Risk capital is more readily available for the promotion of new enterprises in mature economic nations than in underdeveloped areas. In general, money capital is more mobile within a nation than when it must cross international boundaries.

A major distinction between the advanced and underdeveloped areas of the world is the existence of highly developed money and credit systems (31). The advanced nations possess credit associations, savings banks, stock markets, industrial development corporations, and insurance services. These organizations provide the capital for the establishment of industry. For example, the development of the milk processing industry in the southern United States was based to a degree on the farmers' ability to obtain credit from local banks in order to expand their dairy herds (73–96).

If capital is not available, the basic question is how to secure it. Capital can accumulate only from domestic savings or outside sources. In areas near the subsistence level, there can be little savings because the margin between consumption and production is small. In such societies, capital can be accumulated only through forced savings. When this economic process is occurring, inevitable economic misery exists within the society, forcing the immediate level of living to a still lower stratum. If this procedure of capital accumulation is not initiated, the capital must be secured from outside the area. However, there are frequently obstacles that hinder the international movement of capital. The risk may be high to the investor. Paradoxically, the overseas investor so essential to the economic growth of a developing country may also be a target for much criticism and abuse.

Besides money capital, there is also capital in the form of equipment. The two are closely allied because money capital is used to obtain equipment. Nevertheless, the two forms of capital have distinct differences (30–97). Equipment has much less mobility than money. This is particularly the situation with the heavy equipment so fundamental to industrial progress. Because of large investment, long life of equipment, and difficult mobility, industries may be stabilized in a region when other localizational factors are no longer favorable. The inability to move equipment is a dominating factor in geographic inertia.

Labor

The cost, availability, stability, and productivity of labor are vital factors in every manufacturing enterprise (3). The growth and future of any industrial area are jeopardized if these labor conditions are not favorable. Labor requirements for industries are not uniform. Certain industries require a large number of skilled workers; other industries require a large number of unskilled workers; and still others require varying numbers of each.

COST.   When considering the characteristics of labor, cost factors are among the vital items. It must be recognized that wide variations in wages exist between regions, between large cities and smaller communities, and even between neighboring cities. In general the lowest wage scales in the United States exist in the Southeast. The highest wages are found most often in the Pacific coastal cities. The wage scale is affected by many factors, including the skill of the workers; the type of industries within an area; and competition for workers. It has sometimes been felt in recent years that differentials in wages are disappearing because of a number of factors. Federal legislation does not permit discrimination in wages between whites and nonwhites and between males and females for similar jobs. Unions have also made serious efforts to reduce wage differentials. However, the geographic spread in wage rates continues (Table 2.1).

Wage differentials have tended to persist because of a variety of circumstances (36). It was once felt that when a rural area industrialized, wages would rise rapidly. This situation has occurred in southern California, where competition for labor has been high. In contrast, low wages persisted in North Carolina for decades when there was little competition among industries. This situation has been altered because labor became scarce. As a result, the lower-wage indus-

Table 2.1

Work Week and Wage Rates in Manufacturing, Selected States

	Average Weekly Hours Worked			Average Hourly Earnings		
	1952	1960	1975	1952	1960	1975
Michigan	41.0	40.8	40.7	$1.98	$2.75	$5.94
Illinois	41.4	40.0	39.3	1.67	2.45	5.26
California	41.3	39.8	39.3	1.79	2.62	5.08
Colorado	41.2	40.6	38.8	1.63	2.42	4.91
Pennsylvania	40.0	38.9	38.4	1.61	2.31	4.88
New York	39.0	38.8	38.0	1.65	2.31	4.81
Massachusetts	39.1	39.2	38.2	1.53	2.09	4.38
Texas	42.4	41.1	40.2	1.57	2.17	4.49
Tennessee	40.0	39.8	37.9	1.29	1.84	3.86
Georgia	39.9	39.4	37.8	1.20	1.66	3.78
North Carolina	38.3	39.7	36.3	1.17	1.54	3.46

Source: *Employment and Earnings,* Washington, D.C.: U.S. Department of Labor, Bureau of Labor Statistics, vol. 21, May 1975.

tries of North Carolina are experiencing difficulties. In general, wage differentials are the smallest in skilled occupations, even though significant differences do exist. For example, in a survey by the U.S. Bureau of Labor Statistics in 1972, it was found that workers in the machinery industry earned $3.43 in Greensboro–Winston Salem–High Point, $3.66 in Dallas, $4.16, in Los Angeles–Long Beach, $4.47 in Pittsburgh, and $5.58 in Detroit. The wage level in manufacturing is generally higher in large metropolitan centers than in smaller cities (Table 2.2).

A basic reason for wage differentials lies in the expenditure standards of individuals in the different areas. In the larger cities, although individual commodities may be priced the same as in the smaller cities, there is a wider choice in how dollars are spent; this results in increasing inducements to spend. It is much more difficult to be thrifty in a large city. Pleasures and luxuries are simpler, less expensive, and probably less frequent in the smaller cities. Living in metropolitan areas entails expensive housing and commuting. As a consequence, the cost of living is usually higher in areas of concentrated economic activity that have dense nonagricultural populations. Thus it is evident that labor costs are significantly raised as a result of both intangible and tangible expense factors.

When the labor costs are an important proportion of total delivered-to-customer costs of a given product, the selection of a particular labor cost area may become a critical factor. There are at least two types of locations that have conditions conducive to low labor costs. One type is a place where population pressures are great in that expansion of employment opportunities has lagged behind the growth of the labor force. As a result people are willing to work for

Table 2.2

Wage Levels in Manufacturing for Selected U.S. Metropolitan Areas, 1975

Average Hourly Earnings	Area
$6.32	Detroit, Michigan
5.74	Pittsburgh, Pennsylvania
5.73	Seattle–Everett, Washington
5.58	Milwaukee, Wisconsin
5.53	Rochester, New York
5.47	Cleveland, Ohio
5.37	Indianapolis, Indiana
5.27	St. Louis, Missouri
5.19	Kansas City, Missouri
5.04	Columbus, Ohio
5.03	Cincinnati, Ohio
4.94	Erie, Pennsylvania
4.92	Birmingham, Alabama
4.91	Denver, Colorado
4.78	Boston, Massachusetts
4.72	Anaheim-Santa Ana-Garden Grove, California
4.65	New York, New York
4.52	Bridgeport, Connecticut
4.43	Knoxville, Tennessee
4.04	Dallas, Texas
3.83	Greensboro-Winston Salem-High Point, North Carolina
3.48	Greenville-Spartanburg, South Carolina
3.43	Charlotte-Gastonia, North Carolina

Source: *Employment and Earnings,* Washington, D.C.: U.S. Department of Labor, Bureau of Labor Statistics, vol. 21, May 1975.

lower real incomes than elsewhere. The Piedmont area of the South in the late nineteenth century was able to attract the textile industry from New England largely because of its excess labor supply; people were unable to find other economic opportunities and were willing to work for low wages. This labor situation also applies to economically depressed areas where the economy is in transition. An example of this condition existed in the anthracite region of Pennsylvania from 1920 to about 1960, where there was an excess labor supply because of the decline of mining. The textile and apparel industries were the initial industries attracted to the region because of low-cost labor.

The second type is a place where the nature of local employment and the size and structure of the local labor market develop an unusually productive or adaptable labor force, resulting in higher productivity per man-hour. This type of labor force develops in the older industrial regions, such as New England, where skills have been acquired for generations. The advantages are based largely on the efficiency of the local labor force, which is related directly to the economies of scale resulting from specialization and organization of a firm for maximum production.

AVAILABILITY AND STABILITY.   The availability and stability of different types of labor supply are important localizing factors. If an industry uses a variety of types of labor, it is best able to satisfy its needs by locating in a metropolitan area. This is particularly the situation when unskilled labor is required since reservoirs of this kind of labor are normally largest in urban centers. Consequently, many factories are established at centers that lie in the midst of a labor supply.

The availability of labor depends to a considerable degree on its mobility. Unskilled labor has been exceptionally mobile in modern times. The unskilled worker is rarely tied to a particular locality by property holdings and may not have developed strong regional social ties. The automobile and good roads have made it possible for workers to travel quickly to areas of greater economic opportunity. This is reflected in the recent mass movement of workers from the southern Appalachians to such northern cities as Chicago, Detroit, and Cleveland. At times migratory workers appear in unwanted numbers at the merest suggestion of a factory job. As a result of the mobility of unskilled workers, the influence of labor as a locative factor in manufacturing has lessened.

In contrast, skilled labor behaves in an entirely different manner and its influence as a locative factor is much greater. Once a skilled-labor group develops in an area, it constitutes an entity of a relatively permanent character. Such concentrations of skilled labor are a definite factor affecting the location of certain types of industrial enterprise. For example, the Naugatuck Valley, which produces about half the nation's brass, has a concentration of skilled brass workers. Similarly, the workers of New Britain, Connecticut, have been producing hardware for generations, and the Connecticut Valley cities are noted for firearms. Skilled labor becomes significant in locating industry in cases when labor costs are a major proportion of the total cost of manufacturing.

Labor stability is of great significance to the successful pursuit of manufacturing. Unsatisfactory labor relations have forced plants to close or to migrate from a region. The causes of difficulty between management and labor are changing. Since unions have become better established and stronger, relatively few work stoppages have occurred due to the fundamental question of whether a union organization should exist. Wage increase demands, amount of fringe benefits, and jurisdictional disputes are still important items of conflict. There can be no assurance that a community will be free of labor disputes. However, a good indication of the future is revealed by the past history of labor relations in a region. A community that has long experienced industrial peace is a much better prospect for good labor relations than one in which there has been a lengthy history of industrial strife. The number of labor strikes and their duration are barometers of management–employee relations.

Labor instability may be evidenced in ways other than strikes. An adamant attitude on the part of employees, employers, and unions in the final settlement of a problem can stifle industrial growth. Other facets of labor trouble are manifested in excessive absenteeism, labor turnover, tardiness, and a disrespect for work rules and regulations. An annual absentee rate of 3 percent can be expected in a well-run plant. A labor turnover is even a greater indicator of unrest, particularly in industries where training costs for developing worker skills are high.

PRODUCTIVITY.   Since the beginning of the Industrial Revolution a rising trend in labor productivity has been a persistent industrial phenomenon. This is not only a general trend but for every industry for which an index can be provided there has been a long-term growth in output per man hour. Thus, this trend in labor productivity reflects more than an advance in a few selected progressive industries. In a recent study measuring labor productivity trends since 1889, labor productivity in the private economy experienced an average annual growth of 2.4 percent in the United States. In contrast, when both labor and capital inputs were utilized to measure productivity the annual growth rate was only 1.7 percent. This reveals that the output provided by an hour's work has risen half again as fast as the combined efficiency rate. Had the tangible and intangible capital per man hour remained unchanged, labor productivity could not have risen more rapidly than the combined efficiency rate.

It is, however, not only difficult to obtain statistics to produce an index of labor productivity, but frequently the statistics need interpretation to provide a reliable index. For example, in the mid-1960s a controversy arose over the steel industry's ability to raise wages without raising prices. A crucial factor in the deliberations concerning wage levels was the rise in the steel industry's output per man hour. The labor productivity index of the Bureau of Labor Statistics revealed that between 1959 and 1964 the average growth in man output per hour in the steel industry had been 2.2 percent. However, the Council of Economic Advisers of the President felt that this index did not reveal the true rise in labor efficiency because the output of the steel industry is sharply affected by strikes and general economic slow-downs. Therefore, an index was prepared that omitted the quarter years with unusually low operating rates. As a result the rate of growth of labor productivity rose from 2.2 to 3.3 percent. This provided an entirely different perspective in the ability of the steel industry to raise wage levels.

Several factors enter the determination of labor productivity. In the studies of labor efficiency it is evident in essentially all industries that the rise in labor productivity reflects not only a rise in capital available per worker, but also the efficiency with which labor and capital are utilized. Labor productivity, however, entails more than calculating the physical output per man hour. This ignores such qualitative aspects as the degree of skill of the worker, age levels, and the physical and mental abilities of the labor force. Such differences affect directly and indirectly labor productivity over time and from one area to another. However, labor quality is difficult to measure. Frequently the quality of labor input is assumed to coincide with the skill levels of the workers and is thus measured by the scale of prevailing wages. This is based on the assumption that there is a relationship between qualification for a particular activity and labor quality reflected by differences in the wage rates.

The idea has long persisted that there is a strong relationship between the educational level of workers and their productivity. As a consequence vocational schools, industrial training programs, and continuing education classes have become widely established to improve the educational levels of workers. For example, South Carolina provides specialized industrial training programs for specific industries, thus removing the cost from industry for in-plant and on-the-job training programs.

To enhance the belief that an educated labor force is needed, an increasing proportion of the unemployed since 1940 has consisted of workers with less than a high school education. As a result there has arisen the idea that modern industry can utilize only relatively highly educated workers. A number of studies have investigated this assumption. Most of these studies reveal, however, that there is no discernible relationship between changes in output per worker on a particular job in an industry and changes in the educational level of the worker. However, since employers have shown a preference for higher skilled workers, the regions where training opportunities are available are more likely to attract and retain industry. The long trend indicates that regional differences in the educational levels of workers will influence their industrial potential.

Another vital question has been whether there is evidence that the better educated workers exhibit greater mobility moving from industries that are experiencing small increases in output to those industries with larger increases. Recent studies have shown that there has been out-mobility at all educational levels from the slower growing industries. Conversely, at all educational levels there has been in-mobility for the rapidly growing industries. There is thus strong evidence that the rate of worker mobility within and between regions depends primarily on employment opportunities rather than the rate of technological change.

Because labor is a major component of the manufactural costs, the per capita output in manufacturing in different countries of the world reveals a great deal about labor productivity in a given area. The labor productivity in Canada, United States, western Europe, and Japan is extraordinarily high compared with the level in most other countries. There is strong evidence that the differences in per capita output are caused primarily by differences in labor productivity. Thus labor productivity attains major importance in determining the level of industrial output.

RURAL VERSUS URBAN LABOR. Although urban areas have developed concentrations of manufacturing, certain types of industry persist in rural areas. Those most important are food products, textiles, apparel, lumber and wood products, paper products, chemicals, and electrical machinery (68). Lonsdale indicates that labor costs constitute a large proportion of production costs in these industries, and the achievement of labor economies is considered essential to maintain a competitive market position. For the most part, rural factories use unskilled workers who can be trained for routine tasks in a short period of time. The number of managerial and technical workers is usually small. In recent years some exceptions to this labor situation have developed. Some raw-material-oriented industries, such as pulp and paper and chemicals, have high labor costs in rural areas.

In contrast to the importance of labor to the localization of rural industries, labor costs are usually less critical as a locational factor in urban industries. Industries in urban areas require more skilled labor and therefore higher costs. As a result, such other factors as transportation costs, the availability of entrepreneurial talents, nearness to an airport, or a cultural environment are considered desirable. As Lonsdale states, "they are firms where a rural location is not dictated by such solid cost considerations as availability of lower-wage labor and/or opportunity to avoid labor unions" (68–12).

The industrial growth in rural areas in recent times has been based largely on securing a greater share of the low-cost labor-intensive industries rather than the high-labor-cost industries that have been experiencing a high national growth rate. For example, between 1950 and 1968 North Carolina increased its share of the nation's textile industry from 23 to 32 percent. During the same period the state increased its total manufacturing employment by more than 60 percent. This increase was based on the expansion of slow-growth, low-wage industries, which amount to almost 70 percent of the total industrial employment in North Carolina.

In recent times there has been a growing tendency for companies to locate large plants in rural areas isolated from other manufacturing. Some of these plants have a work force of from 2,000 to 3,000 persons. This is possible because rural residents have demonstrated that they are willing to commute long distances. The development of good roads has made it possible for industry to recruit its labor supply from a distance of at least 30 miles from the factory. The utilization of rural labor in factories has provided many advantages to the area. When other economic opportunities are not available, the rural factory provides an alternative to out-migration, thus stabilizing the population. Many subsistence farmers have been able to supplement meager incomes. The availability of work in a rural area has given numerous people the opportunity to maintain their accustomed ways of life.

Rural locations offer advantages to a company other than labor availability. These include cheap land with plenty of space to expand, favorable tax structures, local governments that are sometimes willing to provide subsidies, and the opportunity to escape some of the growing economic and social problems of large cities. There are, of course, some handicaps to the development of industry in rural areas. While certain types of labor exist in rural areas, these regions usually lack trained professional and technical personnel. This type of labor must be imported, which sometimes creates a problem in housing and other services such as educational, financial, and shopping facilities.

DETERMINATION OF LABOR COSTS IN MANUFACTURING.   A basic question in the modern industrial economy is how much of the manufactural costs can be assigned to labor. The answer to this question is basic to the health of a modern economy (38). In reality, President John Kennedy's confrontation with the steel industry in 1962, the general strike in France in 1968, and the labor difficulties of the United Kingdom in the 1970s all had their origins in this fundamental issue.

The recognition of the need to determine the cost of labor in manufacturing is old. Thomas Aquinas posed the question of how a "just wage" could be determined in relation to a system of "just prices." This viewpoint is similar to the modern equivalent of the problem of adopting an appropriate policy for incomes and prices in an economy. The basic difference is that the area of judgment has moved from that of ethics and morals to that of economics. It is now a question of what is desirable for the economy. This change is primarily related to the enormous progress in material prosperity.

There is considerable difficulty in measuring the importance of labor in manufacturing. The general level of wages is the result of a multiplicity of factors, both current and historical, that have been integrated in a variety of ways to bring about the present distribution of the joint product of labor and capital in manufacturing. The fundamental problem is that "the equilibrium level of wages" of modern economic theory has not proved amenable to statistical measurement. As economist Paul Samuelson states, "the final labor cost is almost as indeterminate as the haggling between two millionaires over the price to be paid for a rare oil painting" (95–603).

Nevertheless, there are empirical procedures for determining the percentage of the labor factor in the production cost. One method is to calculate the ratio that total wages and salaries receive in the manufacturing process in relation to the total of the value added. This is thus a measure of the share of labor in relation to other costs in the manufacturing process (67).

TRENDS OF LABOR COSTS IN THE UNITED STATES. Because of the historical availability of statistics in the United States, the importance of labor in relation to value added can be traced from 1899 (Table 2.3). Since then the ratio of wages and salaries to value added for all manufacturing has varied from a low of .45 to a high of .57, while the average of the ratio is .52. The changes in the ratio from one period to another reflect variations in the general economy. During the 1930s depression, value added in manufacturing declined greatly, but the importance of labor declined even more precipitously. As a result labor's share of total costs was at its lowest value in 1933. During World War II and the early postwar period, labor's share of the manufactural costs rose to a high of .56 in 1953 and 1954. Since then labor's ratio has declined slightly and in 1975 was .50. In recent years labor's share of the production cost has had a one-year lead over the parity rule; that is, the payroll of each year tends to the parity point when related to the value added of the following years. This phenomenon is likely related to the general pricing policies of industry.

INTERNATIONAL LABOR COSTS. Table 2.4 reveals that labor's share in the manufacturing costs varies remarkably little among nations. In all developed nations the cost of labor is approximately 50 percent of the value added. Thus the share of labor is about equal to that of the other factors of production plus depreciation. In general, labor's share of the production costs has declined, which indicates advancement in mechanization. The trends are an impressive indication of the similar forces in all countries that shape the underlying economic forces which determine the cost factors in manufacturing. The

Table 2.3

Ratio of Wages and Salaries to Value Added: U.S. Manufacturing Industry, 1889–1975

Year	Ratio	Year	Ratio	Year	Ratio
1889	.54	1939	.52	1963	.52
1899	.47	1947	.53	1964	.52
1904	.50	1950	.53	1965	.51
1909	.50	1951	.55	1966	.50
1914	.54	1953	.56	1967	.50
1919	.52	1954	.56	1968	.50
1921	.57	1955	.53	1969	.50
1923	.53	1956	.53	1970	.51
1925	.51	1957	.54	1971	.50
1927	.50	1958	.55	1972	.50
1929	.47	1959	.53	1973	.50
1933	.45	1960	.54	1974	.50
1935	.52	1961	.54	1975	.50
1937	.51	1962	.53		

Source: Census of Manufactures. Washington, D.C.: U.S. Department of Commerce, Bureau of the Census.

forces that induce uniformity in labor costs prevail despite variations in size of the industry, technology, length of the working day or week, and differences in economic management between capitalist and socialist nations.

Within individual countries there has also been a stability of the wage ratio, from the late nineteenth century to the present. This stability may provide a guideline for determining income and price policies. Further, those industries that deviate from this average exhibit a certain stability in their relation to the average.

LABOR COSTS IN SELECTED COUNTRIES. When labor's share of the manufacturing costs is determined as a ratio of value added, the ratios deviate from the parity value in similar ways in all countries. Table 2.5 shows the ratio of wages and salaries to value added for 20 industrial groups in 14 countries. The average wage ratio for all countries is .494, with variation from a low of .367 in Japan to a high of .572 in Sweden.

The ratio is highest for the transportation equipment industry in almost all countries. Although the transportation equipment industry has, in general, a high ratio, there are considerable variations—from a low of .354 in Japan to a high of .795 in Rhodesia. The highest wage ratios in the transportation equipment industry are found in those countries—Rhodesia, Australia, Finland, Norway, Israel, and the Netherlands—where motor vehicles are assembled largely from imported parts. Outside of Japan, the United States has the lowest ratio, .513, although wage rates are high. The high wages are overcome by advanced technology.

The lowest labor ratios are for the tobacco industry, .259, the beverage

Table 2.4

Ratio of Wages and Salaries to Value Added in Manufacturing: Selected Countries

Country	Year	Ratio	Country	Year	Ratio
Australia	1953–54	.58	Netherlands	1953	.46
	1958–59	.54		1958	.51
	1963–64	.52		1963	.46
	1970	.52		1971	.50
Canada	1953	.50			
	1958	.50			
	1963	.49			
	1971	.52			
Finland	1954	.54	Norway	1953	.45
	1958	.52		1958	.50
	1963	.51		1963	.51
	1971	.50		1971	.52
Ireland	1953	.53	South Africa	1953	.47
	1958	.53		1958	.48
	1963	.51		1963	.45
	1971	.49		1971	.45
			Sweden	1953	.58
				1958	.57
				1963	.57
				1971	.53
Japan	1953	.40	United	1954	.55
	1958	.41	Kingdom	1958	.57
	1963	.37		1963	.53
	1970	.35		1970	.53
Luxembourg	1953	.53	United	1954	.54
	1958	.44	States	1958	.52
	1962	.52		1963	.49
	1971	.53		1971	.46
			USSR	1958	.55
				1963	.45
				1964	.45

Source: Statistical Office of the United Nations. New York: United Nations.

industry, .296, and the petroleum and coal products industries, .312. Of all industries, the tobacco industry has the lowest wage ratios, varying from .068 in Norway to .570 in Rhodesia. Although the labor ratios for petroleum and coal products, on the average, are low, the variations are also rather large: from .172 in Finland to .500 in New Zealand.

Of the 20 industrial classifications, the United States, in spite of high labor costs, has an average wage ratio in 8 industries that is below the average for all countries. The wages ratios in Japan for each of the 20 industries is below the average for all countries. In contrast, only five industries in the United Kingdom are below the world average labor ratio. In general, a low wage ratio is a competitive advantage and a high ratio is a disadvantage for an industrial country seeking world markets.

Table 2.5

Ratio of Wages and Salaries to Value Added in 20 Industrial Groups in 14 Countries, 1970

	Australia	Canada	Finland	Ireland	Israel	Japan	Netherlands	New Zealand	Norway	Rhodesia	South Africa	Sweden	United Kingdom	United States	Average
Food	.428	.474	.395	.513	.491	.304	.419	.562	.675	.420	.354	.397	.443	.405	.449
Beverages	.322	.284	.424	.353	.190	.240	.161	.250	.196	.303	.342	.430	.303	.351	.296
Tobacco	.244	.353	.261	.400	.074	—	.161	.333	.068	.570	.210	.247	.254	.196	.259
Textiles	.544	.546	.595	.529	.521	.414	.652	.600	.528	.452	.402	.588	.568	.548	.535
Apparel	.584	.636	.561	.600	.456	.432	.609	.680	.554	.517	.547	.636	.610	.568	.571
Wood and cork products	.563	.581	.630	.667	.557	.465	.548	.565	.552	.524	.533	.596	.621	.585	.571
Furniture and fixtures	.557	.618	.642	.667	.415	.455	.548	.625	.564	.538	.586	.626	.650	.562	.575
Paper and paper products	.417	.457	.420	.600	.360	.348	.455	.363	.574	.418	.372	.526	.498	.474	.449
Printing and publishing	.555	.573	.500	.600	.647	.413	.452	.545	.499	.621	.573	.593	.554	.526	.553
Leather and leather products	.563	.642	.640	.333	.556	.428	.523	.666	.543	—	.500	.622	.559	.589	.551
Rubber products	.558	.541	.476	—	.389	.358	.523	.500	.582	.402	.394	.601	.537	.509	.490
Chemicals and chemical products	.312	.381	.349	.333	.405	.252	.288	.375	.391	.314	.358	.417	.353	.330	.347
Petroleum and coal products	.173	.350	.172	—	.405	.228	.288	.500	.271	—	.303	.347	.397	.305	.312
Nonmetallic mineral products	.470	.464	.545	.444	.382	.348	.481	.470	.458	.432	.431	.523	.548	.456	.461

Basic metals	.478	.415	.486	—	.444	.460	.373	.333	.472	.597	.437	.613	.569	.513	.476
Metal products except machinery and transport equipment	.585	.561	.634	.667	.541	.413	.582	.571	.532	.591	.569	.634	.550	.545	.567
Machinery except electrical machinery	.607	.540	.593	.500	.322	.416	.582	.600	.536	.535	.605	.634	.582	.543	.543
Electrical machinery, apparatus and appliances	.597	.565	.598	.429	.470	.333	.486	.461	.490	.509	.500	.603	.565	.560	.512
Transportation equipment	.675	.518	.681	.636	.667	.354	.603	.641	.656	.795	.520	.650	.614	.513	.609
Other manufacturers	.516	.531	.574	.400	.628	.407	.613	.555	.544	.396	.500	.551	.533	.493	.517
Total industry	.517	.493	.513	.505	.460	.367	.463	.542	.507	.502	.454	.572	.529	.485	.494

Source: Statistical Office of the United Nations. New York: United Nations.

Transportation and Transfer Costs

The location of manufacturing is greatly influenced by the availability and cost of transportation. As Moore states, "If transportation facilities serve to consolidate regions, it must also be observed that freight rates are to regions and to cities what tariffs are to nations. They form a part of the cost of connections with other regions and may be manipulated to the advantage or disadvantage of a given region in almost exactly the same way" (77–2).

The location of industry in any given area may depend directly on the type of transportation present (20). It must be remembered, however, that the type of transportation and freight rates will vary in different industries. If freight rates are a major portion of the cost of production, or high relative to the value of the final product, they may be a controlling factor in the location of industry. In contrast, if freight rates are a small portion of the cost of production or low relative to the value of the product, they will have little or no influence on the location of the industry.

In the early stages of industrialization, when raw materials were usually obtained locally and the finished goods marketed within a restricted district, transportation played a lesser role in localizing industry. As a result manufacturing was highly decentralized. As transportation facilities developed and greater efficiency in the movement of commodities ensued, areal specialization increased.

In the early stages of the industrial age, road transport was slow and extremely expensive. As a result waterways soon assumed a major role in transporting industrial goods. Cities located on navigable waterways and coastal locations possessed a significant advantage and became the first industrial centers. Such European cities as Bruges, Antwerp, and London are excellent examples.

The natural waterways were soon supplemented by canals and improved river channels. The construction of the canal system in the United Kingdom was a forerunner to the growth of large-scale heavy industry. In the United States, the Erie Canal greatly accelerated the expansion of industry in the cities along its route and in New York City and the Midwest. The canal reduced the freight rate from Buffalo to New York City from $100 to $5 a ton. In the Ruhr of Germany, the raw materials and the heavy finished products of the iron and steel industry made transportation costs a relatively high proportion of total cost. As a result low-cost river and canal transportation assumed great importance in the location of industry.

Waterways had many limitations because not all areas could be served. Canal traffic was also slow, and many canals were narrow and shallow. Improvements were frequently difficult and costly. Consequently, when the railroads appeared, they frequently replaced water transportation. The railroads made possible a more rapid movement of goods and were usually more easily constructed and maintained. Further, railroads permitted the movement of raw materials and finished products to a larger number of locations. The last half of the nineteenth century was the era of railroad transportation dominance.

Motor transportation has assumed a significant role in the twentieth century (61). The expanded road networks have given truck transportation a greater flexibility than that enjoyed by the railroads. The use of road transport has made it possible to coordinate the delivery of raw materials and distribution of finished products in a more efficient manner.

Other forms of transport have developed to serve particular functions. The pipelines have become leading carriers of liquids and gases. In recent years the aircraft has grown in importance for moving special high-priced cargoes. To date, however, air terminals have had little influence on the location of industry.

The influence of transportation as a localizing factor is evident in every modern manufacturing region (44). Every major transportation center in the United States is also a significant manufacturing center. The growth of a manufacturing zone along the Penn Central Railroad from New York to Chicago in such cities as Schenectady, Syracuse, Rochester, Buffalo, Cleveland, and Toledo illustrates the importance of transportation. This route, following the lowlands through New York State and skirting south of the Great Lakes, reflects the importance of a lowland route. All transportation routes seek the lowest grades and thus, as far as possible, circumvent natural barriers.

TRANSPORT AND TRANSFER COST SYSTEMS. Transportation costs frequently play a significant role in determining the ultimate price of a product. Consequently, to gain a competitive position, freight rates are sometimes manipulated. Three basic pricing policies have been utilized at different times: basing-point pricing; zonal, or group rate, systems; and the distance rate (f.o.b.) system. Of these three, only the last is basically nondiscriminatory.

Basing-Point System. The basing-point system was one in which products were sold at an identical delivered price by all producers (69). This price was determined by the price at the basing point plus the set freight rate from the basing point to the destination of the product. Once the price plus the freight rate was determined, it was applied to all products whether delivered from the basing point or from other producing points. This system protected the competitive advantage of a particular location. Every producer, regardless of location, was free to charge the freight rate established at the basing point, but he could not charge less. The producer at the basing point could not be undersold anywhere in the country. Thus the purchaser paid more freight than was incurred on the shipment if he purchased from a source closer than the basing point. In contrast, he paid less freight than was incurred on his shipment if he purchased from a producer located farther away than the basing point.

The basing-point system of determining freight rates began about 1880, when it was established by the iron and steel producers in Pittsburgh. That industry's system came to be known as "Pittsburgh Plus." The basing-point system was also utilized by the glucose and corn syrup industry. Chicago became the basing point for these industries. As a result other centers of production, such as Decatur and Kansas City, supposedly had a competitive disadvantage to Chicago.

About 1924 the single-basing-point system was gradually replaced by the multiple-basing-point system. This multiple-basing-point concept survived until 1948, when basing-point systems were declared illegal by the U.S. Supreme Court. At that time 18 products or groups of products were using a system of single or multiple basing points. These included—besides iron and steel—cement, wood pulp, wood products, and corn oil.

The most important general basing-point systems were the Texas Common Point System, the Southern Basing Point System, and the Transcontinental Terminal "Basing Line" System. The Texas Common Point System blanketed eastern Texas under a single rate system. The southern and transcontinental systems provided low interregional rates to more distant large centers that were established basing points. For example, freight moving from the North to a nonbasing point in the South took the rate of the southern basing point plus the difference in the rate between it and the basing point.

The West Coast port terminal cities constituted basing points in the transcontinental system (33–395). To illustrate, in 1909 a cargo of 10 tons of first-class freight from Chicago to Reno cost $858 to ship. However, the freight cost from Chicago to Sacramento was only $600 because Sacramento was a basing point. The Reno charges were determined by the cost of the movement from Chicago to Sacramento plus the additional charges to Reno. It is obvious that the intermediate points between basing points were at a distinct freight cost disadvantage.

The influence of the basing-point system on the location of industry has been widely considered (104). The system had its greatest effect when the basing point was central to the market area involved and when the market was served by all manufacturers. Agglomeration would then take place at the basing point. If, however, the basing point was eccentric to the market area, and manufacturers could gain economies in production and at the same time possess a local market, the basing point had little effect on the location of new plants. For example, from 1910 to 1925 the steel industry grew most rapidly outside the Pittsburgh region, which was the basing point for the industry. Other factors besides transfer costs were more important in the establishment of new centers of iron and steel production.

Group Rate System. The characteristic feature of the group (regional or blanket) rate system entails the areal grouping of points of origin and/or destination. Thus transportation rates are the same within a single region regardless of distance to the region of destination. Rate changes occur only when a product is transported from one region to another.

The development of group rates resulted from a variety of factors. Because of the complexity of freight rates, they evolved in an attempt to simplify rate structures. Further, a regional system greatly reduced the number of specific rates that needed to be established. Possibly more important, the group rate system was devised to reduce market competition. Because it was possible to have higher rates for shorter hauls than for longer hauls over the same route group rates were established. This group rate scheme developed because a low through rate due to competition became the maximum rate that could be charged at intermediate points.

Group rate systems are numerous (26). The regions vary considerably in size depending on the commodity. For example, New England has frequently been designated as a uniform rate region for freight originating from points west of Buffalo and Pittsburgh. Many of the other regions are large. For example, certain commodities, originating on the Pacific coast, have a single rate for destinations east of the Mississippi River.

Distance Rate System. The simplest form of rate structure is one in which the transfer costs are related to distance. However, in the typical situation the rates do not increase uniformly with distance. Instead, a distance block system is used (Fig. 2.1). For example, rates will increase at 5-mile intervals up to 100 miles, then at 10-mile intervals up to 250 miles, at 25-mile intervals up to 2,000 miles, and at 50-mile intervals for greater distances.

A number of factors favor the use of the block system of rate increases. First, terminal costs are the same regardless of the length of haul. The longer the haul the greater the distance over which the constant terminal costs can be spread. Second, the line haul costs per ton-mile are lower for distant movements of freight because through freight trains make fewer stops and operate more efficiently. Third, if rates increased directly in proportion to distance they would soon be so high they would prohibit the movements of freight. The tapering rate system prevents the transfer costs from restricting the movement of long-distance traffic (Fig. 2.2).

Three advantages prevail in the use of the distance rate system over other systems. First, it is simple and easily understood, whereas other schemes are considerably more complex. Second, the distance rate scheme conforms to the principle that the cost is proportional to the service performed. Third, this system preserves for each locality the advantage of its specific location. Localities are grouped in other schemes, thus losing this uniqueness of location.

FACTORS AFFECTING FREIGHT RATES. Although the freight rates are of the utmost importance to a manufacturer, they are extremely complex to determine and are possibly even more difficult to generalize into geographic patterns (112–326). The freight rate structure includes not only direct freight costs, usually called "transport costs," but also other costs that influence the ultimate rate. The total rate is known as the "transfer cost" (27).

Distance, Volume, Weight, and Value. Basically, transport costs are a function of distance the product is to be carried relative to its volume, weight, and value. The ideal product to transport is one that has low volume and weight and high value. However, the problem of transporting each product must be considered. For example, limestone has great weight and low value, but these disadvantages are partly offset by the ease of loading and unloading and no danger of damage in transit.

The variability of transfer costs in relation to distance, volume, weight, and value depends on technology and facilities available. Carriers operating on water, such as barges or tankers, have large capacity and thus have little limitations of high-weight and low-value commodities. In contrast, motor vehicles have a relatively small carrying capacity and are subject to specified statutory weight

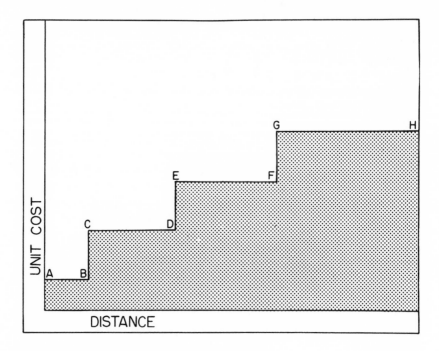

Figure 2.1. A distance block transfer system.

limits. As a result there are greater distance limitations and higher costs in the use of motor vehicles. For example, equal transfer costs would limit the use of trucks in the carriage of coal up to 500 miles and the use of trains up to 1,500 miles; but coal could be carried by barge for the same cost up to several thousand miles. Clearly, the technology of the various types of transportation affects the freight rates.

Common Costs. A carrier frequently provides several types of service. For example, because a railroad may provide both passenger and freight services, certain costs are common to both. The cost of maintaining tracks and facilities such as signal systems is influenced little by the nature of the class of service provided. Carriers are continuously attempting to develop standard equipment that will be adaptable to a variety of uses. When highly specialized equipment is required, freight rates normally increase. When more than one service can be provided by a carrier, the freight rates can normally be lowered. Thus, in areas where facilities serve a multiple purpose, a manufacturer will usually have the advantage of lower rates.

Variations in Scale of Operation. Because there are fixed costs in all transportation services, the scale of the operation becomes important. All transportation companies seek to operate at maximum capacity. If, however, only a portion of the facilities can be utilized, the cost of transportation services rise.

If a small company is located in an isolated region and produces only

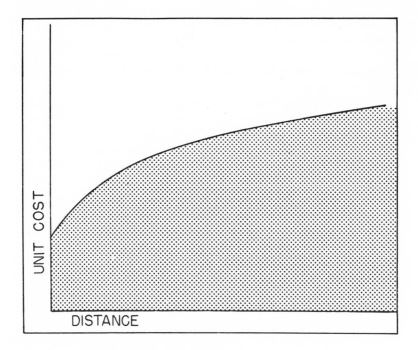

Figure 2.2. A tapering rate transfer system.

enough goods to make up a partial shipment and no other manufacturer is able to complete the shipment, the company will possess a transportational disadvantage. If on the other hand a small plant is located in an industrial complex and produces only a partial load of goods, a transportation company will be able to complete the load from other companies in the area. This situation gives a cost advantage to a company locating in an industrial complex.

Backhaul Traffic. The freight rate on a commodity will depend to a degree on the ability of the carrier to develop a balanced traffic flow. If a carrier has cargo going in one direction only, an uneconomic return of empty vehicles will result. A two-way traffic flow also spreads fixed costs. Those regions on transport routes that have little or no backhaul traffic are at a disadvantage in attracting manufacturing. When a common carrier serves large urban centers, the traffic flow between these centers is likely to be well balanced. The more isolated the area, the greater the possibilities for a one-way flow of commodities.

A number of industries produce so specialized a product that there is little possibility for a return cargo. For example, the tank trucks that transport refined petroleum products are so specialized that backhaul traffic is highly unlikely. As a result transportation costs assume a greater role to the manufacturer. There is thus a greater tendency for plants to be market oriented in order to reduce transportation costs.

Transit Privileges. The disadvantage of a manufacturer being located at a point lying between raw materials and markets may be overcome by the establishment of transit privileges. The transit privilege gives the shipper the right to perform certain processes upon the raw materials en route without increasing the freight rate applied to through shipments. This procedure gives all intermediate points the same advantage.

When transit privileges are granted, there is a wide choice of points where manufacturing can occur. For example, if there is a particular type of labor at an intermediate point, the manufacturer can take advantage of this situation. Because the transit privilege encourages the use of existing facilities, it tends to minimize distance as a factor, thus protecting the market interests of the more distant shippers.

Transit privileges have been granted to a number of manufacturers. Grain milling and finishing timber are well-known industries possessing these privileges. If these privileges were not granted, the millers located at the source of the grain, at the market, and at "rate-breaking" points would have advantages over other sites. All other millers who were charged rates from the grain to the milling point and from the milling point to the market would find that they possessed a competitive disadvantage over millers located at the grain source or market. The transit privilege has made it possible for the grain milling industry to be widely decentralized in the United States.

Competitive Freight Rates. Common carriers have had a long tradition of adjusting freight rates to meet competition. By this practice, they can develop and maintain industries in unfavorable locations and can retard the growth of industries in favored locations. This power is limited by the legal requirement that rates must be just and reasonable, not discriminatory or unduly preferential or prejudicial. Nevertheless, the freight rates established in a given region can greatly influence the attractiveness of locating or maintaining industry in that area.

As early as 1878 an agreement was reached between railroads to charge higher rates from the Midwest to the South than from the East to the South on certain manufactured articles produced in the East; at the same time higher rates from the East to the South were maintained on goods produced in the Midwest. This arrangement encouraged specialization in each region and, naturally, retarded changes in industrial location.[1]

As a result of these practices, the idea developed that a function of transportation is to equalize the competitive position of widely separated manufacturers. This position is justified on the basis that the products produced in distant regions and thus normally receiving higher freight rates would soon disappear, and the railroad would lose business. The extra cost incurred as a result of the discrimination in favor of the more distant manufacturer must be recovered by transferring this amount to other traffic. This practice, if carried to the extreme, can increase rates so greatly that the entire traffic pattern could be deranged and result in the ultimate demise of the carrier. This pricing philosophy may have had some

[1]Freight Bureau *v.* Cincinnati, New Orleans, and Texas Pacific R.R. Co., 6 ICC 195, 216, 241–46 (1895).

validity at an earlier time, but it has little merit in a modern, relatively mature industrial economy attempting to develop sound long-range transportation policies that will ensure efficient utilization.[2]

Railroads have developed many types of freight rates favorable to developing manufacturing along their routes. Examples can be found of low rates from distant points to enable remote producers to sell goods in a given locality in competition with nearby producers. For example, the freight rates for most of New England's manufactured products are the same as the rates for the New York area. This enables the New England area to compete successfully with the New York area. Another notable example of this policy was the preferential rates given New England textile mills over southern mills in marketing textiles in the Midwest in the late nineteenth and early twentieth century. The price of cotton textiles from the southern mills had to be lowered for them to compete with the New England producers.[3]

Services. There are some relatively intangible factors that affect transfer costs. These include speed of delivery, care of the product in transit, courtesy of the shipper, and many others that are difficult to measure. Shippers often cite these factors as being of great importance in the establishment of an industry in a particular area.

Market

The market as a location factor in manufacturing is increasing in importance (29). There is frequently a cost advantage when a substantial local market exists, and this situation is enhanced when a good competitive position is maintained by serving important adjoining market areas. The attraction of the market may then be based on a weight or bulk gain in the process of manufacturing or on higher freight costs of the finished products than of raw materials.

FACTORS AFFECTING MARKET LOCATION. There are several factors that influence a firm to locate in a market area.

Weight Increase. An orientation to market may be based on a weight increase in the process of manufacturing. This occurs when a large quantity of some ubiquitous material like water is necessary in producing the product. As a result the weight of the product may exceed the total weight of the imported raw materials. A ubiquitous material is one that is obtainable everywhere at essentially equal costs so that it has no transfer costs. It does add to the weight of such products as beverages and inks and gives the manufacturer an inducement to locate as near the market as possible to reduce distribution costs.

Bulk Increase. When the bulk of the product is increased in the manufacturing process, a market location is desired. Such items as machinery, pianos,

[2]National Transportation Policy, Committee on Interstate and Foreign Commerce, U.S. Senate Special Study Group on Transportation Policies in the United States, S. Res. 29, 151 and 244 of the 86th Congress, January 1961, p. 386.

[3]Smith Bros. Manufacturing Co. *v.* Aberdeen and Rockfish Railway Co., 181 ICC (1931), p. 137, 139.

barrels, furniture, and automobiles are in this category. For example, an automobile when assembled occupies five to six times the space of its parts. Parts factories are not necessarily market oriented, but the final assembly into a bulky machine tends to be done in assembly plants within market areas.

Fragility. A market location is also encouraged for fragile products because it is usually cheaper to transport raw materials than it is to transport the finished products. It is thus more economical to locate the processing plant near the consumer than the source of raw material. The reasons for this situation reflect a fundamental concept in manufacturing. As products pass through successive stages of production after bulk-reducing, purifying, or preserving operations and gradually assume the form to be delivered to the consumer, they become progressively more difficult to pack and handle, more valuable in relation to weight, and differentiated into more types and sizes. This fragility increases the transfer costs of finished products.

Perishability. Factories that produce perishable products are usually market oriented. Perishable products, including bakery goods, ice cream, ice, and newspapers, must be marketed quickly or their value declines rapidly. Although modern transportation facilities, such as air freight, have made possible the quick distribution of products to distant places, the transfer costs are usually so high that many low-cost perishable products cannot utilize these facilities. However, improved techniques of transportation have a tendency to weaken the market orientation of these types of manufacturing.

Value of the Product. There may be an advantage for a factory to be located near its market if the product is of low value. The transfer costs of low-cost products can become a major portion of the selling price. As the value of the product increases, the market orientation is lessened. For example, cement, which is of uniform quality and low value in relation to its bulk, is oriented to its market because distribution costs would be excessive if production were concentrated and a national market existed. In contrast, many electronic factories are not market oriented because the transfer costs of the high-value products are an insignificant portion of the total cost.

Consumer Requirements. When a manufacturer needs to have an intimate knowledge of his customer's needs and possible changes in specifications of the products manufactured, nearness of producer to consumer is desired. Historically, the concentration of the textile machinery near the textile industry in southern New England led to technical developments that increased productivity in the textile industry. Industries that are experiencing rapid technological changes today, such as the electronic and electrical machinery industries, are frequently oriented to their markets. For a company to remain competitive, it is desirable to be located where the technical changes are occurring. The concentration of the electronics industry around Boston and Anaheim-Garden Grove illustrates this type of location. The advantage of proximity of producer to consumer also applies to the women's apparel industry, where style changes require a massive market for their acceptance.

Market Capacity. As a result of modern mass production techniques, many industries find maximum economies in production only when they produce at an enormous scale (103). These industrial giants include, for example, the motor vehicle and household appliances industries and even basic industries such as iron and steel. The location of these industries is obviously affected by the market capacity of an area to consume the massive output.

The production of iron and steel, even though a raw-material-processing industry, is frequently oriented to a market. The iron and steel industry of the western Pennsylvania–eastern Ohio iron and steel region, although localized near coking coal, is a superb example of an industry being situated in a favorable regional market location. This region produces an excess of iron and steel. Thus the products are sold in the huge market area of the American Manufacturing Belt.

In the twentieth century, most of the new iron and steel centers have been situated near markets, as demonstrated by the growth of Gary, Indiana, near Chicago; the establishment of the Fontana plant east of Los Angeles; and the construction of the Fairless Steel Works, which provided the reason for the building of Levittown, Pennsylvania, on the Delaware River north of Philadelphia.

LOCAL, REGIONAL, AND NATIONAL MARKETS.   The size of the market varies considerably for different types of manufacturing. The market is concentrated for certain types of manufacturing. For example, the textile machinery industry began in New England close to the textile centers. The farm machinery industry has traditionally been concentrated in agricultural regions of high productivity. As a result the farm machinery industry is highly localized in the Midwest. The concentration of industry in these market areas indicated the influence of lower transfer costs and the advantages of contact between producer and user.

In contrast to the concentrated market, there are markets that are widely dispersed. These include such products as food, drink, and some newspapers. When these products are of relatively low value, and sometimes high bulk, it is most desirable to have a large number of plants widely dispersed to reduce transfer costs.

A different market situation exists when there are relatively few factories that serve a national, or even international, market. The products produced are normally of high value and can withstand relatively high transfer costs. Examples of this type of product include electrical machinery, electronic products, and scientific instruments. The plants for these products may be oriented to the largest markets, at a good distribution point, or at a point where there are advantageous factors of production. Thus these factories have a wide choice of plant locations.

DETERMINATION OF MARKET REGIONS.   When two plants exist in a region each plant controls the market where it maintains an advantage in production and transportation costs. When a plant loses its cost advantage in a particular area, the market reverts to a lower-cost plant.

The market area for three plants can be demonstrated by a simple diagram.

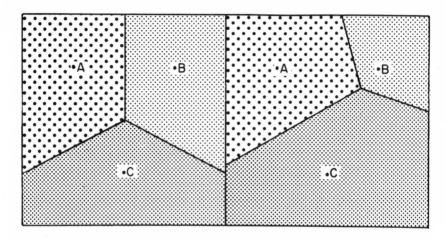

Figure 2.3. Market areas: three plants.

First let us suppose that there are three plants at an equal distance apart from each other; they are located at A, B, and C, produce identical products, and have equal production and transfer costs. The market area in which each of these plants has a comparative cost advantage is identical in size (Fig. 2.3). If the production costs of the plant at B increase, the costs at A and C remain the same, the market area for B is reduced while the market areas of A and C are enlarged (59–38).

When this concept is extended to the distribution of multiple plants, market areas will form either a uniform or a random pattern. This is illustrated by Fig. 2.4. When factories are uniformly distributed and produce identical products at uniform production costs and equal transfer costs, the market area for each plant is theoretically defined by a hexagonal area (25). The perfect hexagonal pattern will be altered if the production and/or transfer costs for each plant differ, or if the plants have a random pattern.

COEFFICIENT OF LOCALIZATION. The size of the market of a region may be estimated by the development of a coefficient of localization using personal income as an indicator of market potential. Personal income is an indicator of the total amount of money available to be spent in the area. It reflects not only the size of the population, but also the economic level of the region. A number of implications on the market potential can be drawn. For example, if there is the same percentage of manufacturing and income in a region the implication is that the industry is market oriented. If, however, manufacturing has a much higher percentage than the income in the region, the implication is that a large proportion of the product is exported. If the income has a much higher percentage in the region than the manufactured product, the implication is that there is a movement of the product into the region.

A measure of the geographic distribution of manufacturing in relation to the

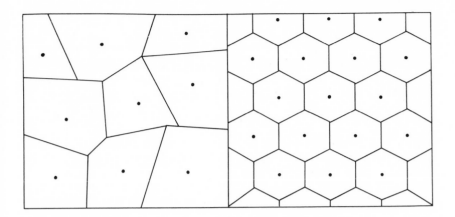

Figure 2.4. Market areas: random and uniform patterns.

market potential is revealed by the coefficient of localization (35–107). To determine the coefficient, the following steps are required:

1. Compute the percentage of total U.S. (other areal units may be substituted) personal income received in each areal unit.
2. Compute the percentage of value added (employment may be substituted) in each industry that is produced in each areal unit.
3. Substract the percentage of personal income in each areal unit from that of value added by each industry in each areal unit.
4. For each industry, sum either the positive or negative differences for all areal units and divide by 100. The number is the *coefficient of localization.* If manufacturing were distributed exactly as personal income, the coefficient would be 0. If all the manufacturing were in one region, the coefficient would be 1.

Table 2.6 shows the distribution of personal income by the nine census regions of the United States in 1971, the distribution of value added for each of 21 two-digit SIC manufacturing industries among the nine census regions, and the coefficient of localization for each industry. There were wide variations in the coefficients of localization. The tobacco industry, with a coefficient of .7113, was the most concentrated industry; the local market is limited so that a national market is served from a concentration of manufacturing. In contrast, the coefficients of localization for stone, clay, and glass products, food and kindred products, and paper and allied products were lowest. Their coefficients were .0710, .0937, and .0954, respectively. This indicates that the manufacture of these products is more closely related to the distribution of personal incomes than the coefficient of any of the other industries.

The coefficient of localization will vary depending on the type of industrial group. The coefficient for all manufacturing in the United States in 1971 was

Table 2.6

Coefficient of Localization: Groupings of Manufacturing Industries, 1971

Industry	United States (in $Millions)	New England	Middle Atlantic	East North Central	West North Central	South Atlantic	East South Central	West South Central	Mountain	Pacific	Coefficient of Localization
Personal income	$857,100.0	6.24	20.55	20.61	7.61	13.96	4.79	8.13	3.82	14.23	
Food and kindred products	34,109.8	3.60	16.55	24.11	12.01	11.09	5.45	8.35	3.20	14.72	.0937
Tobacco manufacture	2,559.9	0.23	5.63	2.01	—	73.79	16.09	—	—	—	.7113
Textile and mill products	9,995.2	8.50	17.09	3.44	0.36	58.60	8.64	1.38	—	—	.5075
Apparel and related products	12,448.4	4.83	40.04	9.25	3.98	17.62	10.40	6.00	0.76	6.90	.2876
Lumber and wood	6,760.9	3.97	5.99	10.20	4.13	15.60	9.01	8.07	6.36	36.37	.3054
Furniture and fixtures	5,226.9	4.34	15.02	23.54	4.27	23.92	9.57	6.64	1.09	11.63	.1767
Paper and allied products	11,682.1	9.70	18.02	21.94	6.87	15.47	8.03	7.61	0.79	11.39	.0954
Printing and publishing	18,086.4	6.64	31.13	24.29	8.18	9.40	3.54	4.66	2.10	10.01	.1523
Chemicals and allied products	29,431.5	3.42	24.15	21.46	5.57	15.86	8.60	13.83	1.00	5.67	.1586
Petroleum and coal	5,616.8	1.05	14.16	16.90	6.29	3.73	2.54	37.78	2.86	14.41	.2983

Census Regions: Percentage Distribution

Rubber and plastic	9,521.2	9.54	15.68	34.74	6.40	9.98	8.41	5.61	—	4.83	.2105
Leather and leather products	2,760.8	24.38	24.56	15.60	8.98	6.30	8.49	7.65	—	0.93	.2722
Stone, clay, and glass	10,757.8	3.40	21.32	25.70	6.06	13.97	6.02	7.85	3.19	10.92	.0710
Primary metal industry	21,133.1	4.09	24.58	40.66	2.65	7.46	6.36	4.60	2.90	6.63	.2565
Fabricated metals	21,966.3	6.58	18.49	39.94	5.48	7.85	4.37	6.51	1.46	9.05	.1967
Machinery (excluding electrical machinery)	30,680.9	8.02	18.97	39.33	9.01	5.40	4.44	4.96	1.69	8.00	.2190
Electrical machinery	27,874.2	8.80	22.23	30.02	4.85	8.90	6.58	4.44	1.77	12.25	.1544
Transportation equipment	34,845.0	4.09	12.06	41.67	8.02	8.86	2.98	4.84	0.82	16.39	.2363
Instruments and related products	8,385.9	14.63	47.39	15.85	4.61	4.95	1.64	2.59	1.25	6.99	.3523
Miscellaneous manufacturing	5,707.3	17.50	31.30	19.86	5.31	5.83	4.53	3.43	1.58	10.35	.2201
Ordnance and accessories	4,601.3	7.10	4.26	8.34	11.28	6.79	3.15	5.55	6.55	47.42	.4045
Total manufacture (value added)	$314,151.7	6.32	20.76	27.88	6.64	12.38	5.94	6.86	1.87	11.18	.0871

Source: Census of Manufactures. Washington, D.C.: U.S. Department of Commerce, 1971.

.0871, indicating that total manufacturing production was distributed similarly to that of personal income. However, the coefficients for the major industrial groupings ranged from .071 to .711. There were also wide variations in concentration within individual industrial groupings. The rubber and plastics group had a coefficient of localization of .2105, but when this group is subdivided the coefficients of the individual components would be both higher and lower. For example, the production of rubber tires is much more concentrated than rubber products in general.

The coefficient of localization will also vary depending on other conditions. An important aspect is the size of the physical unit necessary to produce at maximum cost advantage. There may not be a sufficient market in some regions to justify the establishment of an industry. The lack of production in such an area, however, may not indicate that the industry is not centrally located in regard to a market. The level of the coefficient of localization for an industry is thus likely to vary with the size of the region utilized (84–68).

The coefficient of localization will also vary according to the type of consumer. Today many industries do not produce for direct consumers but for other producers. As a result the market for the producer industries may not be the same as that of the ultimate consumer. The coefficients thus vary to a degree depending on the intermediate and ultimate consumers.

MARKET POTENTIAL.   The market potential of a region can be measured in a number of ways. In a classic paper, Chauncy Harris used the concept of an abstract index of the intensity of the possible contact with markets.[4] In this model, the market potential P is defined as the summation (Σ) of markets accessible to a point M divided by their distances from that point d, or $P = \Sigma (M/d)$. In the empirical application of the model, retail sales were considered a good measure of the total markets for goods. For the measure of distance d, transport costs were considered superior to physical miles.

To determine the market potential P for a given city, a summation (Σ) is made of the market potentials for that city and for all counties in the area. The market potential of each county is the retail sales of that county divided by the transport cost of reaching the city for which the potential market is being calculated (M/d). In the calculations, Harris made two assumptions: (1) that the shortest distance on a map was proportional to actual route miles and therefore it was not necessary to calculate data for individual routes and (2) because of the large number of counties, it was necessary to group the counties into class intervals. Concentric circles representing transport costs (at selected intervals) are drawn around each selected city (Fig. 2.5). The retail sales of each concentric circle are calculated by adding the retail sales of all counties within the band

[4]This section is based on Chauncy D. Harris, "The Market As a Factor in the Localization of Industry in the United States," *Annals of the Association of American Geographers*, 44 (1954), 321–326.

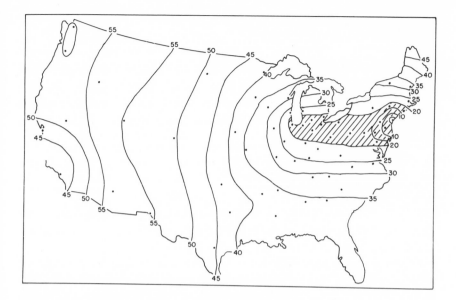

Figure 2.5. Market potential in the United States.

included by that circle and not by a smaller circle. The market potential of each band is then calculated by dividing the total sales of the band by the cost of reaching it from the selected city. The total market potential for this city is then obtained by adding the market potentials for all concentric circles. Dots on the maps indicate the cities for which these detailed calculations were made. On the basis of the value determined for these points, lines of equal market potential are drawn on the map. For easier comparisons, the figures are expressed as percentages of the city with the highest value.

The validity of market potential rests on the concept that there is a progressive decline in the quantity of goods transported as distance increases. Thus the market potential is a measure of the spatial interaction between the producer and the markets.

The map prepared by Harris revealed that the market potential for the United States reached its highest level in a broad zone extending from Massachusetts to Illinois, with the maximum centering on New York City. This zone of high potential is relatively narrow declining sharply to the north and south. The zone of maximum potential reflects not only the high density of population but the high buying power of the region. Southeastern United States possesses modest market potentials. The western areas of the United States are in general characterized by low market potentials. The potential rises in southern California, and a minimum occurs in the Pacific Northwest.

SECONDARY FACTORS

Besides the primary locational factors, there are many other factors that affect the cost of production. These factors are not essential to the manufacturing process in themselves, but may so affect cost structures that they become vital in the localization process.

Physical Environment

The influence of the physical environment on the localization of manufacturing has changed through time. In the early days of the aircraft industry, for example, extensive level sites were sought for airports. Today, however, the availability of level land at a given place may or may not be of importance in the development of an aircraft plant because of the ability to create level areas with mammoth earth-moving equipment. It becomes only one of many factors that enter into the cost analysis of the establishment of a plant.

TOPOGRAPHY.   Because manufacturing is a relatively small space-consuming activity, topography becomes a factor in location in only a few industries. Nevertheless, some industries do require a certain type of topographical setting. For one, the shipbuilding industry requires a gently sloping ocean-front setting. As ships become longer, the basically level space required increases. Topography is also an important consideration in the petroleum refining industry. Vast tank farms desire a topographical setting, either natural or man-made, in which the oil will flow by gravity through the plant.

In recent years, industrial districts have been created with the desired topography. Poorly drained areas have been drained, and lakefronts have been filled. At times the use of a desirable type of topographical setting for industry, such as the sand dune area at the southern end of Lake Michigan, has received adverse publicity because of other competitive uses of the land such as for recreational purposes.

CLIMATE.   Climate may influence the initial location of an industry and, later, may affect its operations. The importance of the climatic factor depends on the type of manufacturing in question. Prior to the artificial control of atmospheric conditions in factories, industries with special requirements frequently sought particular environments. For example, the cotton textile industry requires humid conditions to prevent the breakage of thread in weaving. Thus in the past the regions of high humidity, such as New England and Lancashire (England), were favored over areas with lower humidity.

The climate of a region has a direct influence on the cost of industrial output. The warmer regions of the United States have a comparative cost advantage over colder areas. For example, a southern industrial worker might have a salary 10 to 20 percent lower than a worker in New England, but still have the same standard of living. This is because heavy winter clothing is unnecessary, heating bills are smaller, housing costs are lower, and some foods produced locally are obtained at lower costs.

In manufacturing for which large open buildings are required, such as aircraft production, a warm climate has sometimes been sought in the hope of reducing heating costs. Evidence, however, indicates that aircraft companies in cooler regions such as Boeing in Seattle and McDonnell in St. Louis have secured as high a profit as the southern California firms. The availability of sunshine is of vital importance to some industries. The drying of fruit out-of-doors depends on a continuously sunny, dry environment. Likewise, the testing of aircraft is much more easily done in areas where there is a maximum amount of sunshine during the year.

The weather conditions of an area may also be of considerable importance in the selection of a particular site of a plant. The velocity and direction of prevailing winds may affect the ventilating problems of large plants. This is particularly important if the plant generates fumes, heat, or noxious odors.

One of the most widespread problems confronting industrial meteorologists is that of atmospheric pollution. Although air pollution is man-made, the atmospheric conditions at a particular place affect the rate of diffusion of the contaminating agents. The foreign materials in the atmosphere come from many sources, but industrial operations account for a large part of the smoke, dust, and noxious gases. For example, in October 1948, 21 persons died in Donora, Pennsylvania, because of severe atmospheric pollution. On later investigation, it was found that many individuals in this area were suffering from chronic respiratory diseases. Since this incident Donora has lost much of its original industry and has not been able to attract new industrial development. Air pollution can be a major deterrent to industrial growth.

Climate as an amenity has become an important factor in attracting industry to a particular region. The attractiveness of a climate may be a factor in inducing labor to migrate to a new area. For example, the dry, sunny climate of Arizona has been a significant factor in attracting labor. Climate is thus an indirect factor in the industrial growth of Arizona.

There are many other ways that weather and climate can affect plant operation. Storms can cause damage to a plant and equipment, hamper outdoor activities, and reduce worker efficiency. Wind and low relative humidity increase the fire hazard in factories, especially if combustible and explosive materials are processed. A number of processes require temperatures within specified limits. If the temperature of the area lies outside these ranges, special provisions must be made. Atmospheric cooling towers and condensers in hot areas attest to the effect of air temperature on certain processes.

WATER. An adequate and proper water supply is an essential consideration for the initiation and continued growth of industry. Manufacturing in the United States requires about 15,000 billion gallons of water annually and is increasing at a rate exceeding 300 billion gallons. Fortunately only a small percentage of this amount is consumed, the large proportion either being recycled or discharged from the plant, primarily into streams, for use by other industries.

Water Use in Manufacturing Industries.   Of the 20 major industrial classifications of the U.S. Bureau of the Census, 4 consume about 85 percent of the total. Of these, the primary metal industries use 33 percent of the total; this is followed by chemicals and chemical products, 28 percent; pulp, paper, and products, 15 percent; and petroleum and coal products, 10 percent. Of the industrial users, the primary metals and chemical industries have the highest average intake per plant. The pulp and paper and textile industries are the largest users of water for other than cooling purposes. These figures indicate that the mammoth use of water is concentrated in a few types of industries and in a relatively small number of large plants.

Evaluation of an Industrial Water Supply.   In evaluating the use of water for industrial purposes, it is fundamental to recognize that each local water supply has distinct characteristics and each manufacturing plant has particular requirements. Therefore two aspects must be evaluated. First, there must be a sufficient quantity of water not only for the manufacturing process, but also for fire protection. Second, the chemical character and related water quality must be carefully evaluated in regard to the manufacturing process.

An engineer must match the water requirements of a plant with the options available at the site that will provide the highest economies. In general there are three categories of water available to the manufacturer. First, there is high-quality water that is not seriously affected by the manufacturing process. A typical example of this situation is provided when water is used in the cooling process. In cooling, water is normally held in a nearly closed system and is essentially unchanged except in temperature. The cooling is often done in an open tower. Thus some water is lost through evaporation. The actual amount depends largely on the temperature of the region. There is, consequently, less loss of water in cool regions. Therefore, except in dry regions where water is limited, the availability of high-quality water when utilized only for cooling purposes appears to have little influence on the location of manufacturing.

A second situation is found where there is a demand for low-quality water such as hard water that will be seriously polluted by the manufacturing process. Federal and state environmental laws now largely control the discharge of such water from a plant because of the pollution caused when it flows directly into streams without treatment. Consequently polluted, low-quality water is normally treated so it can be recycled back into the manufacturing process. Further, expensive chemicals must be added to the water in many manufacturing processes and can be recovered only if a recycling occurs.

Finally, there is high-quality water that will be seriously affected by the manufacturing process. Because most water supplies fall into this category, there is frequently competition by many users for the available water. If the water supply is inadequate, its availability may become an important factor in the localization of industry. To assure an adequate supply of water, recycling of water is becoming increasingly important. However, as recycling increases, the influence of high-quality water as a localizing factor decreases.

Future Water Demands and Industrial Localization.   As the industrial demands for water have risen, there has been an increasing concern over the adequacy of a satisfactory supply. However, a study of the U.S. Corps of Engineers has indicated that most areas in the United States will have an adequate supply of fresh water through year 2020. Problems are developing in a number of areas where water is mined or used at rates exceeding replenishment. Nevertheless, the report states that the nation has the basic water resources to meet the doubling of municipal and the tripling of industrial needs in the next half century.

Although there appears to be an adequate water supply available in the United States for all demands, and therefore water should have little influence on the location of industry, the situation may not be so simple. The problem in maintaining water quality may be the willingness or, in some cases, the ability by private and governmental agencies to provide the institutional arrangements needed to manage water resources so that the rising demands will be effectively met.

Governmental Policies

Governmental policies—local, state, or national—may influence the location and growth of all types of industry in a region. Government influence can be either positive or negative. For example, the industrial development of a region may be hastened by government action. By contrast, governmental policies restricting investment may retard the economic growth of a region.

GOVERNMENTAL AID AT THE NATIONAL LEVEL. There are two fundamental ways that governmental actions influence industrial plant location. First, a government agency may construct and operate a plant directly. Corollary to this are privately owned plants built near government installations that utilize their products. There is thus direct and indirect governmental economic assistance provided to industry. Second, legislative and legal actions of the government are frequently directed toward improving the economic environment. The establishment of government-owned projects may change the economic attractiveness of the area.

Government Ownership. The federal government has had a long tradition of ownership of certain types of factories. In 1794 the Springfield Arsenal was built by the federal government. Until World War I, the federal government largely limited its manufacturing ownership to the realm of national defense. However, since then the federal government has entered many fields of manufacturing. The government has justified this invasion of the field of private enterprise on the basis of (1) the existence of a national emergency, (2) demands of a wartime situation, and (3) the development of projects that are not adaptable to private industry because of their nature and magnitude (70–154). The Hoover Commission, the commission to investigate government control of industry, found that there were no fewer than 2,500 separate industrial or commercial facilities owned by the armed services alone in 1945.

It was during World War II that the federal government assumed a major role in the location of industry. For example, there were 73 government-owned ordnance plants built in all parts of the country; they employed over 400,000 persons (18–37). Even more significant from a long-range viewpoint was the establishment of two new industries—synthetic rubber and nuclear energy—and the massive enlargement of the aluminum industry. Although the U.S. government sold many of its wartime plants to private industry, it remains a major manufacturer. Since the 1960s there has been a revival of governmental engagement in industry. This has been particularly noticeable in government-established factories in the space and missile industry.

Governmental Influence.   Governmental influence on industry assumes many forms. In recent years the federal government has shown concern about the economic improvement of depressed areas. Programs have been set up that attempt to locate, establish, and expand manufacturing in such areas. Direct loans at low interest rates granted to firms that will establish new firms in a depressed area are a common governmental procedure. In 1947 the Office of Area Development was established in the U.S. Department of Commerce to aid communities in solving their problems, including industrialization. For example, rapid tax amortization was given to qualified companies that built new plants in areas of chronic unemployment.

Although the 1947 act expired, the Area Redevelopment Act of 1961 and the Appalachian Development Act of 1965 were designed to aid "distressed or redevelopment areas." These acts provided for assistance to areas of chronic unemployment through loans and grants to communities for new auxiliary facilities necessary for industry to flourish. No aid was given directly for industrial plant construction, but an attempt was made to create an adequate economic atmosphere. These acts have had only a modest influence on the industrial development of Appalachia.

The government has also influenced the location of private industry in times of national emergency. For example, during the Korean conflict the National Industrial Dispersion Act encouraged the construction of new industrial facilities in areas that were not considered vulnerable to attack. However, this act had little influence on plant location because of the development of intercontinental ballistic missiles.

Many governmental actions indirectly affect the growth of manufacturing in an area. For example, the Tennessee Valley Authority (TVA), begun in 1933, was not developed primarily to develop industry. Nevertheless much of the industry that now flourishes in the Tennessee Valley owes its existence directly to low-cost power, water supply, navigation, and other economic inducements directly related to the TVA. Prime examples of such industry are the chemical complexes around Florence, Alabama, and Calvert City, Kentucky.

The government has also influenced industrial location by its control of transportation. This control became effective in 1887, when the Interstate Commerce Act was passed. The basic purpose of this act was to regulate interstate commerce. For example, the Interstate Commerce Commission controls rates on all interstate rail freight traffic. This agency is thus in a position to strongly influence the regional transportation costs for an industry.

The federal government has been responsible for the development of the inland and coastal waterway systems. Many industries have been attracted to flood-free sites along navigable waterways. One of the notable developments in recent years has been the chemical and basic metal complexes in the upper Ohio River Valley and its tributaries, and the petroleum-chemical concentration along the Gulf Coast and the lower Mississippi River Valley (114).

In 1956 the federal government instituted the Interstate Highway Program. This program envisions 41,000 miles of limited-access highways that will be 90-percent supported by federal funds. By 1975 over 90 percent of the interstate system had been completed. The importance of these highways in attracting industry is attested to by the growth of manufacturing at the major interchanges and at the termini of many of the routes.

Air transportation has also been subsidized by the government. Without such aid many airlines could not operate successfully. Thus the subsidizing of air routes has indirectly aided industry by making areas remote from main plants more accessible for branch plants.

Government control of labor and working conditions has become increasingly stringent since the 1930s. Labor controls that have most effectively influenced industrial location are minimum wage laws, laws governing collective bargaining, rulings regarding employee job rights, and regulations regarding working conditions. The minimum wage laws can influence the advantages possessed by certain low-paying industries by reducing regional labor cost differentials. Laws governing collective bargaining have encouraged the growth of labor unions. From a locational standpoint, it is significant that certain regions have five times as high a percentage of organized labor as do other areas. In recent years court decisions on employee job rights have directly influenced plant location. For example, one federal court decision required a company to hire old employees at a new location. The court's decision was based on the premise that seniority is a vested right earned by long-time employees in a firm.

Governments have also influenced plant locations by such measures as safety regulations, health requirements, and hours of work. If these are national laws, they give no advantage to a particular region; but if they are state or local regulations, the locational advantage of a particular place may be directly affected. For example, in New England it was illegal, until recently, to employ women after 6:00 P.M. Southern states did not have this regulation, so firms who wished to employ women on night shifts realized an advantage by migrating to the South.

The influence of government aid in one region may affect the development in another. Capital for expenditures in one region frequently originates in other areas. Governmental expenditures may not be based on economic considerations, but rather on political, strategic, or social conditions. For example, the recent industrial growth of the space industries in California, Colorado and Texas has been influenced by governmental expenditures based on national goals. Thus certain regions are favored although the tax money to support their industrial programs is collected largely in all states.

Governments can also influence the location of industry by the control of land use. Large tracts of land are owned by federal and state governments. Local governments control land use by zoning procedures. The control of land use is even more stringent in Europe than in the United States. Therefore, in both the United States and Europe, selected areas are prohibited from industrial uses.

Legal and Legislative Actions. There are many ways that governments have influenced the location and development of industry through legal and legislative actions. Traditionally, governments have aided infant industries by providing a protective tariff against competition from foreign countries. The United States passed its first tariff on imported manufactured goods in 1794. In the late nineteenth century, the federal government began to exert legal controls over industry. For example, in 1890 the Sherman Anti-Trust Act restricted industry—including concentrations of plant locations—by prohibiting mergers or agreements that produced restraint or a monopoly in interstate trade. Legal and legislative action has continued to influence the locational patterns of industry even more strongly.

Court decisions have frequently affected the locational advantages of one region over another. One of the most important decisions affecting industry was made by the U.S. Supreme Court in 1948, when it declared the regional basing-point freight rate system illegal. Prior to this time more than 20 industries, including cement and steel, established freight rates from basing-point locations. Opinion varies as to the influence of this freight system on plant location. However, the American Iron and Steel Institute states, "Many plants have been located in places . . . which would not be desirable places from which to distribute steel products if the basing-point method of quoting prices were not continued" (69–236). The decision of the Supreme Court provided a stimulus for the decentralization of industry, but to the present has not caused a change in the basic locational patterns of the country.

STATE AND LOCAL INDUCEMENTS. As the American economy has become more highly urbanized, communities have depended increasingly on manufacturing to maintain themselves. The attraction of new industry has become the primary goal of many chambers of commerce, and millions of dollars are spent annually to induce new industry to an area. The goal of both local and state plans is to accelerate industrial growth through raising total income and employment, which in turn expands the tax base (15).

The securing of new industry in a given area is becoming increasingly difficult. Competition between states and cities is keen. Since 1936, when Mississippi introduced its "Balance Agriculture with Industry" and Puerto Rico its "Bootstrap" program, essentially every state government has established an agency to promote industrial development. Thousands of communities have created some form of industrial development program.

Estimates of the number of organizations working at industrial development are placed at about 20,000. About 100,000 persons were employed in this field in 1975. Advertising by the organizations involved in industrial development has become an important source of revenue for many magazines and newspapers throughout the nation. State advertising alone, according to Loraz Advertising and Marketing Publications of Greensboro, North Carolina, is over $12,000,000 annually.

To inform corporations about the advantages of particular communities and states, departments of industrial development or similiarly named agencies have been established throughout the country to advertise and promote their areas. For example, the New York State annual budget for such activities exceeds $1,400,000, and New Jersey spends about $250,000. New York City spends about $350,000 a year for industrial development, and Jersey City's Area Development Council has a budget of about $50,000. The activities of these agencies range from visits by governors or leading businessmen to corporations to the preparation of economic and feasibility studies that document assertions made by developers.

Many types of subsidization schemes have been implemented over the years. The traditional inducements include direct loan programs, free industrial sites, municipal plant financing, and tax abatements or concessions (9). More recent subsidies include local, general, or revenue bond issues to support industry, direct state financial assistance using public funds to finance industry, low-interest mortgages, and the development of state- or regional-chartered development credit corporations. The basic types of subsidies vary little from state to state.

The operation of an industrial promotion program has a number of aspects. One of the first steps is the preparation of a data book listing information pertinent to the localization of manufacturing. Making initial contacts with industrial prospects and arranging visits to the community are also necessary considerations. The efforts of the promotional group may extend to other endeavors. For example, the evaluation of the physical appearance of the community may be critical in attracting new industry. Good hotel facilities, well-paved and well-lighted streets, well-maintained homes and parks, good schools, and hospitals—all these create a receptive attitude in the minds of prospective manufacturers. Many towns do not gain industry because of traffic congestion, outmoded retail sections, or areas of slum dwellings. This is particularly true when a firm plans to transport its executive staff to a new location. The industrial promotional group may thus have the problem of considering many aspects of the cultural and economic environment of the town not directly associated with manufacturing.

The significance of subsidies in attracting industry must be seen from two viewpoints: that of the industry concerned and that of the community. In recent surveys the view of industrial management has varied from complete approval to complete disapproval. Most companies that accept direct subsidies do so because of the immediate savings which result. Companies frequently will accept a building under a long-term loan or lease agreement. This type of inducement is regarded as a subsidy only insofar as the cost is amortized at interest rates below the prevailing market level. Some companies will accept minor subsidies in the belief that they indicate strong local interest and tie the community more closely to the industry.

The firms opposed to community subsidies give various reasons for their attitude. Some companies fear that, in the long run, they will have to pay the communities for the subsidies they receive. Some companies suspect that the acceptance of financial subsidies will handicap their operating decisions. Also, many companies feel that communities which can attract industry only by special inducements do not provide a satisfactory economic environment for industry to thrive.

Communities, as well as companies, have divided opinions about the value of industrial subsidization. On the plus side, a subsidy may compensate for a community's minor shortcomings in attracting a desired industry. A subsidy may also be the means by which a community will arouse a company's interest in its industrial potential. A subsidy program may also force a community to evaluate its economic situation and therefore organize its resources for industrial development.

But as subsidization becomes more widely accepted, the incentives to attract industry must be increased. As a result the tax burden in the community may outweigh the advantages of securing the new industry. A concentration on industrial subsidies may result in an unbalanced program in the community. Other services may be neglected in favor of industrial growth. When public credit is utilized to obtain funds for industrial development, many fundamental problems of community welfare must be considered. The Municipal Finance Officers Association cautions communities on the use of public bonds to finance plant construction because "(1) it can adversely affect the traditional immunity from taxation of the income from municipal obligation, (2) the sovereignty of federal, state and local governments can be thrown off balance, and (3) subsidization forces local governments to issue obligations for purposes that are not usually regarded as governmental functions."

The influence of community or state subsidization in attracting industry to a particular locality is difficult to evaluate. Recent industrial surveys present evidence that subsidization has had little influence in the location of industry. A survey of 1,180 plants that expanded or relocated in seven southern states between 1956 and 1960 revealed that financial aid had little influence on plant location. Of a group of 16 locational factors, economic aid ranked last (11). A survey in Michigan indicated that only 2 percent of the management personnel of new plants listed local concessions and inducements as a major factor in industrial localization (80).

Although subsidization has gained much attention in recent years, the evidence of its effectiveness is still to be proved. In isolated instances there can be little doubt that subsidies have played a constructive role in inducing new plants to an area. However, it is highly questionable that the massive efforts that have evolved are effective, and they may involve serious risks for both industry and communities.

A number of important trends are now emerging in industrial planning, including regionalism, diversification, and tie-ins with tourism. In many areas single large industrial units are replacing a number of smaller ones. Neighboring regions have recognized a mutuality of interest and have developed cooperative efforts. For example, the Northeastern Minnesota Association has built an auditorium in Duluth to demonstrate to industrialists and tourists that the economy is good not only for tourists but also for industry. The Piedmont Triad in North Carolina is coordinating the development and improvement of two counties and three cities.

States and cities are coming to recognize, moreover, that the factory is not the only symbol of area development. Other income-producing units urgently sought today are warehouses, office buildings, shopping centers, financial institutions, hospitals, laboratories, and research units. Manufacturing is thus not the only activity that will bring economic security to a region. The major emphasis is how to attract capital for the initiation of a more balanced economy. Further, it is recognized that some land is too expensive to attract industry. This type of land should be utilized for those activities that it can support such as commercial and service functions.

COMMUNITY ACTION. The following is an example of community action taken in Horseheads, New York, to induce a new company to locate there. The Chemung County Development Corporation learned from the New York State Department of Commerce that Company X was interested in establishing a new plant in New York. The name of the company was unknown. This company was seeking a 100-acre, level, relatively square tract having sufficient rail facilities to accommodate 5,000 cars annually and having adequate roads for 30,000 trucks. Besides the normal gas and electric requirements for a plant of this size, the company also needed a water supply with associated facilities for 2 million gallons' delivery a day.

Still without knowing the name of the company, the development corporation began the search for suitable land. It found a desired site near Horseheads on Route 17, which was slated to become a four-lane, limited-access, toll-free highway and was adjacent to the Erie-Lackawanna Railroad tracks. Preparation of the site required many months and involved relocating businesses, securing options, and convincing reluctant farmers to sell their land. The 104-acre site consisted of 14 individual parcels, two local roads, and the Lackawanna right-of-way. The development corporation then began dealings directly with the Great Atlantic & Pacific Tea Company (A & P). During the entire period Chemung County had to combat the pressures of neighboring communities that also wanted the plant. Counterpressures, fieldwork, and spying were elements in the local industrial development operations.

The A & P was willing to pay $2,000 an acre for the 104 acres after it was cleared and ready for construction. This figure was based on the going price for real estate in similar communities in the area. However, the cost of buying the various parcels of land, preparing the site, and meeting all required preliminary expenses amounted to about $300,000 more than the $208,000 allocated by the company. The development corporation then undertook a public subscription campaign to raise the difference. Within a short time cash and pledges from 540 businesses and from industrial and professional men oversubscribed the desired amount. The A & P then bought the land and began development operations.

Today a $25-million, 1.5-million-square-foot food processing plant and bakery are located on the tract.

ENVIRONMENTAL CONTROL PROGRAMS.   The environmentalists have taken an active role in the development of industrial pollution control in the state legislatures. Industry-enticing legislation, so evident in the 1960s, has been largely ignored in the legislatures of the 1970s. In its place has been the enactment of antipollution measures. Environmental protection is now an official policy in many states, and it affects manufacturing directly; controls have been enacted to enforce the policy.

As a result of the antipollution controls, the growth of "clean" industries is being encouraged and the growth of "dirty" industries is being discouraged. "Environmental Bills of Rights" (all people have the "inalienable right" to a decent environment) have been enacted in New York, Rhode Island, Virginia and other states. A citizen in Michigan or Illinois can file a suit to protect the air, water, and other resources in his or her area.

A major problem in industrial pollution control remains the lack of national standards. Instead there is a plethora of federal, state, regional, and local regulations. For example, California, which has one of the best-organized antipollution programs, has no single set of water standards. The State Water Control Board controls water quality through the establishment and enforcement of waste discharge requirements by the nine California Regional Water Quality Control Boards for specified waters and for the protection of enunicated beneficial uses of water. Waste discharge requirements are generally established on a case-by-case basis, but do not adhere to the water quality objectives contained in water quality control plans adopted by the regional boards and approved by the State Board. Many states have even less of a coherent approach to industrial pollution. A common approach is, go ahead with operations as usual—we'll let you know when you've broken the pollution laws.

A variety of antipollution controls have been enacted. State legislation was proposed in Arkansas in 1970 to give a fast tax write-off for pollution control equipment. Legislation in California is aimed at improving the quality of air, land, and sea environments. The 1970 Water Quality Act, revising the state's water pollution law for the first time in 20 years, increases the penalties for violations to as high as $6,000 a day. In Florida, the Division of Environmental Resources and Pollution is responsible for reviewing all proposed industrial projects for their effects on the environment. Research was started by the Florida Department of Commerce on ways to attract selected industries—those that will raise income levels, upgrade the labor force, and not damage the environment. The philosophy of the Florida Department of Commerce is to attract those industries to Florida that will benefit the state the most economically, but industrial growth for the sake of industrial growth is not desired by the state agency. The Georgia legislature defeated several proposals that would have increased the Department of Industrial and Trade's package of plant location incentives. Maine's so-called Site Selection Bill gives an Environmental Improvement Commission veto power over industrial development that it deems harmful to the environment. The Air Quality Development Authority was created in Ohio to help government agencies finance air pollution control efforts.

There is much evidence that the location of industry is affected directly by the antipollution laws. Maine's Environmental Improvement Commission refused permission to a company to build an oil terminal on Long Island in Portland Harbor because of the potential adverse affect it would have on the environment. The Minnesota Pollution Control Agency stated that the U.S. Steel plant in Duluth had to conform to a pollution abatement schedule. The plant officials said that because the plant was noncompetitive and the cost of antipollution control could not be justified, the plant had to be abandoned. In Virginia, the Olin Corporation decided to close a large soda ash plant rather than request lighter regulations of the recently tightened water pollution standards. The Water Control Board permitted the company to phase out its operations in order to cushion the loss of 600 jobs in the Saltsville area. The New York courts filed a suit against the Georgia-Pacific Corporation in 1970 for allegedly allowing wastes from its Lyons Falls pulp and paper mill to contaminate the Black River. The New York courts also sought an injunction against the International Paper Company, charging the firm with the pollution of Lake George from its mill in Ticonderoga.

Taxes

A continuing controversy has centered on the importance of tax differentials in influencing the location of manufacturing. There has been the universal argument that new taxes will drive industry out of an area. Areas have frequently used claims of low taxes in attracting industry; many southern states have attempted to attract industry with the inducement of low taxes. Although many studies have been made of the effect of taxes on the location of industry, they have rarely been sufficiently sophisticated in their techniques to be of great value (7).

RELATIVE TAX BURDENS AND GROWTH RATES. Two studies have investigated relative tax burdens in relation to growth rates. One of these studies used correlation in an attempt to measure the relations between growth in manufacturing and capital outlays of manufacturers in relation to increases in tax collections in the periods 1939–1953 and 1947–1953 (13). This study revealed a small positive correlation between states that had the highest taxes and those that had the highest growth in manufacturing. This indicated that other factors besides taxes were influencing the development of manufacturing. In a more elaborate study using modern econometric techniques, Thompson and Mattila concluded that there was no significant correlation of interstate tax differentials and employment growth in 29 selected manufacturing industries (109).

Most studies of the influence of taxes on industrial location have a number of weaknesses. For example, they do not answer a basic question: If the tax structure had been different, would manufactural growth have been at an even higher level? They also ignore the influence of different types of taxes. Nevertheless, they do reveal that higher taxes have not had a measureable effect on the growth of manufacturing in a particular locality.

INTERVIEW SURVEYS.   Several surveys of the influence of taxes on industrial location using the interview and questionnaire approach have been made. *Business Week* conducted a survey on the importance of different factors on industrial location (119). Of 747 plants surveyed in regard to location decisions, only 5 percent referred to taxation, and some of these were limited to property tax influences at a particular site. The Federal Reserve Bank of Boston undertook a survey of industrial location factors in Massachusetts which is one of the highest taxed states in the country (105). Of the 196 firms interviewed, only 16 percent indicated that local taxes had influenced their location decisions, and 19 percent indicated that state taxes had been a factor.

ROLE OF STATE AND LOCAL TAXES IN COSTS.   A common type of study has related the importance of taxes to total costs in manufacturing. These studies approach the problem by the use of actual data on firms operating in more than one state or region, or by the construction of hypothetical models. A Pennsylvania firm operating in several states showed that a ratio of state and local taxes to net investment varied from 4.34 percent in Wisconsin to 0.57 percent in Delaware. A comprehensive study by Yntema on relative tax costs in relation to actual operations in Michigan and neighboring states for 1956–1957 showed that the percentage of state–local taxes in other states to Michigan taxes ranged from 33 in Illinois to 78 in Wisconsin (115–2).

Floyd developed a number of hypothetical studies on the influence of taxes as a locational factor. He ascertained tax costs for firms in industries in a variety of locations. Significant differences were revealed between industries. For example, the variation in state and local tax costs in hosiery mills between the highest and lowest locations was equal to 2 percent of sales and, for furniture factories, 3.40 percent. A study by the Federal Reserve Bank of Boston revealed that taxes on a typical manufacturing firm had wide variations from state to state. State taxes per unit valuation ranged from $4,105 in Illinois to $28,468 in Massachusetts; local taxes ranged from $16,788 in Burlington, Massachusetts, to $65,862 in Chicago. These studies do not reveal the exact influence of taxes on industrial location, but simply give information on tax ranges.

TAX COSTS IN MANUFACTURING.   A number of studies have analyzed the importance of state–local taxes in total industry expenditures. A Michigan study revealed that state taxes constitute about 1/2 to 1 percent and local taxes about 1.5 percent of value added in manufacture (118–86). The Pennsylvania Economy League showed that the tax differential from the lowest to the highest state equaled 0.3 percent of sales. It would appear from these and other studies that the state–local taxes represent such a small percentage of total cost that they have little significant effect on location.

TAXATION AND INDUSTRIAL LOCATION.   Taxes may influence location decisions due to an emotional response. Certain states have gained a reputation for having high tax structures. Among these are Massachusetts, Pennsylvania, Michigan, and Wisconsin. These reputations are the result of a variety of forces: extent of unionization and state policy toward unions and management, unemployment and workmen's compensation legislation, financial responsibility of the state, magnitude of state debts, and tax levels and structures.

Another factor is the magnitude of taxation, particularly when related to industry. This depends on the general level of state–local expenditures. Another is the type of tax. Many industries have developed a dislike for the corporation franchise tax. This type of tax frequently becomes an issue for disagreement between liberal and conservative groups.

The role of taxation in the decision process is frequently somewhat irrational. Some firms will reject an area before investigation simply because it has a "bad" image. Because of high federal taxes, management often has a strong antitax emotional bias. When legislatures are considering new taxes, industrial groups frequently spread exaggerated propaganda about the effects of taxation on the maintenance or growth of industry.

Although other crucial factors of location (e.g., proximity to markets, adequate labor supply, and available raw materials) make tax considerations of little importance in the selection of a large geographic region, taxes may be important in the selection of a particular state or even a site within a state. For example, in a study of Massachusetts and neighboring states, the highest tax for a hypothetical corporation with net profits before taxes of about $298,000 was $76,171 as compared with the lowest tax, $23,305—a difference of $53,000, or 18 percent of profits (91–31). A recent study reported that the tax burdens on a hypothetical plant in the highest tax state would be 13 times greater than in the lowest tax state. While the primary factors must be evaluated first in making industrial location decisions, a manufacturer can minimize the tax costs by exercising care in the selection of a particular site.

Research

As the industrial structure of a nation becomes more complex, there is a greater need by industry for a research program to maintain technical competitiveness. Today a research scientist may be a greater asset to a community's economy than a major raw material resource (93). Scientists and engineers generate new ideas for the development of products, which leads eventually to the establishment of firms and industrial areas. In addition, scientists attract other scientists and engineers, and these in turn attract firms that require a ready pool of research talent. As a consequence, competition has been intensifying among regions to develop research and development (R&D) talent and retain it as an economic asset (57).

MATURE INDUSTRIAL REGION.   The traditional manufacturing belt of the United States, which lies in the rectangle from Boston and Baltimore on the east to Chicago and St. Louis on the west, has special reasons for its interest in securing the skills of scientists and engineers. Many of the industries of this region were established on the basis of factors that have long disappeared. As a result, many of the traditional industries have declined. Many industries are thus able to survive only if they can adjust to a new set of locational factors. The role of research may become vital as a localizing factor.

A number of metropolitan areas in the old manufacturing belt have been observing critically the country's shift of economic power to the South, Southwest, and West Coast. The response has been for the older industrial communities to examine their economies closely in order to revitalize their industries. The metropolitan areas of Boston, Philadelphia, Baltimore, St. Louis, and Chicago have made strenuous efforts to increase local participation in the "research revolution." These areas have vigorously promoted their regions' advantages for the location of science-oriented industries.

Boston had one of the earliest starts in developing its scientific and engineering capacity. The Charles River area of Boston now possesses one of the greatest concentrations of scientific, engineering, and research talent in the world in the research centers at Harvard University, Massachusetts Institute of Technology, Boston University, and Boston College, as well as industrial and research laboratories. Route 128, a bypass around Boston, is known as "the space highway" because of the presence of more than 225 electronics, missiles, and science-related industries built since 1955. These industries manufacture products valued at more than $150 million annually and employ over 35,000 workers. They employ mostly university-trained personnel and rely heavily on the universities for consultation, research, and recruitment of new personnel. The establishment of new research facilities was the greatest single factor in the revitalization of New England's economy in the 1950s and 1960s. The industry of New England became increasingly characterized by high-value-added products. The advanced engineering and electronic industries became the leading growth industries while traditional industries such as textiles and leather declined in importance. In the early 1970s, with the cutback in the space programs and the reduced demand for scientific products, this area suffered a decline that resulted in serious unemployment.

RESEARCH AS AN INDUSTRIAL GENERATOR. Several regions have attracted industry as a response to their research complexes. A leading "research triangle" has developed in the South centering on three universities—Duke University (Durham), University of North Carolina (Chapel Hill), and North Carolina State University (Raleigh). These universities provide the scientific know-how for a dynamic industrial region. As a result, a host of industrial research laboratories and manufacturing facilities has been attracted to the area. In California the California Institute of Technology has had a considerable influence on the industrial geography of America and is one of the reasons for the great cluster of high-technology firms in southern California.

Of all the research-oriented industrial areas, it is likely that none surpasses Santa Clara County, California, where some 800 pioneering technology companies are clustered; they form one of the densest concentrations of innovative industries in the world. The region that leads in such fast-expanding fields as semiconductors, lasers, medical instrumentation, magnetic recording, and educational and consumer electronics is located along the southwestern shore of San Francisco Bay, centered in such towns as Palo Alto, Mountain View, Sunnyvale, Cupertino, and San Jose (17).

The origins of this industrial area date from possibly 1912, when the vacuum tube was perfected as a sound amplifier and generator of electromagnetic waves in Palo Alto by Lee de Forest. The development of the vacuum tube permitted the later development of such electronic miracles as radio, television, and radar. However, it took decades before the area developed enough scientists, companies, and capital to form a critical mass sufficient to attract the formation of new companies.

Why did the industrial complex grow at this location? Possibly the greatest catalyst was that this is a particularly inviting environment in which to live and work; it has a beautiful physical landscape, and the climate provides a garden of nature where flowers bloom in February. Few places in the world mix so effectively hedonistic delights with the excitement of urbanity. Whereas, industries traditionally clustered at such places as raw material sites or intersections of transportation routes, the high-technology industries depend on research; so they try to attract researchers by locating at places where life is most satisfactory. Stanford University provided the research impetus for many of the original companies. Particularly important was the emphasis placed on research by the College of Engineering. This emphasis was spearheaded in the 1920s and 1930s by Frederick Terman, dean of the College of Engineering and later provost at Stanford. He not only encouraged faculty research but developed regular courses in company classrooms. Most important, he aided in the establishment of the Stanford Industrial Park. The goal was to create a center of high technology. The 665-acre park has acted as a magnet to innovative companies and now has 55 companies who employ 17,000 people.

The concentration of brainpower in the Santa Clara region is impressive. The area now has more than 4,000 Ph.D.'s—one out of six in the state. Since 1950 the number of workers in high-technology companies has increased from less than 3,000 to more than 150,000. Along with freedom from traditional factors of localization, the Santa Clara companies have evolved a freer management style. Many Santa Clara executives work in sports shirts and eat their lunches on outdoor patios. As a response there has been an influx of highly educated and talented young people. This group has come to be known as a "high-voltage population."

It is thus remarkably easy to begin a new company in the Santa Clara area. There is an intellectual and business atmosphere that venturesome entrepreneurs need in order to succeed. The thousands of skilled people who already live there provide the nucleus for the research required to sustain high-technology industry. Many New York capitalists now consider Santa Clara County the new success area of investment geography.

GROWTH POTENTIAL. The growth of research and development in a region depends on a number of factors, one of the most important being its present scientific base. An area in which scientists and engineers participate to a great extent in research and development has a decided advantage over its competitors. The growth of an R&D center appears to be a cumulative process. Scientists attract scientists and the firms that use brainpower.

The use of scientists and engineers specializing in R&D in the Boston, Philadelphia, Baltimore, Chicago, and St. Louis areas is analyzed in the National Science Foundation's National Register of Scientific and Technical Personnel. Of these areas, Boston ranks first in percentage of specialists in R&D, followed by the Philadelphia, Baltimore, Chicago, and St. Louis regions. The ranking is on the basis of the number of scientists and engineers working in R&D compared to total employment in the region. There is a suggestion that the East Coast has greater attraction for research activities than the Midwest.

The type of employers of scientists and engineers varies considerably within these five selected cities. In the Philadelphia and St. Louis areas, about 60 percent of the scientists and engineers are employed in private industry, 25 percent are employed by educational institutions. Chicago and Baltimore have 50 and 30 percent in industry and education respectively. Boston is highly unusual in that the science talent is almost evenly divided between the two primary employers.

When the scientists and engineers are separated, the employment pattern is more mixed. Scientists are less committed to any one type of employer than are engineers. In all five areas, over 70 percent of the engineers are working for private industry. Scientists are more widely employed. For example, of the five areas, the highest proportion employed by any one sector is the 55 percent working for private industry in Philadelphia.

There are similarities with respect to the specializations of the scientists within these five regions. For example, about 80 percent of the scientists in each area work in the fields of chemistry, biology, and physics. In all areas except Boston, chemistry holds first place. In Boston, physics is the leading industry employing scientists. Scientists not in these three fields are primarily mathematicians, meteorologists, and earth or agricultural scientists.

The engineers within the five regions concentrate on a limited number of market demands. In Philadelphia, over half the engineers produce electrical or electronic equipment, chemicals, and aircraft parts. Two-thirds of Boston's, Chicago's, and Baltimore's engineers produce electrical or electronic equipment, services, or construction materials. The market orientation of St. Louis engineers is toward construction materials first, followed by aircraft parts and services. In meeting these various market demands, engineers perform different functions for the firm. For example, an engineer's role in producing an electronic device may range from basic research to production of the prototype through quality control on the assembly line.

TRAINING AND RESEARCH.   The talent and training of scientists and engineers are obviously what makes them an economic asset to their community. However, it is difficult to measure talent by the number of college degrees in an area because many of the workers in R&D receive a large part of their training on the job. In addition, many important research contributions have originated with college, if not high school, dropouts. Nonetheless, in order to perform R&D today, engineers and scientists find it increasingly important to have a degree above the bachelor's level.

Management

As companies become larger and control a greater proportion of the output of an industry, locational decisions are centralized. As a result, the decision to build a plant in a particular area may be based on a strategy to serve a regional or national market. The choice of a given location is greatly widened under these conditions. For example, a plant site may be chosen not because present factors are particularly favorable, but because of future prospects. A large firm having considerable assets may develop a plant in an area that is presently classified as a high-cost area.

An established industrial region is usually one in which managerial skills have developed. This may be a factor in the location of a new enterprise. Although managerial ability has high mobility, a company normally recruits a portion of its executive staff from the local area. If a managerial group must be recruited, regional amenities may play an important role. For example, the physical environment of the Southwest is considered to be an asset in attracting managerial talent. Although this physical environment does not affect production directly, it provides the type of living conditions that attract the managerial class. The factors of production are thus augmented by amenities considered desirable by the managerial group.

Efficient management is a prerequisite for the growth of a manufacturing economy. The development of managerial skills in a region progresses at about the same rate as that for scientific and technological personnel. Inefficient management can raise production costs greatly, even when other factors of production are favorable. By contrast, skilled management, by ingenuity and innovation, can offset the poor economic environment in areas where some of the factors of production are unfavorable.

Regional Perception

The perception of a region's industrial potential can play a role in the selection of a particular place to locate a new plant. The people who choose industrial locations frequently have mental preference maps that give certain areas an advantage over other areas. Each individual will have a different perception of the value of an area for industrial development. The variations are basically attributable to two principal factors (1–3). First, the individual selecting a site cannot possibly have knowledge concerning all alternative areas that can qualify as potential locations because of financial and time limitations. Second, there are emotional and psychological restraints that influence the selection of a particular place by an individual.

Several studies have been completed in recent years on how people in one region perceive the importance of another area. Possibly most notable is the mental map of the United States by a New Yorker. On this mental map New York City assumes a disproportionate size, as does the state of New York. Many of the large states of the Midwest and West essentially disappear and are visualized as being of little importance. As a result of this kind of perception, numerous areas may receive little or no attention in the industrial decision process. Vast areas are simply not considered desirable for factory locations and are not investigated as potential sites for new plants. By contrast, the economic disadvantages of certain regions may be overlooked as a result of their emotional appeal.

The research on mental maps of regions is still in its infancy. In the industrial location decision process, there is a need to include the behavioral factor in the forecast model. Such aspects to be investigated should include the mental maps of people at different socioeconomic levels in the same area. For example, it would be interesting to investigate how the mental maps of people have changed over time in perceiving the industrial potential of such new and expanding industrial areas as Colorado and Florida. Further, and equally important, would be a study of what factors were important in altering this regional perception.

Personal Considerations

The initial location of a plant may be due to a personal decision that has little to do with favorable locational elements. The establishment of a factory may be a response to the accident of residence in a given community, the knowledge of existing capital in a locality, the favorable impression of a chamber of commerce, the desirability of the community, or even simply a "hunch" that a particular community is a good place to work. Findings from a study by Hunker show that about 60 percent of the firms surveyed virtually ignored the primary industrial location factors in selecting Columbus, Ohio, as a place to locate their plants (49).

There are many examples of plants located at places where basic industrial location factors were initially ignored. For example, a cement plant was built in central Ohio because the inventor of a cement plant machine lived in the area. In another example in the same area, an individual purchased chemical formulas from a defunct company and developed a successful operation. There are also cases where a plant has not entered an area because of adverse reactions from the people in the region. For example, an automotive company wanted to build a plant near a residential section in Columbus, Ohio. Because the local inhabitants objected to a change in the zoning requirements, the company refused to enter the area although new zoning regulations were developed. The plant was built in Indianapolis.

Although the reasons for selecting a new plant may not be based on the fundamental factors of location, these elements must be satisfied if the plant is to have a successful future. Many plants that are located according to personal preference are unsuccessful because the primary and critical secondary factors of production are not fulfilled.

INDUSTRIAL GROWTH

A given set of primary and secondary factors of industrial localization are determinants in initial industrial location decisions. However, these initial factors may not be effective in explaining the present locations of industry, for another set of factors may now play a more dominant role, or why certain areas attract new growth while other areas decline in importance. Thus other considerations have become important. These include the economies of scale that provide the effective size of an industry, technological innovation, geographic concentration, industrial linkage and splintering, geographic inertia, and development controls. These factors have influenced the location of individual industries as well as regional concentrations.

Economies of Scale

The achievement of an optimum level of production may depend on the scale of production (39). The optimum level of production may be defined as that output where profits are maximized, or that level of production that attains the lowest average unit cost. Robinson has stated that the scale of output that maximized profit may result from elements of monopoly or other economic imperfections (94). As a result, the average unit cost of production is likely to be a more satisfactory means of determining the optimum scale of production because it is determined largely by technical considerations. The scale of operation of a plant and its location are mutually interdependent variables where imperfect competition exists (21). Only where there is perfect competition could an optimum scale of plant and location be obtained automatically.

INTERNAL ECONOMIES OF SCALE. The internal economies of scale are achieved by an increase in the rate of production resulting in a lower average cost of output. The total operation of a firm resulting in internal economies of scale may be divided into three basic functions: production, management, and marketing.

Production Optimum. Production costs decrease with increases in output. The lowest production costs will depend not only on the divisibility of certain factors of production, but also on lowering the costs of indivisible factors. For example, as the size of the plant increases, such indivisible factors as labor and marketing can be utilized more intensively. Further, the bigger plants can purchase raw materials in substantial quantities, thus reducing costs. In many instances the larger plants can also utilize by-products that are frequently wasted in the smaller plants.

Managerial Optimum.   As size of a plant affects production costs, the cost of management is also related to size. In general, costs of management tend to decrease with increased size because of the indivisibility of managerial ability. The bigger plants can utilize managerial skills more effectively than the smaller plants. Larger plants can effect economies in management because the management functions increase at a slower rate than the production functions. For example, the forecasting of production costs and future sales does not increase in direct proportion to volume of production. Finally, the larger companies are frequently able to employ the most competent managers.

Marketing Optimum.   Scale economies are also operative in the marketing procedures. As a factory increases in size, and frequently product differentiation, the size of marketing organizations does not increase at the same proportion as the increase in production. As a result the larger firm has a cost advantage over the smaller firm. For example, the clerical work is little different for a large or small scale. However, when a single product is produced and can be sold in an organized market, the large firm may have little cost advantage over the smaller firm.

Variations in Optima.   Ideally, the lowest-cost plant would be one in which the scale economies are most effective for the basic three factors—production, management, and marketing. But in practice, the most efficient plant size for one of these factors rarely coincides with the most efficient size for the other two.

Thus the optimum size of a plant for production may not be the managerial or marketing optimum. If the production optimum is smaller than the managerial or marketing optimum, it may be desirable to construct a number of plants. This may reduce a number of the production costs. Also, at times of low demand, production can be concentrated at those plants that have the lowest transportation costs to markets.

In other situations, the marketing optimum may exceed the production optimum. When this occurs, the range of products produced is likely to change. The advantage of mass marketing may induce a manufacturer to produce a range of goods rather than one or a few products. The tendency for managerial and marketing optimum size to exceed production optimum size plus lowered transportation costs for a market orientation has been a major incentive for the development of branch plants. In certain instances, the savings in transportation costs from branch plants result in the building of plants at locations where optimum production scales do not exist.

EXTERNAL ECONOMIES OF SCALE.   External scale economies, which Weber called "social agglomeration forces," are also important locational determinants.[5] The following are examples of the influence that these external

[5]This section draws heavily on J.A. Guthrie, "Economies of Scale and Regional Development," *Papers and Proceedings of the Regional Science Association,* 1 (1955), J1–J10.

scale economies have on location. The lowest production cost for a firm may be one that has a particular mix of product output. Consequently the size of the industry at a given location may have an influence on the cost of production at all other locations. Research facilities are strengthened if firms of the same type are geographically concentrated rather than dispersed. It is also common practice to have linkage of firms in order to secure scale economies. For example, the waste product of one firm may be the raw material for another manufacturer.

When the plant increases in size, the securing of raw materials and the marketing of the finished product are likely to become more efficient. Specialized brokers are organized to serve the needs of the industry. The individual firm is frequently forced to purchase and store large quantities of raw materials, thus requiring much greater capital assets and further freezing the assets for long periods in nonproductive endeavors. A large firm has more ready access to organized exchanges and to the securing of raw materials on short notice. When a raw material and a finished product are able to be handled in massive quantities, the freight rates are normally reduced. This is a factor aiding the concentration of industry.

Industrial concentrations may develop in areas where firms make specialized machinery and other equipment needed by a particular industry. The development of the textile machinery industry in southern New England was a contributing factor to the mammoth expansion of cotton textile production in that area in the nineteenth century. When firms specialize in the production and repair of specialized machinery in the area in which it is used, there is considerable saving not only in freight rates but also in delivery and repair time. Further, advancements in machinery design are more likely to occur when the producer and consumer are in close proximity. The availability of a skilled labor supply is an advantage to any region in attracting industry.

There may be external economies of scale within an industrial area that affect the cost structure of a particular plant although they are only indirectly related to that plant. For example, all plants that produce related products in an area may have advantages in purchase and storage of raw materials, lower freight rates, lower repair and maintenance costs, by-product utilization, and other things because of the concentration of many firms in a single area. To illustrate, if there are two firms that use the same raw material but produce a different product, there may be advantages of scale economies by locating in close proximity.

The external economies of scale do not dictate that industry be geographically concentrated in a single area. A number of concentrations may exist. Robinson divides scale economies into "mobile" and "immobile" (94–142). Certain external economies are not dependent on the size of an industry within a particular locality, but rather on the size of the total industry in a larger area. These are classed as mobile economies and include the use of new research techniques, organized marketing practices, and improved efficiency as a result of better techniques. By contrast, immobile economies are available only to a firm that is concentrated in an area. These include access to specialized firms that produce parts directly for the industry, utilization of by-products, repair services, and use of local storage facilities. Immobile economies also include the lower cost of bulk purchases of raw materials and low transportation rates.

PLANT SIZE AND REGIONAL DEVELOPMENT.   The economies of scale of a plant have important implications for regional economic development.[6] The size of a plant may influence locational patterns in several ways (58). First, the proportion of the total production of the industry that a single plant can supply at its most efficient level will affect the extent to which regional dispersion or concentration is vital in the goal of minimized production costs. Bain states, "In any industry, the minimal scales of plant and of firm which are required for lowest production costs—when these scales are expressed as percentages of the total scale or capacity of the industry and are taken together with the shapes of the scale curves at smaller capacities—determine the degree of concentration by plants and firms needed for reasonable efficiency in the industry" (8–15).

Second, the productive efficiency in relation to the proportion of the market served by an individual plant will greatly affect its potential competition. If a plant or firm supplies only a small portion of the potential market, it will have little influence on the development of other plants. If, however, a plant or firm supplies a large percentage of the market, it will provide a strong deterrent to the entry of other firms. There are also situations where an existing plant is uneconomical because it has not been able to achieve scale economies. If such a plant must be increased in size to be efficient, the new plant operating at scale economies would lower industry selling prices and thus induce unfavorable cost situations in established firms.

Third, the amount of capital required for investment in an efficient plant or firm—as determined by size—may affect the availability of capital for other new investments in the area. When the supplier of capital needed for new investment is limited or when interest rates are high, the lack of the availability of capital will definitely discourage the development of new plant capacity.

DISECONOMIES OF SCALE.   As production of a plant or firm continues to expand, cost does not continue indefinitely downward per unit of output. As shown in Fig. 2.6, the unit cost is the same for output at the R and T levels. Diseconomies may occur as a result of many possible factors. As a plant expands, it may have to secure its raw materials and power from more distant sources, thus increasing the assembly costs. At a given point in the production schedule, there can be no further division of labor; or the further use of specialized machinery can bring no reduction in production costs. The cost of labor may also be increased in response to labor union demands in the specialized production centers. Further, when a plant expands more space is required so that land values usually rise, particularly in congested urban areas. As a result of these, as well as other factors, unit price will decrease to a level and then rise as production continues to increase.

[6]This section relies heavily on J.S. Bain, "Economies of Scale, Concentration, and the Condition of Entry into Twenty Manufacturing Industries," *American Economic Review*, 44 (1954), 15–39.

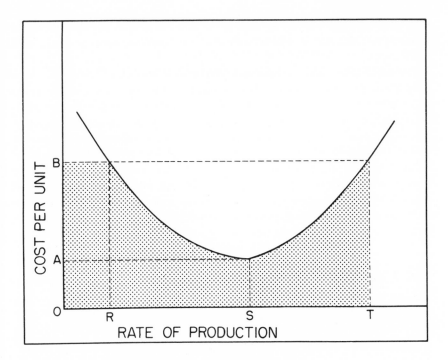

Figure 2.6. Economies of scale: rate of production.

PERSISTENCE OF SMALL PLANTS. Although a major trend has been the concentration of industrial production in fewer and fewer plants, the small plant has been most persistent in its survival (97). For example, in the United States the number of plants with 20 employees or fewer increased from 196,000 in 1954 to 210,000 in 1971. The small plant remains a characteristic feature of a number of industries. Of 2,697 meat-packing plants in 1967, 1,170 had between one and four employees, and the employees' group of 20–49 had the largest number of factories. The bottled and canned soft drinks, natural and processed cheese, and bread, cake, and related products industries had similar employment structures.

There are a number of reasons for the persistence of the small factory. The application of automation is possible only to industries that have a mass market. As a company must market its product to more distant places, increases in the cost of transportation can overbalance the production economies of scale. Today transfer costs may be as much as 80 percent of the delivered cost of a product. When high transportation costs occur, the forces for decentralization of production become operative. Although the small factory may have higher production costs than a larger firm, it persists at a particular location because it has a lower delivery cost for its product to a market than the more distant lower-cost plant.

Transportation costs are dynamic through time, and as a result the market area of a product is also subject to change. For example, suppose that a large company can produce a product for $8.00 and that transfer charges to a specific market are $2.00, making a total delivered-to-customer cost of $10.00. At the point of consumption, a small producer has a production cost of $10.00 for the same product, and a delivery charge of $1.00, making a total delivery cost of $11.00. Thus the larger, more distant plant has a distinct economic advantage over the smaller local plant. If, however, production costs remain stable, but transportation costs increase over time by 75 percent from the more distant distribution point, the economic advantages shift. The more distant, larger plant now has a delivered-to-customer cost of $11.50 while the smaller local plant has a delivered-to-customer cost of $11.00. The smaller plant now dominates the local market, and the market area of the larger but more distant plant has become restricted to a smaller area.

Technological Innovation

A technological innovation may create an entirely new industry or it may alter the original factors in the location of an existing industry (5). When either of these occurs, the pattern of production may be altered greatly. New areas of production may emerge, and the older areas may stagnate and gradually disappear. Technological change may cause not only plant relocation, but also the growth of new plants in new and different locations. There are thus three major types of scientific and technological innovations that influence the location of industry: changes that affect individual industries, changes that affect the overall structure of industry, and changes that affect one or more factors of production.

INNOVATIONS AFFECTING INDIVIDUAL INDUSTRIES. Technological change affecting the location of industry is not a new phenomenon but is as old as industry itself (28). For example, the changes in the location of the iron and steel industry over the centuries were frequently associated with a change in technology. Each invention of a new iron furnace, such as the catalon, Bessemer, and Thomas-Gilchrist, gave a particular area an advantage in the growth of the iron and steel industry.

The development of a new process that, for example, utilizes a different raw material usually affects the location of an industry. The changes in the location of the paper industry in the past century are largely a response to technological change. For centuries paper was made by hand from rags. As a result paper production was widely distributed, being oriented to a supply of rags. As the demands for paper increased, research began to broaden the raw material base. In 1840 a method was devised in Germany for producing wood pulp mechanically. The wood was shredded and mixed with rag pulp. Although this procedure increased production, the paper discolored quickly and was used primarily for newsprint. Nevertheless this technological change resulted in a change in the location of paper production, orienting it partly to the new raw material source. A second technological change came in 1867, when the sulfite process was developed in Sweden. This process, which boils wood chips to produce a pulp, could use only nonresinous woods. Because the market for sulfite pulp was large, not only in the paper industry but when bleached as a raw material for rayon, plastics, and other products, there was a concentration oriented to the nonresinous forest resources. Late in the nineteenth century the sulfate process was developed in Sweden. Its great advantage was in being able to use resinous pine woods as its raw material. As a result plants began to develop in such areas as southern United States, where resinous pine forests existed. In 1930 a bleaching technique for sulfate pulp was discovered. This allowed production of pulp as white and cheap as the sulfite pulp, but stronger. As a result there was a stronger orientation to the resinous forests of the world. In 1958 the magnesite process, developed in the United States and Canada, made it possible for the sulfite process to utilize both resinous and nonresinous woods. This technological change once again created the possibility for locational changes in the industry. The pulp and paper industry has been strongly raw material oriented throughout its history; when a technological change occurs that affects the location of the raw material utilized, plant locational changes take place.

Essentially all industries have experienced locational changes due to technological innovations over a period of time (86). Thus technological advances become a major factor in the growth or stagnation of an industry in a particular region. The location of the cotton textile industry illustrates how important technological advancements can influence the localization of an industry. Before the Industrial Revolution, the cotton textile industry was centered in India. With the application of power in operating the new mule spinner after 1779 in the United Kingdom, India's dominance declined rapidly and for a long period the United Kingdom dominated. However, with the early twentieth-century development in other countries of a number of newer automatic looms that provided a cost advantage, the United Kingdom's cotton textile industry declined to insignificance; newer centers, such as Japan, arose.

CHANGES IN THE STRUCTURE OF INDUSTRY. There is little question that the industrial world is changing dramatically and that the rate of change is increasing markedly. These changes are usually related directly or indirectly to increases in the application of scientific knowledge to technology. Since about 1940 in the United States there has been a planned increase in funding research and development projects for the development of new products. Research and development expenditures have grown from about $1 billion in 1941 to about $16 billion in 1963 and to over $40 billion in 1975, with visible and spectacular results. Many of these efforts have been stimulated and financed by the federal government in response to specific demands. For example, after the launching of the Soviet satellite in 1957, there was renewed impetus for scientific progress in space exploration. From this basic knowledge has been drawn the technology to change the industrial structure of a number of industrial regions in the United States.

As a response to technological change some regions are expanding rapidly, others are nearly stable, and still others are declining in importance. For example, in the past quarter of a century the electrical machinery and electronic industries have experienced dynamic growth. As a response to this vast expansion, the structure of industry within such large regions as southern New England and southern California have experienced significant changes. New industrial centers, such as Anaheim, California, have developed. In contrast, the lack of technological change in the textile industry has been a factor in its stagnation in various regions of the United States.

In a modern, dynamic, industrial economy, technological change plays a significant role in maintaining the position of a diversified industrial region. It is often quoted that 40 percent of the products used today were not in existence 25 years ago. Old plants have been converted and new plants built to produce these products. Many of such older industries as food processing and fabricated metals have been completely transformed.

The manufacturing process has become increasingly complex as technology has advanced. As a result there is an increasing number of steps between the initial processing of the raw material and the finished product. This trend influences the location of industries in various ways. The additional steps may make it more difficult to define the area of least cost or maximum profit. In certain instances there may be a tendency to centralize the production of a product at a highly automated center where all processes are centralized. This type of location reduces the transportation costs as the product moves through various stages of processing. On the other hand, when a product is assembled from a variety of complicated parts (e.g., an automobile), the parts manufacturers may be widely dispersed. This situation prevails when there is a tremendous output of the product and the concentration of the total industry within a small area could create diseconomies in scale.

CHANGES IN FACTORS OF PRODUCTION.   Scientific and technological innovations continuously change the relative importance of the different factors of production. These changes frequently influence the locational pattern of industry. A change in the raw material sources is likely to alter the location of the industry. For example, until 1900 only relatively high-quality copper ores could be utilized. With the development of the froth flotation process, the low-grade copper ores could be mined. As a result the copper smelter locational pattern of the United States was greatly changed.

Technology has continuously sought to increase the efficiency of the utilization of energy. As a result energy's share of the cost of production has steadily decreased. While the total consumption of energy has risen remarkably, energy has not increased its importance as a factor of location. As energy becomes cheaper and more easily transported, its role as a location determinant decreases. With each increase in distance of electrical transmission, the localizing influence of electrical power decreases.

As a response to technological innovations in transportation facilities, not only have transfer costs been lowered but the entire cost structure has been altered. In time this has altered the importance of distance decay in localizing an industry. As a result new locations achieve a cost advantage that they did not previously possess. In general, as the quality of the service has improved, there has been a decrease in transfer costs. The effect of this trend is to decrease the importance of transfer costs as a locational determinant and to increase the importance of processing costs. Industries that serve a regional or national market are able to transport their products greater distances at lower costs. This influences not only the location but the concentration of the industry. Transportation efficiencies are thus related directly to economies in scale of production. There are therefore larger, more efficient processing units serving larger market areas. In the same manner industries that secure materials from dispersed sources can concentrate their operations in larger, more efficient operations.

Technological changes also have an impact on labor requirements. In general, as technology advances industry becomes increasingly automated, thus reducing the demand for labor. It is estimated that in the 1960s automation caused 200,000 workers to lose their jobs permanently. In the early stages of the Industrial Revolution, labor was attracted to urban centers in response to the demand for greater and greater numbers of workers. Although the total labor supply in manufacturing has grown, its relative importance as a localizing factor has declined because of the continually increasing mechanization of factory processes. The development of new technological processes has created the need for continual growth of new skills that require retraining.

Changing technology has indirectly changed the market potential of regions. Transportation advancements have freed manufacturing to a considerable degree from locating at points of immobile production inputs. In response to the weakening locational influences of such factors as raw materials and power, the market has increased its attraction for industrial location.

Geographic Concentration

It has long been known that industry attracts industry. In general, industries in the major industrial regions of the world are growing at a much more rapid pace than those in the underdeveloped areas. There are many reasons for the concentration of industry (117).

The initial establishment of industry in a region may be due to such factors as available power or raw materials. If the initial industry thrives, similar industries will be attracted to the area. At the same time, other industries that utilize the products of the initial industries may develop in the region. As the labor supply grows, the increasing variety of skills will add another incentive to industrial growth. Other industries may then enter the region to avail themselves of particularly favorable conditions developed to serve the initial industries—such as an established transportation network and a generally favorable economic environment. Thus, once industry is firmly established, there are fundamental reasons why growth occurs.

Geographic concentration may also provide economies of scale in production that would not exist at an isolated plant. Economies of scale are usually most easily achieved in an industrial complex. This may be accomplished in a number of ways. An individual firm may contract out the making of certain parts, which results in a specialized firm that can concentrate on producing a superior product. Quantity production is most likely to occur where there is a large market (88). The development of subcontracting has become a part of most large modern industries. This practice influences location. For example, the American automobile industry subcontracts for a large portion of its manufactured products. As a result scores of communities in the Midwest are maintained in Detroit's hinterland by producing motor vehicle parts.

In a modern industrial complex in which the sources of power and raw materials and the ultimate market are not local, transportation assumes a dominating role. Thus in an industrial complex transportation facilities are better developed, giving a company a considerable advantage in marketing its product. As an industrial concentration grows, the labor supply not only increases but the variety of skills is also enlarged; this makes possible a wider range of industries.

There are other advantages in the geographic concentration of industry. Many essential services will develop in an industrial area because of the magnitude of operations. These include such services as banking and insurance. Research institutions will be attracted to the area to provide essential technical advice. Repair and maintenance services are improved in areas of concentration; these services are particularly important if many of the companies are small and cannot maintain their own service departments economically. Educational facilities (e.g., continuing education) that will serve the needs of industry may also be provided. In recent years, as amenities have become increasingly important as a factor localizing industry, the larger centers have provided cultural, entertainment, health, and other facilities not developed effectively in isolated areas.

There are also some disadvantages to industrial concentrations. The industrial complexes in vast areas of modern cities are frequently old and decadent, which creates urban slums. Diseconomies may result because of obsolescence and congestion. The cost of services may rise as the complexity of the region grows. Union activity is usually greatest in an established industrial region, resulting in demands for higher wages and other costly benefits. In times of war a major segment of a nation's industry can be destroyed with a single air attack, which is one of the most important reasons for the decentralization of industry.

Linkage

Industrial linkage refers to the "economies of locational integration" (47–117). There are more steps between the raw material and the finished product as manufacturing becomes more specialized. As a result the interchange among plants in a region increases, and the successful operation of a single plant becomes increasingly dependent on its securing of materials from a nearby plant. Perloff argues that "intra-industry absorption is perhaps the most significant of the input-output relationships for manufacturing" (89–395).

A traditional form of linkage occurs when all stages of production are integrated. This is known as *vertical integration*. The interrelationships of the modern iron and steel industry illustrate this situation. The blast and steel furnaces are normally linked into a unit operation. All the processes in this unit require heat; consequently there is a considerable savings if the metal is transformed from one stage to another in the molten state rather than starting from a solid state in each operation. Further, the by-product coke industry is usually found in close association with the furnaces. The utilization of the by-product coke gases at the plant to heat the furnaces also reduces cost. In addition, process scrap in furnace charges further extends the economy of vertical integration. The linkage between coke production, iron ore smelting, steelmaking, and rolling mills is usually so unified that the processes are controlled by a single company.

A second type of linkage is *horizontal*, or *lateral, integration*. The development of horizontal integration may be a major factor in the growth of an industrial complex. Within recent years numerous examples of this type of linkage have occurred where separate firms produce a variety of products that are later assembled into a finished product. The best example of this type of integration is found in the motor vehicle industry. There are thousands of factories in the United States producing individual parts that are shipped to an assembly plant for the ultimate production of an automobile.

A third form of linkage is known as *forward*, or *diagonal, integration*. In this form of linkage, a firm produces a product or provides a service that is needed by another plant in the region. Hunker and Wright give an excellent example of the development of forward linkage in the growth of a chemical complex in Ashtabula, Ohio (51–109–113). The first plant in the complex was built in 1943 by the federal government to produce ferroalloys and certain chemical by-products. A second plant entered the area in 1949 to manufacture sodium by utilizing Michigan salt and local power and water. These two plants formed the nucleus for later developments. In 1950 a plant was constructed to produce chlorinated solvents; chlorine, a by-product of sodium production, was purchased from the adjacent plant. In 1952 a fourth plant located beside the ferroalloy plant to purchase calcium carbide for the manufacture of acetylene and liquid carbon. In 1954 a synthetic rubber company was attracted to the area because of available materials for producing resins. Other plants entered the area in 1955 and 1956 to process titanium using the sodium reduction process. Within the complex there are now at least nine manufacturing facilities, two power plants, and a private water company. At least 20 products are produced for consumption by other industries in the area.

Another type of forward integration occurs when there are two or more industries that use the same type of raw materials and produce complementary products. For example, in New England the electrical machinery industries have frequently attracted other electrical machinery producing companies, and scientific equipment companies have clustered in Rochester, New York. Once the factors of production—such as a particular type of labor, raw material, and market—are established, other industries will take advantage of the favorable economic environment. Thus industries with similar factors of production are attracted to the same region.

Market-oriented industries may be attracted to an area by the presence of an industry to which they sell. This is called *backward integration* because it involves the transmission of an effect to manufacturing further back in the sequence of operations. Backward integration is common because so much manufacturing in a region produces for the local market. The larger the region, the greater the importance of the internal market. An example of backward linkage is the production of tin cans in a petroleum refinery region that emphasizes the production of motor oil. A second example would be the development of a printing industry that prepares reports for companies in the region.

Another type of linkage results from *technological integration*. In this type of linkage, industries will utilize common processes found in the local region. For example, there are numerous processes in the metal fabrication industries that are related to one another, and numerous products can be produced from a common or slightly varied process.

The integration of different types of labor forms another type of linkage. Different types of industries using similar types of labor may be located in the same region. The nineteenth-century classic example of this type of labor association developed in the anthracite region of northeastern Pennsylvania. The men were employed in the coal mines and the women, supplementing meager family incomes, were employed in the textile mills. The textile industry in this area was an example of a parasitic industry: it existed only because of a complementary industry, coal mining.

The linkages that have developed between industries are making it increasingly difficult to establish plants in new locations (16). To be outside of established centers may greatly increase the risks for success. An isolated location frequently results in the inability to share in the economies available to the area of geographic concentration. Further, new centers may not be able to market their products because information is not available as to quality. The close proximity of related plants provides the possibility for the economies of concentration. In the ultimate, linkages between plants lead to the concentration of industry in larger production centers.

Industrial Splintering

Industrial splintering refers to the growth of industry in a region through the creation of a new company by an individual or group who has left the employment of an existing company. There are many reasons why individuals will leave an existing company to establish a new firm. The experience they have gained in management in the older firm may make them realize that opportunities may exist elsewhere. Other individuals may have invented a new product or created a new process that they want to utilize under their direct control. There may also be personal dissatisfaction with the policies of the older company and a desire to develop under a different industrial environment.

The splinter companies are usually located in the same area as the older firms. The new firms are thus able to exist under similar favorable factors of production. The new firms will attempt to attract labor from the older plants, use existing transportation facilities, have access to existing raw materials and power, and in general adapt to the existing economic conditions of the area.

There are many examples of industrial splintering in the United States. Several of the machine tool companies in Cincinnati and the Miami Valley of Ohio are the result of industrial splintering. The best example of industrial splintering, whereby a great industrial complex was created in a single region, was the growth of the automobile industry in southeastern Michigan in the first three decades of the twentieth century. Scores of splinter firms were established by automotive workers, managers, and engineers who felt that they could produce a better vehicle. Although over 98 percent of these companies failed or were later incorporated into the present-day automotive giants, many made notable contributions to the advancement of the industry.

Geographic Inertia

Manufacturing, once established in an area, has a tendency to persist over time. There appears to be a resistance to change in numerous regions. An industry survives even though the factors that were favorable for the introduction of the industry may have been altered or even disappeared and a new set of factors may have been established. It is important to recognize that, over time, new industrial factors will sustain an industry in a region. This does not imply that geographic inertia will sustain all older industrial regions. If the original factors of industrialization decline and disappear and no new factors replace the original ones, the industrial region will fall into decay.

Geographic inertia will aid in maintaining an industrial region, initially because the plant and equipment are highly immobile and frequently have a long life. If a plant is moved the investment in it must be written off, and perhaps only a portion of the equipment can be moved. Owners of a plant will then attempt to maintain operations at a particular site as long as possible. In this same connection, it is usually much less costly to expand the facilities at an existing plant than to build a completely new plant at a different location. For example, it is estimated that a new petroleum refinery will cost three to four times as much to build as to enlarge an existing plant of equal capacity.

Besides the direct influence of equipment in stabilizing the location of manufacturing, there are other factors that may be equally, or even more, important. For any manufacturing region to exist, the six primary factors of production must exist in some type of relationship. Thus, for example, an industrial region has a certain type of skilled labor, transport facilities have been built to serve the area, and a market has been developed for the product. Also, the established industrial region has developed a number of services necessary to the functioning of manufacturing. It is usually thought that it is much easier for an area to maintain its existing industrial structure than it is to attract new and different industry.

The degree of mobility of an industry varies considerably. Those industries with low capital investment are frequently the most mobile. An example of this type of industry is the apparel industry in New York City. Many apparel manufacturers rent equipment for short periods of time and are thus able to move locations with few limitations. In contrast, heavy industries that cannot be readily dismantled are more rigidly tied to a particular location.

Development Controls

As an industrial economy matures, there is a tendency for some regions to develop concentrations of industry and for other regions to stagnate or decline. To cope with this type of disparate development, government policies have sometimes evolved to control further agglomeration and at the same time develop those areas that have lagged.

INDUSTRIAL AGGLOMERATION.   The development of industrial agglomerations is the result of two basic forces. First, the improvements in transportation have had a centralizing effect on industrial activities. Second, the market forces have a tendency to cluster manufacturing in specific localities. Such agglomeration is well illustrated in the European industrial economy. Of the concentrations of industry, Paris is an excellent example of concentrations that result from transport and market forces. The Paris area has approximately 20 percent of total French industry, and in many specific industries the percentage is much higher. For example, about 70 percent of the pharmaceutical, 60 percent of the aircraft, 50 percent of the automobile, 40 percent of the chemical, and 32 percent of the apparel industries are situated in this region. Other great agglomerations of industry occur in the Ruhr area, London, and Milan-Turin.

Many countries have enacted legislation to control the growth of these concentrations. In France, as early as 1950–1951, plans were laid for the *Aménagement du Territoire*. A small fund was established for the economic development of areas outside the Paris region. At the same time provincial areas developed regional planning and industrial development commissions. Although there was a modest development in the provinces of France, a policy based on persuasion was of limited importance in accomplishing a major decentralization. In 1955 the *Société de Developpement Regionale*, through private funds, and the *Société d'Equipment*, through public funds, made loans available for decentralizing industries. A third means of controlling the centralization of industry in the Paris region came with the development of zoning laws in 1959. Under these regulations the development of new plants requiring floor space of more than 500 square meters, or old plants expanding more than 10 percent of their space, could be prohibited.

There has been a decentralization of industry in France and a decline in the percentage of French industry building in Paris as a response to these efforts. Since the 1960s new industry has developed farther and farther from the Paris region. Although Paris is still the leading center of manufacturing, its dominance has declined.

The centralization of industrial activities has been a major trend in recent decades. Such large industrial centers as those centered in London, Milan, Tokyo, and New York have continued to grow. The governmental efforts to check the increasing centralization of economic activities has, at best, had limited success. The means of controlling growth have not been particularly effective in areas with a high level of aggregate demand and with well-established industrial facilities.

INDUSTRIAL LAG.   Several areas have suffered noticeable lag in their industrial growth. The differences between northern and southern Italy illustrate these disparate economic trends. Northern Italy has evolved a modern, dynamic industrial economy centered in the Milan–Turin area. In contrast, southern Italy, the Mezzogiorno, has long been noted as a depressed region.

In the early 1950s, the Italian government began an intensive program to develop southern Italy. The first of the plans to have a major impact on the Italian economy was the Vanoni Plan of 1954. One of its goals was a large-scale investment program in the south to speed economic growth in Italy's least developed regions. In recent years a large proportion of the investment was directed to southern Italy. For example, in the 1966–1970 plan 40'percent of investments, from both government and private sources, were designated for southern Italy. The Industrial Reconstruction Institute and the National Office of Hydrocarbons have been established to encourage development. Government-controlled industries have been built in the south; steel mills, petrochemical industries, and mechanical industries are now operating south of Rome. Private business firms, attracted by fiscal advantages, have built new plants in the south. Although industrial development is occurring in southern Italy, the north still dominates and growth continues unabated.

There are many areas in the world that have lagged economically and have received public and private funds for their development. For example, the Appalachian area in the United States has received national attention in recent years in an endeavor to encourage economic development.

PROBLEMS OF REGIONAL DEVELOPMENT.   The processes that influence concentration or decentralization are still not well understood. Policy decisions concerning industrial locations are frequently made without complete understanding of their implications. Industrial growth is encouraged in some areas but discouraged in other areas by policy-makers who may not know the optimum amount of industry at a given place. In many instances the pattern of decentralization is not clear; that is, it is not clear whether decentralization means even distribution or a number of centers of concentration. Different agencies frequently work at cross-purposes in the development of a regional economy. For example, most plans for transportation development in recent years have favored the centralization of activities. For industrial decentralization to succeed transport facilities must be developed to encourage, rather than hinder, the policies of decentralization. At the present time the forces affecting regional economies and regional growth are not sufficiently understood to make realistic judgments on optimum industrial development.

MODELS FOR REGIONAL ANALYSIS

Many useful techniques for analyzing industrial location have been developed. Although it is beyond the scope of this book to consider and evaluate all of them, brief descriptions are given for several procedures that have been found generally useful. These techniques are comparative cost analysis, industrial complex analysis, input-output techniques, and correlation and regression analysis. For the construction of other statistical tests, useful treatments can be found in a number of books on quantitative methods, either in statistics books or in books applied directly to locational analysis. [7]

Comparative Cost Analysis

Comparative cost analysis is a procedure for comparing locational costs for a plant at different sites. Although theoretically an industry can have an unlimited number of locations, in reality the choice is always much more restricted. As Isard states,

> If we can assume that the firm's decision is to be made on the basis of an established or anticipated pattern of markets and a given geographical distribution of raw materials and other production factors used in the industry, the objective of the comparative cost study is to determine in what region or regions the industry could achieve the lowest total cost of producing the required output and delivering to the market. Such studies frequently reveal that certain component costs do not vary among sites. For instance, labor costs may be fixed by union contracts, in which case such costs can be ignored. Accordingly comparative cost studies need compare

[7]For statistical references, see J.P. Cole and C.A.M. King, *Quantitative Geography* (New York: Wiley, 1968). O.P. Duncan, R.D. Cuzzart, and B. Duncan, *Statistical Geography* (New York: Free Press, 1961). S. Gregory, *Statistical Methods and the Geographer* (London: Longmans, 1963), and Leslie J. King, *Statistical Analysis in Geography* (Englewood Cliffs, N.J.: Prentice-Hall, 1969). For books applied directly to locational analysis, see H.L. Alder and E.B. Roessler, *Introduction to Probability and Statistics* (San Francisco: Freeman, 1962); A.R. Baggaley, *Intermediate Correlational Methods* (New York: Wiley, 1964); M. Ezekiel and K.A. Fox, *Methods of Correlation and Regression Analysis* (New York: Wiley, 1959): M.J. Hagood and D. Price, *Statistics for Sociologists* (New York: Holt, Rinehart & Winston 1952); D.V. Huntsberger, *Elements of Statistical Influence* (Boston: Allyn & Bacon, 1961); S. Siegel, *Nonparametric Studies for the Behavioral Sciences* (New York: McGraw-Hill, 1956); and A.G. Wilson and J.M. Kirby, *Mathematics for Geographers and Planners* (New York: Oxford, 1975).

only those costs which are known, or believed, to be affected by the choice of location. (53–7)

Comparative cost studies normally consider economic factors of production initially because cost of production is critical to the successful location of an industry. However, comparative cost studies may consider noneconomic factors that may affect the location of an industry. For example, in recent years governmental pollution controls have been effective in the restriction of sites that are economically feasible.

Comparative cost studies have proven advantageous in some types of industrial developments. When there is a change in the factors of production, new areas may gain economic advantages that attract industry while traditional areas may lose certain of their advantages. A technological change frequently alters the locational advantages. An expanding market may justify the building of plants in regions where none exist at the present time. The development of new types of transportation may open a region to new industrial development. In each of these situations, comparative cost studies could provide information for the location of new or expanded industry.

CASE STUDIES. Comparative cost studies that have been prepared in recent years generally have been confined to those industries for which only a relatively small number of alternative locations need to be evaluated. Thus the utilization of a cost surface technique has not been applied. Further, the studies have been confined to industries for which the number of critical inputs are limited.

Iron and Steel Industry. In the early 1950s Isard and Cumberland prepared a comparative cost study of potential iron and steel sites for New England (54). This study assumed initially that transport cost differentials were critical in localizing the iron and steel industry. It was also assumed that differences in costs of raw materials, fuel, labor, and other inputs were much less important than transportation costs. A number of potential sites in New England—including Fall River, Massachusetts, and New London, Connecticut—for which to determine costs were selected. To provide comparisons with competing centers, cost studies were prepared for established iron and steel centers on the Atlantic Coast and in the Pittsburgh region. After an empirical investigation of all factors, the study concluded that the cost of assembling coal and iron ore at the production site and the cost of transporting the finished products to market were the fundamental variables. Thus the transportation costs for each actual and potential location were calculated. For example, it was determined that the transport cost for the assembly of raw materials and fuel and the delivery of finished steel from New London, Connecticut, to New York City would be $17.90 compared to $16.34 from Sparrows Point, Maryland, $19.03 from Buffalo, New York, $16.42 from Bethlehem, Pennsylvania, and only $13.13 from Trenton, New Jersey. Isard and Cumberland found that the cost of producing iron and steel in New England was higher than for eastern sites in the Middle Atlantic area. It was thus concluded that New England sites would not be favorable for development of an iron and steel industry.

Petrochemical Industry.   Isard and Schooler also used a comparative cost analysis to determine favorable cost sites for the petrochemical industry (52–235–240). First, they determined the factors of production that were expected to have regional cost differences. Of these factors fuel, raw material, electric power, labor, and transportation were isolated as potentially having the greatest regional variations in cost.

The second step was to determine the regions that provided the best potential for establishment of the industry. After a study of the critical factors of production, the major consideration was whether the best location would be a raw material site on the Gulf Coast or a market site in the Northeast. After analyzing production costs for a plant producing ethylene glycol near Monroe, Louisiana, and one at Cincinnati, Ohio, it was found that regional differences in transport costs and economies of scale due to differences in plant size were the only major cost variables in localizing the petrochemical industry.

In analyzing these factors, it was recognized that the size of the plant will be dependent on the market. Further, it was recognized that a raw-material-oriented plant would serve several market areas while a market-oriented plant would be restricted to a single market area. It was concluded that although transport costs favored a market orientation, the economies of scale were sufficiently great to override this cost advantage. In reality, a comparison of the scale advantages of even a moderate-sized plant at Monroe ($2.45) would more than offset the transport advantage ($.60) of a small plant at Cincinnati. Thus in this instance a comparative cost analysis revealed that a raw material orientation was more desirable than a market orientation.

ADVANTAGES AND LIMITATIONS.   The comparative cost analysis is an effective analytical tool when confined to a single industry. Most important is the use of substitution analysis so that the comparative cost analysis can consider alternative locations. Thus if one factor can be substituted for another, the advantages of a specific location can be altered. The ultimate location would be one where no further substitution at another location could result in a cost reduction. This analysis is thus within the Weberian framework of least cost analysis. In essence each of the regional cost differentials measures the effect of a single substitution or a combination of substitutions in attempting to locate the least cost region.

In theory each industry in a region could be analyzed on a comparative cost basis, and ultimately an understanding of the total regional structure would be developed. However, this would be a most laborious, if not impossible, task. Further, comparative cost studies assume that the price/cost structure and the market are given. These assumptions are likely not warranted where the geographic patterns of the industry have a marked influence on such factors as income, demand, prices, and costs in one or more regions. These assumptions are untenable where the totality of a region is analyzed industry by industry for the market and price structure is highly dependent on the amount of industry found in a particular region. As a result other types of analysis are superior when interrelations of an industrial region are to be analyzed.

Industrial Complex Analysis

To analyze a complex of manufacturing in a region, Isard, Schooler, and Vietorisz developed a methodology that lies intermediate between the comparative cost analysis and the more detailed interindustry relations revealed by the complex input-output studies of Leontief (55).

The Isard approach to industrial complex analysis begins in a traditional fashion with a survey of the factors of production. This step normally reveals certain initial advantages and disadvantages that the region possesses for the development of manufacturing. As a result meaningful interindustry links are established, and the basis for investigating a meaningful complex evolves. It is now presumed that investigation will reveal whether an industrial complex can evolve or, if one exists, whether it can be enlarged.

The industrial complex analysis follows specific prodecures. The first step requires the construction of a table showing the various inputs and outputs associated with each individual process or combined industrial processes. In the table, each column represents one activity; commodities that are inputs are indicated with a minus sign and outputs are indicated with a plus sign. In preparing the table, only those inputs and outputs that cause variations in cost and revenue need be included.

After the initial table is prepared, it is necessary to prepare a detailed structure of each of the complexes considered meaningful. This requires the elaboration of several types of manufacturing, with a further specification of specific output levels. This is followed by a computation of total inputs and outputs associated with each of the selected production complexes. In this manner the investigator determines the structure of specific complexes, each detailed in terms of production inputs as well as the outputs. It is now possible to proceed with a comparative cost analysis on the regional complex of industry.

COMPARATIVE COST METHODOLOGY. The most comprehensive treatment of applying a modern Weberian framework to industrial locational analysis has been prepared by Walter Isard.[8] Because transportation is a basic location factor, it is the first to be analyzed for an industrial complex. By determining the weights and quantities of inputs, the minimum-cost-transportation location may be determined. Once the minimum transport cost point is determined, the analysis proceeds to other factors of localization. These cost differentials must be related to each other so as to determine which of the factors are significant. As Isard indicates, if labor and transportation costs are analyzed, the transport cost differentials must be computed to determine the cost disadvantages of the cheap labor site as well as the labor cost differential with which to determine the labor cost advantage of the low-cost labor site (52–394). Other cost factors in production, such as raw materials, power, and so on, are analyzed in this same fashion.

After the cost differentials are analyzed, the Weberian approach investigates

---

[8]Walter Isard, *Location and Space Economy* (Cambridge, Mass.: MIT Press, 1956), chaps. 4 through 6.

agglomeration economies and diseconomies. These economies (or dis-economies) normally include scale, localization, and urbanization. Scale economies are those achieved through a change in the level of production when the level of other production and external variables are held constant. Scale economies thus become important in the locational process. The advantage due to scale economies requires extensive cost-revenue computation for each activity. At least two major steps are required. First, the level of production at a given location is determined. For each new level of production, the change in revenue is calculated. This is followed by a calculation of the change in total input cost of production. This step requires estimates of the unit cost of production at every level to be considered.

> Thus the excess increase (or decrease) in total revenue over the increase (or decrease) in total input costs equals the amount by which the profitability of the reference industry at the given location is increased (decreased) by the specific scale change for the given activity. This amount also indicates the adjustment required in dollar-advantage estimates for the changed reference industry at its given location, when compared with industries elsewhere whose scale has not been changed. (52–402)

The analysis of localization and urbanization economies follows next in the Weberian framework. The economies of localization result from concentration at a given place, while those of urbanization are linked with regional develop-ment processes. The economies of localization include such inputs as adminis-trative economies, elaboration of production at different stages, effective quality control, and social welfare gains. When localization and urbanization econo-mies are combined, they are termed "spatial juxtaposition economies."

Industrial complex analysis is concerned basically with regional patterns of industrial development. In the Weberian approach used by Isard and his coauthors, there is the attempt to develop a framework for an analysis of loca-tional interdependence using an interactivity matrix. It is felt that the industrial complex approach can be applied to a number of industrial regional problems. The specific procedures will vary from complex to complex and region to region. As Isard states,

> It can identify and evaluate profitable situations and activity combinations which cannot be accurately assessed, either by industry-by-industry com-parative cost studies or by strictly linear interindustry techniques. In one sense, the industrial complex approach is a hybrid approach: it can effec-tively isolate and evaluate the interplay of key variables among groups (subsystems) of highly interrelated activities. (52–411)

Case Study. The use of industrial complex analysis is well illustrated by the study of the potential development of the petrochemical industry in Puerto Rico by Isard, Schooner, and Vietorisz (55). This study began with a survey of the Puerto Rican economy to find potential advantages for the growth of such an industrial complex. This study revealed that Puerto Rico's greatest resource was an abundant supply of unskilled labor. Although there was little local fuel or energy, the area was close to Venezuela's oil supplies. Further, the large market of the United States was readily accessible. As a response to these favorable factors of production, it was felt that a petrochemical industry could be the basis of a potential industrial complex.

After it was determined that a petrochemical complex appeared feasible, a table was prepared giving hypothetical oil refining inputs and outputs. A great number of products are produced from the refining process that can be used as inputs for other products. For example, methane can be used to produce hydrogen, which is converted into nitric acid, ammonium nitrate, urea, and ultimately fertilizer. Further, methane is the basis for the output of synthetic fibers.

The next step was to define the specifics of the petrochemical complex. A fundamental decision was the choice of particular refinery activities to be implemented. It was determined that the production of intermediate products should be limited to the internal requirements of the complex. The level of demand was determined by the market potential.

The inputs and outputs associated with the petrochemical industry were then calculated. For example, one of the complexes was designated "Dacron A." It was estimated that a plant producing 36.5 MM pounds of dacron staple was required for this complex. For each complex detailed input and output analyses were prepared.

Isard, Schooler, and Vietorisz then applied the modern Weberian framework to provide a study of comparative regional costs. The analysis began with a study of transportation costs at alternate locations. With a presumed market for refinery products on the eastern seaboard, fibers for the South, and fertilizer for Puerto Rico, a comprehensive cost computation indicated that the Texas-Louisiana Gulf Coast was generally the area of minimum transport cost.

The next step was to determine whether Puerto Rico's low-cost labor could provide a cost advantage over its transportation cost disadvantage. Using the interindustry matrix, labor requirements for the chemical-petroleum industry were calculated.

It was estimated that the skilled labor required for a petrochemical complex would be more expensive in Puerto Rico than on the Gulf Coast by about $1.00 per hour. This resulted in a second cost disadvantage for the establishment of the industry in Puerto Rico. On further study, however, it was revealed that Puerto Rico possessed a major labor cost advantage over the Gulf Coast for the textile industry. When the two labor costs plus the transportation costs were summarized, the following was revealed:

$$+\$4,861,000 \quad - \quad \$263,000 \quad - \quad \$2,229,000 \quad = \quad +\$2,369,000$$

Textile Labor	Transportation	Petrochemical Labor	Cost Advantage for Puerto Rico vis-à-vis Gulf Coast

Such other cost factors as power, capital, taxes, water, and land were considered, but the cost differentials were found to be minor. Thus this comparative cost study revealed that Puerto Rico possessed cost advantages for the establishment of a textile industry based on a petrochemical complex. This case study illustrates how the industrial complex analysis using a Weberian approach can be used to derive specific locational decisions in the industrial planning process.

Input-Output Technique

Input-output theory is fundamentally concerned with the interrelations arising from production. Its major purpose is to measure the magnitude of the flow of goods and services from one level of production to another. The input-output method of analysis is thus an attempt to combine economic theory with an empirical approach to the study of production. As Leontief, the modern developer of the model, states, "it takes advantage of the relatively stable pattern of the flow of goods and services among the elements of our economy to bring a much more detailed statistical picture of the system into range of manipulation of economic theory" (64–15).

The basic premise of the input-output model is that it is possible to divide all productive activities in an economy into sectors whose interrelations can be meaningfully expressed in a set of input functions. Several assumptions are necessary for such a procedure to be theoretically meaningful. First, it must be possible to form the productive sectors so that a single production function can be assumed for each one. This is a fundamental concept in all general equilibrium models. Further, Leontief makes several special assumptions. The most important of these are that (1) a given product is supplied only by one sector, (2) there are no joint products, and (3) the quantity of each input is directly proportional to the level of output of that sector (19–12). Although there are too many variables to treat each individually, it is possible to reduce the number by aggregating them into groups. This is the procedure used in input-output analysis in attempting to improve the grasp of economic theory as applied to real-world situations.

INTERINDUSTRY ACCOUNTING SYSTEM. The input-output analysis is developed by the construction of a transactions table. This table is a matrix that shows how the inputs and outputs of each industry are distributed among other industries and sections of the economy. Its significance is summarized by Leontief as follows:

For the economy as a whole the input-output (coefficient) table reveals the structure of the interlocking interdependencies that tie the highly differentiated and specialized parts of the system together as a whole. It represents, in effect, a working model of the system. As such it can be employed for the experimental study of a great many theoretical and practical questions about the economy . . . Input-output analysis derives its conceptual framework from recognition of the fact that all the possible interconnections of the different sectors of a national economy can be regarded as special instances of the general solution of a single large system of equations in matrix algebra. (65–148)

CONSTRUCTION OF THE TRANSACTIONS MATRIX.   The input-output table is compiled by a system of double entries. The total inputs of the various goods and services that are required in an industry are listed in the vertical columns. The horizontal row shows how the products of the industry are distributed. Because each figure in the horizontal row is also a figure in the vertical column, the output of one sector is shown to be an input in another sector. Thus the total final demand for all industries is equal to the total value of inputs.[9]

A simplified hypothetical table of industrial production is presented to illustrate the input-output technique (Table 2.7). The processing sectors are shown in the upper left-hand corner. This shows the inputs and outputs for six theoretical industries. For example, industry A has 10 intraindustry transactions. Further, industry A purchases 5 units from industry B, 7 from industry C, and so on.

Besides the processing sectors of the table, there are also the payment and the final demand sectors. The payment sectors include the other inputs. Gross inventory depletion includes the consumption of accumulated raw materials, intermediate goods, and finished products. Imports include the value of goods purchased by each industry. The payments to government represent payments in the form of taxes as well as such items as security and fire protection. Depreciation allowances represent the cost of plant and equipment depleted in the manufacturing process. Finally, householder payments represent wages, salaries, dividends, interest, and similar payments. The large figures here mostly represent labor inputs.

The final demand sectors indicate purchases outside of direct industry consumption. Gross inventory accumulation includes the addition of inventories to each industry. Typically, manufacturers have a stock of goods on hand that they produce. Exports are those goods exported from each of the processing industries. Many industries have sales to governments. Gross private capital formation are the sales to consumers who use their purchases for capital formation. The households sector of final demand represents the purchase of finished goods by the ultimate consumer.

The final row and final column give the total gross outlays and outputs.

TECHNICAL COEFFICIENTS.   After the gross value input-output table has been constructed for a given year, it may be more useful if technical coefficients are developed from it. A technical coefficient is *the amount of inputs required from each industry to produce one dollar's worth of the output of a given industry.* The technical coefficient table requires two steps in its preparation. First, the gross output is adjusted by subtracting gross inventory depletion from

[9]The following material is summarized from and Tables 2.7 through 2.11 are taken from William H. Miernyk, *The Elements of Input-Output Analysis* (New York: Random House, 1965), chaps. 2 and 3.

Table 2.7
Simplified Hypothetical Transactions Table of Industrial Production

Outputs[1] / Inputs[2]	Processing Sector (1) A	(2) B	(3) C	(4) D	(5) E	(6) F	Final Demand (7) Gross inventory accumulation (+)	(8) Exports to foreign countries	(9) Government purchases	(10) Gross private capital formation	(11) Households	(12) Total Gross Output
(1) Industry A	10	15	1	2	5	6	2	5	1	3	14	64
(2) Industry B	5	4	7	1	3	8	1	6	3	4	17	59
(3) Industry C	7	2	8	1	5	3	2	3	1	3	5	40
(4) Industry D	11	1	2	8	6	4	0	0	1	2	4	39
(5) Industry E	4	0	1	14	3	2	1	2	1	3	9	40
(6) Industry F	2	6	7	6	2	6	2	4	2	1	8	46
(7) Gross inventory depletion (−)	1	2	1	0	2	1	0	1	0	0	0	8
(8) Imports	2	1	3	0	3	2	0	0	0	0	2	13
(9) Payments to government	2	3	2	2	1	2	3	2	1	2	12	32
(10) Depreciation allowances	1	2	1	0	1	0	0	0	0	0	0	5
(11) Households	19	23	7	5	9	12	1	0	8	0	1	85
(12) Total Gross Outlays	64	59	40	39	40	46	12	23	18	18	72	431

Industry Producing · *Payments Sector* · *Processing Sector*

[1]Sales to industries and sectors along the top of the table from the industry listed in each row at the left of the table.
[2]Purchases from industries and sectors at the left of the table by the industry listed at the top of each column.

Source: William H. Miernyk, *The Elements of Input-Output Analysis.* New York: Random House, 1965, Table 2-1.

the gross output. This is accomplished by subtracting column 7 from column 12 of Table 2.7. The second step consists of dividing all the entries in each industry's column by the adjusted gross output for that industry.

To illustrate, the adjusted gross income for industry A is equal to $63 (total gross outlay minus gross inventory depletion). To compute the coefficients for column 1, each entry in this column is divided by $63. Similarly, the adjusted gross output for industry B is $57, and this divided into each entry in column 2 of Table 2.7 gives column 2 in Table 2.8, and so on.

Table 2.8 shows that for each dollar's worth of production in industry A it will require direct purchases from other industries as follows:

Intraindustry transactions of	16 cents
Purchase of industry A from industry B of	8 cents
Purchase of industry A from industry C of	11 cents
Purchase of industry A from industry D of	17 cents
Purchase of industry A from industry E of	6 cents
Purchase of industry A from industry F of	3 cents
Total direct purchases	61 cents

From the technical coefficients, it is possible to calculate the amount of direct purchases required from each industry along the left-hand side of Table 2.8 as a result of a change in the output of one or more of the industries listed at the top of the table. If, for example, the output of industry B were increased by $100 (assuming constant technical coefficients), the direct inputs of industry B (purchases from other industries) would be increased by the following amounts:

Inputs from industry	would be increased by
A	$26.00
B (intraindustry)	7.00
C	4.00
D	20.00
E	0.00
F	11.00

This type of analysis could have important locational implications for an industry. By using such a table, an industry can determine how much it must purchase directly from supplying industries.

DIRECT AND INDIRECT PURCHASES. Table 2.8 shows the direct purchases made by a given industry from all other industries within the processing sector for each dollar's worth of output. This does not, however, reveal the total addition to output resulting from additional sales to the final demand sector. When the final demand changes, these changes will affect every industry in the processing sector. Thus an integral part of the input-output analysis is the construction of a table showing the direct and indirect effects of change in final demand.

Table 2.8

Input Coefficient Table—Direct Purchases Per Dollar of Output (in cents)

	Industries Purchasing					
Industries Producing	A	B	C	D	E	F
A	16	26	3	5	13	13
B	8	7	18	3	8	18
C	11	4	21	3	13	7
D	17	2	5	21	16	9
E	6	0	3	36	8	4
F	3	11	18	15	5	13

Source: William H. Miernyk, *The Elements of Input-Output Analysis.* New York: Random House, 1965, Table 2-2.

The following procedure, used by Miernyk, is one of several that can be used to develop the direct-indirect table. Let us assume a 1-dollar increase in the demand for the products of industry A. This will increase the intraindustry transactions by 16 cents (see row 1, column 1 of Table 2.8). Thus the gross output of industry A will increase at least to $1.16. But when the output of industry A increases, the firms in this industry will increase purchases from industry B. Sales from industry B to industry A will increase an additional 9 cents (1.16×0.08) as a result of the increased activity of industry A. Similarly, sales from industry C to industry A will increase 13 cents (1.16×0.11) and so on down column 1 of Table 2.8.

This procedure could be continued to include each industry in the processing set; then by summing all of the direct and indirect figures, a new table would be created (Table 2.9). Fortunately, the table can be created by the use of a high-speed electronic computer. This involves taking the difference between an identity matrix and the input coefficient matrix and, finally, computing a transposed inverse matrix.

INPUT-OUTPUT AS A PREDICTION TOOL.   The transactions table can be utilized for future projection. As Almon states, "The output of each industry is consistent with the demands, both final and from other industries, for its products."[10] This procedure has come to be known as *consistent forecasting.* Its major advantage is that it ensures that projections for individual industries and sectors will add to a total projection.

Consistent forecasting requires two steps. The first step is the projection of each entry in the final demand sectors of the input-output table. After this is completed, a new transaction table is projected on the basis of the assumed changes in the final demand. After the components of the final demand have

[10]Clopper Almon, Jr., "Progress Toward a Consistent Forecast of the American Economy in 1970," paper presented at the Conference of Economic Planning, Pittsburgh, March 24–25, 1964 (mimeographed), p. 2.

Table 2.9

Direct and Indirect Requirements Per Dollar of Final Demand

	A	B	C	D	E	F
A	$1.38	.25	.28	.41	.27	.23
B	.45	1.21	.16	.19	.12	.24
C	.27	.38	1.38	.23	.17	.39
D	.35	.25	.25	1.53	.65	.41
E	.35	.26	.31	.39	1.28	.25
F	.38	.35	.22	.30	.21	1.32

Source: William H. Miernyk, *The Elements of Input-Output Analysis.* New York: Random House, 1965, Table 2-3.

been projected, the individual final demand columns are aggregated to form a single column. This is called the final demand column (Table 2.10). In the actual forecast, each of the final demand components is projected separately. Table 2.10 shows the hypothetical projected final demand.

To prepare a projection for Table 2.7 it is assumed that the changes will occur as indicated on the basis of projections in the final demand of Table 2.10. Also, it is assumed that during the projection period the technical coefficients of Table 2.8 will remain constant. The projected transactions table (Table 2.11) is prepared as follows:

1. Compute adjusted projected final demand by first multiplying the original projected final demand by the ratio of capital consumption and inventory depletion to final demand in the base year, then subtracting this amount from the original projected final demand.
2. Multiply each row of the table of direct and indirect coefficients (Table 2.9) by the adjusted final demand figure for that row. The result will be another table of the same size as Table 2.9.
3. Sum the columns of the matrix obtained in step 2 to obtain new adjusted total gross outputs for each industry. Transfer the row that is thus obtained to the bottom of the table of direct coefficients (Table 2.8).
4. Multiply each column entry in the table of direct coefficients by the adjusted total gross output at the bottom of the column. The result is the processing sector of the projected transactions table.
5. To obtain the total gross output figure shown in Table 2.11, add the appropriate inventory adjustment which was substracted in step 1 to the adjusted total gross outputs found in step 3.
6. Insert the original projected final demand figures in a column to the right of the projected sector, and insert the total gross output figures obtained in step 5 as a column to the right of final demand. The result is the projected transactions table illustrated by Table 2.11. (74–35–36)

As expected, the largest increases are predicted for those industries that

Table 2.10

Final and Projected Demand

Industry	Original Final Demand	Projected Final Demand	Percentage Change
A	25	30	+20.0
B	31	26	−16.0
C	14	17	+21.5
D	7	10	+43.0
E	16	15	− 6.5
F	17	20	+17.5

Source: William H. Miernyk, *The Elements of Input-Output Analysis.* New York: Random House, 1965, p. 34.

experienced the largest increases in both final demand and in interindustry transactions. For those industries, B and F, for which the final demand declined, the values of the interindustry transactions increased slightly.

The above example is relatively simple. It has its greatest value for short-term forecasting because it assumes no change in the technical coefficients. Its accuracy for prediction is dependent on the final demand projections. Over time the technical coefficients will change as a result of changes in relative prices, the appearance of new industries, and the effects of technological change.

SPECIALIZED COEFFICIENTS.   The technical input coefficients are always expressed in value terms. Other coefficients may provide information for special purposes. Leontief has noted that the technical structure of each industry can be described by a series of technical input coefficients—one for each separate cost element (63–144). It is not possible to prepare coefficient tables for all factors for a particular industry. As an example, the importance of labor may provide a useful input coefficient. This coefficient shows labor inputs in physical terms per unit of output. It can easily be converted to employment and thus determine the effects on employment generated by a change in final demand. But how stable is the labor input coefficient? It has been found that the labor coefficients are quite stable for the short term. However, over time the labor coefficients are less stable than the basic technical coefficients. Nevertheless changes will be gradual and will tend to be in the same direction.

Another useful measure is the capital coefficient, defined as "the quantity of capital required per unit of capacity in an industry." Thus a table of capital coefficients shows capital requirements per unit of capacity by industry of origin for each industry or group of industries in the input-output system. The amount of capital needed at a given time is determined by technological considerations. This type of table helps reveal the stage of development of industry in an area.

REGIONAL AND INTERREGIONAL INPUT-OUTPUT ANALYSIS. The early input-output interindustry studies in the 1940s were national in scope,

Table 2.11

Projected Transactions Table with Changes in Final Demand

Industry Producing	A	B	C	D	E	F	Projected Final Demand	Projected Total Gross Output
			Industry Purchasing					
A	11.7	15.4	1.2	2.4	5.7	7.1	30	74
	(10)	(15)	(1)	(2)	(5)	(6)	(25)	(64)
B	5.8	4.1	8.5	1.2	3.4	9.5	26	59
	(5)	(4)	(7)	(1)	(3)	(8)	(31)	(59)
C	8.2	2.0	9.7	1.2	5.7	3.6	17	48
	(7)	(2)	(8)	(1)	(5)	(3)	(14)	(40)
D	12.9	1.0	2.4	9.8	6.9	4.8	10	48
	(11)	(1)	(2)	(8)	(6)	(4)	(7)	(39)
E	4.6	0	1.2	17.2	3.4	2.4	15	44
	(4)	(0)	(1)	(14)	(3)	(2)	(16)	(40)
F	2.3	6.1	8.5	7.3	2.3	7.2	20	54
	(2)	(6)	(7)	(6)	(2)	(6)	(17)	(46)

Final demand and total gross outputs shown in parentheses from original transactions table.
Source: William H. Miernyk, *The Elements of Input-Output Analysis.* New York: Random House, 1965, Table 3-2.

and interest in regional analysis has grown in the past 25 years. Input-output studies with a regional orientation have been classified in a number of ways. One major distinction is between regional and interregional models. Another distinction is made between balanced regional models and pure interregional models. A balanced regional model is constructed by disaggregating a national input-output table into its component regions; the pure interregional model is composed by aggregating a number of regional tables.

The interregional models are more complex than the regional models because interindustrial and interregional interdependence must be blended. To date, the interregional input-output tables have been rather highly aggregated. A number of interregional models have been constructed. For example, Leon Moses has blended an interregional input analysis and a linear programming technique to make an empirical study of regional comparative advantage in the United States (79).

The initial interregional and regional input-output studies were based on input coefficients from the national table. The method of construction of the table was to obtain total gross output for each industry in the region or regions to be analyzed. These figures were then multiplied by national input coefficients. The table was thus based on the assumption that regional input patterns were identical to national input patterns, which was obviously a major limitation. However, the lack of data on a regional basis forced this type of expediency.

Advances have occurred with time. A major refinement was developed in a study by Hirsch on the St. Louis area. The national coefficients were not utilized to obtain interindustry flow. Rather, input and output data were obtained by direct surveys for most large and medium-sized companies operating in the St. Louis area (45). The companies actually assigned staff personnel for a three-month period to prepare the input-output table. This procedure provides a study of great accuracy. This type of study provides a matrix of information that is most helpful in the selection of industries which have the greatest cost advantages in a given area. However, the method is extremely expensive and time consuming.

INPUT-OUTPUT ANALYSIS AND ECONOMIC DEVELOPMENT. Leontief says that the "input-output table is not merely a device for displaying or storing information, it is above all an analytical tool" (65–149). Input-output tables have been prepared to analyze the economy for more than 40 countries, and input-output analysis has been applied to planned as well as unplanned economies. How economic development occurs is not simple, and there are wide differences of opinion about why differential rates of economic growth exist among the industrialized nations. Of all analytical tools, however, the input-output technique is possibly best for the analysis of the structure of development—including industrial growth. It is almost axiomatic that if a country wishes to industrialize it adopts the structure of an advanced economy. Leontief further states, "The process of development consists essentially in the installation and building of an approximation of the system embodied in the advanced economies of the U.S. and Western Europe and, more recently, of the U.S.S.R.—with due allowance for limitations imposed by the local mix of resources and the availability of technology to exploit them" (65–159). Input-output analysis can thus provide one procedure for the analysis of the process of industrial development in an area or a nation.

LIMITATIONS. There are numerous problems in the utilization of input-output analysis. Of greatest importance is that the construction of an input-output transaction matrix is extremely complex. It requires tremendous personnel and capital resources. Also, input-output analysis is an econometric blending of theoretical, mathematical, and statistical techniques. The fundamental literature is thus couched in abstract mathematical language.

The availability of data has also placed strict limitations on the use of input-output analysis. It appears most successful at the national level; at spatial levels below the national, data problems become serious. There have also been questions as to the adequacy of input-output analysis for such aspects as economies of scale, localization economies, and regional cost variations.

Correlation and Regression Analysis

Correlation methods provide measures whereby the relationship between two or more variables can be calculated. If more than one causal factor is involved, multiple correlation and regression analysis are employed. Some correlations are direct and obvious, as the relationship between population and manufactural employment. However, in many instances it is not easy to visualize cause-and-effect relationships. Sometimes the correlation that is shown to be valid depends on a complex set of intermediate factors. Correlation methods can thus establish connections, but a valid interpretation is necessary to explain these relationships. Before attempting to draw conclusions it is necessary to have considerable experience with particular examples.

MULTIPLE CORRELATION AND REGRESSION ANALYSIS. To analyze the complex variables that are normally related to understanding the spatial location of industry, multiple correlation and regression analysis have evolved as valuable analytical tools. They are, however, somewhat difficult to utilize because multivariate analysis requires a computer to process the large amount of data required. Because the process is adequately described in a number of statistical texts, it will only be summarized in this section.

A simple regression analysis can be used when it is assumed that a single causal location factor dominates. In this situation, the coefficient of correlation r indicates the importance of the observed relationship between two sets of variables. When there are a number of independent variables, the multiple regression model is expressed as follows:

$$Y = a + b_1x_1 + b_2x_2 \ldots + b_nx_n + e$$

Y is the dependent variable, x the independent variables, a the intercept constant, b the regression coefficient, and e the error term.

The coefficient of multiple correlation measures the strength of the relationship between the dependent variable and the independent variables. Multiple regression analysis thus provides a model for testing a specific hypothesis.

Multiple regression provides a fairly flexible model because it can use a variety of data sources. For example, the effect of market can be measured by spatial differences in income or sales. However, great care needs to be given to the selection of critical variables that measure causal factors of localization. Spiegelman states the rationale for using regression analysis for industrial location problems as follows:

> Multiple regression can explain location patterns that result from the location decisions of individual owners and managers when these decisions are economically "rational" and are based upon past experience and knowledge of existing area characteristics. Regression can also explain location patterns that are created by a process of differential economic success. For example, if economic success is awarded to electronic plants that locate near universities, a close correlation of growth in electronics employment with distribution of universities may result either from the actual decisions made by entrepreneurs to locate their plants near universities, or by a process of differential success in which plants so located expand while plants located elsewhere fail to expand. (102–4)

Thus the location of an industry can frequently be explained as a function of a set of measurable variables.

There are some limitations to the use of regression analysis. For the model to be significant, a variety of high-quality data must be available. Further, data for the intangible factors of industrial location may not be available because of measurement problems. Regression analysis is also limited in its application in that it explains locational patterns on the basis of conditions at a particular time. In a mature industrial economy, many industries were established under factors of localization that changed over time. Finally, a strong statistical relationship, as shown by high correlation coefficients, does not necessarily indicate a strong cause-and-effect relationship.

Approaches to Regression Analysis. There are two basic approaches to the use of regression analysis. The first is known as the "stepwise approach" (60–145). This analysis begins with the recognition of a relatively large number of independent variables and, by a process of elimination, the factors that influence the localization of the industry are isolated. The first variable to be considered is the one with the highest simple correlation with the dependent variable. After this initial two-variable regression is completed, partial correlations between the dependent and all other independent variables are computed. The independent variables among these that have the highest partial correlation are then included in the second step. A new regression equation now involving two independent variables is derived. The partial correlations are computed for the remaining variables, with the two held constant. The selection of the next variable is made on the basis of these values. Thus, at each step, the adjusted partial regression coefficients and multiple correlation coefficients are obtained. The stepwise procedure continues until all selected independent variables are included. The analysis can be stopped at the point when the addition of more variables brings no new explanation of localization.

The second approach involves the testing of a specific hypothesis developed by either deductive or inductive reasoning. This method is best applied when there is a relatively small number of independent variables. By correlation and regression analysis the hypothesis will be accepted, rejected, or modified according to the results of the test. The following example illustrates the "hypothesis approach."

The Machinery Industry. A study by McCarty, Hook, and Knos in which three hypotheses on the localization of the machinery industry were tested illustrates the procedures of regression analysis (71). As a general hypothesis, it was assumed that manufacturing activities are likely to be oriented with respect to raw materials and markets. Generally, locational variations are a response to differences in the cost of transporting materials and/or finished products. Consequently, if the material loses weight or bulk in the manufacturing process, or if transportation rates for the materials are as high or higher than rates for the finished products, there would be a cost advantage in locating the processing plant near the market.

By using this hypothesis it would appear that the machinery industry should be located near its market because there is little weight loss in the manufacturing process. The raw materials are, in the Weberian concept, "pure." At the same time there is a substantial increase in bulk so that freight rates are higher for the finished product than the materials. However, it is difficult to test a hypothesis involving market orientation because of the difficulty of determining what the market is and the ultimate difficulty in data collection. Consequently it is necessary to inquire into the characteristics that form the various stages in the production chain of manufacturing.

For this investigation, three hypotheses were formulated for testing. The first was:

Area Specialization Hypothesis. This hypothesis stated that the areal importance of the machinery industry will vary directly with the degree of industrial specialization. There was thus the assumption that the machinery industries are market oriented and that this market consists mainly of the manufacturers of other metal products. Also, since the degree of industrialization in an area was known to vary directly with the importance of its metal products manufacturing, it was expected that the volume of employment in the machinery industries would vary directly with the degree of industrialization.

This hypothesis was tested directly, by measuring the degree of association between specialization in manufacturing and machinery, and indirectly, by determining the extent to which those associations also appear in other industry groups whose locational characteristics appear to differ from those of machinery. This hypothesis thus measured the association between the number of employees in machinery and the degree of specialization in manufacturing by using the Pearson coefficient of correlation method. The coefficients for different areal units, together with coefficients of determination and tests of statistical significance, are shown in Table 2.12.

It was revealed that there were significant correlations between the percentage of workers in manufacturing and the number of workers in machinery manufacturing in each of the test areas. The study further indicated that

the degree of association is small, however, in the counties and metropolitan areas of the United States where variations in percentages of workers engaged in manufacturing "accounts" for less than ten per cent of the variation in the occurrence of the machinery industry. When we compare these coefficients with coefficients between the specialization variable and other industries which, according to our theory, would not be associated with specialization in manufacturing, we find that machinery is more closely associated with specialization than are the other industries in all of the universes under study except metropolitan areas. These differences, furthermore, appear to be relatively large. (71–80)

Table 2.12

Coefficients of Correlation (*r*), Explained Variation (*r²*), and Significance of Correlations Between Numbers of Workers in Machinery (35) and Percentages of Workers Engaged in Manufacturing in Each of Four Universes

Data	*r*	*r²*	Significant
States, 1950	.564	.318	Yes[1]
Counties, 1950	.277	.077	Yes[2]
Metropolitan areas, 1950	.306	.094	Yes[3]
Prefectures of Japan, 1948	.841	.707	Yes[4]

[1]The least significant value of *r* with *N* = 49 is .276.
[2]The least significant value of *r* with *N* = 414 is .098.
[3]The least significant value of *r* with *N* = 152 is .159.
[4]The least significant value of *r* with *N* = 46 is .285.
Source: Harold H. McCarty, John C. Hook, and Duane S. Knos, *The Measurement of Association in Industrial Geography*. Iowa City: Department of Geography, State University of Iowa, 1956, Table 26.

The empirical observation appears to support the hypothesis when applied to states and counties of the United States and the prefectures of Japan. The hypothesis therefore provides a partial explanation of variations in the spatial distribution of machinery within the selected universes.

The Production-Sequence Hypothesis. The second hypothesis suggested that "an industry at any given stage may be expected to be located near other industries which occupy the same position or adjacent positions in the production sequence; since they would tend to provide materials and (or) markets for that industry. The general hypothesis may therefore be stated as: The occurrence of the machinery industry (35) will vary directly with the occurrence of those industries which occupy the same or adjacent stages in the production sequence. (71–64)

In the formulation of the production-sequence hypothesis, it was assumed that industries forming the later stages of production tended to be market oriented. Since it appeared that industries with varieties of customers would concentrate in population centers, it seemed reasonable to assume that they would tend to seek locations in the same general area.

Industrial groups that have been hypothesized as belonging to the earlier and later stages of the production sequence are shown in Table 2.13. All coefficients between the later-stage industries and machinery are statistically significant. These associations are thus consistent with the hypothesis. Nevertheless, there are considerable variations in the degree to which the variables are associated; the percentage of the variations of the dependent variable explained by variations of the independent variables (*r²*) is, on the average, relatively high

Table 2.13

Coefficients of Correlation (*r*), Determination (*r²*), and Standard Errors of Estimate (σys) Between Group 35 (Machinery) and Other Metal-Consuming Industries, for States, 1950

Industry (SIC)	*r*	*r²*	σys	Significant[1]
Later Stages				
Iron and steel foundries (332)	.879	.773	21,700	Yes
Nonferrous metal rolling and drawing (335)	.614	.377	35,800	Yes
Nonferrous foundries (336)	.959	.920	12,900	Yes
Miscellaneous primary metal industries (339)	.927	.859	17,000	Yes
Cutlery, hand tools, and hardware (342)	.741	.549	30,500	Yes
Heating and plumbing equipment (343)	.896	.803	20,200	Yes
Structural metal products (344)	.817	.668	26,200	Yes
Metal stamping and casting (346)	.954	.910	13,600	Yes
Fabricated wire products (348)	.842	.709	24,500	Yes
Electrical machinery (36)	.876	.767	21,900	Yes
Motor vehicles and equipment (371)	.514	.264	38,900	Yes
Earlier Stages				
Blast furnaces and steel mills (331)	.657	.432	34,200	Yes
Primary nonferrous metals (333)	.145	.021	44,900	No
Secondary nonferrous metals (334)	.802	.643	27,100	Yes
Machinery (35)	Mean = 26,200		σy = 45,400	

[1]The least significant value of *r* with *N* = 49 is .276.
Source: Harold H. McCarty, John C. Hook, and Duane S. Knos, *The Measurement of Association in Industrial Geography*. Iowa City: Department of Geography, State University of Iowa, 1956, Table 29.

(69.1 percent). Results of these tests appear to substantiate the reasoning that machinery is more closely associated with groups in the later phases of the metal production sequence than with those of the earlier stages.

Two basic questions were then raised: Are each of the related industries significantly associated with machinery when variations in all other industries are taken into account? And to what extent are these variables associated with machinery when all of them are considered simultaneously? These assertions are based on the assumption that all other relevant variables remain constant, an assumption that is unlikely in reality.

To answer the above questions, multiple correlation and regression analysis were employed. Eight of the eleven later-stage industry groups were combined with the specialization variable, employment in manufacturing, in a multiple regression analysis. The eight groups were selected largely on the basis of the size of the simple coefficient of correlation with machinery. A matrix showing inter-

Table 2.14

Results of Multiple Correlation and Regression Analysis, States, 1950 (5 Variables)

Variable	Beta	t	Significant[1]
Nonferrous foundries 336	.4445	5.9425	Yes
Structural metal products 344	−.1431	3.4902	Yes
Metal stamping and casting 346	.4306	5.8906	Yes
Electrical machinery 36	.2873	5.4105	Yes
$R = .986$			Yes[2]
$R^2 = .972$			

[1]The least significant value of t is 2.021.
[2]The least significant value of R with $N = 49$ and $m = 5$ is .440.
Source: Harold H. McCarty, John C. Hook, and Duane S. Knos, *The Measurement of Association in Industrial Geography.* Iowa City: Department of Geography, State University of Iowa, 1956, Table 33.

correlation between all of the variables was prepared. These coefficients were inserted in the matrix for solution by the Doolittle method.

The next step in the analysis was to derive the partial regression coefficient b and the multiple regression equation from the β's coefficents (the partial regression coefficients expressed in standard deviation units) computed in the foregoing analysis (Table 2.14). When the variables were considered in the multiple regression model, five of the variables (SIC groups 332, 339, 348, 371 and the percentage of the workers in manufacturing) were considered unimportant in explaining the localization of machinery industry. This was due to the high degree of correlation between the independent variables and the four remaining variables. With the elimination of these five variables, the final regression equation is:

$$\gamma_c = 8.24(336) - 1.08(344) + 2.79(346) + .05(36) + 103.23$$

Y_c is the estimated number of workers employed in machinery (35) in hundreds, and the numbers in parentheses refer to the SIC classifications. The coefficient of multiple correlation is now .986 and $r^2 = 0.972$.

The regression equation for predicting the number of workers in machinery performed most poorly in many of the states that had the largest numbers of workers in machinery. The equation underestimated by more than one standard error the number of workers in New York, Massachusetts, New Jersey, Pennsylvania, Ohio, Illinois, Wisconsin, and Iowa. Thus those states had more workers than would be expected in machinery from an examination of the number of workers in industries 336, 344, 346, and 36. Because of the nature of the distribution, the regression equation did not overestimate by more than one standard error in any state. It was concluded from these results that at the state scale for 1950, the production-sequence hypothesis was substantiated in terms of the association between the dependent and independent variables taken both singly and collectively.

Related Industries Hypothesis. The third hypothesis stated that the machinery group will be more closely associated with other metal-using industries than with non-metal-using industries. It was based on the assumptions that technologically linked industries tended to agglomerate spatially and that the metal-consuming industries as a group were of that type.

To test this hypothesis, correlation and regression analysis tests were applied as in the previous hypothesis. The analysis revealed that the machinery industry was more closely related to the metal-using industries than the non-metal-using industries. Thus the hypothesis was substantiated.

SELECTED REFERENCES

1. Aangeenbrug, Robert T., "Regional Perception and Its Effect on Industrial Location," *Kansas Business Review*, 21 (January 1968), 3–6.
2. Ahluwalia, M.S., "Taxes, Subsidies, and Employment," *Quarterly Journal of Economics*, 87 (August 1973), 393–409.
3. Alejandro, C.F.D., "Industrialization and Labor Productivity Differentials," *Review of Economics and Statistics*, 47 (May 1965), 207–214.
4. Alexander, John W., S. Earl Brown, and Richard E. Dahlberg, "Freight Rates: Selected Aspects of Uniform and Nodal Regions," *Economic Geography*, 34 (1958), 1–18.
5. Ames, E. and N. Rosenberg, "Changing Technological Leadership and Industrial Growth," *Economic Journal*, 73 (March 1963), 13–31.
6. Arianin, A.N. and S.A. Nikolaev, "An Intra-Regional Model of Optimum Plant Location," *Papers, Regional Science Association*, 24 (1970), 163–170.
7. Armstrong, Robert, *Location of Industry as Influenced by Taxation and Special Inducements*. Detroit, Mich.: Public Library, Municipal Reference Library, n.d.
8. Bain, J.S., "Economies of Scale, Concentration, and the Condition of Entry into Twenty Manufacturing Industries," *American Economic Review*, 44 (1954), 15–39.
9. Baker, Robert M., "Tax Exemption as a Means of Attracting Industry," *George Washington Law Review*, 20 (January 1952), 253–263.
10. Beckmann, Martin J. and Gunter Schramm, "The Impact of Scientific and Technical Change on the Location of Economic Activities," *Regional and Urban Economics*, 2 (August 1972), 159–174.
11. Bergin, Thomas P. and William F. Eagan, "Economic Growth and Community Facilities," *Municipal Finance*, 23 (May 1961), 146–150.
12. Blackbourn, Anthony, "Locational Decisions in the International Corporation," *Proceedings of the Association of American Geographers*, 5 (1973), 22–24.
13. Bloom, C.C., *State and Local Tax Differentials*. Iowa City: Bureau of Business Research, State University of Iowa, 1955.
14. Borovits, Israel and Arthur Carol, "International Comparison of Industrial Structures Using Input-Output Analysis," *Long Range Planning*, 6 (March 1973), 63–68.
15. Bridges, B., Jr., "State and Local Inducements for Industry," *National Tax Journal*, 18 (March and June 1965), 1–14, 175–192.
16. Britton, John N.H., "A Geographical Approach to the Examination of Industrial Linkages," *The Canadian Geographer*, 13 (Fall 1969), 185–198.
17. Bylinsky, Gene, "California's Great Breeding Ground for Industry," *Fortune*, 89 (June 1974), 129–135+.
18. Campbell, Lewis H., Jr., *The Industry-Ordnance Team*. New York: McGraw-Hill, 1946.
19. Chenery, Hollis B. and Paul G. Clark, *Interindustry Economics*. New York: Wiley, 1959.
20. Chinitz, Benjamin, "The Effect of Transportation Forms on Regional Economic Growth," *Traffic Quarterly*, 14 (1960), 129–142.
21. Chisholm, Michael, *Geography and Economics*. London: G. Bell and Sons, 1966.
22. Cigno, A., "Economies of Scale and Industrial Location," *Regional Studies*, 5 (1971), 295–301.
23. Close, F.A. and D. E. Shulenburger, "Labor's Share by Sector and Industry, 1948–1965," *International Labor Relations Review*, 24 (July 1971), 588–602.
24. Czamanski, Stanislaw, "Some Empirical Evidence of the Strengths of Linkages Between Groups of Related Industries in Urban-Regional Complexes," *Papers, Regional Science Association*, 27 (1971), 137–150.
25. Dacey, Michael F., "Analysis of Central Place and Point Pattern by a Nearest Neighbour Method," *Lund Studies in Geography, Series B, Human Geography*, 24 (1962), 55–75.
26. Daggett, Stuart, *Principles of Inland Transportation*. New York: Harper and Row, 1955.

27. —— and John Carter, *The Structure of Transcontinental Freight Rates*. Berkeley: University of California Press, 1947.
28. Domar, E.D., "On the Measurement of Technological Change," *Economic Journal*, 71 (December 1961), 709–729.
29. Dunn, Edgar S., "The Market Potential Concept and the Analysis of Location," *Papers, Regional Science Association*, 15 (1956), 183–194.
30. Estall, R.C. and R. Ogilvie Buchanan, *Industrial Activity and Economic Geography*. London: Hutchinson University Library, 1961.
31. Evans, M.K., "Study of Industry Investment Decisions," *Review of Economics and Statistics*, 49 (May 1967), 151–164.
32. Fahle, V.L. and H.R. Hertzfeld, "The Role of Transport Costs and Market Size in Threshold Models of Industrial Location," *Papers, Regional Science Association*, 28 (1972), 189–202.
33. Fair, Marvin L. and E.W. Williams, *Economics of Transportation*. New York: Harper and Row, 1959.
34. Farris, P.L., "Market Growth and Concentration Change in U.S. Manufacturing Industries," *Antitrust Bulletin*, 18 (Summer 1973), 167–179.
35. Florence, P. Sargent, W.G. Fritz, and R.C. Gilles, *Industrial Location and National Resources*. Washington, D.C.: National Resources Planning Board, 1942.
36. Fuchs, Victor R., "Hourly Earnings Differentials by Region and Size of City," *Monthly Labor Review*, 90 (1967), 22–26.
37. Garrison, C.B., "New Industry in Small Towns: The Impact on Local Government," *National Tax Journal*, 24 (December 1971), 493–500.
38. Gujarati, D., "Labor's Share in Manufacturing Industries, 1949–1964," *Industrial and Labor Relations Review*, 23 (October 1969), 65–77.
39. Guthrie, J.A., "Economies of Scale and Regional Development," *Papers and Proceedings of the Regional Science Association*, 1 (1955), J1–J10.
40. Hansen, Niles M., *Location Preferences, Migration, and Regional Growth: A Study of the South and Southwest United States*. New York: Praeger, 1973.
41. Hansen, R.W. and G.M. Munsinger, "Prescriptive Model for Industrial Development," *Land Economics*, 48 (February 1972), 76–81.
42. Harris, C.C., "Forecasting the Location of Industries," *Review of Regional Studies*, 1 (1970), 1–4.
43. Harris, Chauncy D., "The Market as a Factor in the Localization of Industry in the United States," *Annals of the Association of American Geographers*, 44 (1954), 315–348.
44. Healy, K.T., "Transportation as a Factor in Economic Growth," *Journal of Economic History*, 7 (1947), 72–88.
45. Hirsch, Werner Z., "Interindustry Relations of a Metropolitan Area," *Review of Economics and Statistics*, 41 (November 1959), 360–369.
46. Hodge, G. and C.C. Wong, "Adapting Industrial Complex Analysis to the Realities of Regional Data," *Papers, Regional Science Association*, 28 (1972), 145–166.
47. Hoover, E.M., *The Location of Economic Activity*. New York: McGraw-Hill, 1948.
48. Hopkins, Frank E., "Transportation Cost and Industrial Location: An Analysis of the Household Furniture Industry," *Journal of Regional Science*, 13 (1972), 261–278.
49. Hunker, Henry L., *Industrial Evolution of Columbus, Ohio*, Monograph No. 93. Columbus: Bureau of Business Research, Ohio State University, 1958.
50. ——, *Industrial Development*. Lexington, Mass.: Heath, 1974.
51. —— and Alfred J. Wright, *Factors in Industrial Location in Ohio*. Columbus: Ohio State University, 1963.
52. Isard, Walter and others, *Methods of Regional Analysis: An Introduction to Regional Science*. New York: Wiley, 1960.
53. —— and others, *Ecologic-Economic Analysis for Regional Development*. New York: The Free Press, 1972.
54. —— and John Cumberland, "New England as a Possible Location for an Integrated Iron and Steel Works," *Economic Geography*, 26 (October 1950), 245–259.

55. ———, Eugene W. Schooler, and Thomas Vietorisz, *Industrial Complex Analysis and Regional Development, with Particular Reference to Puerto Rico.* Cambridge: The MIT Press, 1959.

56. ——— and Pangis Liossatos, "Industrial Location: Agglomeration and Feedback Analysis," *Papers, Regional Science Association,* 28 (1972), 7–36.

57. Jay, R.A., "Effective Use of Research and Development Resources," *Advanced Management Journal,* 32 (July 1967), 34–38.

58. Jewkes, J., "The Size of the Factory," *Economic Journal,* 1952, pp. 237–252.

59. Karaska, Gerald J., "The Partial Equilibrium Approach to Location Theory: Graphic Solutions," in Gerald J. Karaska and David F. Bramhall, *Locational Analysis for Manufacturing.* Cambridge: The MIT Press, 1969.

60. King, Leslie J., *Statistical Analysis in Geography.* Englewood Cliffs, N.J.: Prentice-Hall, 1969.

61. Kohl, John C., "Highways as a Factor in Plant Location," *Michigan Business Review,* 10 (March 1958), 1–6.

62. Leonard, W.N., "Research and Development in Industrial Growth," *Journal of Political Economy,* 79 (March-April 1971), 232–256.

63. Leontief, Wassily, *The Structure of American Economy, 1919-1939.* New York: Oxford University Press, 1951.

64. ———, "Input-Output Economics," *Scientific American,* 185 (October 1951), 15–21.

65. ———, "The Structure of Development," *Scientific American,* 209 (September 1963), 148–166.

66. Loewenstein, Louis K., "New Factors and Facts of Industrial Location," *AIDC (American Industrial Development Council) Journal,* 3 (July 1968), 25–34.

67. Loftus, P.J., "Labour's Share in Manufacturing," *Lloyds Bank Review,* 92 (April 1969), 15–25.

68. Lonsdale, Richard E., "Rural Labor as an Attraction for Industry," *AIDC (American Industrial Development Council) Journal,* 4, no. 4 (1969), 11–17.

69. Machlup, Fritz, *The Basing Point System.* Philadelphia: Blakiston, 1949.

70. MacNiel, Neil and Harold W. Metz, *The Hoover Report 1953-1955.* New York: Macmillan, 1956.

71. McCarty, Harold H., John C. Hook, and Duane S. Knos, *The Measurement of Association in Industrial Geography.* Iowa City: Department of Geography, State University of Iowa, 1956.

72. McGregor, John R., "Water as a Factor in the Location of Industry in the Southeast," *The Southeastern Geographer,* 10 (1970), 41–54.

73. McLaughlin, G.E. and S. Robock, *Why Industry Moves South.* Washington, D.C.: National Planning Association, 1949.

74. Miernyk, W., *The Elements of Input-Output Analysis.* New York: Random House, 1965.

75. Miller, E. Willard, *A Geography of Manufacturing.* Englewood Cliffs, N.J.: Prentice-Hall, 1962.

76. ———, *A Geography of Industrial Location.* Dubuque, Iowa: Wm. C. Brown, 1970.

77. Moore, Harry E., *What Is Regionalism?* Southern Policy Papers, No. 10. Chapel Hill: University of North Carolina Press, 1937.

78. Morgan W.D. and W.E. Brownlee, "The Impact of State and Land Taxation on Industrial Location: A New Measure for the Great Lakes Region," *Quarterly Review of Economics and Business,* 14 (Spring 1974), 67–77.

79. Moses, Leon M., "A General Equilibrium Model of Production, Interregional Trade, and Location of Industry," *Review of Economics and Statistics,* 42 (November 1960), 373–397.

80. Mueller, Eva and James N. Morgan, "Location Decisions of Manufacturers," *American Economic Review,* 52 (May, Supplement 1962), 204–217.

81. Nelson, R.H., "Economies of Scale and Market Size," *Land Economics,* 48 (1972), 297–300.

82. Nicholls, A.F., "Transportation Development and Löschean Market Areas: An Historical Perspective," *Land Economics,* 46 (February 1970), 22–31.

83. Nishioka, H. and G. Krumme, "Location Conditions, Factors and Decisions: An Evaluation of Selected Location Surveys," *Land Economics,* 49 (May 1973), 195–205.

84. Nourse, Hugh O., *Regional Economics: A Study in the Economic Structure, Stability, and Growth of Regions*. New York: McGraw-Hill, 1968.
85. Nurkse, R., *Problems of Capital Formation in Underdeveloped Countries*. Oxford: Basil Blackwell, 1955.
86. Osborn, D.G., *Geographical Features of the Automation of Industry*. Chicago: University of Chicago, Department of Geography, Research Paper No. 30, 1953.
87. Osleeb, Jeffrey P., "The Optimum Size of Plant for the Uniform Delivered Price Manufacturer," *Proceedings of the Association of American Geographers*, 6 (1974), 102–105.
88. Pashigan, B. Peter, "Market Concentration in the United States and Canada," *Journal of Law and Economics*, 11 (October 1968), 299–319.
89. Perloff, Harvey S., et al., *Regions, Resources and Economic Growth*. Baltimore: Johns Hopkins Press, 1960.
90. Poindexter, J.C. and C.P. Jones, "The Effect of Recent Tax Policy Changes on Manufacturing Investment," *Quarterly Review of Economics and Business*, 13 (Winter 1973), 79–88.
91. Purcell, H.I., "State and Local Taxes: A Significant Site Selection Variable," *Industrial Development and Manufacturers Record*, 137 (November-December 1968), 30–35.
92. Qualls, D., "Concentration, Barriers to Entry, and Long Run Economic Profit Margins," *Journal of Industrial Economics*, 20 (April 1972), 146–158.
93. Redmond, J.C., "Essential Elements of Research in Industry," *Research Management*, 10 (May 1967), 175–185.
94. Robinson, E.A.G., *The Structure of Competitive Industry*. Chicago: The University of Chicago Press, 1958.
95. Samuelson, Paul, *Economics*. New York: McGraw-Hill, 1951.
96. Schmidt, Charles G., "Firm Linkage Structure and Structural Change: A Graph Theoretical Analysis," *Economic Geography*, 51 (January 1975), 27–36.
97. Shen, T.Y., "Economies of Scale, Expansion Path, and Growth of Plants," *Review of Economics and Statistics*, 47 (November 1965), 420–428.
98. Sherman, R., "Entry Barriers and the Growth of Firms," *Southern Economic Journal*, 38 (October 1971), 238–247.
99. ———— and R. Tollison, "Technology, Profit, and Market Performance," *Quarterly Journal of Economics*, 86 (August 1972), 448–462.
100. Silbertson, A., "Economies of Scale in Theory and Practice," *Economic Journal*, 82 (March 1972), 369–391.
101. Smith, Wilfred, "The Location of Industry," *Institute of British Geographers Transactions and Papers*, 21 (1955), 1–18.
102. Spiegelman, R.G., *A Study of Industrial Location Using Multiple Regression Techniques*. Washington, D.C.: Agricultural Economic Reports 140, Economic Research Service, U.S. Department of Agriculture, 1968.
103. Stekler, H.O., "A Note on the Size of a Market," *Journal of Industrial Economics*, 9 (July 1961), 251–254.
104. Stocking, George W., *Basing Point Pricing and Regional Development*. Chapel Hill: University of North Carolina Press, 1954.
105. Strasma, J.D., "State and Local Taxation of Industry," *Federal Reserve Bank of Boston: Bulletin*, 1959, pp. 12–18.
106. Struyk, Raymond J., "Evidence on the Locational Activity of Manufacturing Industries in Metropolitan Areas," *Land Economics*, 48 (November 1972), 377–382.
107. ————, "Spatial Concentration of Manufacturing Employment in Metropolitan Areas," *Economic Geography*, 48 (1972), 189–192.
108. Swan, P.L., "Decentralization and the Growth of Urban Manufacturing Employment," *Land Economics*, 49 (May 1973), 212–216.
109. Thompson, W.R. and John M. Mattila, *An Economic Model of Postwar State Industrial Development*. Detroit: Wayne State University Press, 1959.
110. Turner, Robert G., "Industry Location Factors and the Role of State Agencies in the Location Decision," *Atlanta Economic Review*, 21 (1971), 32–34.

111. Turner, W.H.K., "The Significance of Water Power in Industrial Location," *Scottish Geographical Magazine*, 74 (September 1958), 98–115.
112. Ullman, E.L and H.B. Mayer, "Transportation Geography," in *American Geography: Inventory and Prospects*, Preston E. James and Clarence F. Jones, eds., Syracuse: Syracuse University Press, 1954.
113. Weiss, Leonard D., "The Geographic Size of Markets in Manufacturing," *The Review of Economics and Statistics*, 54 (1972), 245–257.
114. Will, R.A., "Federal Influences on Industrial Location: How Extensive?," *Land Economics*, 40 (February 1964), 49–57.
115. Yntema, D.B., *Michigan Taxes on Business*. Holland, Mich.: Hope College, 1959.
116. Yotopoulos, P.A. and J.B. Nugent, "A Balanced-Growth Version of the Linkage Hypothesis," *Quarterly Journal of Economics*, 87 (May 1973), 157–171.
117. *Economic Concentration: New Technologies and Concentration*. Washington, D.C.: U.S. Senate Committee on the Judiciary, Subcommittee on Antitrust and Monopoly, hearings, pt. 6, 19 September-6 October 1967, pursuant to Senate Resolution 26, 90th Congress, 1st Session, 1968, pp. 2551–3438.
118. *Michigan Tax Study: Staff Papers*. Lansing: State of Michigan, 1958.
119. "Plant Site Preferences of Industry and Factors of Selection," *Business Week Research Report*, 1958, pp. 1–20.

III

LOCATIONAL ANALYSIS: SELECTED INDUSTRIES

The first two parts of this volume provided the theoretical and empirical framework for the study of industrial location. A logical progression is to utilize this material in the analysis and interpretation of the localization of selected industries. It is fundamental that the study of the selected industries be grounded in reality. Therefore the material in this section depends heavily on empirical information. Nevertheless any analysis that reflects complex spatial relationships must have theoretical abstract models.

The selection of industries is difficult and each reader is likely to reflect, based partly on personal considerations, why a particular industry and not some other was chosen. The eight industries analyzed in Part III were selected to illustrate some of the more important factors that play a role in the localization of manufacturing; the approach is thus analytical rather than synthetic. Further, industries that have a national or international localization were selected for study. At all times, however, emphasis was placed on an interpretation of the spatial aspects. The United States provides a locational case study for each of the industries considered.

The first industry analyzed is that of iron and steel. This traditional industry of the Industrial Revolution demonstrates how factors of localization change over time. This industry was traditionally oriented to fuel and/or raw materials. With technological advancement the localizing influences of fuel and raw materials declined and other factors, particularly markets, have increased in importance. As a consequence the spatial patterns of this industry have been dynamic. Further, this industry illustrates that as a response to changing factors of localization the theoretical framework can also be altered. The industry originally evolved under the Weberian concept of seeking a least cost site, but the Löschian framework of securing a maximum market location has dominated in recent times.

The aluminum industry provides an excellent example of a power-oriented industry. From its earliest period, the aluminum industry has always sought the lowest cost power available and therefore has developed within the Weberian framework of seeking a least cost location. Emphasis is placed on the migration of the industry in its search for new sources of power as the demand for aluminum increases.

Three engineering industries have been selected for analysis, each having a different combination of factors that influence its localization. The machine tool industry, which provides the foundation for all modern engineering industries, illustrates the dominance of labor and markets as principal localizing factors. Emphasis is placed on the spatial stability of the machine tool industry in the twentieth century.

The motor vehicle industry illustrates the development of a modern oligopolistic industry. It is a supreme example of an industry seeking the maximum market orientation and has thus developed within a Löschian theoretical framework.

The agricultural machinery industry provides a study of an orientation to a particular type of agriculture. Market orientation has thus dominated the factors localizing the industry. In contrast to the motor vehicle industry, with its national mass consumption market, the agricultural machinery industry represents a special type of market orientation.

The petroleum refining industry illustrates how the factors of localization vary from place to place. Raw materials and markets appear to be dominating influences in the establishment of the world's refinery pattern. Most important, these two factors frequently do not coincide spatially, but operate individually in influencing the patterns of petroleum refining. To complicate the spatial pattern, large refinery centers have developed at intermediate points between the raw materials and the final market. In the selection of one of these types of location, transportation costs frequently become a critical locational factor, as do such factors as governmental influences and company strategy.

The portland cement industry is one that produces a heavy, bulky, relatively low-cost commodity and has been consistently oriented to raw material sources and markets. Transportation costs thus become the critical factor in the siting of a plant.

The cotton textile industry has consistently sought the least cost point of production. Labor costs are a critical locational factor. This industry illustrates that, as the labor increases in skill and thus rises in cost, new locations are sought. Traditionally, the quantity of labor has been more important than the skills it possessed. However, with the modern development of a capital intensive industry in contrast to the labor intensive industry of the past, the future locational pattern may be based on a different set of criteria.

A major purpose of the case studies is to demonstrate the importance of a desirable combination of factors of production. An industry will exist in an area depending on its competence in marshaling the critical factors of localization. Thus the ability of a manufacturing industry to exist and expand will depend on being located where a satisfactory combination of locational factors exist.

IRON AND STEEL INDUSTRY

Archeologists date the beginning of the Iron Age, when man smelted ore and used the resulting metal to produce useful articles, from about 1500 to 1400 B.C. Because iron ore and wood for charcoal were widely distributed and the amount of iron produced was small, the industry developed in widely separated regions over the centuries. Nevertheless, the important early centers evolved where artisans developed steels that possessed a superior quality. For example, Damascus and Toledo swords could be bent from hilt to tip and at the same time take a cutting edge; their reputation was based on craftsmanship and on the strength and flexibility of Wootz steel that came from the Hyderabad area of India. Because processes developed in a particular area were highly guarded secrets, the art of producing quality steels did not become widely known. As a result technological advances in different areas were greatly limited.

For more than 1,000 years during the Dark and Middle ages, the technology and economic organization of the iron industry remained practically unchanged. Beginning in the fifteenth century, charcoal furnaces were developed in western Europe and the industry began to expand. The charcoal furnace not only provided greater efficiency in fuel and labor, but also had a larger output. Because the iron was of a better quality, its uses were greatly extended. When the forges were small, raw material sources were not important localizing factors. As production increased, the overcutting of forest stands for charcoal became an important limiting factor in production. In general iron ore deposits were not exhausted in the countries of western Europe, but timber resources did become scarce in many areas. The centers of the iron industry gradually localized in areas where charcoal could be made from vast forest reserves. As a consequence Sweden, with its abundant charcoal supplies, became a leading iron center; by the middle of the eighteenth century it produced some 30,000 tons of pig iron a year. Nevertheless the iron industry continued to thrive in other nations. For example, in 1788–1789 the Bureau de Commerce of France indicated that more than 600 charcoal furnaces were operating in the country. The small charcoal ironworks were relatively cheap to build and easy to operate. Furthermore, the finished metal was in universal demand and its costly transport made it desirable that the local market be supplied from local furnaces and forges. The charcoal furnace had its greatest period of dominance in Europe during the latter part of the eighteenth century.

Long after coal became the dominant fuel for smelting iron ore in western Europe, charcoal persisted as the major fuel in the United States because of the vast forests on the East Coast and the inaccessibility of the interior coal deposits. By the middle of the eighteenth century the British colonies were producing almost as great a quantity of pig iron as England, perhaps 25–35 percent of the world output. After the American Revolution, the iron industry in the United States did not expand rapidly and gradually lost its significant world position. In contrast to the great technological progress in Britain, iron continued to be smelted by charcoal in the United States until the introduction of anthracite in eastern Pennsylvania as the major smelting fuel in the 1830s.

The next phase in the localization of the iron and steel industry was related intimately to the Industrial Revolution, which was primarily a revolution in power and metallurgy. A series of inventions and improvements established the basis for the modern iron and steel industry. The great changes in the smelting of iron ore and the shaping of iron were initiated about 1784, when the puddling furnace was developed in England. This furnace used coal (later coke) rather than charcoal for its fuel. Because the furnace reduced the cost of manufacture and yielded a larger quantity and more uniform grade of iron, the center of iron production rapidly shifted to the British coalfields. The use of coal in iron ore smelting freed Britain from its greatest iron industry handicap, a shortage of fuel. With rapid technological advancements, Britain soon assumed world leadership. In 1820 Britain produced about 25 percent of the world total, but increased its share to more than half by 1860.

In the second half of the nineteenth century, the iron and steel industry grew rapidly in coal-producing countries. For example, after 1840 iron manufacturing forged ahead in Germany as a result of the rapid growth of railroads and a series of inventions that improved the quality of cast iron and made it in some respects superior to the British product. Output in the United States also began to increase, first under the stimulus of the anthracite furnaces in eastern Pennsylvania in the 1840–1860 period, later because of the use of coke blast furnaces in western Pennsylvania. As a result of the growth in American production, the United States became the world's leading iron and steel producer by 1890. In the early twentieth century production continued to be concentrated in the United States and coal producing European nations including the Soviet Union.

The expansion of world steel capacity since 1945 has been spectacular. The first stage was from 1945 to the early 1950s, when the steel industry was being reconstructed after World War II. During this period the increase in capacity was particularly high in Europe, the Soviet Union, and Japan. The second period extended from the early 1950s to the early 1960s when countries were expanding their capacity to meet growing domestic demands. During this period the number of steel-producing countries grew from 34 to over 40. The present period, beginning in the mid-1960s, is characterized by a growth in capacity sometimes based on a potential international market. At the present time at least 60 nations have become iron and steel producers. Nevertheless, seven nations—the Soviet Union, the United States, Japan, West Germany, the United Kingdom, France, and China—still produce nearly three-fourths of the world's steel.

Theoretical Locational Framework

In the nineteenth and early twentieth centuries, the iron and steel industry developed within the Weberian concept of seeking the least cost points of operation. Because the iron and steel industry was a major consumer of bulky, heavy raw materials and a massive consumer of fuel, it sought the lowest costs point for the assembly of these materials. In the United States a combination of factors—a single coking coal seam in western Pennsylvania and the fact that two tons of coal were required for each ton of iron ore smelted—produced a least cost area that secured a near monopoly situation for many years.

As technology advanced in the twentieth century, the consumption of coal per ton of ore smelted declined. As a result other factors of production increased in importance, making it increasingly difficult to determine the area of least cost production. Consequently the least cost advantage of western Pennsylvania declined. Other regions could produce iron and steel at a satisfactory profit. In essence transportation costs for raw materials and fuel declined as localizing factors and the market increased in importance. Thus the market concepts of Lösch gradually assumed the greatest importance in localizing the iron and steel industry. Because iron and steel could be produced at essentially the same costs at numerous locations, the greatest profits could be secured where the largest markets exist. In the past 25 years few, if any, new iron and steel plants have been raw material or fuel oriented. A Löschian framework of seeking a maximum market site is thus the locational objective of the present-day iron and steel industry throughout most of the world.

Factors of Location

The factors that have influenced the location of the iron and steel industry have changed with time, primarily because of technological advancements, sources of raw materials, transportation costs, and size of market.

COAL. Coalfields exerted the dominating influence in locating the early iron furnaces. In Britain the early centers of the industry were found on the coalfields of the Midlands, Yorkshire, Derbyshire, and South Wales. In 1820 about 90 percent of the industry in Britain was located in these areas. The importance of coal as the dominant locational factor was due to the fact that the amount of coal required to smelt a ton of ore and process the pig iron greatly exceeded the total weight of the ore plus the finished product.

Efficiencies in fuel consumption in iron ore smelting and steel production were introduced at an early date. As a result there has been a constant decline in coal consumption. The coal requirements to produce a ton of iron fell from about ten tons in 1790 to three tons in 1850 and was further reduced to an average of 3,247 pounds in 1913 and about 1,900 pounds in 1975. The coal requirements to produce a ton of steel fell from about eight tons in 1870 to only a little over one ton in 1975. The Bessemer furnace and later the Thomas and Gilchrist process and the Martin and Siemens process, and still later the oxygen process, reduced the consumption of fuel in the steelmaking process. The continuous processes of taking the iron directly to the steel converter in the molten stage has greatly reduced fuel requirements. Thus, while fuel requirements for pig iron have fallen significantly, the fuel requirements to produce steel have declined at an even greater rate. As a result the coalfields have declined in importance in locating the iron and steel industry. In recent years other factors have influenced the localization of the iron and steel industry.

IRON ORE.   With the declining importance of coal in the production of iron and steel, the relative importance of iron ore has increased. In the nineteenth century, when four tons of coal were required to produce one ton of metal and one ton of slag, the orientation was to the coalfields. But under present conditions in many regions, when two tons of coal are required to produce one ton of metal and one ton of slag, the same amount of coal as iron ore has to be transported. As a result the coalfields and iron ore deposits have an equal attraction. In this situation, other factors may be more influential than either coal or iron ore in localizing the industry.

As the rich iron ore deposits have declined in recent years, lower-grade deposits have been exploited. When a 25-percent ore is utilized, it requires approximately two tons of coal to produce one ton of metal, but there are three tons of slag produced in the process. Under these conditions there is obviously a transport cost advantage in orienting the industry to the iron ore deposits. In reality, however, a 25-percent ore is rarely, if ever, utilized in a blast furnace. Rather, the ore is beneficiated, producing ores of 50–60 percent iron content. As a result the attraction of the ore deposit for the establishment of the blast furnaces is lessened. The ability to beneficiate ores has increased the importance of other localization factors, particularly the market. Further, it has tended to stabilize production in already developed areas.

A number of iron and steel centers have been oriented to iron ore deposits. The establishment of the modern industry at iron ore sources began in Britain about the middle of the nineteenth century. Blast furnaces were built near Cumberland and Lancashire ores, and by 1880 this region was the second largest pig-iron-producing area in Great Britain. In Britain it appears that the demand for iron and steel was so great, and the transport distances so short, that both coal and iron ore deposits attracted the industry.

The attraction to ore fields is also evident on the European continent. In a number of countries that possessed iron ore but little or no coal, iron and steel industries were oriented to iron ore deposits; notable examples are Lorraine in eastern France and Luxembourg. In more recent times iron and steel industries have developed on the Urals and Ukraine iron ore deposits of the Soviet Union. The transport of coal from the Kuznetsk Basin and eastern Ukraine to these iron ore deposits has been a major achievement in the Soviet iron and steel industry.

As the influence of the coalfields declined in the United States, the importance of the ore deposits in localizing the industry has increased. The first major shift away from the coalfield orientation came with the development of the industry in Cleveland. Iron ore was received in Cleveland from the upper Great Lakes by lake freighters, and coal came from the interior Appalachian fields. At a later date other iron and steel centers developed on the lower Great Lakes at Buffalo, Detroit, Gary, and other lake ports. This trend in developing the iron and steel industry at lower Great Lakes ports illustrates the lessening attraction of coal and the growing importance of securing iron ore, the processing taking place at a break in transportation at an intermediate point.

SCRAP. With the development of the open-hearth and electrical furnaces, scrap became a major raw material in the steelmaking process. Since 1915, when steel began to exceed pig iron production in the United States, this nation has consumed about 2,000 million tons of scrap. Converted into terms of ore, this is equivalent to about 3.3 billion tons of Mesabi hematite. If scrap had not been utilized, the high-grade Lake Superior iron ores would have been long exhausted.

There are a number of technological and economic reasons for utilizing scrap rather than pig iron in the steelmaking process. There is a major economy in using scrap in the open-hearth and electrical furnaces because the steel has already been refined. The scrap reduces the percentage of impurities to be burned out; it thus reduces the amount of fuel consumed and enables the process to be completed in a shorter time period. The electric furnace, more costly to operate than the open-hearth, normally uses only scrap. Thus the great use of scrap increases the capacity of the furnace and reduces the cost of fuel in relation to total production.

A second economy in the greater use of scrap is associated with smelting. Scrap replaces pig iron and thus reduces the demand for smelting capacity. The blast furnace operation—with its auxiliary smelting, coking, hot blast, and other necessary operations—requires higher capital investment than the construction of a steelwork. Thus the use of scrap reduces not only the primary costs in steel production, but also in plant construction.

Scrap becomes available from a variety of sources. Most metal consumed by the metal fabricating industries is ultimately recovered as scrap. Only small portions are lost through corrosion and such events as the sinking of ships. Although scrap is generated from the moment pig iron is produced, the principal sources of scrap are trimmings and clippings from metal-consuming industries. For example, the motor vehicle industry is the largest producer of process scrap. Another major source of scrap is machinery and metal products that have become obsolete and are junked. With the decline in the consumption of coal and iron ore and the increase in the consumption of scrap, the attraction of the industry to iron ore and fuel sources has greatly declined. Scrap is most readily available in the steel market areas. If the iron and steel industry were located in other areas, it would necessitate the transportation of scrap to these centers. Thus the locational attraction of the market is measurable by the difference in the sum of the weights of the scrap and the finished products if the former is located at the market.

The relative decline of a number of the older centers oriented to fuels is due partly to the persistent scarcity of scrap. The Pittsburgh–Youngstown–Johnstown region's production capacity has always far exceeded its local market. As a consequence, the local supplies of scrap are inadequate and the area must import a large percentage of this raw material. By contrast, the Chicago area has a much larger supply of scrap because of its metal fabricating industries. The rise of the Detroit iron and steel industry reflects not only a large steel-consuming market, but also the availability of scrap.

The availability of scrap has made it possible for small steel plants to develop in a market region even if no blast furnaces exist in that region. The Pacific Coast of the United States did not possess a blast furnace industry until the World War II period, although there were a number of steel-producing plants. Under this situation the furnace charge was made up of about 85 percent scrap. Thus the steel industry was able to orient itself to its market, overcoming locational disadvantages of access to traditional raw materials.

MARKET.   The earliest iron centers were usually oriented to local markets. The bulk and weight of iron as well as the poor transportation facilities limited the market area. When anthracite became a major fuel in eastern Pennsylvania, the furnaces were not developed directly on the coal deposits; instead they were developed at intermediate points between the fuel and the markets of the eastern states. Later, when bituminous coal became the principal fuel, the iron and steel industry localized in the northern portion of the Appalachian coalfield as near as possible to the large northern market. The western Pennsylvania–eastern Ohio iron and steel region occupied a central position between Boston and Chicago and was thus able to supply the nation's leading industrial centers.

In recent times the market position for the iron and steel industry has been greatly enhanced; a number of factors have encouraged this trend. With the decline in the consumption of coal per ton of steel produced, the attraction to fuel and iron ore sources has greatly lessened. At the same time there has been an increase in scrap consumption. Scrap is most readily available in the steel market areas. If the iron and steel industry were located in other areas, it would necessitate the transportation of scrap to these centers.

The changing sources of fuel and raw materials have also encouraged a market orientation. Traditionally the fuel and iron ore were obtained by a plant from single sources. At the present time fuel and iron ore may come from several sources that are widely separated. As a result these materials are assembled in the region where the finished product will be utilized in order to reduce the transportation costs. To illustrate, since 1950 the coastal steel mills in the Common Market countries of Europe have grown more rapidly than interior plants. These mills secure their fuel and iron ore from world sources, with the hinterlands of the ports providing the major markets.

A significant trend in the iron and steel industry has been the increase in the size of the plant. This change has been largely a response to technological advancements that have lowered costs in the production of finished steel in vertically integrated plants. Economies of scale are significant in the larger furnaces. For example, 25 years ago a 1,000-cubic meter blast furnace was considered huge. Today the 2,000-cubic-meter blast furnace is common, and many new furnaces have a capacity of 3,000 cubic meters. Because of the larger quantities of steel produced, a market orientation is of great importance in reducing transportation cost for the finished products.

There is still another aspect that illustrates the attraction of major markets in the establishment of new iron and steel centers. People have long wondered why no primary iron and steel industry has developed in New England. In a 1950 study Isard and Cumberland investigated the possibilities of establishing such an industry (17). It was generally concluded that costs of production were not unfavorable to a New England iron and steel industry. However, the authors questioned whether the market was sufficiently large to justify an iron and steel industry. Although it was estimated that New England industry required an annual consumption of 1,250,000 tons, it needed a large number of specialized steels; many of these steels could not be produced profitably in New England because of limited demand. The New England steel market is thus complex, and a total annual demand figure may provide a misleading impression that the regional market will support an iron and steel industry. Further, because of its peripheral location New England is in a disadvantageous location for competing with other iron and steel producing centers in supplying markets in the United States. It appears that New England's iron and steel needs should continue to be supplied from outside the region. Thus regions that have a considerable demand for iron and steel may not develop a local industry if a supply can be obtained nearby at what appears to be reasonable costs.

Once a modern iron and steel industry is established, rarely does it disappear. The sources of fuel and iron ore may change, but new sources are normally substituted. However, there are a few places where an iron and steel industry was established with the expectation that a limited market would expand; in some cases, though, the market did not develop and the industry was abandoned. One major example of this situation was the integrated iron and steel plant built near Duluth and oriented to the iron ore sources of Minnesota. This plant was built over 50 years ago to take advantage of the low rates for coal on the backhaul of ore carriers. The pendulum principle of locating iron and steel plants at the termini between coal and iron ore sources is illustrated by this location. Nevertheless the Duluth plant was abandoned in the early 1970s because the potential market had not materialized and the antiquated equipment needed to be replaced to meet modern environmental protection standards.

Another example of abandoning production in a plant is provided by the iron and steel industry at Wheeling, West Virginia. This plant developed a large market for cut nails in the nineteenth century. However, although the demand for this type of nail declined in the twentieth century, the plant was not modernized. As a consequence the market gradually disappeared and the profitability of the plant declined below the acceptable margin. Thus the iron and steel industry in Wheeling disappeared as a response to the inability to adjust to changing market conditions.

LOCATIONAL INERTIA. There is a strong tendency for the iron and steel industry to persist in regions where it was originally established, even though the factors responsible for its initial development have long since disappeared. The present iron and steel industry of Sheffield, England, is an example. Sheffield has had an iron and steel industry for at least 600 years. In the early centuries Sheffield possessed many advantages for an iron and steel industry. Ironstone was found locally, and charcoal came from the forests of the Don Valley. The Don River provided power for working the bellows and forges. Refractory material was found in abundance in the coal measures. Limestone was found in deposits in Derbyshire, less than 15 miles from the blast furnace. Coal, when it replaced charcoal, was found within the political boundaries of Sheffield. Thus Sheffield was as ideal a site as any in England, and it became the leading iron processing center in the nation. Although the fuel and iron ore must now be imported, the industry persists as a response to the presence of skilled labor and long-established markets.

The huge capital investment in an iron and steel plant has been a major factor in the locational stability of the industry. A modern iron and steel plant requires hundreds of millions of dollars of capital outlay and may exceed a billion dollars. It is difficult, if not impossible, to move much of the equipment to a new location. As a result an iron and steel plant once established, will normally persist at its original location until the equipment is so antiquated that it is no longer profitable to operate. The basic equipment of an iron and steel plant has a remarkable longevity. Furthermore, the equipment does not deteriorate as a unit, and parts can be repaired or replaced. For example, some furnaces originally constructed in the nineteenth century have been rebuilt many times. Although efficiency of the older plants decreases, making it difficult for them to compete with newer and more modern plants, a profit may still be obtained. Thus the huge capital investment in an iron and steel plant becomes a principal factor in the locational inertia of the industry.

LABOR.   The iron and steel industry has changed from a labor intensive to a labor extensive industry. In the last decades of the nineteenth century and for much of the first half of the twentieth century, technological changes had only moderate influence on the demand for labor. In contrast, technological changes in recent decades have revolutionized the labor requirements. A major goal in the industry is to link isolated units of production in a steelmill into one continuous process, with computer controls assuming normal operations.

Employment in the steel industry in the United States reached a peak in 1953, when it was 544,000. By 1975 there were fewer than 425,000 employed. The United Steel Workers Union (USWU) says that the number of workers needed to produce a ton of steel is declining at the rate of 3 percent per year. The man-hours per ton of steel has declined from about 33 in 1935 to 14.5 in 1950 to less than 9 in 1975.

There has not only been a decline in the labor requirements, but there has also been a lowering of the skills needed on many jobs. For example, the "first helper" on an open-hearth furnace once had to possess skills acquired through long years of training. The length of time the batch of steel remained in the openhearth depended on how accurately he could judge the chemical composition of the molten steel from its color. In the change to the basic oxygen furnace, this job is performed more accurately by automatic controls. In the changeover to the oxygen converter, the first helper becomes the "furnace operator," a job that entails little more than button pushing. Consequently, the skill level of the first helper goes down seven job classifications under the job classification of the USWU.

Although labor may not have been a decisive factor in the early localization of the iron and steel regions of the world, it played an important role in creating high densities of population. More important, the skill of the labor supply played a role in the rise of the principal regions. As the demands and skills of the labor requirements have changed, it has made it easier for many of the lesser developed nations to become steel producers. A nation can now import labor for the few highly skilled engineering jobs, and not as highly trained workers can perform the necessary semiskilled jobs. It can be expected that there will be a further reduction in the number of semiskilled jobs because of the technological advances that are now being introduced into the industry. Conventional advances in such things as plant layout and materials handling have reduced the labor requirements. Only a few mills are automatic, with closed-loop controls. But when these mills become commonplace, there will be a drastic reduction in labor requirements.

The decline of employment in regions where iron and steel provides the major economic base has created many problems. In certain regions, iron and steel production has been so dominant that a diversified economy has not evolved. Some of the basic questions that these areas must cope with are: How do new industries develop in mature heavy industrial regions to absorb an excess labor force? What is management's responsibility for retraining a displaced worker? What is the role of unions in such a region? Other questions of a similar nature can be raised.

ECONOMIES OF SCALE.   Capital and operating costs in the iron and steel industry are considerably lower in large plants than in small plants, providing operations are at full or near full capacity. The capacity of plants has increased greatly in recent years. One-third of the steelworks in the United States can produce about 3,000,000 tons annually, and one plant—the Sparrows Point (Maryland) plant of Bethlehem Steel—has a capacity of 7,500,000 tons. In 1946 in Britain, about 93 percent of the steelworks had a capacity of less than 1,000,000 tons. By 1970 only 35 percent had a capacity below 1,000,000 tons, and 10 percent had a capacity in excess of 3,000,000 tons. The largest market for steel is for standardized finished products, for which there is a steady demand and in which the economies of large-scale production are best realized.

Site Factors

The iron and steel plant is one of the largest industrial operations developed in modern times. A prime requisite in selecting a site for an iron and steel industry is the availability of level land, not only for buildings but also for the disposal of waste slag. A modest-sized iron and steel plant will extend a mile in length and several hundred yards in width. The development of a modern iron and steel industry in an established urban area is today virtually impossible because of the land requirements. This is well illustrated by two modern examples. The Fontana plant located east of Los Angeles was built in a farming section. Similarly, the Morrisville plant north of Philadelphia was constructed on some of the best agricultural lands in Bucks County, Pennsylvania.

A second factor affecting the site of an iron and steel industry is the availability of a water supply. Because water is used in this industry in larger quantities than any raw material except air, the availability of water—from underground, streams, or lakes—is the most important factor in determining the specific site of an iron and steel plant. Lack of water may prove a limiting factor in the growth of the industry in a particular place. The American iron and steel industry uses between 13 and 15 billion gallons of water daily. A single blast furnace may use the same as a city of 30,000 people in a single day.

Water is needed for a number of purposes. Millions of gallons of cold water are required to circulate around the essential parts of the furnace. Water at a pressure of 1,000 psi is jetted to remove mill scale on steel slabs in the milling process. In the coking process, as much as 50 million gallons of water are used daily in a single plant. A distinction must be made between water that is circulated and water that is used up. Because of the tremendous quantities needed, little water in an iron and steel mill is used up. For example, of the 65,000 gallons needed in producing a ton of finished steel in a modern plant, only about 1,000 gallons are lost to the system. It is now estimated that the entire flow of the Monongahela is used seven times by the iron and steel industry before the river empties into the Ohio at Pittsburgh.

Water used in the iron and steel industry must possess a particular quality. Cold, clear, and soft water is desired. It should be free of silt and other impurities. If water does not possess these qualities, it must be treated. For example, hard water must be treated with lime or soda. Algae in water may become troublesome in summer if the temperature rises to 100°F. These organisms will adhere to pipe walls and clog the circulatory system in a short time.

The cost of water varies from area to area according to the quality of the water and the use to which it is to be put. The lowest water costs in 1970 were for plants on the Great Lakes, which averaged between 0.2 and 0.5 cents per 1,000 gallons. By contrast, the cost of water for the Fontana plant was about 2 cents per 1,000 gallons. If water is available, its cost is rarely, if ever, a decisive factor in the location of a plant.

The availability of transportation facilities is also a factor in locating the site of a plant. For a plant to function effectively, there must be a continuous flow of raw materials into the plant and finished materials outward to a market. A tremendous amount of raw material is consumed in the iron and steel plant. To produce 1 ton of pig iron normally requires 2 or more tons of iron ore, 1 ton of coke, 1/2 ton of limestone, 4 tons of heated air, and 57 tons of water. Besides the 1 ton of pig iron produced, there is also 1/2 ton of slag and 5 tons of gas. To assemble such a vast quantity of raw materials, the cheapest transportation is sought. Therefore the location of a steel plant on a navigable waterway where large docks can be constructed is greatly desired. If this is not possible, the second choice for the site of a steel plant is at the convergence of land transportation routes, particularly railroads.

United States

EARLY LOCALIZATION.   The iron industry was one of the first types of manufacturing to develop in the United States, with the first iron furnaces being built in Massachusetts in 1629. The industry was widely dispersed from the establishment of the first iron furnace until the middle of the nineteenth century. Iron ore deposits were found in many places, and charcoal from the virgin forests was omnipresent. Because fuel and raw materials were widely scattered, the major factor in the establishment of a furnace was the demand for a local iron supply. Since transportation facilities were limited and iron was heavy, the operation could not bear the costs of long-distance hauling. Centralization was also impossible because the iron ore deposits were small and no local area could provide sufficient charcoal to supply the furnaces for any extended length of time. Accordingly the early iron industry was migratory, with furnaces being moved or abandoned when one or another of the local raw materials became depleted.

The first concentration of iron furnaces developed in eastern Pennsylvania when anthracite was introduced as a fuel in 1839. Although charcoal produced a higher-quality iron, anthracite permitted the use of furnaces with greater capacity, and these were better able to serve the expanding market for iron in factories and railroad construction. Anthracite, although not a perfect blast furnace fuel, grew rapidly in importance, maintaining its dominance until the early 1870s.

Because anthracite was found only in northeastern Pennsylvania, the location of the iron industry was fuel oriented. However, the anthracite mining region developed only a small iron industry. This area was isolated and contained a minimum market for the finished iron. Consequently, anthracite was shipped out of the region, moving toward the iron ore deposits and, more important, the iron market of the East Coast. The precise location of the iron industry was determined by water routes such as the Lehigh and Schuylkill rivers. Coal could easily be floated down the canalized streams by barges, and iron ore was available from many small but widely scattered deposits. In the 1860s about 100 small iron ore mines also were operating in the region, and the area was the country's major producer of iron ore. At this time southeastern Pennsylvania was producing more than half of the nation's pig iron.

FACTORS IN THE MIGRATION TO SOUTHWESTERN PENNSYLVANIA.   A number of technological changes in the late 1850s resulted in the rapid migration of the iron industry center from southeastern to southwestern Pennsylvania. This movement began in 1856 with the invention of the Bessemer converter in England. The Bessemer converter was a major technical advancement because it was larger than the anthracite furnace and provided a cheap means of producing large quantities of steel. The demands for iron and steel were growing rapidly because of the expanding domestic economy, and the Civil War period stimulated these trends. Use of the Bessemer furnace spread rapidly after its introduction in the United States in 1864 at Wyandotte, Michigan. The Bessemer converter required a strong fuel that would not crush under the burden of the ore. Coke made from bituminous coal is sufficiently strong to sustain, without crushing, as much as 1,500 tons of load in the furnace. It is also porous and permits the hot blast of air to permeate it freely. Because it is nearly pure, it does not contaminate the metal. As a result, at almost the peak of the use of anthracite as a smelting fuel a technological change made it desirable for the industry to shift to the bituminous coal area of southwestern Pennsylvania and adjacent states.

This area was particularly favored because it contained the famous Pittsburgh coal seam. In the nineteenth century coke was made by the beehive-oven process, which requires a particularly high grade of bituminous coal with an absolute minimum of impurities such as sulfur, iron oxide, or shale. Few coal seams could meet these requirements. The Pittsburgh seam, being 57–65 percent fixed carbon content, 30–35 percent volatile matter, 4–14 percent ash, and less than 1 percent sulfur produced an excellent coking coal; in addition, with its high reserve, it assured a supply of fuel for an indefinite period of time.

Although western Pennsylvania possessed a well-developed iron industry based on charcoal and local iron ore when the Bessemer converter was introduced, the local supply of iron ore was inadequate for the large furnace. As a result, iron ore had to be secured outside the local area. The nearest major reserve was in the Lake Superior region. This source of ore was made available with the construction of the Sault Sainte Marie canal in 1855. Production began in the Marquette range and was followed in the Menominee in 1877, the Vermilion and Gogebic in 1884, and the Mesabi—the largest of the ranges—in 1892. The Lake Superior region owed its importance in iron ore production to the abundance, high quality, ease of mining, and low-cost transportation of the ore, which was shipped by lake freighters to the lower-lake ports.

YOUNGSTOWN–WHEELING–JOHNSTOWN   METALLURGICAL TRIANGLE.   In the late nineteenth century the greatest iron and steel region in the world developed in the industrial zone outlined by the cities of Youngstown, Wheeling, and Johnstown. The Pittsburgh District in the heart of the area was the first center and long dominated the industry. However, a single district could not satisfy the rising demands, and three nearby areas—Johnstown, the Mahoning and Shenango Valleys, and Steubenville–Wheeling—developed as heavy metallurgical centers. This region, with its mammoth industrial concentration in the river valleys, became, like Germany's Ruhr, a citadel of heavy industry. Pittsburgh is so closely associated with the iron and steel industry that most think of the city as the steel capital of the world.

Pittsburgh District.   The development of the Pittsburgh District as the nation's principal iron and steel center in the late nineteenth century was primarily due to its strategic position in the assembly of Lake Superior iron ores and

Pittsburgh seam coal from the Connellsville-Uniontown coke area. For the processing of the iron ore, the integrated iron and steel industry developed at the place of greatest advantage in transportation for the assemblage of raw materials and marketing of the finished products. This location was along the valleys of the Monongahela, Ohio, and Allegheny rivers, which provided the low-level routes through the district. Because it required two tons of coal to smelt one ton of iron ore, the Monongahela Valley, lying nearest the coalfields, developed the greatest concentration of iron and steel furnaces.

In the 1870s and 1880s the Pittsburgh District became the metallurgical heart of the nation. As the district's iron and steel industry grew in importance, new industries that depended on steel migrated to the area, not only to be near this basic raw material but also to save in freight charges on the transportation of the crude steel. The iron and steel industry and associated functions occupied most of the level land in the valleys. Scores of blast furnaces and associated rolling mills belched smoke into the congested valleys, and Pittsburgh became known not only as the "Steel City" but also as the "Smoky City." The industrial landscape was particularly striking at night, when the Bessemer converters lit the sky with their radiance. Thousands of immigrants crowded into the narrow valleys until scarcely a square foot of space remained. Here developed the ultimate example of a heavy metallurgical region.

Although the modern iron and steel industry developed in this district nearly a century ago, the original factors that localized it are still present. Its relative share of the nation's iron and steel output has declined with the development of new areas, but it has maintained its nationwide market. Possibly the most significant trend in the district's iron and steel industry has been the growing emphasis placed on the production of specialty stainless steels and other steel alloys. The iron and steel industry in the Pittsburgh District, as the cotton textile and leather industries of New England, is combating the rise of new, competitive steel areas by applying acquired skills toward producing quality steel. In this manner the Pittsburgh District remains a dynamic steel-producing center.

Mahoning and Shenango Valleys. The evolution of the iron and steel industry in these valleys was similar to that of the Pittsburgh District. The industry evolved through a series of stages from the use of local fuels and raw materials to the assemblage of raw materials from distant sources and the growth of interregional markets. Although the transportation cost for coke from the Connellsville area was higher here than for the plants in the Monangahela Valley, the delivery cost of Lake Superior ore was lower. Today a steel industry, centered in Youngstown and Canton, dominates all other phases of economic activity. Of all the steel centers in the United States, Youngstown has the greatest concentration in steel production. The primary phases of the steel industry predominate—including the output of sheets, strips, structural shapes, rails, and bars—rather than the production of finished steel products. The production of primary steel employs about 50 percent of the workers in the Mahoning and Shenango valleys, whereas in the Pittsburgh District only about 40 percent of the workers are in basic steel. The economic well-being of the district depends on the quantity of steel produced.

The local market absorbs only a small percentage of the steel production. Therefore the area depends on a national market. About two-thirds of the steel is sold in Ohio, Michigan, and Pennsylvania, but one-third must seek more distant markets. The largest single user of the valleys' steel is the automobile industry in Michigan. Fortunately, large regional markets are nearby so freight costs on crude steel are relatively low.

Wheeling–Steubenville District.   Within this district, the first iron mill was constructed in 1832 at Wheeling, West Virginia, on the Ohio River. The city possessed two advantages for the growth of the industry. There was an abundant supply of coal in the local area, and because it was the reliable head of navigation on the Ohio, it had access to the western markets. Wooden buildings were in vogue in the nineteenth century, so that nails were in great demand. Wheeling, by using the latest techniques in iron making and by producing a better cut nail, soon became the nail capital of the nation. However, by the end of the century the wire nail came into use. Wheeling nail producers failed to comprehend the importance of the new nail and between 1885 and 1900 lost most of their nail market. After 1900 Weirton, West Virginia, and Steubenville, Ohio, emphasized the production of such primary steel products as bars, sheets, pipes, and tin plates. These two centers, which have specialized, grew rapidly in importance as Wheeling's position declined. In the early 1950s Wheeling disappeared as a steel-producing center.

Johnstown.   The Johnstown District lies to the east of Pittsburgh in the valley of the Conemaugh River. The city gained its first impetus as an iron manufacturing center because it was at the head of the western branch of the Pennsylvania Canal. Johnstown has become a miniature Pittsburgh. It is basically a one-industry town, dominated by the Bethlehem Steel Corporation, whose plants—strung along the narrow valley—occupy more space than all other manufacturing combined. This congested valley presents a striking picture of intensive industrial use. In 1974 the plant operations were threatened by environmental pollution; this problem must be solved if the industry is to have a secure future. The steel plants are aligned in the center of the valley, and residential areas cluster around the huge buildings. It is a typical nineteenth-century city, having been constructed when transportation was poor and workers were forced to live near the plants. In only a few places has the city been able to climb to the plateau, where there are beautiful homes and spacious shaded lawns. The fresh environment of these upland residential suburbs is in striking contrast to the smoke pall that fills the valleys and begrimes the workers' homes.

Importance of Valley Localization.   One of the significant aspects of the localization of the iron and steel industry in this triangle is its concentration in the river valleys. These valleys possess many advantages for the establishment of a heavy metallurgical industry. Fundamental to the successful operations of the iron and steel industry is the opportunity to have uninterrupted assemblage of the bulky raw materials and to move the new crude steel to its market without delay. Railways hug the riverbanks that have the least grade for the movement of the heavy materials. The rivers provide the lowest-cost transportation in the region.

Coal, coke, and limestone are transported by barge from the mines and quarries to the steel plants, and increasing tonnages of steel are shipped by inland water routes from the Pittsburgh area to cities on the Mississippi River system and to the Gulf Coast. The movement of raw materials and iron and steel industry products makes the traffic on the Monongahela River the heaviest of all rivers in the United States.

Because of the tremendous consumption of soft water in the iron and steel plants for cooling and other industrial purposes, the riverside location of the plants is of considerable value. There is an adequate supply of water at a reasonable cost. It would be impossible to supply the water requirements of the steel industry in this region from underground wells. But a pollution problem has developed because of phenol and acids that enter the rivers from coal mines, by-products from coke ovens, and from the mills themselves. As a result the most critical water problem in Pennsylvania is in the Pittsburgh area.

Although the river valleys have proved the most desirable location for the iron and steel industry, there are a number of disadvantages. The massive plants require a large amount of space. Thus the narrow ribbons of land along the rivers are congested and make expansion difficult. Some of the plants are dispersed because of lack of space. A number of plants have been forced to establish branches in various portions of the valley, or have migrated to small islands in the rivers, such as Neville Island near Pittsburgh. In a number of places, such as Carnegie, Etna, Monessen, and Aliquippa, the giant works are located near the center of the city, creating problems of congestion, dirt, and grime. Another serious problem is floods. Flood stages obviously present problems to mills lining the banks of the rivers. Because it is not feasible to discontinue operations during high water, the mills must be assured of water during flood stages. To partially solve this problem most companies have constructed massive caisson-type intakes, placing horizontal pumps at the bottom and projecting the walls above maximum flood stage. Regardless of these disadvantages, the importance of transportation and available water outweighs the negative factors of inadequate space, water pollution, and floods.

Dominance of the Youngstown–Wheeling–Johnstown Triangle. In the period between the Civil War and World War I, this metallurgical triangle grew to be the major iron and steel region in the United States. In 1914, at the peak of its dominance, it was producing about $674,000,000 of iron and steel out of a total of $918,664,000 in the United States, or about 70 percent of the nation's total.

The rise to dominance was due to a number of factors. Of primary consideration was the limited number of coal seams in the United States that could be utilized in the beehive coking process. The Pittsburgh coal seam was the only one in the northern Appalachians that had sufficient reserves to supply coke to the dynamically growing iron and steel industry. This is a supreme example of the orientation of the iron and steel industry in the nineteenth century to a coal source.

As the markets for iron and steel became more widely dispersed, there was a growing demand for new centers of production. However, economic policies were initiated to discourage competition. The most important of these was the institution of a controlled freight-rate system known as "Pittsburgh Plus." Its primary purpose was to stabilize the industry in the region by discouraging competition. The policy operated in this manner: If a Kansas City, Missouri, buyer purchased steel from a Gary, Indiana, plant, he paid the f.o.b. Pittsburgh price and also the freight rate (the "plus") that would have been assessed against shipment from a Pittsburgh mill. In 1900 the cost of producing iron and steel was lower in the Pittsburgh region than anywhere else in the country. However, shortly after 1900 the cost of producing iron and steel in a number of places, notably Chicago, fell below that of Pittsburgh. As a result of this system of freight charges, Pittsburgh was given a tremendous competitive advantage over all other regions.

A number of other factors were important in making this region dominant. The transportation system was one of the best developed in the nation, giving it access to a national market. The industry of the region was directed by a group of aggressive industrial and financial giants. Of them, the Pittsburgh steel industry owes the most to the organizing capacity of Andrew Carnegie. He entered the iron and steel business in 1863, and within a few years he merged a number of small companies into the Carnegie Steel Company. In the succeeding decades he built blast furnaces to supply his steelworks, gained control of the largest coke company in the Connellsville area, and controlled a large share of the Lake Superior ores to ensure a steady flow of ore to his mills. He also owned or controlled steel fabricating plants to secure a guaranteed market for his basic steel. When Carnegie retired in 1903, his company became the nucleus for the United States Steel Corporation. For many years he dominated the entire economic structure of Pittsburgh and was respected as the steel magnate throughout the world.

DECENTRALIZATION OF THE IRON AND STEEL INDUSTRY. Since early in the twentieth century several forces have favored the decentralization of the U.S. iron and steel industry. Possibly the most important of these was the country's mammoth economic growth. The market had increased so greatly that it was no longer feasible to supply the demand for iron and steel from a single region. New important industrial centers required nearby sources of iron and steel.

As the nationwide market was developing, an important technological advance aided the decentralization of the steel industry. Until about 1910, coke for the steel industry was made mostly by the beehive process. Between 1910 and 1925 the wasteful beehive process was largely replaced by the by-product coke oven. In the beehive coke oven, the only product was about 1,000 lb of coke per ton of coal. In the by-product oven, the yield was about 1,200 lb of coke, plus 10,500 ft^3 of gas, 7.1 gal of tar, 2.4 gal of oil, 20–25 lb of ammonium sulfate, 5–6 lb of liquid ammonia, and a little toluol.

Since 1930 beehive ovens have been important producers of coke only during periods of national emergency when by-product ovens could not supply the demands. The by-product ovens had a number of advantages over the older beehive process. They not only saved the valuable coal tars and gases but made possible a wider distribution of the coke industry. A much greater range of coals could be used, and the fuel supply was no longer so geographically restricted. Because the gases from by-product ovens were utilized to preheat the furnaces as well as the plant, these ovens were developed at iron and steel plant sites instead of mine sites, as were the beehive ovens. It thus became advantageous to transport coal to many market-oriented iron and steel plants.

Other factors also encouraged decentralization. Among these were the alterations of the preferential freight rate structure. With the rapid growth of the industry, particularly during World War I, it was no longer possible to maintain the artificial freight-rate structure imposed by the Pittsburgh Plus system, and this freight rate was declared illegal by the U.S. Supreme Court in 1924. In its place the multiple basing-point system of determining freight rates was instituted. This was a modification of the Pittsburgh Plus system in that, instead of using a single point to determine the price for transporting iron and steel to the national market, a number of centers were established (e.g., Chicago and Birmingham) to serve as regional basing points for freight rates. As a result, prices for iron and steel were quoted in terms of the nearest basing point—called the "government basing point"—plus the appropriate charges for transportation and extras. This in reality established a system of regions in which a plant or group of plants had a competitive freight advantage.

Both the single and multiple basing-point systems were sources of considerable controversy. The major criticism was that the basing-point system provided the basis for geographic price discrimination because it eliminated regional price competition. After 24 years of operation, the iron and steel industry abandoned the basing point system when, in July 1948, the U.S. Supreme Court declared it illegal. Since 1948 the price of steel at any destination has been determined by the f.o.b.-mill pricing policy. This system is based on the price of the steel plus freight charges from the point of origin to the point of destination. As a result of the changed freight structure, a number of companies have built plants in new areas to compete in the steel market. A notable example of this trend is the development by the United States Steel Corporation and the Bethlehem Steel Company of iron and steel facilities on the Atlantic Coast.

Changing sources of raw materials have also affected the location of the iron and steel industry. Although the original reserve of high-grade iron ore in the Lake Superior ore ranges was enormous, huge demands for more than three-quarters of a century have reduced the supply of high-grade ore, so much so that the industry is beginning to face a depletion problem. The iron and steel industry has recognized that Lake Superior ores are exhaustible and that new sources must be sought in such countries as Canada, Venezuela, and Brazil. Because these ores enter the United States through port cities, there has been a growing tendency to develop iron and steel plants at such port sites as Baltimore, Philadelphia, and Houston.

Governmental policies have also encouraged the decentralization of the

American iron and steel industry. Iron and steel plants have been constructed in strategic locations under government subsidies during national emergencies. For example, the Fontana plant east of Los Angeles was built by the government during World War II to supply steel to West Coast shipyards and other war plants.

COMPARATIVE CHANGE, 1947–1969.   Between 1947 and 1969 the U.S. production of steel increased from 84.78 million tons to 141.24 million tons, an increase of 66.59 percent. Within the United States, 9 of the 11 districts delimited by the American Iron and Steel Institute (AISI) experienced a comparative growth, while two districts experienced a comparative decline (Fig. 3.1). The Pittsburgh District, with a comparative decline of 10.17 million tons, had 60.1 percent of the total comparative decline. Youngstown, with a comparative decline of 6.75 million tons, had the remaining 39.9 percent.

The comparative growth was more evenly distributed than the comparative decline. The comparative growth ranged from 4.83 million tons in Detroit to 800,000 tons in Chicago. Thus the oldest areas were experiencing a comparative decline while the newer areas were experiencing the highest comparative increases. The districts that were able to introduce the basic oxygen furnaces had the largest comparative growth.

The AISI has not released production figures since 1969 for iron and steel producing districts, but general statistical evidence indicates that the pattern of production has not been significantly altered in the 1970s.

LOCALIZATION OF THE INDUSTRY.   U.S. steel production is concentrated in six regions. The Lower Great Lakes region, made up of the AISI districts of Chicago, Detroit, Buffalo, and Cleveland, produced about 38 percent of the nation's steel in 1969. In 1947 this area produced about one-third of the country's steel. The Chicago District has maintained a nearly constant relative position by producing about 20 percent of the country's total. Partly as a result of the decline of the importance of the Pittsburgh District, Chicago became the nation's leading steel-producing district in 1960 and has maintained a small lead since then. Detroit's share has increased from 3.7 percent to slightly over 7 percent of the total. The Cleveland and Buffalo districts each produce about 5 percent of the nation's steel.

The Pittsburgh–Youngstown region, composed of the two districts of Pittsburgh and Youngstown, in 1969 produced nearly 28 percent of the steel output. These districts have, however, experienced a long and steady relative decline. In 1947 this region produced 39.5 percent of the nation's steel. The Pittsburgh District has declined from 26.3 to 19.1 percent of the total. The Youngstown District has also experienced a pronounced decline, going from 13.2 to 8.4 percent of the total.

The Northeast Coast has increased its relative position from 12 to nearly 14 percent of the total. Actual production increased from 10.3 million tons to over 19.3 million tons. The inland Midwest, composed of the St. Louis and Cincinnati districts, produced 4.9 percent of the nation's steel in 1947, but increased its share to over 7 percent in 1969. The Western District increased its share from

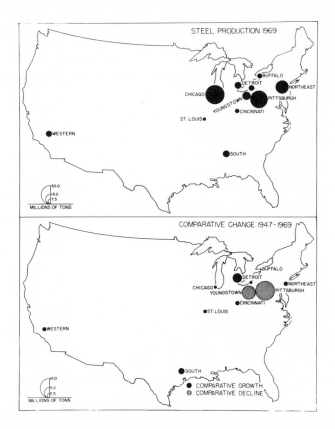

Figure 3.1. Comparative change of iron and steel production in the United States, 1947–1969.

5.1 in 1947 to 6.5 percent in recent years. The Southern District has also increased its proportion from 4.7 to 5.9 percent of the total.

ALUMINUM INDUSTRY

Aluminum production began in the late nineteenth century with the discovery of the electrolytic process of extracting the metal from bauxite. For decades, however, production was limited to a few countries. As late as 1940 seven countries—Germany, the United States, the United Kingdom, the Soviet Union, France, Italy, and Japan—produced about 82 percent of the world's aluminum. Germany, the largest producer in 1939, had an output of only 240,000 tons—about 30 percent of the world's total.

As a response to the demand for the light metal, primarily in the aircraft industry, output in nearly all producing countries increased in the early war period. Subsequent wartime destruction by military action, sabotage, and economic curtailment reduced plant capacities in Germany, Hungary, the Soviet Union, Norway, Italy, and to a lesser extent France. The United States and Canada emerged during the war as the great aluminum-producing nations. In the period from 1940 to 1945, these two nations increased their proportion of world output from 33 to about 70 percent of total ingot capacity.

Although aluminum production was stable for a few years after World War II, every producing country has had a rise since 1950. The total output has risen from 1,480,000 tons in 1950 to 4,950,000 tons in 1960 to over 12,000,000 tons in recent years. Aluminum production is located in at least 37 nations and has become particularly important in highly industrialized countries and where low-cost hydroelectric power is found. The largest producers are the United States, the Soviet Union, Japan, and Canada—with about 63 percent of the world's primary output. Europe produces about 25 percent of the world total; Norway, West Germany, and France are the leading producers. Australia has developed an important production in recent years. A number of the developing nations, such as India and Ghana, are developing an aluminum industry.

The pattern of aluminum production has undergone rapid change, and it cannot be assumed that the present-day pattern will provide the model for the localization of the industry in the future. The prospect that between 1975 and 1985 the industry will more than double its production offers wide opportunities for a new locational pattern to evolve.

Theory and Location

The aluminum industry, from its earliest period, has been influenced by the Weberian concept in seeking the least cost point of production. Because energy costs have dominated all other factors, they have dominated the industry's location. When a single locational factor dominates, it is relatively easy to determine empirically where the lowest-cost production areas are to be found.

Although with increasing national and world markets the type of energy consumed has been altered, largely because of available supply at a particular plant, new sites have always sought the lowest-cost energy. The changes in the pattern of production in the United States illustrate the continuous quest for the least cost area. For example, three new regions of aluminum production—the Northwest, Gulf Coast, and Ohio Valley—have developed since 1940 in the United States. As each region initiated production, it was located at the lowest-cost area in order to supply a rising demand. Although rising demand has maintained most of the earliest aluminum-producing areas, the earliest center of production (Niagara Falls) and the high-cost centers built during World War II have disappeared. These production points did not fall within the profitability range imposed by the industry's ceaseless search for a least cost point. There is essentially no evidence that the market theory of maximum profit or the concepts of general equilibrium theory, such as industrial concentrations, have played a role in the localization of the aluminum industry.

Locational Factors

There are three basic procedures in the production of aluminum: (1) the mining of bauxite, (2) its conversion into alumina, and (3) the production of aluminum from alumina. Because each of these steps entails a cost consideration, each is discussed individually in regard to the factors affecting localization.

MINING AND BAUXITE-PROCESSING PLANTS. The production costs in mining bauxite vary considerably depending on such factors as location, technology, geology, and transportation. Most bauxite operations in tropical countries are on a scale of production of at least 300,000 tons per year and are highly mechanized. This scale is usually considered necessary to achieve an economic mining operation in a remote location where all facilities, such as electric power, transportation, and housing, have to be provided and amortized by the mining company. In countries where such facilities are readily available, the mining operations can be considerably smaller.

The scale of operation is important in affecting production costs because substantial economies of scale are possible in bauxite mining. The initial cost for fixed investment includes stripping equipment, internal transport, crushers, drying kilns, warehouses, port facilities, and housing. Data available indicate that fixed equipment costs vary considerably. To illustrate, the cost per ton of capacity in the late 1960s was over 40 percent higher in Jamaica than in Ghana. At both sites the costs included, in addition to mining and drying equipment, the cost of buildings, storage facilities, piers, docks, and transportation. Variations in costs are primarily due to differences in accessibility, geologic aspects of the deposits, and labor cost differentials.

Geologic conditions affect mining costs directly. The amount and nature of the overburden are of primary consideration. Overburden up to 150 feet thick is removed in some bauxite mining operations. Dry, sandy overburden is cheaper to remove than wet, clayey overburden covered by dense vegetation. The overburden that can be removed depends directly on the quality of the bauxite. In general, for a high-grade bauxite, the economic limit is usually 5–8 times the amount of bauxite recovered.

Other direct costs may also be associated with the mining operation. The hardness of the bauxite will affect the cost of grinding, and the moisture content will affect the cost of drying. Additional costs are added if beneficiation is required. Some bauxites require washing and classification to remove clay and excessive silica. In certain countries there is also the cost of restoring the mined area so that other economic activities can be resumed.

Although bauxite mining is highly mechanized, labor costs cannot be ignored. With an increase in scale of production, labor costs decrease. Further, open-pit mining offers possibilities for labor-capital substitution. In a Ghana project labor requirements are estimated to decrease by 50 percent, from 3.1 to

1.6 man-hours per ton, with an increase in output to 2 1/2 times (from 400,000 tons to 1,000,000 tons annually). Labor requirements vary considerably. In Ghana one mine with an output of 1,360,000 tons of bauxite has an estimated labor requirement of 3.5 man-hours per ton of bauxite. In the United States the labor requirements of 0.54 man-hour per ton of bauxite indicate greater mechanization. Because of the need for a regular flow of bauxite to aluminum plants, there is a need for labor-saving techniques when labor costs are high in order to secure large-scale and efficient operations. Bauxite is becoming highly competitive on the international market, so the lowest-cost operations must be maintained.

Fuel is an additional cost in preparing the bauxite at the mine. The amount of fuel needed depends on the water in the ore. Crude bauxite may contain 5–30 percent water. If the bauxite is converted to alumina at the mine, it may not have to be dried. The fuel requirements, when drying is necessary, will vary not only with the moisture content, but also with the size and design of the drying kiln. For drying bauxite with a high moisture content, between 1,000,000 and 1,100,000 Btu's per ton of ore are usually required. Eight to 10 times this amount of fuel is needed for calcining bauxite (removing chemically combined water) for use by the abrasive industry. Natural gas or heavy oil rather than coal is used as fuel to avoid contaminating the bauxite with ash.

Other production costs in mining are power and explosives. Electric power is needed for grinding bauxite to a desired size and thus varies with the hardness of the ore. The ore can range from a friable deposit, as in Jamaica, to a hard rock, as in Greece. In the United States the demand for electric power varies from 3.8–5.5 kwh per ton of ore processed. In most of the open-pit operations, the ore must be blasted with low-strength dynamite to loosen the bauxite. This is usually a small, but persistent, cost.

Because bauxite is relatively low valued and bulky, transportation costs are of prime importance. In Jamaica, Surinam, Guyana, Greece, and Australia, the developed deposits are on the coast or a navigable waterway. In Europe, where distances are shorter, bauxite is shipped by rail from southern France, Yugo-slavia, and Hungary. When bauxite deposits are far into the interior, the ore is frequently processed into alumina to raise its value by reducing its bulk and thus lowering transportation charges. The cost of transporting bauxite has decreased rapidly with the use of very large ore ships. The larger vessels, however, require deep-water docks for loading and unloading. Sometimes larger ships are used to export the bauxite to major ports, and then the bauxite is loaded onto barges for shipment to the processing plants.

Because the bauxite is mined and processed exclusively by the international aluminum companies, and no uniform system has been devised to report costs, it is possible only to estimate the cost range of bauxite delivered to alumina plants. Until 1953 all bauxite was processed in alumina plants located in the aluminum companies' home country. Since then the bauxite processing has developed near the mine in those countries where conditions are economically and politically satisfactory. Consequently sizable savings can be secured in the shipping costs of bauxite. The lowest costs are for bauxite processed near the mine, and the higher costs involve the transportation of bauxite great distances. The shipping costs will depend on the distance shipped, the size of the vessel, the quantity shipped, and the terms of the shipping contract.

ALUMINA PLANTS. The principal factors affecting the location of alumina plants are the capital costs of plant construction in relation to cost per ton of output, the costs of converting the bauxite into alumina, and the transportation charges on the bauxite from the mine and, if necessary, on the alumina to the reduction plant. Most of the output of alumina is used in the production of aluminum. The remainder is used in producing abrasives and in the chemical industries. The Bayer process is the only economically feasible process, but some variations have been developed to process low-grade ores. The Bayer process is the conventional process in processing bauxite containing less than 10 percent silica. There are two principal variations: The American Bayer process is used in treating trihydrate bauxite, and the European Bayer process treats monohydrate bauxite. The basic differences between these two are that the latter uses a greater concentration of caustic soda, a higher digestion temperature, and a longer digestion period.

Fixed Investment. [1] The fixed investment of an alumina plant varies considerably depending on capacity. Economies of scale are significant with increasing capacity. At the present time 330,000 tons per year is the optimum size for a single plant. A larger plant will consist of two or more parallel production units.

Investment will also vary with the process that is used. The European Bayer process requires an investment between 10 and 15 percent higher than the American Bayer process; the combination of these processes requires an additional investment of between 20 and 30 percent, depending on the quality of the bauxite treated.

Production Costs. Production costs will also vary with the size of the plant. A 330,000-ton-capacity alumina plant will have production costs between 25 and 30 percent lower than a 60,000-ton-capacity plant. In the larger plants, economies of scale are achieved in labor, electric power, capital costs, miscellaneous supplies, and general expenses.

Labor requirements per ton of alumina produced vary with the process used, with the size of the plant, and with local labor costs. Plants using the European Bayer process and those treating low-grade ores require between 20 and 40 percent more labor than do comparable plants using the American Bayer process. In the United States, the cost of producing alumina is reduced by one-half when the size of the plant is increased from a capacity of 60,000 to 330,000 tons. An alumina plant using the American process and having a capacity of 60,000 tons has a cost of approximately $15.00 per ton of alumina produced. When the annual capacity of the alumina plant is increased to 330,000 tons, the labor costs are reduced to $7.50 per ton. If the alumina plant is integrated with a mining operation or reduction plant, labor costs may be lowered due to sharing

[1]*Pre-investment Data for the Aluminum Industry* (New York: United Nations, Studies in Economics of Industry, 1966) pp. 6–9.

maintenance and other direct expenses. In contrast, an alumina plant in an isolated location may require considerably more labor. However, in a developing tropical country, higher labor inputs of a lower cost may replace capital to some degree. Consequently low-cost labor may provide some inducement to attract a maximum-sized alumina plant to a tropical country that produces bauxite.

The power consumption in an alumina plant also depends on its size. A 330,000-ton-capacity plant will have power costs about one-third lower than that of a 60,000-ton-capacity plant. Power consumption also depends on the hardness of the bauxite used. Large quantities of energy are required to grind hard bauxite.

Capital costs are lowered with increasing plant size. The depreciation on fixed capital will decline about 40 percent per ton of alumina produced in plants ranging from an annual capacity of 60,000–300,000 tons. In the same situation, interest on fixed capital will likewise decline by about 40 percent per ton of alumina produced. Miscellaneous supplies of general expenses will also show a similar decline.

Other input costs in an alumina plant include bauxite, caustic soda, steam, fuel for calcination, and materials and equipment maintenance. These inputs may vary. The amount of bauxite needed in alumina production depends on the quality of the bauxite, and the amount of extractable alumina may be estimated from the alumina and silica content of the ore. The silica causes alumina to be lost as part of the insoluble residue. The amount lost is approximately equal to the silica content of the bauxite. About 3–4 percent of the bauxite is also lost in the plant process.

In the Bayer process, caustic soda or soda ash in combination with burnt lime is consumed. Certain amounts of caustic soda are needed to replace that lost as insoluble residue in the process of producing alumina. Consumption of caustic soda varies widely, depending primarily on the silica content of the bauxite and, to a lesser extent, on the amount of residue washing. Caustic soda losses are equivalent to approximately 90 percent of the silica content of the bauxite used in the production of alumina.

Fuel input is used mainly for the production of steam and calcination of the alumina. The quantity of heat consumed depends on the efficiency of the heat exchange. A heat exchanger with high efficiency requires additional investment, which has to be weighed against the lower cost of the fuel. Steam consumption per ton of output also decreases with the increase in size of plant and with the higher grades of bauxite. Higher steam consumption is required for treating monohydrate as compared with trihydrate bauxite because of the higher digestion temperature and pressure needed for the former.

Localization. Because of economies of scale in fixed investment and in cost per ton of alumina produced, alumina plants are increasing in size. The production of alumina is thus a capital intensive industry requiring huge investments and companies must be assured that a new plant will be economically feasible. This entails a number of basic considerations in the location of alumina plants. First, an alumina plant can be constructed only where huge reserves of bauxite are available to assure long-term operations. Second, since capital outlays are great, companies will select areas where there is adequate assurance of political and economic stability. If these conditions are met, transportation costs play a dominant role in localizing the alumina plant. Because bauxite and alumina are transported at the same rate, it is necessary to reduce the bulk of the ore at the earliest opportunity. In recent years alumina plants have been attracted to the mining sites. If, however, a country possesses an aluminum industry and must import bauxite, the alumina plant is frequently built at the breaking point of transportation. In recent years the international trade in bauxite has diminished, and the trade in alumina has expanded rapidly.

Changing Locational Pattern of Alumina Production. Alumina production was initially localized in the countries of primary production of aluminum. However, the traditional pattern of alumina production has been greatly altered in the past 15 years, with many of the bauxite-producing nations becoming alumina producers. Alumina plants have been built in such bauxite regions as Guinea, Australia, Surinam, the Virgin Islands, and Greece. These plants illustrate the current trend for alumina plants to be built at bauxite sources to reduce transportation costs. The development of the alumina plant at Alcan, Jamaica, initiated the trend. The international consortium of Olin-Mathieson has built an alumina plant in Guinea. Alcoa has followed this trend with an alumina plant in Surinam, and Kaiser has built a plant in Australia. These developments are partly a response to the shifting development of bauxite production, but also reflect real economic incentives that are sometimes politically motivated.

ALUMINUM REDUCTION. Of the factors affecting the localization of aluminum reduction plants, power costs are most important. Other factors include fixed investment, labor, capital requirements and general expenses, and alumina costs.

Power. The aluminum industry was traditionally oriented to low-cost hydroelectric power resources. About 12 kwh of electricity are consumed in the production of 1 lb of aluminum, an amount sufficient to keep a 40-watt light bulb burning continuously for over 12 days. Thus, next to alumina, the cost of electrical power is the largest item in the cost of aluminum production. In the United States, the cost of power is 20–30 percent of the final price of the metal. This makes the energy cost the most important factor in siting an aluminum reduction plant.

Although power costs do not vary with the size of the plant, there are constant attempts to reduce the total power requirements to produce a ton of aluminum. In the average plant about 60 percent of the electric current is lost in transmission and in the electrolytic cells. It has been found that, with the development of larger-capacity cells and improved electric circuit designs, the amount of electricity can be reduced.

For example, with the expansion of cells in a plant from 26,000 amp to between 42,000 and 52,000 amp, there could be an expected reduction in current from 20,000 kwh to about 18,000 kwh per ton of aluminum produced. Lower direct current consumption figures of 14,500 kwh per ton have been reported for a modern French plant using 100,000-amp cells and an elaborate electric system.

Because larger cells are more expensive, the decreased use of power must be weighed against the increased cost of investment. Thus in countries with large quantities of low-cost power, such as Canada and Norway, it is more economical to use smaller cells and consume greater quantities of electricity. In contrast, countries where electricity is in greater demand, such as Germany, the larger cells become economical.

Power costs vary considerably from country to country and even within a nation. The cost of energy in 1970 for electrosmelting in the United States ranged from 2 mills per kilowatt-hour in the Pacific northwest up to 4.8 mills per kilowatt-hour for the eastern and midwestern reduction plants. The range of power costs in Canada was between 1.5 and 3.5 mills per kilowatt-hour. In Europe and Japan the range was from 1.8 to 8.0 mills per kilowatt-hour.

It is difficult to determine the range in power costs on a world basis, but it is estimated that the energy costs per ton of primary metal varied in 1970 between $34 and $136. The differential of $102 per ton of aluminum represented about 20 percent of the market price of primary aluminum (about $500 per ton).

In isolated regions, new electric power facilities must be built in association with the reduction plants. Investment in electric power facilities is normally high in such regions. For example, investment in hydropower facilities in Ghana have been from 30 to 60 percent higher than in Norway. The additional investment for power facilities may be equal to from one-third to two-thirds of the total plant investment in the developing countries.

Fixed Investment.   The fixed investment in a reduction plant decreases up to a certain size because the costs of several important items of equipment, such as rectifiers and transformers, increase less than proportionally with an increase in capacity. It is believed that the lowest investment per unit of output is achieved with a furnace size of approximately 70,000–80,000 amp. A further increase in furnace size requires an increase in unit plant investment because of the more than proportionate increase in the size of the furnace associated with a given increase in amperage. Also, better ventilation is needed, as is a more complex electric system to counteract the increasingly serious magnetic disturbance.

There is a slight difference in the cost of plants depending on whether they use the prebaked or the Soderberg process. This difference narrows as the size of the plant approaches 100,000 tons per year. Elasticities of investment in respect to plant capacity are 0.72 for the prebaked and 0.80 for the Soderberg process. Using the prebaked process, a 200,000-ton plant will have an investment per ton of from 45 to 50 percent less than that of a 20,000-ton plant.

Capital requirements for identical plants vary considerably from country to country. For example, fixed investment in Norway is higher than in most European countries because of the modifications required in building construction due to rugged terrain and a rigorous climate. Construction must also vary in cold and hot climates. In the cooler climates, it is customary to install two parallel rows of cells arranged end to end; this arrangement allows adequate ventilation. However, in tropical climates, one line of cells arranged end to end is best because of the need for greater ventilation space. This increases the building area and the number of cranes and other facilities that must be constructed, resulting in a high capital investment.

Labor.   Labor requirements vary with the type of reduction plant, the scale of operation, the size of the electrolytic cells, the degree of mechanization, and the differences in performance of individual plants. A greater amount of labor is required in a prebaked plant than in the Soderberg anode system to manufacture and handle the individual anodes. Unit labor requirements decline as plant capacity increases; but the extent of this is rather small because a large part of the labor force is engaged in operations that require repetitive service at the unit level.

Capital-labor substitution is achieved in a reduction plant chiefly in the handling of materials and in auxiliary facilities. However, because of the repetitive nature of the labor requirements, such activities are readily mechanized and automated. A United Nations technical report indicates that the total labor requirement could be reduced from a level of 132 man-hours per ton to 29–38, depending on the size of the cells used. In some newer, highly mechanized plants in the United States and France, the labor requirements have been reduced to 11–14 man-hours per ton of aluminum produced.

A high proportion of the labor required in an aluminum reduction plant must be semiskilled and skilled. As a consequence, securing the necessary type of labor may be a problem in developing countries. The maintenance of mechanized equipment also presents a problem in reduction plants. Further, experience has shown that the operations in a reduction plant are performed by mechanics more efficiently than by hand labor. Consequently, available labor may be a limiting factor in the establishment of reduction plants in some developing countries.

Capital Requirements and General Expenses.   The largest economies of scale in a reduction plant can be secured from lowered capital charges and general expenses as the size of the plant increases. For an American plant, it was estimated in 1970 that the fixed investment for a 20,000-ton-capacity plant was $19,600,000; for a 100,000-ton plant, it was only $72,000,000. The depreciation costs per ton of output for a 20,000-ton plant were about $72, but decreased to $53 in a 100,000-ton plant. Likewise, interest on fixed capital declined from $53 to $38 per ton of output. The miscellaneous and general expenses also declined from $50 to $38 per ton of output.

Alumina.   Alumina consumption per ton of output does not vary with the scale of operations. Approximately 1.91–1.95 lbs of alumina are required for each pound of aluminum produced. The cost per ton of alumina varies between $45 and $70 depending on whether the primary aluminum producer is a fully integrated company or whether the alumina must be secured from an alumina producer. The cost of alumina will thus range from $86 to $134 per ton of primary metal produced.

Other Inputs.   Other inputs include cryolite and carbon. Fluorides are used in the form of cryolite. Engineering estimates for fluoride consumption are given at 25 kg and 35 kg per ton of output for prebaking and Soderberg plants respectively. Because fluorides are expensive, they are partly recovered in some plants from the gases and from used cathode linings. About 1/2 ton of carbon electrodes is consumed in the production of 1 ton of the metal. Consumption of anode carbon in the form of petroleum coke does not depend on scale of operation, but rather on the quality of the raw material, the manner of manufacturing the carbon paste, and the pot-room operating practice.

Total Production Costs. As a result of economies of scale, the total production costs for producing a ton of aluminum decline with an increase in size of the reduction plant. For a hypothetical U.S. plant of 20,000 tons annual capacity, the cost per ton of aluminum was about $502 in 1970. If the plant capacity were increased to 100,000 tons, the cost per ton of aluminum would decline to $450. Smaller plants exist within nations where the market is limited. By contrast, if a plant is required to compete on the international market, increased size is desired to lower the production costs.

Geographic Cost Differentials. The capital requirements for a reduction plant vary considerably depending on local economic conditions. In the developing nations, plant costs are usually high because most of the equipment must be imported. In addition domestic markets are small, so plants will be small and unable to take advantage of economies of scale unless an export market is secured. To offset these high costs, labor costs are usually lower, as are those for raw materials and electricity. Thus a country that possesses bauxite or hydroelectric power reserves may establish an industry even when the domestic market is limited. Because reduction plant capacity is characterized by relative divisibility, a small plant may be enlarged as the market expands. In plants producing for the international market, economies of scale favor large-scale operations. Because low-cost power is essential to remain competitive, an even more important factor favoring large-scale operations may be the economies of scale obtained in the generation of hydropower.

Localization. Because of economies of scale and variations of costs for such factors as power and capital requirements between regions, the aluminum reduction plants are localized where they can take advantage of cost reductions. It does not appear that a small plant can be economically developed. Most significantly, aluminum reduction plants are localized in regions where the lowest-cost electric power can be obtained.

United States

EARLY LOCALIZATION. The first aluminum reduction plant in the United States was constructed by the Aluminum Company of America (Alcoa) at Pittsburgh in 1888; but it was soon moved 30 miles north to New Kensington on the Allegheny River. The high cost of electrical energy in this area caused the reduction plant to be dismantled and moved to Niagara Falls in 1895. As the demand for aluminum grew, this reduction plant was expanded and new sites were developed. The Massena, New York, plant on the St. Lawrence River was constructed in 1903. In 1914 a reduction plant was completed at Alcoa, Tennessee, on the Little Tennessee River, and two years later the Badin, North Carolina, plant was built on the Yadkin River. These sites were chosen because there was little or no competition for the great quantities of available hydroelectric power. These hydroelectric sites were developed by the Aluminum Company of America. No other reduction plants were built in the United States until the World War II period. There was a slow but steady increase in the production of aluminum, from nearly 70,000 tons in 1920 to 187,000 in 1939.

Prior to 1902 the alumina consumed in the industry was imported, but in that year Alcoa built its East Saint Louis plant. This plant remained the single source of alumina in the United States until 1938. East Saint Louis is situated between the bauxite of Arkansas and the reduction plants of the East. The plant was oriented to the low-cost coal from the Illinois fields. It was also well situated for supplying the midwestern industrial markets with alumina outside the metallurgical industry. Bauxite was also obtained from South America by way of New Orleans and the Mississippi River. In 1938 Alcoa built its second alumina plant at Mobile, Alabama. This plant was in an excellent position to process Caribbean ores at a break in transportation after they entered this country. The alumina was then shipped northward to the reduction plants in Tennessee and North Carolina.

WORLD WAR II EXPANSION. Consumption was unprecedented during World War II, particularly because of the enormous production of aircraft, for which aluminum is the principal material. Aluminum was the first metal placed under priority ruling during the war, but production increased so rapidly that it was also the first metal freed from priority control.

The tremendous growth was accompanied by an expansion of facilities by private capital and the development of vast government projects. Alcoa expanded its existing facilities and in 1941 built the first aluminum reduction plant on the northwest Pacific Coast, at Vancouver, Washington. By 1942 the annual capacity of Alcoa's plants was approximately 400,000 tons. Although this company was the sole producer of primary aluminum until 1941, the Reynolds Metal Company, originally engaged in fabrication only, became a producer of the metal that year. This company built an alumina and reduction plant at Listerhill, Alabama, and also erected a reduction plant at Longview, Washington. These plants were oriented to hydroelectric power resources.

Because private companies did not expand the industry sufficiently, the U.S. government became a large producer of the metal. It erected two alumina plants, one at Hurricane Creek, Arkansas, near the domestic bauxite deposits, and the other at Baton Rouge, Louisiana, to process Guiana ore. The annual capacity of the Arkansas plant was 778,000 tons and that of the Louisiana plant was 500,000. Both plants were operated during the war by Alcoa. Between 1941 and 1943 the government also built nine additional reduction plants, eight of them leased and operated by Alcoa and one by the Olin Corporation. These plants were located at Maspeth (Queens, Long Island) and Massena, New York; Jones Mills, Arkansas; Los Angeles and Modesto (Riverbank), California; Troutdale, Oregon; Burlington, New Jersey; and Mead (Spokane) and Tacoma, Washington. These nine government plants, with a combined capacity of over 635,000 tons annualy, were sometimes located where excess electricity existed, although it was sometimes high in cost. As a result of the expansion by private companies and the erection of government plants, aluminum production trebled between 1941 and 1943, when 920,000 tons were produced.

At the conclusion of hostilities the government's Defense Corporation plants were declared surplus, and the most economical plants were sold to private companies (7). Under the terms of the Surplus Property Act and the rulings of the attorney general, Alcoa was prohibited from acquiring any of the surplus government plants that would tend to perpetuate its adjudged monopoly (19). The alumina plant at Hurricane Creek was sold to the Reynolds Metal Company, and the Baton Rouge plant was sold to the Kaiser Aluminum and Chemical Corporation, a newcomer in the industry. Of the reduction plants, the Trout-dale, Massena, and Jones Mills works were purchased by the Reynolds Metal Company, and the Mead (Spokane) and Tacoma plants were sold to the Kaiser Aluminum and Chemical Corporation. The high-cost plants at Los Angeles, Modesto, Maspeth, and Burlington were dismantled.

RECENT LOCALIZATION TRENDS.   For a few years after World War II, U.S. capacity was sufficient to meet demands. However, by 1950 it became evident that a large expansion in production facilities was required to meet the growing metal market (7). Requirements for civilian consumption were increasing steadily, and military needs rose sharply because of the Korean hostilities. The enactment of the 1950 Defense Production Act enabled the government to offer the following incentives to the aluminum industry for expanding production: "certificates of necessity" that allowed accelerated amortization for tax purposes, government guaranteed loans, subsidies to offset excess power costs, and a guaranteed market for metal produced from new facilities.

The major problem of the aluminum industry's expansion in the 1950s was that of securing adequate low-cost power. The traditional regions of low-cost hydroelectric power in the southern Appalachians and in the Northwest were able to offer only a few new sites. Three new plants were oriented to hydroelectric power sources. Two of these were in the Northwest, at Wenatchee, Washington, and The Dalles, Oregon; the third was situated at Columbia Falls, Montana. These plants have a combined capacity of 295,000 tons per year.

By the early 1950s the demand for hydroelectric power for industrial and commercial uses increased rapidly in the Northwest. Political controversies over water utilization policies that restricted growth also developed. As a result power sources other than hydroelectric were sought. The largest potential source of untapped power available in the early 1950s was the natural gas of the Southwest. This energy source could be used directly for operating gas-diesel engines and for generating steam for turbine-driven generators. To utilize this source of energy, two plants were built in Texas, in Point Comfort and San Patricio; one was built in Chalmette, Louisiana; and one was built in Arkadelphia, Arkansas. Another plant was constructed at Rockdale, Texas, to utilize lignite as its power source. These plants in 1975 had a combined capacity of about 900,000 tons of aluminum annually. To provide alumina for the expanding industry, new alumina plants were built at Bauxite, Arkansas, to process domestic ore and at Point Comfort and La Quinta, Texas, to process Caribbean ores imported primarily from Jamaica and the Guianas.

Another localization trend became evident in the aluminum industry in the middle 1950s. Until this time the industry had been concerned primarily with production costs. The distribution costs and the market had been relegated to secondary consideration. With the growth of the industry in the Ohio Valley, the market became greater in importance as a localizing factor. In 1956 the Ormet Corporation began construction of the first plant in the area—at Hannibal, Ohio. The Kaiser Aluminum and Chemical Corporation followed with a plant at Ravenswood, West Virginia. Alcoa was the last company to enter the area, with a plant at Evansville, Indiana. The Ormet Corporation built an alumina plant at Burnside, Louisiana, and the Kaiser Corporation built an alumina plant at Gramercy, Louisiana, primarily to supply this region. By 1960 the three aluminum plants had an annual total capacity of 485,000 tons; by 1975 this had been increased to 688,000 tons.

The orientation to the Ohio Valley was a response to a number of factors. Each of the three companies has indicated that the regional market played a decisive role. The plants were located within a few hundred miles of approximately two-thirds of the nation's aluminum market. The Kaiser and Ormet companies have rolling mills in conjunction with their reduction plants.

The aluminum plants distribute a large portion of their output to processing plants in the region. Kaiser has a forging mill in Erie, Pennsylvania; a container plant in Wanatah, Indiana; extrusion mills in Chicago and Baltimore; and foil and fabricating plants in Belpre and Newark, Ohio. The Ormet plant sends part of its output to its wire and cable plant in Chattanooga, Tennessee, and to its extrusion mills in Baltimore, Maryland; Chicago, Illinois; and Nesquehoning, Pennsylvania. Alcoa sends most of its aluminum to its extrusion and rolling mill in Davenport, Iowa, and its rolling mill in Fayette, Indiana.

The regional market can be reached in two to three days from the Ohio Valley plants. By contrast, it requires from 20 to 30 days for delivery to the region from plants in the Northwest. Because of the Ohio Valley plants the storage of aluminum is greatly reduced and the specific requirements of the market are better served.

The market potential is determined largely by transportation costs. Two aspects must be considered: the transfer costs for alumina and the costs for transporting the finished product. The Ormet Corporation processes Surinam bauxite at its Burnside plant and transports the alumina by barge to its reduction plant. Alcoa and Kaiser secure most of their alumina by railroad transportation. As a response the railroads have reduced their charges because of the possible competition from water routes. The Waterways Freight Bureau has indicated that the rail rates for alumina are below cost, which is keeping the traffic out of river barges. The aluminum companies have indicated that alumina shipments would not be sufficiently large to justify the use of barges. Regardless of which type of transportation is used for the movement of alumina, the expensive cross-hauling of alumina and aluminum to and from the Northwest is eliminated. Besides, aluminum—which moves at a higher freight rate than alumina—is produced closer to the market.

The reduction plants of the Ohio Valley possess a considerable cost advantage in freight rates over the Northwest plants. Freight costs on aluminum sheets from the Northwest to Cleveland are approximately 4.8 cents per pound, while the costs from Ravenswood are 1.4 cents per pound. The differential is even greater for foil, 6.72 as opposed to 1.49 cents per pound.

The Ohio Valley plants were the first American aluminum plants to be oriented to coal for their supply of power. Because of the lower costs of coal due to mechanization, reduced transport costs due to larger and more efficient coal barges, and greater efficiency in steam-generating plants, the cost of electricity from coal declined. Electricity produced by thermal plants cost about 0.4 cents per kilowatt-hour in the early 1960s. This was almost twice the rate of hydroelectric power in the Northwest, but compared favorably with rates in the Tennessee Valley and the Gulf Coast area. It requires 12 kwh of electric energy to make a pound of aluminum. Thus the power cost in the Northwest for a pound of aluminum was 1.89 cents compared with 3.6 cents in the Ohio Valley. This discrepancy was somewhat reduced by 1970 due to increasing efficiency in thermal plants.

Each of the companies in the Ohio Valley secures its power in a different manner. Alcoa built its own power plant at Boonville, Indiana. This plant provides 375,000 kw, assuring the company of an adequate power supply. Kaiser purchases its power needs from the Ohio Power Company on a 40-year contract. Kaiser has, however, purchased coal reserves in Kentucky for future power development. Ormet has chosen a middle position: It has established a generating subsidiary that owns two of three generators in the Ohio Power Company's plant at Cresap, West Virginia.

Other factors, for example, the available labor supply, have been of small importance in localizing the aluminum industry in the Ohio Valley. The aluminum industry was located in an area of declining employment in the coal industry. The expanding employment in the aluminum industry that now employs about 8,000 workers has been of great importance in reversing a declining economy.

CHANGING PATTERN OF PRODUCTION.   As a result of the changing geographic pattern of aluminum reduction plants, the pattern of aluminum production has also been altered greatly since 1940. Before World War II all facilities were located in the eastern United States. As a result of the expansion in the western United States, approximately 40 percent of the metal-producing capacity in 1950 was concentrated in Washington and Oregon. About 10 percent was located in Arkansas, and approximately 50 percent remained in the East. By 1975, the East had declined to about 38 percent of the total. The Northwest had also declined to 32 percent of the total. However, the South had increased to 30 percent of the nation's total output (Fig. 3.2).

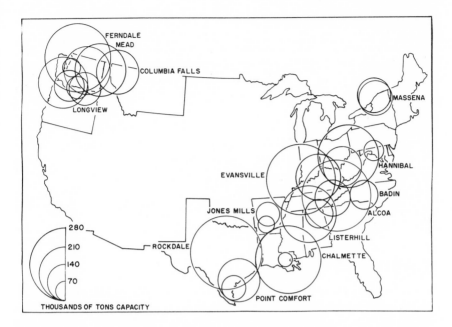

Figure 3.2. Localization of aluminum production in the United States, 1975.

MACHINE TOOL INDUSTRY

Machine tools are absolutely essential to the industrial advancement of a nation. Nevertheless many countries still lack the technical ability to produce them. Only the industrially advanced nations have developed a significant machine tool industry. Based on value of production, the United States is the leader, followed by the Soviet Union, West Germany, and Japan. The United States produces more than one-fifth of the world's machine tools. The nine leading western European nations—West Germany, the United Kingdom, France, Italy, Switzerland, Austria, Belgium, the Netherlands, and Sweden—produce about two-fifths of total world output. The Soviet Union and the eastern European nations—Poland, Czechoslovakia, and Hungary—produce about one-third of the world total. Japan has experienced remarkable growth in the machine tool industry in recent years. The relative importance of the United States has declined with the expansion in other countries. A number of developing countries, such as India, Brazil, and Mexico, have begun producing machine tools.

Locational Factors

The manufacture of machine tools is one of the most complicated of all mechanical industries. Because of the great value added in manufacturing, the primary factors localizing machine tool production are the availability of highly skilled mechanical labor and a market. Because skills are acquired only after a long period of training, skilled labor is essentially always found in mature industrial regions. The migration of labor to the newer industrial areas rarely includes a high percentage of skilled mechanics. A huge capital investment is also required to establish even a modest-sized industry, so adequate resources are limited largely to the advanced nations. Because the machine tool is a product of high value, the availability of raw materials or fuels is not a factor in its location. It is also a product of relatively small bulk in relation to its value and can therefore withstand the high costs of shipping over great distances.

Theory and Location

In contrast to most industries that originated early in the Industrial Revolution and sought a least cost point of production, the machine tool industry has always sought areas of maximum profit. The Weberian least cost concepts rooted in minimizing transportation costs have had little influence in the localization of the machine tool industry. It has consistently sought a maximum market orientation and thus has evolved within the Löschian concepts.

The machine tool industry in the United States was initially oriented to its market in the machinery-producing centers of southern New England and eastern Pennsylvania. New machine tool centers developed with the growth of the Midwest market. Because transportation had little influence on the precise localization of the industry, it developed at sites where quality labor existed. Thus a wide number of sites could be chosen within the market region.

There has been little change since the establishment of the spatial pattern of production of machine tools early in the twentieth century. The small new markets have not developed significant centers of machine tool production, and the Löschian influence prevails. Existing centers can produce a sufficient quantity of machine tools for the nation. It would appear from empirical studies that only the largest markets provide the profit incentive for a machine tool company.

United States

EARLY CENTERS OF PRODUCTION. The machine tool industry had its origin in this country in the machine centers of southern New England. It developed, as its relationships to mass production clearly indicates, at the time when the idea of interchangeability of parts in manufactured articles became a part of American industrial enterprise. It is generally agreed that the first application of this idea was made by Eli Whitney in a musket factory near New Haven in 1808. Whitney spent several years making the tools that made the manufacture of interchangeable parts practical. By 1815 this idea was being adopted in gun factories throughout southern New England and soon gained recognition in the making of textile machinery. However, the market was so small that independent machine tool companies were few and machine shops made most of the machine tools. It was not until 1833 that the first company was organized in Providence, Rhode Island, to produce machine tools exclusively. The English machine tools were copied during the early period, and few advances were made in the United States. The industry was characterized by a lack of specialization. In 1860 there were only 17 companies manufacturing machine tools in the United States, with an estimated 450 wage earners. The major centers were in southern New England and Philadelphia.

With the rapid growth of the machinery industry in the Midwest during the late nineteenth century, new machine tool centers developed. Although eastern factories attempted to produce a full line of machine tools, the Midwestern plants specialized in particular machines. By the time of the establishment of the Midwestern centers, many advances had been made in machine tools, and the construction of a single tool was frequently a complex operation. As a result specialization in a single machine resulted in the improvement of the product and economy in its production. Specialization in the manufacturing of machine tools closely followed the differentiation of processes in other lines of industry. Thus a multitude of special machines was created, each designed to perform a single and often simple operation. These refinements in production, which are still in progress, were the major contribution of the United States to the machine tool industry.

By 1900 the basic geographic pattern of the industry was well established. New England, the Middle Atlantic, and Midwestern states had essentially equal divisions of the industry. The four leading states in production were Ohio, Pennsylvania, Connecticut, and Massachusetts. The five leading cities, which produced about one-third of the entire output, were Cincinnati, Philadelphia, Providence, Hartford, and Worcester. The balance of the machine tools came from many cities and a considerable number of small towns having a single establishment, usually making only one type or class of machines.

FACTORS AFFECTING GEOGRAPHIC DISTRIBUTION. Several factors affect the location of the American machine tool industry.

Labor. Labor requirements have acted as a major influence in the concentration of the American machine tool industry. The labor is developed largely through apprenticeship and other on-the-job training programs. From 1954 to 1975 the apprenticeship program produced more than 20,000 machinists. Those who enter this trade must have not only the aptitude but also a willingness to spend years in training, during which the rewards are modest. After a long apprenticeship period, a company will make every effort to employ the worker; further, the individual has usually by that time developed a close relationship with the company.

Labor costs have traditionally been high, averaging 40–50 percent of total production costs. As machine tools have become more complex, labor costs have risen. For example, in 1954 a standard machine tool required an average of 384 man-hours of direct labor to produce. By 1972 the same machine, but far more complex and efficient, required 764 man-hours.

Because the industry is characterized by cyclical periods of growth and decline, it is extremely difficult to maintain an adequate labor supply. Workers cannot be easily recruited during periods of growth because of the long training period. Therefore during these periods the workweek is lengthened; skilled jobs are divided into simpler tasks if possible; workers are promoted from within the company, creating openings at the lower levels. During slack periods the reverse of this situation prevails. Because the machine tool worker has the highest skills in the mechanical trades and therefore receives the highest wages, there is little or no incentive to migrate to other areas during periods of low productivity.

Markets. Machine tools are marketed mainly in the region where they are produced. The production of machine tools has long been concentrated in the northeastern quadrant (census divisions of New England, Middle Atlantic, and East North Central) of the nation. In 1919, measured by value added, 98 percent of the industry was found in this region. Between 1919 and 1947 this region maintained its absolute position, with the area still having 97 percent of the production. In 1947, 81 percent of the machine tools were located in the Northeast. By 1972, about 93 percent of the machine tools were still produced in the Northeast, but the region possessed only about 68 percent of U.S. machine tools, indicating an increase in machine tools in other regions.

Although the production and market for machine tools have exhibited a remarkable stability in the Northeast, a number of locational trends within the region can be recognized. In 1919 New England possessed 36 percent of production, but by 1972 its share had declined to 14 percent. This reflects a gradually declining market; between 1947 and 1972 the number of machine tools in the area declined from 17.7 percent of the total to 10.9 percent of the machine tools in the United States. By contrast, the East North Central region increased its share of production from 48.0 to 57.3 percent of the total from 1947 to 1972. This reflects the expanding market of the Midwest, which now has about 37 percent of all machine tools in the United States.

The general trends in New England and the Midwest are reflected in the positions of the leading states. From the early 1900s until 1967 Ohio was the largest machine tool producer having approximately 25 percent of the U.S. output, but has now declined to second place having 17 percent of the output. Michigan is now the leading producer having grown steadily from about 6 percent of the production in the 1920s to 21 percent in 1972. Illinois' percentage during the same period increased from 6 to 12 percent. Until the 1900s Connecticut was the second largest producer, but it has declined to fourth position.

The Middle Atlantic region has maintained a relatively stable position in machine tool production, with 11.4 percent of output in 1919 and 14.3 percent in 1972. The area has traditionally been a deficit area in production because the region possesses about 21 percent of the machine tools in the United States. Machine tools are obtained from both New England and Midwest plants.

Since 1947 there has been a modest growth of the machine tool industry in the South and the West. The West in 1972 had about 5.4 percent of the machine tool production, but possessed about 13.7 percent of the nation's tools. The South produced 3.2 percent of the tools and had 11.9 percent of the machine tools. The small machine tool industry of these regions illustrates the problems of developing the industry in areas where a relatively small market exists.

Technical Advances. As the machine tool becomes more complicated and consequently more expensive, the small firm that has been a traditional feature of the machine tool industry has greater difficulty surviving. The small firm lacks not only the necessary capital for production but, more importantly, the required research for maintaining and advancing the technology of the industry. Even though they have a short history, numerically controlled tools have become increasingly sophisticated. The small machine-tool-producing firm is gradually disappearing, and the larger firms are those best able to cope with advancing technology. A present-day technological trend encourages a concentration of the industry at a smaller number of larger centers.

Structure of the Industry. The machine tool industry has traditionally been composed of a large number of small companies. In 1974 there were approximately 900 companies building machine tools; about 400 of them employed fewer than 20 workers. The traditional small size of the plants has encouraged decentralization. As a consequence machine tool companies have located in scores of towns.

Because the small company normally does not possess the resources or the market facilities to engage in national distribution, the industry developed the American Machine Tool Distributors Association for marketing machine tools. This organization represents some 225 independent companies serving the United States and Canada. In general these companies are small businesses employing an average of 15 people. The sales personnel of machine tool distributors are technically trained not only in sales, but are also able to specify the best tools for a specific job.

A major trend affecting the traditional geographic structure of the industry began in the early 1960s, when the motor vehicle companies began to develop their own facilities for producing machine tools and associated accessories. In some instances the motor producers have acquired independent companies, but in most cases the motor corporations have developed their own facilities.

There are a number of reasons for this trend. With the development of in-house machine tool facilities, the corporations have greater control over production and labor supply. The automobile industry makes major model changes every three to four years, requiring a complete retooling; in other years the amount of retooling is modest to slight. In the years of heavy demand the machine tool companies, since the early 1960s, have been operating at near full capacity and have not been able to adequately supply the motor vehicle companies. As a result the motor corporations increased their facilities to accommodate their peak demands. However, in the off years the automobile industry had to increase their work load to keep their labor force employed. Under the collective bargaining agreements between the automakers and the United Auto Workers, the machine tool employees are guaranteed an annual income regardless of the work load.

A second factor encouraging the growth of the machine tool industry by the automobile companies lies in the technology of automobile production. It is extremely important in the automotive industry to be able to proceed quickly from the initial design of a new model to production so that the consumer's taste will not have changed. To do this the automobile companies have attempted, through numerical control techniques, to produce the large dies for the production of hoods, fenders, and trunks more quickly. This is an extremely costly operation. It is estimated that for a complete retooling of all models a company could expend as much as $1,000,000,000 and, for a partial retooling of a single line, $50,000,000 to $100,000,000. A single numerical-control machine tool needed for these processes costs more than $500,000. This is a major expenditure for a small company. Further, the small companies cannot be guaranteed that the auto companies will not continue to develop in-house tools.

A third factor for the in-house trend in the production of machine tools and accessories by the automobile industries is the snowballing effect of the auto companies' use of maintenance facilities for machine tools supplied by the small companies. The automotive companies have traditionally maintained small in-house tooling facilities for maintenance and repair work. These facilities cannot be operated economically if they are used only a small portion of the time. Since about 1960 the automakers have utilized these facilities more efficiently in the retooling process. However, the types of machines and labor skills needed for new tooling are different, and gradually new facilities were required so the work force could be utilized at a more stable level.

Government Policies. Government procurement policies are influencing the development of the machine tool industry in a number of areas. A major consideration is the increasing use by government contractors, particularly aircraft companies, of government-owned machine tools. The justification for the government's providing such equipment is that the prime contractors are not able to purchase such expensive equipment for what may be short-term use on government contracts. In certain cases machine tools have been provided to the aircraft companies when similar machine tools with experienced personnel to operate them are available in small nearby companies. Once the machine tools are located in the aircraft companies, the companies begin to develop repair facilities for them. To utilize these facilities, the next step is to produce machine tools. Many of the aircraft companies have now developed substantial in-house tooling and machine facilities far beyond their needs. To keep these facilities operating, they have subcontracted tooling and machinery production to each other. As a result the market for small machine tool companies in supplying the aircraft industry has been adversely affected. Thus the situation is similar to that in the automobile industry in that the machine tool and accessory industries concentrate in localities of large aircraft production.

MOTOR VEHICLE INDUSTRY

The development of the motor vehicle industry has taken place essentially within the twentieth century. Prior to 1900 western European nations, particularly France and Germany, produced the first motor vehicles. However, after 1900 the European countries quickly lost their supremacy to the United States, which has maintained leadership since 1905. Until 1950 the United States produced annually about 80 percent of the world's motor vehicles. When the Canadian output was added to that of the United States, the total rose to 85 percent.

The United States had ideal physical and economic conditions for the development of the motor vehicle industry. In the early twentieth century the country was relatively poorly served by railroads and other transportation. The automobile, a new and inexpensive form of transportation, was universally accepted in a country that was expanding rapidly. The United States also possessed resources well adapted to the development of the industry. American manufacturing is based on labor-saving, large-scale production techniques.

The relative position of the United States has declined greatly in recent years with the growth of the Japanese and European motor vehicle industry. With increasing world prosperity, the demand for motor vehicles has increased at an extremely rapid rate. The growth, however, has been localized in the industrially advanced nations. For example, Japan experienced the most spectacular growth, with production rising from 31,600 vehicles in 1950 to about 5,000,000 vehicles in 1973. The motor vehicle industry has experienced a modest expansion in the Soviet Union. Under Soviet planning, the production of trucks has been emphasized and the output of automobiles has received a low priority. However, a new plant constructed by Fiat on the middle Volga has increased passenger car output to about 1,000,000 units a year.

A motor industry has developed in recent years in some of the smaller industrial nations, such as Belgium, the Netherlands, Denmark, and Yugoslavia. A small motor industry is also expanding in developing nations including Brazil, Argentina, and Mexico. Although their total output is limited compared with the leading nations, production has grown as demand has risen.

The rapid growth of the automobile industry throughout the world was halted when an oil embargo was imposed by the Middle Eastern oil producers in late 1973 and when the embargo was lifted in early 1974 the price of petroleum was increased by about 500 percent. Besides the rising cost of fuel, general inflationary pressures increased the price of automobiles from 20 to 33 percent. The 1974 world output was approximately one-quarter to one-third below that of 1973.

Theoretical Constructs

With the development of mass production in the motor vehicle industry, the Löschian philosophy of market orientation has prevailed. The philosophy was thus not to produce the largest profit per vehicle, but to sell the most vehicles at a satisfactory profit. To achieve this the industry began the process of decentralization by establishing market-oriented branch plants. The maximum profit is consequently secured as a response to volume production.

The theoretical foundations for the location of the motor vehicle industry are typical for most mass production industries. As the market potential grows, there is less and less interest in seeking a least cost point and more and more interest in securing a larger and larger market area. This is frequently accomplished by building plants in new potential market areas. Profits may vary from sites where near least cost conditions prevail to sites where a minimal satisfactory profit can be attained. However, in all instances the goal is maximization of profit through market control mechanisms.

General Factors of Localization

The motor vehicle is a complex mechanical machine requiring thousands of parts that can be produced only in the most advanced industrial economies. In the lesser developed nations, an assembly industry has developed based on importation of the more complicated parts. An integrated motor vehicle industry has evolved only in the advanced industrial nations.

Besides an advanced industrial structure, a nation must possess certain economic and cultural characteristics for an automobile industry to thrive. The industry is the supreme exemplification of mass production. Consequently a massive market is essential. The size of the market is largely dependent on the economic structure of the area. A basic prerequisite is the availability of large personal disposable incomes. However, even in the most prosperous nations, there is not sufficient personal savings to assure a mass market for automobiles. As a result a credit system becomes essential to assure volume sales. Besides, in order to attract a massive market, there must be a wide range of price levels to appeal to all economic groups.

The automobile is, however, a durable machine that will last for years. To maintain a mass market, the motor vehicle industry has fostered the desire to purchase a new automobile at frequent intervals. This has been done partly by mechanical improvements, but largely by yearly style changes. The motor vehicle companies appeal to the general public through extensive advertising programs. Present-day marketing policies are in great contrast to Henry Ford's idea that a person would purchase a car and keep it in operation by simply replacing parts when they wore out. This philosophy could not maintain the modern-day motor vehicle industry.

United States

EARLY LOCALIZATION. The automobile industry has always been concentrated in the lower Great Lakes states. In 1909, when the industry was first listed in the U.S. Census of Manufactures, this region had over 70 percent of the total production, Michigan being dominant with about 35 percent of all output based on value added by manufacture. New York was the only important producer outside the Midwestern states.

A group of factors was influential in the development of this early localization. The lower Great Lakes states had a number of existing industries directly related to the growth of the automobile industry. These include the production of malleable iron, steel, brass parts, springs, rubber tires, paints, and varnishes. Such materials were indispensable to the production of the horseless carriage. This region, with its hardwood forests of oak, hickory, and maple, was also the most important area of buggy and carriage construction in the country. Because the early automobile was essentially a buggy with a motor attached, the horse-drawn and horseless carriages were similar in many ways.

Because of the growing lake-freighter transportation, the lower Great Lakes states had become important producers of gasoline-powered marine engines. In the early period of the automobile industry there was considerable competition between the steam engine, the electric motor, and the gasoline engine. The steam engine to power vehicles had its greatest acceptance in Massachusetts, the electric motor in Connecticut, and the gasoline engine in Michigan. When the gasoline engine proved to be most effective, Michigan achieved a decided advantage over other regions. It is thus important that the initial success of the automobile occurred in the Midwest while most of the eastern manufacturers were having discouraging failures.

Largely as a result of the factors just discussed, there were many pioneer inventors and manufacturers in this area. Since this was a new and expanding economic region, there were also a number of men willing to risk capital in the new industry. Financiers in the East were less willing to provide risk capital for an infant industry. Since the growth of the leading producers was cumulative, the automobile industry soon became centered in the Midwest.

Other factors played a role in the early localization. The topographical element cannot be disregarded. Although much of the east is hilly, the Central Lowlands are relatively flat, and since the early cars had little power this was one of the best areas in which they could function successfully. The Midwest, with its great distances, was more transportation conscious than the East, where distances between towns were shorter. The glacial gravels of the Midwest facilitated road building, and the poorly developed public transportation also stimulated the new industry. Finally, an intense spirit of resourcefulness and enterprise in the Midwest provided an impetus to the infant industry that was generally lacking in the more conservative East.

DETROIT AND THE FORD MOTOR COMPANY. As the automobile industry concentrated in the lower Great Lakes states, the Detroit area, from a very early date, became the leading center of production. The first important factor localizing the automobile industry there was the ability of the Olds Motor Works to produce a successful, luxury car in 1899 at East Lansing on what was then a large scale. The Oldsmobile was possibly the earliest car to make a profit for its producers. With an annual production of over 1,000 this car demonstrated that the automobile could be built and sold in quantity and a profit made in its manufacture. The Michigan people were really the first in the United States to become automobile-minded.

This early success had a number of important implications. It caused a group of early inventors and developers to be attracted to Michigan centering on Detroit; among them were David Buick, Charles King, Henry M. Leland, Elwood Haynes, and the greatest of them all, Henry Ford. Detroit, the leading industrial city, was soon the center of new ideas for producing a better automobile.

By 1903, when the Olds Motor Works was producing 4,000 cars annually, Detroit became the motor capital of the world. Dozens of new companies began to produce cars there. All of these, however, remained small until Henry Ford applied mass production methods, which gave the industry a substantial size and assured Detroit of undisputed leadership. The Ford car was based on the fundamental idea of cheap interchangeable parts. As an old part wore out, a new part replaced it; theoretically at least, the buyer needed only to purchase a car and could keep it in running order indefinitely by replacing parts.

To produce this new car, Ford revolutionized the techniques of automobile manufacturing. Standardization was the key to Ford's mass-produced automobile. This was accompanied by the use of highly specialized machine tools, power-driven conveyor assembly belts, minute subdivision of labor, intensive supervision of labor, and high wages. In 1909 one of the world's largest manufacturing plants was created in Highland Park, Michigan. There the company introduced innovations in factory and shop practice that gave Ford undisputed leadership in the automobile industry for nearly two decades. This innovation which is now used by nearly all assembly industries, is known as the "endless chain production system." In the traditional factory, machines were located in groups according to the type or class of operation. This resulted in a large amount of crisscrossing of the lines of movement and much in-shop transportation. The Highland Park plant was designed to avoid this by having the machines and the employees operating them placed in such sequence that the automobile was completely constructed as it moved from the beginning to the end of a single assembly line. Although this continuous process method had been used by steel companies, Ford pioneered in applying the system to the manufacture of such complex mechanisms as automobiles.

In close correlation with this method was the minute subdivision of labor made possible by the development of specialized machinery designed to perform a specific operation in making the parts of a car. Tasks previously requiring skilled workmen were divided into many operations, skill in any one of which could be acquired in a few hours. The importance of this practice is appreciated when it is recognized that the existence of a large number of skilled mechanics and woodworkers in various localities in the lower Great Lakes region early influenced the location of the initial automobile factories. The scale of the Ford operation, however, would have been impossible had it depended on existing skilled labor. As a result of the Ford Motor Company's success, its techniques were copied by all large motor vehicle companies in the Detroit region.

All automobile companies outside the lower Great Lakes region have failed. The General Motors and Chrysler corporations were formed from smaller successful companies in the area. The phenomenal success of one company in the early period became the magnet around which other companies developed.

FACTORS OF DECENTRALIZATION.   While the automobile companies were establishing their main plants in the Detroit region, they were also establishing branch assembly plants throughout the United States (14). This geographic structure developed as a result of the tremendous growth of the industry. The large manufacturer soon discovered that a single plant could not satisfy the demands of the country. The Ford Motor Company was the first to start this trend with the establishment of a branch plant in Kansas City, Missouri, in October 1910. All other major producers now have branch plants strategically located in market areas throughout the United States, and many have plants in foreign countries. The automobile industry has thus come to be the prime example of a centralized-decentralized organization.

The development of branch assembly plants has many advantages. Transportation costs are minimized by shipping parts instead of finished automobiles because freight cars can be more heavily loaded, carloads of parts receive lower freight rates, and standard boxcars can be used instead of special cars. Because the automobile industry is basically an assembly industry, parts made outside the automobile region can be shipped directly to the branch plants, often saving freight charges. Another advantage is that stocks can be accumulated at the various assembly plants, thus economizing storage. The assembly plants also establish sources of supply in the area in which they are located, thus aiding business in the immediate region.

There is also a significant advantage in the distribution of parts and finished automobiles. Dealers are supplied with finished automobiles and parts directly from the assembly plants. This practice greatly facilitates the physical distribution of the great volume of production. In essence, the individual companies have grown too large to be located at a single point of production.

GENERAL MOTORS—AN EXAMPLE OF A CENTRALIZED-DECENTRALIZED ORGANIZATION.   The General Motors Corporation illustrates effectively the modern geographic structure of an automobile company. This corporation is the largest, most profitable, private manufacturing enterprise in history. In *Fortune* magazine's survey of the 500 largest American corporations, General Motors has been in first place each year in the last quarter of a century. Net sales in 1973 were well over $35 billion, and net income was nearly $2.4 billion. General Motors has an annual output of about half of all motor vehicles in the United States and thousands of units of such other products as refrigerators, ranges, air conditioners, dishwashers, jet engines, automobile components, and oil burners. It employs directly over 760,000 wage and salary earners and, indirectly, about 200,000 more in privately owned sales agencies. To produce its vast amount of manufactured goods, General Motors retains its economic headquarters in Detroit, while maintaining a vast system of decentralized facilities. In 1973 the corporation had 110 plants in U.S. and Canadian cities; it also had assembly, manufacturing, and warehouse operations in 28 foreign countries (Fig. 3.3).

This organization makes possible the most remarkable assemblage of materials and parts in modern industry. For example, suppose a Chevrolet is to be assembled in Baltimore, Maryland, at 9:00 on a Friday morning. To assemble that car, a frame must leave a plant in Milwaukee on Monday afternoon. Its axles leave Buffalo, its engine leaves Flint, and its transmission leaves Cleveland on Tuesday. On Wednesday its fenders are shipped from Pittsburgh. Meanwhile other components are shipped from other places, all to arrive in Baltimore shortly before final assembly. The problem of assembly becomes even more complicated when it is remembered that, for the Chevrolet alone, there are at least 14 body styles, 18 trim and color combinations, and 5 special equipment options. The complexity of making and delivering between 2,000,000 and 3,000,000 of these cars in one year is appreciable.

For years the automobile final assembly line, which can put together a completed car in two hours, has been popularly regarded as the industry's great miracle. The real miracle is the manufacturing and scheduling of all the car's parts to arrive at a certain point at a precise time. That accomplished, final assembly has become a comparatively simple operation.

MODERN GEOGRAPHIC STRUCTURE.   The location of the motor vehicle industry is undergoing a significant change. Between 1939 and 1947, when the number of employees in motor vehicles and parts in the United States increased from 458,723 to 653,169, the number in Michigan rose from 286,477 to 371,795. But even with this great increase in the number of employees, the relative importance of Michigan declined from 62.4 to 56.9 percent of the total employees. In 1947 the next most important states were Ohio (with 9.40 percent of employment), Indiana (8.06 percent), and New York (5.95 percent). The East North Central region continued its dominance, producing 80 percent of all the motor vehicles and parts produced in the United States.

Since 1947 the Michigan area has experienced an absolute decline in employment in motor vehicles and parts. Between 1947 and 1972, when national employment rose from 653,169 to 739,100, employment in Michigan declined from 371,795 to 294,700. The relative importance of Michigan declined from 56.9 to 39.87 percent of employment. In contrast to the employment trends in Michigan, other East North Central states experienced significant gains. Employment in Ohio increased from 61,447 to 112,800, increasing its relative importance from 9.40 to 15.26 percent of the total. Increases also occurred in Indiana and Wisconsin. Although the relative importance of Michigan declined greatly, the East North Central states still maintained 73.88 percent of the motor vehicle employment in 1972.

Outside the East North Central states, the motor vehicle and equipment industry has had its greatest growth on the Pacific Coast. Between 1947 and 1972, employment in California increased from 12,118 to about 30,000. Em-

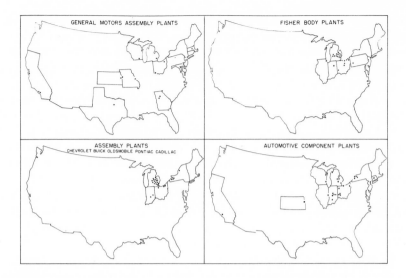

Figure 3.3. Location of General Motors Corporation plants.

ployment in the South during the same period increased from about 10,200 to 64,600, or an increase from 1.55 to 8.74 percent of total employment. The motor vehicle and equipment industry of the Middle Atlantic and New England states has maintained a stable employment, but a relative decline.

The motor vehicle industry has continued to experience a decentralization in recent years. As the market has expanded geographically and freight rates have risen, there has been a growing trend toward greater market orientation.

FACTORS INFLUENCING GEOGRAPHIC AND FINANCIAL CONCENTRATION. Since the early days of the motor vehicle industry, the number of companies has continually decreased until today only four companies remain in the United States. Of these, General Motors produced about 50 percent of total output in 1973, Ford Motor Company about 30 percent, Chrysler about 15 percent, and the American Motor Company about 3.5 percent. A basic question is, why is the motor vehicle industry limited to giant corporations and what are the requirements for entrance into motor vehicle manufacturing?

The first aspect to investigate is the size of the plant necessary for a company to be competitive. A survey of the size of the present assembly operations of existing companies can provide some concept of this. In 1973 General Motors had 46 assembly plants for producing 6,512,263 cars and trucks, or an average of 141,570 vehicles per plant. However, there is considerable variation in output per assembly plant depending on the particular make of vehicle. In 1973 there were 3,349,299 Chevrolets—cars and trucks—produced in 35 assembly plants, or an average of 95,694 vehicles per plant. There were 10 assembly plants for the production of Buicks, Oldsmobiles, and Pontiacs, of which three specialized in one make each. These three divisions of General Motors had an output of

2,608,867 vehicles, or an average of 260,000 units per plant. Cadillac had one assembly plant for producing 307,267 vehicles.

The Ford Motor Company had 18 plants for assembling 3,771,704 vehicles in 1973, or an average of 209,531 per plant. Chrysler had 9 assembly plants for producing 1,947,036 vehicles, or 216,337 vehicles on the average for each plant. The proposed Chrysler plant at New Stanton, Pennsylvania, had a predicted capacity of 200,000 vehicles annually. In 1976 Volkswagen purchased this plant for production of cars. American Motors assembled 446,672 vehicles at its only assembly plant in 1973.

It would then appear that, for plants assembling vehicles, 95,000 to 446,000 vehicles annually would be the desired range of output; it would also appear that there are advantages in establishing a multiplant decentralized system after the higher critical figure is passed. The total assets of the four motor vehicle companies varied greatly in 1973, from a low of $712,000,000 for American Motors to $20,296,000,000 for General Motors. For a company to enter the motor vehicle industry today, nearly $1 billion dollars of initial capital would undoubtedly be required. This tremendous investment provides a major barrier to the development of new motor vehicle companies.

Even if capital is available, there are additional barriers to the entry of new companies into the motor vehicle industry. The modern automobile is a complex piece of machinery offering maximum opportunity for physical product differentiation. Although there is general similarity of gross specifications, there is an appreciable degree of physical differentiation in such items as the body, engine, transmission design, and many other features. Coupled with the pattern of physical product differentiation is one of annual changes in body and mechanical design.

The automobile is bought with conspicuous consumption clearly in mind, with a used-product market offering an alternative to lower-income groups and the new-product market being predominantly a replacement market; demand for new automobiles each year is maintained by successive changes by the producer. The basic pattern that has evolved requires a major retooling every third or fourth year, with smaller efforts on an annual basis. The principle of protective imitation is utilized by all companies, so that over time the physical differentiation between companies does not increase. It is estimated that retooling by the automobile manufacturers is now nearly $1 billion each year. A single model change may be as much as $100,000,000. As a response to this cost, there must be considerable economies of scale attributable to spreading the fixed retooling overhead over large-volume output.

The small producer encounters significant diseconomies in retooling costs per unit of output because it must compete with the larger companies to remain in operation. The practice in recent years for the small independent company has been to make fewer changes between major retoolings. As a result the production of the independent companies has varied, particularly in design, from those of the large companies during the longer periods of stable design. The small producer frequently depends for his market on the minority of buyers

who want a car that is somewhat different in design. Since 1950 small producers have not been able to maintain their market, and all have disappeared
except American Motors. There is thus strong evidence that product identification has created a substantial and durable market for a particular brand.

A company maintains identification of its product by means of advertising
in a variety of media. By this means there is the constant pressure to purchase a
particular brand of automobile. It is estimated that the "Big 3" producers (General Motors, Ford, Chrysler) each spend annually more than $100,000,000 for
direct advertising.

There are other considerations that give the large producer an advantage
and act as a barrier to the entrance of new companies into the industry. The
modern automobile is such a complex machine that the average buyer is unable
to evaluate its mechanical quality. The automobile is also so expensive that the
buyer has limited opportunity to experiment with different makes. Also, there
has been a sufficient number of automobile makes, even by the major producers,
that have not proved satisfactory (e.g., the Edsel and the Corvair); thus buyers are
unwilling to risk experimentation. They therefore depend on the reputation of an
established make. In addition, buyers tend to believe that better automobiles are
those that have the larger sales. Thus a strong market position of a particular
automobile gives it a self-perpetuating position. The smaller producers thus have
a distinct disadvantage in expanding their market position.

The dealer system is an important factor in maintaining a restricted sales
system. Automobiles are sold only through a special, limited system of outlets.
All companies attempt nationwide distribution, but the product is sold by use of
exclusive franchise policies. Further, a dealer is restricted to a brand or brands of
a single company. A huge amount of capital is invested by independent dealers
in land, building, equipment, parts inventories, and like items. Thus the dealers
promote not only sales but also the servicing of a particular make of automobile.
In general the number and geographic density of the dealers determine to a large
degree the volume of the sales. Here again the small manufacturer is at a distinct
disadvantage. He will have difficulty in securing an adequate number of fran-
chises necessary when volume is lower.

There are two distinct advantages for the dealer system. First, buyers give
considerable allegiance to individual dealers, who are expected to service the
automobile. Buyers are reluctant to purchase an automobile if a dealer is not
readily accessible. Second, there is a tendency for buyers to consider it advantageous to purchase a car from dealers who have a high density of location.

Conspicuous consumption has long been a factor in the purchase of a
particular automobile. In the 1920s and 1930s the owner of a Packard was
considered an individual of affluence. Many persons today buy such high-priced
cars as Cadillacs or Continentals as status symbols. This also applies for foreign
makes. This buyer attitude perpetuates allegiance to the more popular cars and
works against the smaller companies.

The motor vehicle companies are becoming increasingly integrated. A
greater percentage of the parts are made by the companies or their subsidiaries to

secure scale-economies. It is general practice for parts-making subsidiaries of the integrated firms to charge their outside customers the same prices as those within the company. However, the prices are so set to provide some margins of excess profits to the parts-making branches. Thus the less integrated companies are at a cost disadvantage. If a new entrant to the motor vehicle industry were to be fully integrated (i.e., beyond body, engine, and parts), there would be an additional capital requirement of possibly $100,000,000.

ENERGY SHORTAGE, INFLATION, AND THE FUTURE OF THE MOTOR VEHICLE INDUSTRY.   The motor vehicle industry has been developed on the basis of unlimited supplies of gasoline at modest prices. Although an energy crisis has long been evolving in the United States, it was dramatically precipitated in October 1973 when Middle Eastern petroleum producers imposed an oil embargo on most industrial nations, including the United States. As a consequence the United States suffered a 15–20 percent oil deficiency until the embargo was lifted in March 1974.

The reduction of petroleum supplies had an immediate effect on the purchasing of motor vehicles. To illustrate, the effects on the General Motors Corporation will be considered. Between January and March 1974 car sales declined 35.7 percent from the same period in 1973. Furthermore, General Motors was exceeded for the first time by Exxon as the nation's most profitable industrial corporation. From October 1973 to March 1974, General Motors closed 15 of its 22 automobile assembly plants and 3 of its 4 body plants for varying lengths of time to reduce its backlog of unsold big cars. In this same period General Motors laid off 65,000 workers and placed 57,000 more on temporary furlough. Probably no American company was so directly affected by the 1973–1974 energy crisis.

Although the energy crisis was eased in March 1974 when the embargo was lifted, there were still many questions to be answered. The price of gasoline had increased by about 80 percent. At the same time the United States was beset by a major inflation. The sales of motor vehicles declined greatly in 1974 because of international political uncertainty, high interest rates, and possibly most important, the most serious economic depression in the past 40 years. Purchasing power declined, unemployment escalated, and consumer resistance to rising prices for cars and gasoline deepened the automotive recession. As a result car sales declined from a record high of 9,700,000 in 1973 to a low of 7,400,000 cars in 1974. Employment in the motor vehicle and parts industries reached a peak in mid-1973 of 950,000 workers but with declining consumption the number of workers decreased to a low of 690,000 in February 1975. In 1975 there was a modest recovery with sales exceeding 8,000,000 and employment had risen to 740,000 by late 1975. Nevertheless the increase in sales was not as strong as in previous postwar economic upturns.

The future of the motor vehicle industry remains uncertain. The sharp rise in car prices has dampened demand. For example, the 1975 Chevrolet Vega was 33 percent higher than the 1971 model and the Datsun's list price was 69 percent higher. There is also uncertainty concerning what Congress will ultimately legislate about pollution control and fuel efficiency.

The car of the future will be much different from that of the past. It appears certain that cars will become smaller in order to reduce gasoline consumption. A number of other aspects are now being considered. For example, General Motors plans to reduce the weight of cars by 500–1000 pounds. Axle ratios will be reduced so the car will utilize less energy, particularly at cruising speeds of 50–60 miles an hour; this, however, will also reduce acceleration speeds. Transmissions will be tightened so that, instead of changing smoothly from gear to gear as in the past, automatics will produce a slight jerk as they shift. But they will also deliver better fuel economy because they will transfer power more efficiently from engine to wheels.

The motor vehicle industry recognizes that it is in a transition stage. There is every evidence that fundamental changes will occur in the immediate future. As of 1975 no plant had been abandoned by the industry. However, how the future locational pattern of the industry will evolve is not clear. If the present decline of production of over 2,000,000 cars continues, what locations will be abandoned in the future is a fundamental question. Will the industry become more concentrated, or will the recent past trends toward decentralization continue? There will certainly be changes in the localization of the industry that will affect the entire American industrial pattern.

AGRICULTURAL MACHINERY INDUSTRY

Although the manufacture of farm implements depends on agriculture, farming itself is still not dependent on the manufacture of machinery. There are millions of farmers who have no more equipment than primitive hoes and sickles. Because of their simplicity such tools are normally produced locally, frequently in small handicraft shops. But overall, agriculture has been revolutionized by agricultural machinery. Because modern farm machinery is complicated and costly to produce, the agricultural machinery industry is localized in particular agricultural regions.

The agricultural machinery industry is concentrated in the United States, Canada, western and northern Europe, and the Soviet Union. An agricultural machinery industry has also developed in such isolated nations as Japan and Australia. These areas not only possess the technological skills necessary for an agricultural machinery industry, but the high prosperity of agriculture makes it possible for farmers to purchase expensive machinery. The growing domestic and foreign demands for food and agricultural raw materials has in general ensured an expanding market and profitable prices for agricultural produce in these areas.

In contrast to the nations where agriculture is highly mechanized, most countries in Asia and Africa have limited use of power-operated farm machinery. Agriculture in those countries still depends for the most part on the use of hand tools supplemented by animal-drawn equipment of simple design. The pressure of population on the land, resulting in smaller farms and a lowering of income per farm, has discouraged the growth of a modern agricultural machinery industry. Most of the agricultural machinery that is utilized in these areas is imported.

Latin America represents an intermediate stage between the highly mechanized agricultural areas and those using mostly hand tools. Although tractor production is still limited, numerous Latin American countries make other items of machinery and equipment. The industry is best developed in Argentina, Brazil, and Mexico. To encourage domestic production, a number of countries have placed import restrictions on agricultural machinery. Nevertheless Latin America still depends to a large degree on imported machinery.

Theory and Location

The agricultural machinery industry has sought those areas where the largest market prevails, thus reflecting a Löschian framework. The westward migration of the industry in the United States in the nineteenth and early twentieth centuries reflects the market influence. Thus the attempt was not to find the least cost point, but rather to secure the greatest profits through the mechanism of the maximum market. Although the goal of the farm machinery companies is to achieve a maximum profit, in reality they are not likely to be able to determine the places where maximum profits can be achieved. But, through empirical studies, they are able to eliminate from consideration those areas that will not provide a satisfactory profit margin. However, changing economic conditions also change the opportunities for profit at a given location. As a result the spatial patterns of manufacturing remain dynamic. Specifically, farm machinery manufacturers seek wider markets by building plants in new potential regions of production.

General Factors of Localization

Physical, technological, and economic factors greatly influence the production and sale of farm implements. The quantity and type of farm machinery available to farmers depends on the technological state of the industry and the development of an agricultural system that is prosperous enough to provide them with sufficient capital to invest in labor-saving machinery. The growth of this system is related to a great number of factors.

The availability of farmland for raising crops is a limiting factor in the sale of farm implements in many areas. Of the more than 1,150,000,000 acres of farmland in the United States, only about half is available for crops; the remainder is used for pasture or woodland. The bulk of the demand for farm implements in the United States comes from those areas where farmlands are planted in crops that require annual planting, cultivating, and harvesting. The vast grazing lands of the West do not provide a large market for farm machinery.

The physical factors of topography, soil, and climate have greatly affected the extent and direction of agriculture and the type and kinds of farm implements used by farmers. To be adaptable for farming, an area must not be too hilly or stony; it must have sufficient rainfall; its soil must be fertile enough so that production costs are reasonable; and its growing season must be long enough to permit a crop to mature. Limitations imposed by physical factors are readily apparent from the fact that of the 1,903,000,000 acres of virgin land in the United States, only approximately 500,000,000 are used for crops and pasture, another 500,000,000 are suitable only for pasture, and about 150,000,000 are suitable only for pasture and forest.

The prosperity of the farmers and the utilization of farm implements are closely related because farm income directly influences farmers' operating expenditures and the extent to which efficient farm management practices may be used. Decreased costs of farm production depend largely on farmers' ability to purchase the most efficient implements and machines. In the United States about half of the farms in the 16 southern states are tenant operated, while only about 30 percent of the farms in the Northeast are so operated. The Northeast has about 50 percent of the total farm income, and the South has about 30 percent.

The technological stage of farm machinery development for different types of crops has greatly influenced the industry's localization. Modern farm machinery was developed first for harvesting small grains and hay crops. Because these crops were produced primarily in the Northeast and Midwestern United States, the orientation of production to a regional market was strong. In contrast, cotton-harvesting machinery did not develop until the location of the farm machinery industry was firmly established. The new, specialized farm equipment developed in recent years has had only a limited effect in the establishment of new centers of implement production.

Also important to the localization of the farm machinery industry are such factors as the availability of raw materials, a well-developed industrial region, and facilities for distributing the finished products. The farm implement industry is a large consumer of raw materials and partially manufactured products. Between 40 and 45 percent of the value of farm implements is represented by raw material costs. Of the materials consumed, between 65 and 75 percent is iron and steel, 5–10 percent is lumber, and 15–30 percent consists of other materials. Thus it is important to locate the farm implement industry in an industrial area that can supply raw materials, particularly steel, and other manufactured products.

The manufacturer also prefers to establish his plant near the market because of the high freight rates charged on farm machinery. High rates are due principally to the large amount of space required to ship farm machinery. Only specialized, high-cost farm machinery can withstand the high freight rates.

It is difficult to evaluate each of the factors just discussed, but it is the collective impact of all the physical, technological, and economic conditions on the farm operators in a nation that finally determines the demand for agricultural implements and machines. The ideal location for the farm machinery industry is in a well-developed industrial region close to a prosperous, diversified farming area.

United States

Farm mechanization has advanced rapidly in the United States. On January 1, 1910, the value of agricultural implements, automobiles, motor trucks, and tractors amounted to about $1.2 billion. This figure is now in excess of $50 billion and is increasing at the rate of about 8–10 percent each year.

INITIAL LOCALIZATION.   As a response to the need for better harvesting machines because of the expanding agricultural land in the early nineteenth century, a number of inventors attempted to produce a satisfactory mechanical reaper. Most of the machines were not of commercial quality. Finally, in 1831 Cyrus Hall McCormick perfected the principle of the reaper and formed the McCormick Harvesting Company, later to become International Harvester. Two years later Obed Hussy also produced a commerical reaper. Both McCormick and Hussy secured patents and formed the only two companies to produce reapers until their patents expired in 1847 and 1848 (15).

Because the market for the reaper remained relatively small, manufacturing centers did not develop rapidly. As late as 1843 McCormick's reaper was produced in his blacksmith shop on the family farm in Walnut Grove, Virginia. In 1847 McCormick built a factory in Chicago in order to be localized in the developing Midwestern market. With the gradual dispersal and increase of the market for harvesting machinery, the McCormick company contracted with other companies to produce the reaper. Because of costly transportation, the production of the reaper was oriented to local and small regional markets. Further, the companies were small and consequently their output was limited. The early production centers were concentrated in the leading grain-producing centers in the East Coast states. Of particular importance were the Central Lowlands of New York State. The Hussy company began production in Cincinnati, but moved its factory to Baltimore in order to serve the large East Coast market. It remained in production until 1860, when Hussy sold his patent to a mowing machine company.

DISPERSAL OF THE INDUSTRY.   From 1840 to 1890, the focal point of competition in the industry was the product itself because of a succession of radical changes and advances in farm machinery. Although the mechanical revolution in farm machinery began with the reaper, the development of the complicated harvester provided the basis for advancement. The harvester provided the means for eliminating the great waste of grain and the exhaustive labor of binding the grain on the ground after it had been raked or swept from the platform of the reaper; it thus demonstrated the desirability of using farm machinery. As a result a variety of new machines were developed, of which the mower was no doubt as important as the harvester.

By the time the patents for the original reapers expired in 1847 and 1848, several small companies were technically capable of producing reapers and other types of mechanical farm equipment (23–34). By 1850 at least 30 new reaper firms had come into existence; by 1857, 176 grain reapers and 62 mowing machines had been patented in the United States. In the development of the industry, the latter part of the nineteenth century was characterized by periodic conflict for patents, patent infringement cases, and pooling arrangements. Although patent protection became a condition of survival, the great expansion of agriculture provided an initiative for the continued growth of the agricultural machinery industry.

During this period the changing geographic distribution of the industry was closely related to the westward migration of agriculture. Between 1840 and 1870, New York was the largest producer of farm implements, having major centers at Auburn, Brockport, and Buffalo. Ohio was second in output, followed by Illinois. By 1880 Ohio had become the leading state, having centers at Canton and Springfield. Illinois and New York were second and third, respectively. The supremacy of Ohio was short-lived. By 1890 Illinois had assumed leadership; Rockford, Rock Island, Moline, and Chicago became centers of production. By this time there was some extension of production into Wisconsin and Iowa. The needs of the market dictated the geographic pattern of production. Thus mower firms usually remained in the hay-producing states, such as New York and Ohio, while the reaper, harvester, and binder producers thrived in the grain areas of the Midwest. During this period, however, no great centers of production rose. The industry remained highly dispersed in a large number of small plants that served local markets.

Although the South remained predominantly an agricultural region, a farm machinery industry did not develop there. The new farm machines of the nineteenth century were not suited to the southern agricultural economy, particularly the cotton culture that dominated large areas.

GEOGRAPHIC MARKET STABILIZATION. After 1890 new trends that affected the spatial patterns of farm machinery production became apparent. This date is generally considered as marking the disappearance of the frontier and the end of the great westward movement. This change directly affected the implement industry in three ways (27–11). First, the distributional pattern of the farm machinery industry stabilized. Second, market stabilization witnessed the disappearance of numerous small firms that had previously produced on contract from the larger companies which held key patents. The small firms were able to survive as long as inadequate transportation provided a significant cost advantage to small producers serving local markets. With improved transportation and a stable market, the need for subcontracting diminished and the major companies increased production in their own plants to gain economies of scale. Also, competition increased and only the efficient producers were capable of surviving. Third, with market stabilization the companies began to reorganize their distribution systems. In the earlier period the implement producers had agents who received farm machinery on consignment and sold within specified areas. When the market was expanding into new areas, little care was given to selecting agents or even to seeing that all regions were served. In most instances the important consideration was simply to have a marketing outlet in a region. With increasing specialization and growing competition, it was necessary to have a more effective marketing organization. The leading companies now attempted to have representatives in all market areas.

CONCENTRATION OF PRODUCTION. The trends of the 1890s culminated with the creation of large companies through mergers and other procedures. Between 1902 and 1931, the modern organizational and geographic structure evolved. The large companies were formed by becoming major producers of a single line of products and then expanding to full-line production of farm machinery. Harvesting machinery companies provided the initial core of companies that formed the International Harvester Company. The John Deere Company's amalgamations centered initially on acquiring tillage machinery companies; Allis Chalmers began as a tractor-producing organization and added farm machinery companies through mergers.

Geographic Concentration. A concentration of production facilities began with the amalgamation of companies. This was accomplished by various actions. For one, production was concentrated at a small number of centers rather than decentralized at numerous locations. For another, there was a concentration of production of a particular type of implement at a specific location to secure economies of scale. For example, when International Harvester acquired the Plano Company's harvesting machinery plant at West Pullman, Illinois, it moved the equipment to Chicago to consolidate production there, and the West Pullman plant specialized in other equipment. Similarly, the Milwaukee Harvester Company's production was transferred to Chicago, and the Milwaukee plant specialized in the production of cream separators and stationary gasoline engines.

Although the regional pattern of production was not greatly changed between 1900 and 1920, scores of small centers disappeared as output became concentrated in a few large centers. The number of establishments declined from 715 in 1899 to 521 in 1919. More significant was the development of the massive centers of production that dominated output. During this same period, total employment rose from 57,254 to 67,177.

The concentration of production is best illustrated by geographic localization of the International Harvester plants in 1920. The major operation was located in Chicago, where four plants produced a total of 675,000 binders, reapers, threshers, mowers, rakes, and corn shellers; 30,000 tractors; 45,000 wagons; and 110,000 tons of twine. Other plants were located at Akron, which produced 15,800 motor trucks and commerical cars; Milwaukee, which produced 150,000 engines, cream separators, and tractors; West Pullman, which produced a total of 150,000 manure spreaders, corn planters, cultivators, and threshers; Rock Falls, Illinois, which produced corn shellers, harrows, hay loaders, and rakes; Springfield, Ohio, which produced a total of 85,000 harvesting and seeding machines, hay presses, and manure spreaders; Auburn, New York, which produced 225,000 harvesting machines and tillage implements and 20,000 tons of twine; Chattanooga, Tennessee, which produced 30,000 plows and evaporators; Canton, Illinois, which produced 10,000 plows, cultivators, and corn planters, and Saint Paul, Minnesota, which produced 12,000 tons of twine.

International Harvester Company. The International Harvester Company, organized in 1902, was the first of the modern companies to be created by merger; the merger consisted of the five largest producers of harvesting machinery. This amalgamation brought under a single company the control of 90 percent of the production of grain binders and 80 percent of the mowers in the United States.

Although the original amalgamation gave International Harvester dominance in the production of harvesting and mowing machinery, the company still lacked facilities to produce a full line of farm machinery. Beginning in 1903 the company began efforts to become a full-line producer. International Harvester not only purchased short-line firms, but also made selling arrangements with specialty companies to market their products under Harvester's name. The company's selling arrangements with other firms during this transition period helped it retain its dealers in the interharvesting seasons even before it became a full-line firm. Finally, in 1919 the company became a full-line manufacturer when it announced its entrance into the production of plows.

A unique problem in the amalgamation involved trade names. For many years International Harvester did not abandon the trade names used by the companies it acquired for fear of losing buyers. For example, by 1912, although the McCormick and Deering lines were the leading sellers, the company still marketed machines under the names Champion, Buckeye, Milwaukee, and Osborne. This situation created severe distributional problems. During the earlier competitive period most of the constituent companies, particularly McCormick and Deering, had developed intensive marketing systems. After the amalgamation the McCormick and Deering dealers were retained essentially in their entirety, as were some of the other outlets. As long as International Harvester remained basically a producer of harvesting equipment, the problem remained manageable; but when the line of farm machines was expanded, it became increasingly difficult to supply all dealers with a full line of machines. For almost 20 years two complete lines of harvesting and tillage machinery were produced. Such a variety of models taxed the planning ability of the company's engineers and the productive ability of its plants. The International Harvester organization believed that

> so long as there is competition it is desirable for the company to maintain five selling organizations for the purpose of getting the largest amount of effort from the greatest number of local agents without expense to the company, and for the purpose of utilizing in its own business as much as possible of the local agency material rather than permit any of it to become available for competitors. [2]

With the development of the International Harvester Company, the U.S. government began an investigation as to possible monopoly infringements on the Sherman Anti-Trust Act. Although the government was frustrated in these attempts, the U.S. Senate in 1912 passed a resolution directing the Bureau of

[2]*Report of the Commissioner of Corporations on the International Harvester Company* (Washington, D.C.: Government Printing Office, 1913), p. 66.

Corporations to investigate the farm implement trade and, specifically, the control of trade by the International Harvester Company. The report of the bureau, published in 1913, indicated that although competition was keen prior to the preamalgamation period, it had not declined as drastically as other companies had claimed. However, the Bureau concluded, "There is no doubt that the principal motive for the formation of the International Harvester Company was to eliminate competition and to secure a dominant position in the trade."[3]

The bureau report surveyed competitive methods used after the establishment of the large companies. These included bogus independents, full-line forcing, monopolizing the best dealers, and resale price maintenance. "Full-line forcing" is a term applied in the implement industry to imply exclusive dealing. The bureau found that International Harvester was able to force dealers to handle new tillage lines under the threat of depriving dealers of its monopolized harvesting machinery lines. The company also negotiated exclusive-dealing clauses in its dealer contracts. This practice was, however, discontinued in 1905 when antitrust proceedings were threatened against the company in several states.

As a response to the bureau report, the U.S. government instituted a suit against the International Harvester Company for violation of the Sherman Anti-Trust Act. The government hoped to divide the company. In 1914 the court ruled in favor of the government, and the company was ordered to be "separated and divided among at least three substantially equal, separate, distinct and independent corporations with wholly separate owners and stockholders."[4] Two months later the company was able to have the order amended to read, "be divided in such manner and into such numbers of parts of separate and distinct ownership as may be necessary to restore competitive conditions and bring about a new situation in harmony with law."[5] The 1914 decision was immediately appealed to the U.S. Supreme Court. The case was inconclusively argued in 1915 and again in 1917, and in 1918 the appeal was postponed for the duration of the war.

In July 1918 International Harvester, desiring to settle the drawn-out negotiations, made a proposal to the attorney general. The two parties agreed to a consent decree that modified the original order. The company requested that the 1914 decision be dismissed and the modified decree replace it. In a report of the attorney general in 1918, the Harvester case was described as "the most fundamental issue which had arisen under the Sherman Act since its constitutionality was determined"(27–20).

The 1918 consent decree specified three stipulations (27–18). The first was that International Harvester could not have more than one agent or representative at any one location. As a response the number of dealers declined from 31,800 in 1917 to 13,860 in 1919. The company discontinued the practice of producing two complete lines of implements having the McCormick and Deering names.

[3]Ibid., p. 66.
[4]*Report of the Federal Trade Commission on the Agricultural Implement Industry* (Washington, D.C.: Government Printing Office, 1938), p. 156.
[5]Ibid., p. 160.

With the restriction of dealerships, the two lines became uneconomical and were combined. A second stipulation was aimed at reducing the number of lines marketed. The company was required to sell the harvesting machinery lines sold under the trade names of Osborne, Milwaukee, and Champion. The purchaser was to be an established producer of farm machinery. The third order required International to offer for sale the plants that produced the Osborne and Champion lines, these being located at Auburn, New York, and Springfield, Ohio. However, no buyers could be found for these plants, and International was permitted by the court to convert them to other purposes.

The consent decree of 1918 appears to have had little influence on reducing the dominance of the International Harvester Company in the production of farm machinery. In 1922 the Department of Justice indicated that International had 75.4 percent of the grain binder, 66.7 percent of the mower, and 70.5 percent of the corn binder trade. The John Deere Company, the nearest competitor, had between 11 and 15 percent of the total trade for these implements. As a result, in July 1923 the Department of Justice filed a petition in the District Court of Minnesota to revise the consent decree and bring about a further dissolution of International Harvester. However, in 1926 the court denied the petition, indicating that International did not have an unreasonable monopoly in the farm machinery trade of the United States. The court indicated that International's share of the market of all harvesting machinery had declined from 85 percent in 1902 to 64 percent in 1925. Furthermore, significant new competitors had developed. The Department of Justice appealed the Minnesota court decision to the U.S. Supreme Court. In June 1927 the Court upheld the lower court's decision. This decision concluded the Harvester's court battle which had extended over the previous 15 years. The Supreme Court decision stated the oft-quoted dictum that "the law does not make the mere size of a corporation, however impressive, or the existence of unexerted power on its part, an offense, when unaccompanied by unlawful conduct in the exercise of its power."[6]

An important question is whether the court actions influenced the localization trends of the industry during this period. No direct evidence is available. However, empirical observation reveals a strong geographic concentration of production, indicating that the court actions had little, if any, influence on locational decisions. The location of the industry was influenced primarily by cost factors rather than political considerations.

MODERN GEOGRAPHIC PATTERN.   The geographic pattern of the farm machinery industry has experienced little change in over 50 years. The East North Central and the West North Central states today have about 80 percent of the value added in the farm machinery industry. Within this region, Illinois leads (with 25 percent of the total), followed by Iowa (about 19 percent) and Wisconsin (12 percent).

With new types of farm machinery designed for the farm economy of the South and the Pacific Coast, these regions are now developing a specialized implement industry. The South produces about 11 percent of the nation's out-

⁶Ibid., p. 162.

put; Kentucky, Tennessee, and Georgia are the leading states. The Pacific Coast produces about 2.5 percent of the nation's farm machinery. The industry there is concentrated in California, which specializes in machinery especially adapted to the agriculture of the region. Farm machinery output in the Northeast has declined from about 7 percent of the total in 1958 to 5 percent in recent years. This reflects the general decline of the market for agricultural machinery in this region.

PETROLEUM REFINING INDUSTRY

The world's petroleum refining industry has been evolving since the first oil well was drilled at Titusville, Pennsylvania, in 1859. Until 1940 the United States was the major oil refining nation, with approximately two-thirds of the world's capacity. This localization reflected the large oil production as well as the huge market demands of the United States. The United States was the only country that possessed a sufficiently large demand to enable refineries to be economically oriented to the market.

In the rest of the world, the refinery industry was largely concentrated in the oil-producing countries. The Soviet Union and the Dutch West Indies (Netherlands Antilles) each possessed about 8 percent of the world's total refinery capacity. Other important early refinery centers oriented to crude oil resources included Rumania, Iran, the Netherlands East Indies (Indonesia), Mexico, and Venezuela.

A small refinery industry developed in Canada, France, the United Kingdom, and Germany—consuming areas that were deficient or lacking in oil resources. However, the total capacity of the market-oriented refineries outside the United States did not exceed 100,000,000 barrels annually. In general the markets were not sufficiently large to justify a large refinery industry. Oil demands could best be met by importing finished products.

During the early 1940s the war demands for petroleum products resulted in a rapid expansion of refinery capacity. The industry expanded in the traditional refinery areas. U.S. capacity between 1940 and 1945 increased by nearly 400,000 barrels daily. The demands of the Western Hemisphere were met primarily by the refineries in the United States and the Caribbean area. The Middle Eastern refineries provided the oil products for much of the Eastern Hemisphere. The largest refinery in the Middle East, at Abadan, Iran, doubled its capacity from about 60,000,000 to 120,000,000 barrels annually.

A new locational pattern has evolved since World War II with the growth of refinery capacity in the major market areas of Europe and Japan. Italy is now the third largest refining center in the world, exceeded only by the United States and the Soviet Union. Following Italy the leading refinery nations are Japan, the United Kingdom, France, and West Germany. Many of the petroleum-oriented areas have declined in their relative position as refining centers. In 1939 Iran was the fourth largest refining center, but by 1975 it had dropped to thirteenth position, and the Dutch West Indies had declined from third to eleventh place.

Another change in the locational pattern began in the 1950s when a number of developing countries, previously supplied by traditional prewar sources by exports from countries where refinery capacity had expanded, began to build their own refineries. The construction of these small national refineries (a national refinery is one that supplies domestic requirements) was justified by the desire to become independent of foreign marketing companies, conserve foreign currency, develop local industrial employment, and improve the prestige of the nation. Petroleum was discovered in a number of developing countries, and even though demand has remained low to this day, the construction of national refineries had further justification.

At the present time about two-thirds of the world's refining capacity is market oriented, and one-third is resource oriented. This is a reversal of the 1939 locations, when two-thirds of the refineries were resource oriented. In 1973 and early 1974 a critical oil shortage was created in the world when the oil-producing, countries of the Middle East imposed an embargo on oil exports to a number of consuming nations. It was well illustrated how fragile the oil refining industry is when a processing nation is denied its source of crude petroleum. The future localization of the petroleum refining industry was clouded in the mid-1970s because of changing sources of petroleum, governmental policies of producing and consuming countries, and altered market patterns.

Theoretical Framework

From the earliest period, the petroleum refining industry has developed under both the Weberian and Löschian frameworks. The refineries oriented to raw materials are in general oriented to least cost sites. Many of the earliest refineries were built in the western Pennsylvania oil fields, in search of the lowest cost point of production. This practice has continued, and some of the world's largest refineries—such as the Abadan refinery on the Persian Gulf and the refineries on Lake Maracaibo—are raw material oriented.

At the same time that the least cost locations were developing, the petroleum refining industry was also being oriented to market regions. One of the earliest centers was on the East Coast of the United States. This trend has accelerated in recent times with the massive refinery-building programs in such areas as the oil deficient European nations. The Löschian orientation to markets reflects the profit motivation of the oil companies in seeking the largest potential markets.

Whether the trend toward a Löschian framework of development will continue in the future is uncertain. Most of the oil-producing nations are now enacting legislation that will require the establishment of domestic refineries. As this develops, the Weberian philosophy of seeking least cost sites for raw-material-oriented refineries will necessarily prevail. The minimizing of transportation costs due primarily to larger tankers also enhances the Weberian approach to seeking least cost refining sites.

Locational Factors

The localization of the petroleum refining industry is influenced by economic, political, and technological factors. The extent of the influence of each of these factors depends on the precise situation of a particular refinery (22).

MARKET INFLUENCES.   The size, location, and nature of the market exert a strong influence in the establishment of a refinery. If size is the dominant factor, the refinery will normally be oriented to a raw material source, especially if the refinery is so situated that it can serve a number of markets (26).

Economies of scale are significant in a refinery operation. "Assuming that the capital cost of a ton of refinery output for a 5 million tons-per-year plant is 100, the comparable indices for 3 million and 1 million ton units are 123 and 190 respectively" (22–185). As a result refineries have become increasingly larger. To illustrate, in 1947 there were 67 refineries in the United States that had an annual capacity of less than 750,000 tons. By 1959, 43 of these were no longer operating and two had increased their capacity to over 2,250,000 tons. The 22 refineries that continued to operate were located largely in isolated areas and possessed a transport cost advantage in serving a local region (21). The number of refineries in the United States decreased from 326 in 1955 to about 275 in 1974. By contrast, the refinery capacity during the same period rose from 8,420,000 to over 11,000,000 barrels daily.

The trend to larger refineries implies that these refineries must have access to large, expanding markets if economies of scale are to be achieved. The economies in transport costs are frequently limited to large markets. Thus if a single market will not support a large refinery, it will likely be more economical to locate the plant at the raw material source or at some intermediate point in order to serve several markets.

A refinery must also consider the pattern of consumption in the regions where its products will be sold. Consumption patterns vary considerably from region to region. For example, in some areas gasoline dominates, in others fuel oil, and in still others distillates. If a market-oriented refinery is to be economical, it must adjust to the consumption patterns of its market region. With the trend to larger refineries, the adjustment to local or regional consumption patterns may be difficult where markets are relatively small. Consequently small market areas may be best served by raw-material or intermediate-oriented refineries.

Market influences play a role in both raw-material and market-oriented refineries. The resource-based plant may have three distinct advantages. First, it may serve several market areas so that, by increasing its size, it may take advantage of economies of scale in refining. Second, the demands of the combined markets may justify a full-scale refinery that produces a wide range of products.

As a result markets with different requirements may be served. Third, there may be a saving in transport costs because a certain amount of crude oil is lost in the refining process.

The market-oriented refineries have three cost advantages in marketing their product. First, the cost of transporting crude oil is generally lower than transporting refined products. Second, oil may be obtained from a number of sources. Third, the products of the refinery can be more easily adjusted to changing local and regional demands.

COMPARATIVE TRANSPORT COSTS. The location of a refinery can be influenced by differentials of transport costs for crude oil and finished products. Within recent years, the differences in the cost of transporting crude oil and products by tankers has continued to widen because of a number of factors. Since the development of oil tankers, there has always been a cost differential between crude oil (clean) and refined products (dirty). The differences in cost have continued to increase because crude oil can be transported in much larger tankers than finished products can (by all but a few of the largest tanker companies). Refined products are rarely transported in tankers of over 30,000 dwt because either the markets are too small or there are drought limitations in ports.

There are other transport cost advantages for crude oil. It is technologically easier to transport crude oil than many refined products. However, it is the totality of cost in transporting all products that must be considered. For example, it is cheaper to transport gasoline from the Midcontinent area to the East Coast than to transport crude oil by pipelines. However, the movement of residual oils, which are transported primarily by rail, from the Midcontinent to the East Coast is considerably higher than that of crude oil, so the total transportation costs for the refined products is higher than for crude oil. This factor has favored the growth of market-oriented refineries.

TANKER CAPACITY. In recent years the size of tankers has been greatly increased. In 1963, 75 percent of the world's tanker fleet had a carrying capacity below 40,000 dwt, and more than 90 percent was below 50,000 dwt. By 1968 only 60 percent was below 50,000 dwt, and about 20 percent of the fleet was above a size that could pass through the Suez Canal with a full load. By 1975 more than 33.3 percent of the tanker fleet was above 100,000 dwt.

The development of larger vessels has had a profound influence on the transport costs of crude oil. To illustrate, to transport crude oil from the Persian Gulf by the Cape of Good Hope route to northwest Europe, a 200,000-dwt vessel has a transport cost of at least 35 percent less per barrel than that of a 50,000-dwt vessel. However, a 100,000-dwt vessel compared to the 50,000-dwt vessel reduces the per-barrel transport cost by only 14 percent.

The reduction of transportation costs on crude oil has influenced refinery location in a number of ways. For one, it has reduced the attraction of refineries to the producing areas. Refineries, in increasing numbers, are being built in market areas at deep-water ports. The larger tankers have also encouraged the building of larger refineries because a refinery must have a significant size in order to be serviced by the larger vessels. For example, if a refinery is serviced by a 200,000-dwt vessel, it must have a capacity of 140,000 barrels daily, or have a storage capacity greater than a 10-day supply of petroleum. If the refinery were smaller it would require additional storage facilities, thus increasing costs.

INLAND TRANSPORTATION SYSTEMS.   A number of factors have influenced the development of inland transportation systems in recent years. The expansion of the market and the shift to lighter products, particularly in Europe, has encouraged the growth of pipelines. A network of crude oil and light-product pipelines has developed in the United States and is evolving in Europe and the Soviet Union. Until recently the development of the product pipeline in Europe was limited because of the high proportion of residual fuel oils produced in refineries in relation to total demands. As a result of the development of a light-product pipeline system, a refinery can be more centrally located to serve a larger market. This encourages the construction of larger refineries, which in turn can secure the advantages of economies of scale.

Another factor influencing the location of refineries in Europe is the increasing tendency of railroads to give preferential rates for the large-scale movement of crude oil and refined products. As a result of this competition from railroads, the construction of a number of product pipelines has been delayed or prevented. For example, in the United Kingdom the railroads have given special rates for block trains of petroleum products from coastal refineries. In Germany the railroads long prevented the construction of a product pipeline from Ingolstadt to Munich by offering lowered rates on refined products. The influence of the railroads is thus to expand the coastal refineries at the expense of inland refineries.

REFINERY SIZE.   There has been a remarkable increase in the size of refineries in recent decades. Prior to World War II there were only three refineries of over 80,000 barrels daily capacity—one in the Middle East, at Abadan, and two in the Caribbean, at Aruba and Curaçao. Today the average refinery has a capacity of nearly 60,000 barrels daily, with at least 86 refineries having an average daily capacity of 145,000 barrels. Between 1960 and 1965 the number of refineries in excess of 80,000 barrels daily increased by 2 1/2 times, and from 1966 to 1975 the number rose from 82 to more than 125.

The economies of scale are linked closely to the size of a refinery. In general the cost of the equipment of a refinery per barrel of capacity is directly related to its size. For example, the equipment costs are approximately the same for a 50,000-barrel-per-day plant as for an 80,000-barrel-per-day plant. Although the cost per barrel of capacity flattens out considerably beyond the 100,000-barrel-per-day plant, the larger the refinery the lower the cost per unit of capacity.

TYPES OF CRUDE OIL TRANSPORTED.   Most crude oils can be transported by pipelines. However, certain crude oils that have desirable qualities (e.g., low sulfur content) but are waxy and have a high pour point cannot be transported by pipeline. Examples of this type of crude oil are found in Libya and West Africa. These crudes must be blended with other crude oils before they can be transported in pipelines. As a result they lose some of their natural advantageous characteristics, and transport costs are increased. As a result refineries using these crude oils have a greater transport cost advantage if they are oriented to a coastal location serviced by tankers.

REFINERY YIELD PATTERN.   A variety of products is produced when petroleum is refined. However, the consumption patterns vary from region to region. For example, the greatest demand in the United States is for gasoline, while in Europe the greatest demand has traditionally been for fuel and diesel oils.

When markets are small and dispersed, the refinery is normally located near its raw material source. This was one of the reasons why refineries were built at Abadan, Aruba, Curaçao, and other resource-oriented refineries prior to World War II. Most countries did not have a sufficiently large market to absorb all the products produced in a large refinery. Most European countries prior to 1940 provided an excellent example of having a limited market demanding a variety of refined products. The postwar development of market-oriented European refineries was due to a great increase in volume of demand and an increase in demand for all the principal refined products.

Only if there is a demand for the total refinery yield can refineries operate economically in consuming areas. Problems have arisen in marketing many of the products produced in refineries built in the smaller consuming areas in recent years.

TECHNOLOGICAL IMPROVEMENTS.   The role of technology in localizing a refinery has changed over the decades. The location of a refinery will be influenced by the amount of crude oil versus the finished products that must be transported. Prior to 1900 the volume of oil was reduced between 25 and 50 percent in the refinery process, and prior to the development of thermal cracking about 5 barrels of oil were required to produce 1 barrel of gasoline. Thus in the early period of refining there was a distinct transport cost advantage for a refinery to be oriented to its raw material base.

Technological improvements have greatly altered this situation. In the present-day refining processes, less than 5 percent of the petroleum is lost, and the cracking processes make possible the desired products the market demands. As a result of these technological changes, there is a much wider choice in the location of a refinery.

Other technological developments affecting costs have been an increasing degree of automatic process control, optimization of operations by means of computers, and automatic blending of products. The physical plan of refineries has become more centralized in recent years. In the past each processing unit was a separate plant with its own control room and laboratories. Modern plants have a single central room, boilers and tanks are concentrated, run-down tanks have been nearly eliminated, and offices have been streamlined. As a result the area of land required by a refinery has been greatly reduced, thus lowering costs for roads and pipes. Maintenance costs have been lowered because of the higher standards of technical equipment. Within the past 15 years plant costs have been decreased by as much as 30 percent.

Furthermore, with a decrease in the variety of yield represented by an emphasis on gasoline, refineries have become simpler. The trend in the past several decades for more sophisticated products has been reversed to some extent. For example, aviation gasoline has been replaced by jet fuel, and high-octane gasoline is now challenged by virgin naphtha; both are straight-run distillation products. These technological changes have encouraged the decentralization of the refinery industry and have been particularly important in encouraging growth in the developing countries.

LABOR. Today the petroleum refining industry is one of the most highly automated industries. As a result the number of employees in a refinery is small. However, the employees are highly skilled and wage rates are high. Labor becomes an important factor in the localization of a refinery only in the less developed countries. Skilled workers have had to be imported in such areas as the Middle East and Africa. Nevertheless the availability of labor plays a minor role in the location of a refinery.

ELECTRICITY. A petroleum refinery consumes a large quantity of electricity. However, the differentials in cost of producing electricity from one region to another are so small that they have no significant locational influences.

GOVERNMENTAL INFLUENCES. In the past 40 years governmental influences have assumed an increasingly important role in the localization of the world's refinery industry. The influences have at times been direct, at other times indirect. Policies have sometimes been legislated, and at other times they have evolved piecemeal.

Direct Influences. A definite policy of governmental influence in refinery construction began about 1928, when the French government built the first refinery in the nation. Although the French refinery industry was highly subsidized and uneconomical, it continued to grow. Other non-oil-producing nations have virtually compelled companies to construct refineries if they were to be permitted to market products within the nation. Under these conditions economic considerations frequently become of secondary importance.

There have also been political pressures to encourage the construction of refineries in petroleum-producing countries. One of the better examples of governmental legislation affecting refinery construction occurred in Venezuela. The Venezuelan Hydrocarbon Act requires that the refinery capacity within the nation be increased so that a given quantity of the Venezuelan production be refined domestically. In a recent agreement between Saudi Arabia and Japan, it was stipulated that a certain proportion of the oil exported to Japan had to be refined within Saudi Arabia.

In recent years many of the developing nations have required that refineries be built, frequently as status symbols. As a result a worldwide pattern of small, but economically marginal, refineries have emerged. These refineries are usually protected by a high tariff—as much as 40 percent on import parity in Africa and Central America. A number of governments have established monopolistic arrangements with the refining companies; examples of this situation exist in Portugal, Ghana, and Tunisia.

Indirect Influences. Many nations have established policies that have indirectly influenced the development of their refinery industry. For example, the United States has created isolated regulations that have, over time, greatly affected the development of the petroleum refining industry. The actions were often complicated and not integrated into a sound national petroleum policy. The evolution of such influences dates from about 1928, when the American oil industry gained its first oil concessions in the Middle East. This operation began the pursuit for petroleum overseas, which ultimately resulted in the neglect of the domestic industry. Over the years the foreign operations were encouraged. Most significant in this encouragement was the foreign tax credit decision by the U.S. State and Treasury departments in 1950. This decision permitted the American companies to allocate part of the royalty they paid to the governments of the oil-producing countries as a tax, and then to credit this amount against their U.S. taxes on a dollar-to-dollar basis. The results were dramatic. In 1950, the Arabian American Oil Company (Aramco) paid federal taxes of $50,000,000; in 1951, $6,000,000.

Tax policies such as these have constituted strong disincentives to domestic exploration, development and refining. For the past quarter of a century, our domestic corporations, the multinationals, have been operating abroad because of the great economic advantages in developing foreign oil resources.

The government established an import quota program in the 1950s that restricted crude oil imports to a set percentage of domestic production. At the same time no restrictions were placed on importing refined products. Domestic production rose slowly during the 1960s, reaching a peak about 1970. At the same time consumption soared, so there was a widening gap between production and consumption. This gap in demand could be met only by importing refined products.

To further the development of foreign oil deposits, particularly in the Middle East, the per-barrel price of crude oil was, until the late 1960s, determined unilaterally by the oil companies, not by the producing countries. A producing-state group, the Organization of Petroleum Exporting Countries, was formed in 1960 in an effort to gain some control over prices. However, this group had little influence until 1969, when Col. Muammar al-Qaddafi seized power in Libya. In 1971 he demanded higher prices for Libyan petroleum, but was initially rebuffed. He resorted to what has come to be known as "Arab salami" tactics by acting, not against the powerful major companies, but against the smaller independents. The first company to yield was Occidental Petroleum, which gave the Libyan government a 30-cents-a-barrel increase and a higher tax rate. After the Libyan government won this concession, the other countries of North Africa and the Middle East gained concessions, first from the independents and then from the major oil companies. Since then the price demands have leapfrogged upward, with oil rising from about $2 per barrel to over $11 per barrel in 1975. There have been attempts by the multinationals to form a united front to regain control over prices. For example, in 1970 the U.S. Justice Department's antitrust division, over some protests, provided an unpublished "business letter of review" to the oil companies. This letter amounted to a guarantee of immunity from civil antitrust prosecution for combining to negotiate jointly with Libya. However, the efforts of the American companies and the government have had little or no influence on the rise in the price of crude oil in North Africa and the Middle East.

The lack of a coordinated energy policy in the United States is evident by the piecemeal procedures and policies of the 1950s and 1960s. Finally, in June 1971 President Richard Nixon presented his first policy statement on the energy problems. However, governmental action was extremely slow. The full extent of the crisis was revealed when the Arab nations placed an embargo on oil to the United States in October 1973 because of this nation's pro-Israel position in the 1973 conflict between Israel and the Arab nations.

As a result of the various actions, or lack of actions, there has been little expansion of the refining capacity in the United States in recent years. The decisions of the multinational companies are so intertwined with governmental actions that it is essentially impossible to separate them. However, there can be little doubt that the size of the refinery capacity of the United States has been directly influenced by decisions on the international level.

FINANCIAL AID.   Financial aid to underdeveloped areas has been used to develop the petroleum refining industry. To illustrate, the Soviet Union, Rumania, and Czechoslovakia have provided loans and technical aid for the construction of state-owned refineries. India's refinery industry has been increased by the Soviet Union's construction of two refineries and Rumania's willingness to build one. The Soviet Bloc nations have built refineries in such countries as Egypt, Syria, Ethiopia, and Cuba. Such aid represents a readily obtainable objective for the Soviet Bloc countries in that the capital outlay is relatively small and personnel can be obtained largely from the expanding labor force of the underdeveloped country. In return for this investment, the Soviet Bloc countries hope for a favorable economic and political response from the countries in which the refineries are built. The petroleum refinery has become a status symbol of progress, similar to a new iron and steel mill.

The building of new refineries by the Soviet Bloc has also aided the developing countries in controlling the operations of the international oil companies. For example, there was much dissatisfaction in Ethiopia with the prices charged by the international oil companies. Because the country was not able to negotiate successfully on lowering prices, it sought capital from the Soviet Union to build a state-owned refinery. This type of development could be a problem not only to the international oil companies, having headquarters in the United States and Europe, but also to the governments of the developing countries. A developing country is frequently obligated to support the commerical interests of the oil companies in the event of conflict with the interests of its own government.

COMPANY STRATEGY.   Several refineries have been built in recent years because of company policies. Companies are frequently reluctant to have their total operations in a single country due to national and international tensions resulting in the destruction of property or expropriation of facilities. As a means of reducing dependence on a single area, international companies will produce their oil in some countries and have refineries in other countries. Thus, if the supply of oil is disrupted from one source, the only problem is to find an alternative source, or if a refinery is expropriated in one country, the crude oil can be diverted to a refinery in another country.

The international oil companies have built refineries for a number of other reasons in recent years. Several international companies have invested considerable sums of money in oil production. In recent years many of these endeavors have been highly successful. However, as the number of countries with refineries has increased, the markets have become more competitive. Certain companies have found it necessary to process the crude oil they produce in the countries having small markets in order to secure outlets for at least a part of their production. In some instances these refineries may be uneconomical and survive only as a result of such government actions as quota controls on imported oil products or the complete exclusion of all products that compete with the domestic refineries.

As a result of present-day trends, the international oil companies have not always been able to build refineries at lowest-cost locations. This situation has created a number of problems. First, the large export refineries usually oriented to crude oil supplies must frequently be operated at less than capacity. Second, and more important, in order to protect their crude oil markets, the companies have been forced to build so-called defensive refineries. These refineries are in themselves uneconomical to operate, but they guarantee that the company can continue to supply the market with products at prices which enable it to achieve an overall profit on its vertically integrated operations.

The competition between refining centers has been increasing in recent years. Until the late 1950s most countries sought refineries and gave protection to the company in order to ensure the local market. As a result a company could assure itself a profit without undue increases in prices of the petroleum products by securing crude at a discount from the posted price. Further, petroleum products in these countries often enjoy a lack of competition; therefore the uneconomical refinery can operate within a given margin and supply its products below import prices (26–131).

As competition has arisen between established international companies and new entrants, countries have gradually imposed more stringent conditions on refining construction. These new relations take on numerous forms. For example, an offer to build a refinery by Mobil Oil was rejected by Ghana in favor of an alternate proposal from an Italian Company, Ente Nazionale Idrocarburi, commonly known as E.N.I. In return for a monopoly in the refinery and marketing operations within the country, the Italian company offered the government of Ghana a 50-percent share in the refinery, without payment, after ten years of operation. Similar arrangements have been made by E.N.I. in Morocco and Tunisia.

In the past the international companies usually did not desire local capital participation because it limited their operating and financial flexibility. National pressures and competition have forced an alteration of this position. In several countries the construction of a refinery is a joint venture between a company and local capital. In recent years this has occurred in such countries as Peru, the Philippines, and Thailand.

The demands for petroleum have been increasing at such a pace that companies are tempted to enter new areas which at the present do not justify refineries. Decisions to do so have been encouraged by the increasingly diverse means of financing refineries in countries where sound economic grounds do not yet exist. There is every indication that this pattern will continue in the newly developing countries.

Site Considerations

Because of the nature of petroleum refining, the selection of a good site is a prime requisite. A refinery, with its many units and the considerable space occupied by its storage tanks, needs an area of ample size. The smallest plant requires more than 100 acres, and the larger plants frequently require more than 1,000 acres. Since this is an expanding industry, the availability of additional space must also be considered when a new plant is erected, as should the cost of the land required.

The modern refinery should be so situated that there can be a gravitational flow of oil from one unit to the next. Thus the tank farm should be placed on the highest ground and the loading platform for the finished products on the lowest ground. For example, if the plant is on the coast and most of the products are exported, a surface sloping gradually to the water's edge is desirable. If rugged land is the only type available, the storage tank farms are normally located on the highest ground. If the refinery is situated along a stream in a narrow valley, the possibilities of flood should be investigated. A flood in an oil yard can have disastrous consequences.

The availability of an adequate water supply is essential to refinery operations. It is frequently said among refinery men that a refinery can never have too much water. The importance of cooling water for the refinery operations, potable water for personnel, and pure water for boilers requires that a thorough study of the water situation be made at the time the refinery site is selected. The amount of water required varies with the type of plant and the temperature conditions of the area's water. Twice as much cooling water will be needed if its temperature is 85° F instead of 60° F. In some locations the amount of water needed can be reduced by the use of cooling towers. In other areas, such as regions of high humidity, the effectiveness of such towers is greatly reduced. In some areas, the silt or alkali content of the water will be too high for effective use in many refinery operations. A supply of pure water is necessary for boiler and treating departments; this is normally about 30 percent of the total amount required. The remainder may be low grade (e.g., saltwater) for cooling condensers, fire fighting, and general use. For a simple refinery with a 25,000-barrel daily capacity, the pure cooling water requirement may be 15,000,000–30,000,000 gal per day.

This is more than the flow of a small stream. To take so much pure water from the local population and return it to a stream as warm, polluted water is impractical and, in certain places, illegal.

Air pollution is another problem that influences the desirability of a refinery site. The prevailing winds, the frequency of atmospheric inversions, and the possibility of smog pockets are important aspects in air pollution. If a community is subject to air pollution from refinery operations, the industry is likely to be subject to local controls. Although air pollution can be controlled, its control is frequently expensive. For example, it is costly to remove the sulfur precipitates from high towers.

One of the most difficult problems in selecting a refinery site is the disposal of waste products, which frequently carry chemicals and refuse oils. In the past many refineries were located on streams, and during high-water stages the sludge pits were opened and the water was allowed to wash the wastes away. This, however, caused extreme pollution, killing fish and destroying the usefulness of the water for towns further downstream. Because most states now prohibit this type of waste disposal, large areas must be provided for the construction of settling pits in which the waste is absorbed.

The availability of transportation facilities is of importance in selecting a refinery site. Because of the tremendous quantity of petroleum processed, the selection of a particular site may reduce transportation costs considerably. The cheapest method of transport is by tanker (Table 3.1). Pipeline operations are generally more expensive than water transport. Railroad transport is the next most expensive method and tank trucking on the highways is the most expensive. The latter is used only on the shortest hauls of finished products. To take advantage of the cheapest assembly of crude oil and the marketing of finished products, refineries are frequently located at ocean or lake sites. Such sites require a good harbor plus docking facilities. At the same time marketing of the finished products in the immediate area usually demands adequate pipeline, railway, or highway facilities.

United States

ESTABLISHMENT OF REFINERY PATTERN. The development of the oil refinery pattern in the United States has always reflected the availability of crude oil and markets. Almost simultaneously with the discovery of oil in the Appalachian Province in 1859, refineries were built in the oil region, in inland market centers such as Cleveland and Pittsburgh, and in the Atlantic Coast cities of Philadelphia, Baltimore, and New York. Until 1890 four states—New York, New Jersey, Pennsylvania, and Ohio—processed more than 95 percent of the crude oil. Within these states the East Coast refineries produced about 60 percent of the total refined products. This concentration in refining can be attributed to the large eastern markets, a growing demand for refined products abroad, and the influence of the Standard Oil Company in developing refineries in market areas.

Table 3.1

Comparative Costs of Transportation of Crude Oil

	Unit Costs Per Barrel Per 100 Miles
Tanker	1.0
Barge	1.1
Pipeline	1.3
Tank Car	7.3–10.6
Truck	53.0–54.0

The period between 1890 and 1910 was one of great geographic expansion of petroleum refining. New oil fields were developed in the Gulf Coast, in the Midcontinent, in Illinois and southwestern Indiana, and in the California provinces. As a result, the dominance of the Northeast in refining declined rapidly. Major new construction was concentrated first in the lower Great Lakes area, next along the Gulf Coast, then in the Midcontinent, and somewhat later in California. By 1910 the East Coast and Appalachian refineries were processing no more than 35 percent of the nation's crude oil. Although the industry has increased greatly in size in recent decades, the basic refining pattern had been established by 1910.

RECENT TRENDS.   Although the basic pattern has remained stable for the past 50 years, not all districts have grown at the same rate. In the period from 1960 to 1972, when refining output increased 38.8 percent, from 3,119,327,000 to 4,332,381,000 barrels, six of the petroleum refining districts experienced a comparative gain and seven districts experienced a comparative loss. The greatest comparative gain was experienced by the Louisiana Gulf Coast, which was oriented to the domestic production of the Southwest. The Texas Gulf Coast experienced the greatest comparative loss because of lagging refinery construction. The comparative loss of output on the East Coast reflected the growing tendency of this region to rely on imported foreign refined products. The Midwestern areas experienced comparative gains because they were less dependent on imported petroleum products. But the inland oil-producing areas experienced a comparative loss because production did not keep pace with oil imports and thus refining output lagged relatively (Fig. 3.4).

FUTURE LOCATION OF REFINERIES.   Within the United States there are three major market areas: the densely populated megalopolis from Washington to Boston, the lower Great Lakes region, and the West Coast, primarily California. Of these three, the California area is the only one where the petroleum and the market are in relatively close proximity.

The petroleum products consumed in the megalopolis can be secured from refineries located there or on the Gulf Coast. The question is, Should new or enlarged refineries be located on the Gulf Coast or in the megalopolis? Of the

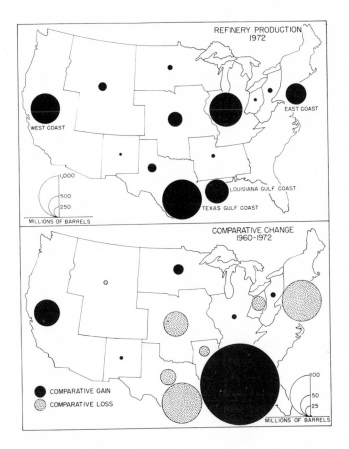

Figure 3.4. U.S. Petroleum Refining Industry. *Above:* Production, 1972. *Below:* Comparative change, 1960–1972.

factors to be considered, the transport costs on crude oil and petroleum products become vital. Once these have been determined, other regional differences in cost can be evaluated. In the consideration of transport advantages, two questions must be considered: (1) Is there a difference in the cost of shipping a barrel of crude oil and a barrel of finished products? (2) How much crude oil is required to produce a barrel of finished products?

A recent study by Lindsay revealed that there were no appreciable differences between the transport costs of crude oil and finished products from the Gulf to the East coasts (20). Using ocean tankers, it costs about 33 cents to ship either a barrel of crude oil or refined products from Galveston to New York City. Thus transport costs favor neither the Gulf or East coast areas as locations for oil refineries. Other factors must be considered.

A certain volume of the crude oil is lost in the refining process. The loss will vary from about 5 to 10 percent, depending on the type of refinery. Thus, in the

30,000-barrel daily capacity refinery, as much as 3,000 barrels are consumed in the refining process. The total transport saving would be about $1,000 per day if the oil were refined on the Gulf Coast.

Fuel costs may also be a major determinant in the location of a refinery. Refineries at all locations burn some portion of their heavy yields. In practice, a refinery on the Gulf Coast will find it cheaper to use natural gas and to ship the residual fuel oil as a product. The difference in the price of natural gas and residual fuel oil on the Gulf Coast is due to the greater cost of transporting natural gas. Specifically, it costs about 13 cents more to move 1,000,000 Btu of natural gas from the Gulf Coast to the East Coast by pipeline than it does to ship 1,000,000 Btu of residual fuel oil by tanker. Because the price of the fuels is approximately the same per Btu, the value per 1,000,000 Btu on the Gulf Coast is about 13 cents higher for fuel oil than for natural gas. Thus the Gulf Coast refinery has an option as to the type of fuel it consumes, while the East Coast refinery does not have a choice. This advantage to the Gulf Coast may be as much as $900 per day in a 30,000-barrel refinery.

Other cost differentials, such as electric power, labor, water, and chemicals, appear to be of little importance. In conclusion, the cost advantages per day for a 30,000-barrel refinery on the Gulf Coast in contrast to one on the North Atlantic Coast will vary from $500 to about $2,000, depending on the type of refinery. The question is whether these savings are sufficient to affect the location of a refinery. By applying ratios published by government agencies in order to determine profits, it is revealed that the pretax profits for a refinery on the Gulf Coast would be 4–13 percent higher than on the East Coast. The more complex the refinery, the greater the differential.

In regard to the third major market area, that in the lower Great Lakes, the locational advantage will hinge on the two interrelated issues of transport and fuel differential costs. Most of the crude oil for the lower Great Lakes area comes from the Midcontinent and West Texas oil fields. Crude oil may be shipped the entire distance by pipeline or by a combination of pipeline and barge. However, for such heavier refined oils as heavy fuel oils and lubricating oils, pipelines cannot be utilized and the products must be moved by rail at least part of the way. The cost of moving a barrel of refined oil from West Texas to Chicago by rail is approximately 27.5 cents per 100 miles, while for crude oil by pipeline it is 1.93 cents per 100 miles. Consequently the transport advantage for a lower Great Lakes refining site is quite large.

In contrast, however, the fuel costs are in favor of the oil fields and not the lower Great Lakes. The reasoning follows much the same line as in the difference between the Gulf and East coasts, except that the refinery not located at the market could buy natural gas at a price below the value of heavy fuel oil. Thus the Gulf Coast refiner burns natural gas and ships the fuel oil to market. In contrast, a West Texas refiner serving the Chicago market finds that natural gas prices are higher rather than lower than the value of his fuel oil; this is because the cost of shipping fuel oil to market by the cheapest combination of transport facilities is still much greater than the pipeline charges on natural gas moving to market. Thus the West Texas refiner will find it to his advantage to sell all refinery gas in the natural gas market and burn additional fuel oils. However, the savings on fuel costs in the oil fields is not sufficient to offset the basic transport cost differentials. The other differentials in cost, such as water, labor, and electric power, are not significant. Thus the least cost location for the lower Great Lakes or Midcontinent–West Texas refinery is at the market rather than the oil field.

As a response to these forces the Gulf Coast area has increased its refinery capacity from 26 percent of the total in 1940 to about 33 1/3 percent in 1974, and the interior district centering on the lower Great Lakes has increased its capacity from 15 to 19 percent during this period. By contrast the East Coast has remained stable, with about 14 percent of the total refinery capacity. Its position has been maintained largely because of the importance of foreign crude oils. The West Coast has declined in relative importance, from 20 to 15 percent of the total capacity, which reflects the declining availability of crude oil; but the market has expanded rapidly during the past quarter of a century. The modern pattern of refining reflects economic forces that are likely to be projected into the future.

PORTLAND CEMENT INDUSTRY

The history of cement can be traced to the days of Babylonia and Assyria. The Egyptians used clay mortar in the pyramids, and the Romans produced a type of cement by mixing volcanic ash and quicklime, which to this day is often free from fissures. Whenever mankind has undertaken to build with rock, stone, or brick, and for any degree of permanence, some form of cement has been an indispensable construction material.

Before the development of portland cement, the principal cements were natural cements and pozzuolan. Natural cements are made from cement rock, a naturally occurring limestone that needs only to be burned and pulverized. This cement industry was localized by available natural cement deposits and local markets. Pozzuolan cement is a mixture of slaked lime and granulated blast-furnace slag, lime and volcanic cinders, or the like. This cement industry was thus frequently oriented to the iron industry, which provided a primary raw material. Because these cements today constitute less than 1 percent of the total output, this analysis of localization will be limited to the production of portland cement.

A patent for the making of portland cement was first secured by Joseph Aspdin, a bricklayer of Leeds, England, in 1824. The new cement did not receive a ready acceptance because of the established reputation of the natural cements. It was not until the 1850s that portland cement gained a wide market in England, and by the 1860s the industry had developed on the European continent, particularly in Germany, France, and Belgium. The industry was well established in Europe before the first patent to produce portland cement was granted in 1872 in the United States.

The world production of portland cement has increased rapidly in the twentieth century, from less than 50,000,000 tons in 1920, to over 700,000,000 short tons in 1975. The cement industry is especially widely distributed, having production in at least 112 countries. Europe, including the Soviet Union, produces about 54 percent of the world total; Asia, 22 percent; North America, 15 percent; South America, 4 percent; Africa, 4 percent; and Oceania, 1 percent. The annual increase in world cement production has varied from 5 to 10 percent in recent years.

Because of the widespread distribution of cement's raw materials, its low cost, its great bulk and consequent high cost of transportation, and its universal use as a construction material, there is a growing tendency for a country to meet its domestic needs by producing its own cement. Adequate supplies of cement are important not only to the advanced industrial nations, but also to the progress of the underdeveloped areas of the world. As a result cement production has been increasing substantially in many of the developing countries in recent years. The cement industry is frequently the first heavy industry to be developed in the underdeveloped countries.

Location and Theory

The localization of the cement industry in the United States illustrates a change from the Weberian concept of least cost location to the Löschian concept of market orientation. The portland cement industry was initially established at the point of least cost in the Lehigh Valley of eastern Pennsylvania. In the period before 1900, the Lehigh Valley possessed essentially the only source of limestone suitable as a raw material and thus monopolized production. In this instance the least cost point of production may have been achieved because of the unique raw material situation of the industry.

After 1900, when a variety of limestones, blast furnace slags, and other types of raw materials became usable to produce cement and the market for cement became widely dispersed, the search for a least cost point was largely abandoned. Thus, a market orientation within the Löschian theoretical framework gradually evolved. Plants thus sought a maximum profit location. In reality, plants have been established where empirical cost studies have indicated that satisfactory profits could be expected.

Locational Factors

Cement is a cheap, heavy commodity; it is manufactured from bulky raw materials, and considerable fuel is used in the process. It can be produced profitably only on a fairly large scale. Consequently, the ideal location for a cement plant is one where supplies of raw materials and fuel are found in close proximity to each other and to a large market. Ideally, the sites of plants are raw material and fuel oriented, and the regional location of plants is market oriented.

RAW MATERIALS. The cement industry is one of the largest consumers of bulk raw materials. When a high calcium limestone plus clay or shale mixture is used, about 225 tons of limestone, 75 tons of clay or shale, 60 tons of coal, and 5 tons of gypsum are needed to produce 1,000 barrels of cement weighing 376 lb each. Thus nearly 2 tons of raw materials and fuel must be assembled to produce 1 ton of cement.

The types of raw material used depend on the geographic location of the plant. In the United States in 1900, when the industry was predominantly centered in eastern Pennsylvania, cement rock constituted over 70 percent of the raw material; limestone and clay or shale constituted only 12 percent, and limestone, mud, and clay but 18 percent, of the raw materials consumed. As the demand for cement increased and new plants were built in other sections of the country, the excellent cement rocks of eastern Pennsylvania were not available and local raw materials were utilized. As a result the use of cement rock decreased from 70 percent of the total in 1906 to about 25 percent at present. There was a corresponding increase in the use of limestone and clay or shale, from 35 percent in 1906 to nearly 70 percent of the total in 1930; the figure has remained at 70 percent since then. In recent years marl, clay, blast furnace slag, and limestone have become sources of raw materials.

There are a number of considerations in selecting the raw material source. The composition of the raw material must have the essential elements. Also, it must be possible to proportion the materials so the essential elements are present within the desired limits. Of the raw materials, limestone exerts the greatest influence on cement plant location. Clay or shale is available in most localities; even if they are not available locally, only about one-third as much clay or shale as limestone is needed. Although deposits of limestone are widely distributed, not all have a composition suitable for cement manufacturing. A cement limestone cannot contain more than 10 percent magnesium carbonate; improper ratios of aluminum, silica, and iron oxide; or excessive impurities, such as silica, iron pyrite, or sulfur.

The raw material must also possess a fair degree of uniformity. If it does not, it requires so many additional analyses and mixing operations that the cost rises greatly. Some physical characteristics are also important. The three most important are the resistance to grinding (grindability), the degree of homogeneity, and a fair uniformity of hardness throughout.

Because the cement industry is a massive consumer of raw materials, the quantity of the deposits is important. A several years' supply of the raw materials is considered necessary for a satisfactory plant location. Essentially all of the raw materials are produced by surface mining. Consequently the cost of quarrying increases rapidly as the thickness of the overburden increases.

ENERGY REQUIREMENTS. Because cement is produced by heating the raw materials in a rotary kiln to sustained temperatures of between 2,400 and 3,000° F, fuel inputs represent a substantial portion of total operating costs. The fuel requirements can be satisfied by the burning of coal, natural gas, or fuel oil. The availability of a fuel determines which type is used. In California, for example, fuel oil is widely used; natural gas is used in the Southwest; and coal is an important fuel in Pennsylvania. In the United States today coal is used to produce about 30 percent of the cement; natural gas, about 18 percent; and oil, 5 percent. A combination fuel of coal, oil, and natural gas supplies nearly 50 percent of the requirements.

A major characteristic of the cement industry is the heavy consumption of fuel and energy. To produce a ton of cement requires about 650 lb of coal and 100 kwh of electricity. The fuel and electrical energy costs are from 50 to 55 percent of total costs. A reduction in the fuel and energy requirements can reduce costs significantly. The principal factor affecting the quantity of fuel is the choice between the two basic processes—wet or dry. The dry process requires about 1.15 million Btu while the wet process requires 1.25 million Btu to produce one barrel of cement. The development of the dry process has influenced the decentralization of the cement industry into regions that are deficient in fuels or into regions where fuel costs are high.

It is difficult to estimate the average cost of fuel used to produce a barrel of cement because of regional variations in fuel costs and because one fuel can be substituted for another. The scale of operation also has some influence on fuel consumption. In general there will be about a 50-percent reduction in fuel when the length of the kiln is increased from 120 to 300 ft. In the 1960s it was estimated that a realistic average cost of fuel was 30 cents per 1,000,000 Btu (8–73). It required an average consumption of 1.2 million Btu to produce a barrel of cement, or a fuel cost of 36 cents per barrel. With a barrel of cement costing $2.25, fuel costs were about 16 percent of total costs (Table 3.2).

The use of electrical power is also an important factor in cement production. In the United States the average unit of electricity consumed to produce a barrel of cement is 23.9 kwh. In recent years over 8.2 billion kwh of electricity have been consumed annually in the cement industry. With an average cost of $0.0089 per kwh, the power costs are about 21 cents per barrel of cement, or about 9.3 percent of the total cost.[7] The consumption of electricity depends on the nature of the raw material, the quality of the finished product, and the level of mechanization. For example, it requires less electricity for grinding soft raw materials, such as marl and chalk, than it does for hard limestones.

MARKETS.   Because the market for a cement plant is regional rather than national, the potential market plays an important role in the establishment of a plant. A company may enter a new market area either by building a new plant or by purchasing an existing plant. From 1950 to 1966, 29 new cement plants were built in the United States, 7 of which constituted entry into new regional markets. Evidence indicates that potential markets are frequently entered by established firms. In recent years, partly as a result of the increasing cost of building

[7]*Statistical Yearbook of the Electric Utility Industry—1966* (New York: Edison Electric Utilities, 1967), p. 49.

Table 3.2

Average Production Costs of a Barrel of Cement

	Actual Cost	Percentage of Total Cost
Labor	$0.67	29.9
Depreciation	0.50	22.2
Fuel	0.36	16.0
Power	0.21	9.3
Miscellaneous supplies	0.20	8.9
Maintenance materials	0.16	7.1
Plant supervision and maintenance	0.15	6.6
	$2.25	100.0

Source: R. S. Harwell, "For the Cement Industry, a Time of Crisis," *Rock Products,* 71 (April 1968), 60.

new plants, entry into new markets has frequently been accomplished by merger arrangements.

Because cement is heavy, low valued, and has a high transportation cost, a number of unique marketing features have developed. A single plant may have several types of markets within its reach. Aggregate cement demands will vary, depending on local trends in demand. As a result a cement company will emphasize the development of one market over another, favoring markets where cost advantages are greatest.

LABOR REQUIREMENTS.   The availability of labor is rarely important in the localization of the cement industry because this industry has long been highly mechanized. Further, there has been a steadily rising labor efficiency. From 1910 to 1950 the average annual rate of labor productivity rose by about 10 percent annually. In 1910 about 1.03 barrels of cement were produced per hour of labor expended. In 1950 about 5.36 barrels of cement were produced per hour of labor expended. Since 1950 labor productivity has increased at a lower rate, probably about 3–5 percent annually.

At the present time the most highly automated plants in the United States produce about 20 barrels of cement per man-hour. This top figure is not likely to change unless there is a significant change in plant maintenance productivity and in the wear resistance of equipment. The average plant is considerably below this level. Nevertheless, the labor required to operate a cement kiln has been reduced to two men for each eight-hour shift.

Although labor is unimportant as a localizing factor, it is the most important single cost factor in cement production. In 1966 there were 29,000 production workers in the cement industry. They worked an average of 41.7 hours per week and received an average of $3.94 per hour. It thus took 63 million man-hours to produce 372,000,000 barrels of cement, or an average labor consumption of 0.1693 man-hours per barrel, or 67 cents per barrel of cement produced. With the average cost of a barrel of cement at $2.25, labor costs were 29.9 percent of the total.

INVESTMENT REQUIREMENTS.   Cement production is a capital intensive, highly mechanized process. Thus the fixed investment in a modest-sized cement plant is large. Fixed investments include quarrying installations; cost of buildings, equipment, and storage facilities; land clearing and improvement; and administration and engineering expenses. Because sufficient electric power is unavailable in many regions where cement plants are being built, electric power generating plants are being installed at plant sites.

The size of the investment will be determined by the size of the plant and its technical facilities. The prime determinants of the size of the plant are the size and number of kilns. All other equipment is chosen in relation to these key items. Kiln sizes are now largely standardized to reduce costs. Considerable flexibility exists in regard to material-handling equipment and the types of automated control devices. Finally, the equipment for dust collection varies widely in efficiency. The type of this equipment will depend on local conditions; for example, if the plant is in an urban region, dust control will be much more stringent.

TRANSPORTATION AND SHIPPING COSTS.   Because of the low value per unit of output, transportation and shipping costs play an important role in determining the location and size of a cement plant. Shipping costs are primarily determined by the size of the market, the distances involved, and the type of transportation available. In many instances transportation costs equal production costs.

In seeking the lowest-cost transportation, the cement industry has developed bulk shipping. This practice is particularly important when the market can be reached by water routes, which involves the construction of huge barges, docks, and automatic loading and unloading facilities. The building of modern, automated distribution terminals for the storage and transshipment of cement in bulk is one of the leading trends in the present-day industry. At least 150 such distribution points are in operation in the United States for the convenience of local markets. This means of shipping provides substantial economies of scale, but they are economical only if there is a large concentrated market.

There are three major U.S. market areas where water transportation is developing: the East Coast, the lower Great Lakes, and the Mississippi River system. The plants oriented to water routes are among the largest in these regions. Six recently built plants along the Hudson River have an average capacity of 4,200,000 tons. Eight Mississippi River plants have an average capacity of 3,800,000 tons, and seven plants on the Great Lakes have a capacity of 4,800,000 tons. New plants in these regions that are not oriented to water transportation have an average capacity of 1,500,000 tons.

It is also a growing practice to construct grinding mills in large cement-consuming centers located at some distance from cement plants. Because cement clinkers are impervious to spoilage and spillage losses, and can be transported at lower costs than cement, additional savings are secured in the market regions. This also permits the concentration of clinker production at the point of lowest cost so that economies of scale can be obtained.

Improvements in land transportation have also occurred in recent years. Special railroad cars have been designed to reduce costs in bulk handling. For example, the Lehigh Cement Company uses pneumatic pressure cars to move cement from its Miami plant to its Jacksonville distribution terminal. Each railroad car holds 107 tons of cement, and low-pressure air is used to fluidize the cement. A car can be unloaded in about 20 minutes.

ECONOMIES OF SCALE. Recent studies have indicated that there are substantial economies of scale in cement production. A plant with a capacity of less than 1,000,000 barrels may have unit costs as much as 70 percent greater than a plant with a capacity of more than 5,000,000 barrels. In a 2,000,000- versus a 6,000,000-barrel plant, the cost differentials may be as great as 40 percent.

A United Nations study reveals that economies of scale are largely in labor, depreciation, overhead, and fixed capital.[8] In a plant of 704,000-barrel capacity, labor costs are approximately four times greater than in a plant of 5,800,000- barrel capacity. In plants of 1,000,000- and 5,000,000-barrel capacity, the overhead, depreciation costs, and fixed capital are more than double per barrel for smaller plants than for larger plants. The costs for raw materials, power, fuel, and water do not vary with the size of the plants. Under present technology it is doubtful if savings can be achieved for plants beyond the 6,000,000-barrel capacity.

Although larger plants have lower costs because of economies of scale, plants with a wide range of capacities exist today. About two-thirds of the existing plants have a capacity of from 1,000,000 to 3,000,000 barrels. In general the new plants are larger than those built in the past. However, there appears to be little difference in the capacity of plants built by small and large companies. The size of the market may be a more important determinant of plant size than economies related to size of the plant.

United States

DEVELOPMENT OF THE NATURAL CEMENT INDUSTRY. The natural cement industry was developed in the United States more than 50 years before the first patent was secured for the manufacture of portland cement. The construction of canals was the greatest impetus to the expansion of natural cements because canals required watertight masonry. Because of this need, the first natural cement was produced in New York State in 1818. The construction of canals furnished the largest market for natural cements for many years, and because these waterways were then the only means of transporting bulky mate-

---

[8]"Cement/Nitrogenous Fertilizers Based on Natural Gas," *Studies in Economics of Industry*, No. 1, (United Nations, 1962), pp. 22–23.

rials, the cement industry developed along canal routes. Then, in 1866, the first cement mill located along a railroad was built. It was a success, and most new cement mills were built either along railroad or canal routes after this date.

The manufacture of natural cement was a comparatively simple operation. The natural cement rock was heated in small upright kilns at relatively low temperatures for approximately one week. Either wood or coal was used as fuel, depending on which was available. The clinkers were then ground between millstones operated by waterpower. Natural cement was thus a direct product of natural rock.

Because the raw material was the most important factor in the quality of natural cement, natural cement deposits greatly influenced the location of the major production centers. By the 1890s there were three areas of production, each originally located on a canal route. The principal center was the Rosendale District in Ulster County, New York. About 50 percent of the total natural cement output came from this one district. The second largest area was developed near Louisville, Kentucky. The quality of this cement was excellent, and it was marketed throughout interior United States. The third center of importance was the Lehigh District of Pennsylvania. Natural cement, utilizing the local natural cement rock, was first produced here when a canal constructed by the Lehigh Coal and Navigation Company created the initial market.

Natural cement gained acceptance in the building trades at an early date and competed successfully with portland cement for more than 25 years. Production of natural cement continued to rise throughout the nineteenth century to a peak in 1899, when 1,683,000 metric tons were produced. At this time output came from 15 states, with 60–70 plants in operation.

CONCENTRATION OF THE PORTLAND CEMENT INDUSTRY IN THE LEHIGH VALLEY. The first portland cement was produced commercially in the United States in the Lehigh District of eastern Pennsylvania in 1875. For the next 25 years the Lehigh District maintained a near monopoly in production. In 1897, the year of its greatest dominance, this single district produced 74.8 percent of the country's total output. The early dominance of this district was due mostly to the availability of large quantities of limestone that was a natural cement rock and its position near the large eastern market. During this period it was believed that the natural cement rock of this region was superior to any other clayey limestone in the United States. Such cement-making communities as Bath, Cementon, Coplay, Egypt, Evansville, Fogelsville, Nazareth, Northampton, and Stockertown developed in the Lehigh Valley.

American portland cement was not readily accepted in this country. Two factors were particularly important in its rather long period of retarded growth. The natural cements had gained a national reputation as quality products, and many builders preferred to use them. Also, European portland cement was imported before the American industry was established. Until about 1890 these cements could be shipped to the United States and sold at a price below that of the domestic portland cement. The foreign portland cements had also gained a good reputation, which gave them a preferred market.

However, by the 1890s the Lehigh District cement was gaining wide acceptance. It was being sent to every section of the country and even developed a small export market. As the industry expanded, it was able to lower production costs and thus compete with the foreign cements. Output between 1890 and 1900 rose from 57,150 to 1,477,000 metric tons. Dating from 1875, it thus took a quarter of a century to establish the American portland cement industry.

DECENTRALIZATION OF THE CEMENT INDUSTRY, 1900–1928. As the nation's cement production expanded, many new cement plants were constructed outside the Lehigh District. In 1900 three East Coast states—Pennsylvania, New Jersey, and New York—produced nearly 80 percent of the country's total. The next most important region, the Midwest, produced about 19 percent. The locational change was so rapid that by 1905 the East Coast produced only 55 percent of the total and output in the Midwest rose to 30 percent. The western states, particularly those on the Pacific Coast, were rapidly expanding production and produced a little over 10 percent of the total by 1905. The number of cement plants in the country increased from 50 in 1900 to 88 in 1905.

The decentralization of the cement industry continued at a less rapid pace after 1905. However, by 1928 cement production was found in at least 27 states. The Lehigh District remained the largest single district, with about 22.5 percent of output. The Midwest and the Pacific Coast combined produced about 40 percent of the total in that year.

California had become the second largest state in production, having about 8 percent of the total. During the period from 1900 to 1928, production rose steadily to 176,299,000 barrels.

FACTORS INFLUENCING DECENTRALIZATION. Several interrelated factors caused the widespread decentralization and growth of the industry. The first factor that made changes possible related to the technological improvements in cement production, which greatly reduced the cost of production. In the two decades from 1900 to 1920, complete mechanization of the industry was achieved. The introduction of the rotary kiln was the most significant technical advancement. It revolutionized the making of portland cement, while at the same time greatly widening its markets. The operation became continuous when the reclining rotary kiln replaced the old upright batch burners that ran in repeated cycles of loading, firing, coking, and unloading.

The rotary kiln was also able to use a wider range of fuels. The early success of this kiln was made possible with the introduction of powdered coal. Coalfields were located near many of the new areas of cement production, and from 1900 to 1920 coal furnished 80–85 percent of the fuel consumed. Early in the period natural gas was also found to be excellent fuel and attracted the industry to areas when it was readily available, particularly the Midcontinent oil and gas fields. Petroleum also became a source of fuel during this period.

With the introduction of the rotary kiln, it was soon realized that a standard, uniform quality of cement could be produced from a wide range of raw materials. Thus the cement industry was no longer restricted to those areas where natural cement rock was found. For example, a variety of raw materials was utilized in the Midwest. The availability of Michigan marl deposits provided the raw material orientation for some plants; the limestone deposits of northern Ohio were also used. A technological interdependence also developed between iron blast furnace and cement production. This linkage was evident in such centers as Duluth and Chicago. Furnace slag became an important raw material for cement production. Blast furnace slag was not the only raw material used by the cement industry in the iron and steel centers. However, because the blast furnaces required limestone and coal, there was an obvious locational advantage for cement production. In addition the heavy industry centers also provided a large market for cement.

Increased mechanization greatly reduced the price of cement. In the early days of the portland cement industry, one of the significant problems was the high price of American cement. From the earliest times the manufacturer was confronted with high-priced labor, and economy in this direction was one requisite of success. Labor costs per barrel of cement declined eventually because of the increased speed in processing. The time required to convert the rock at the quarry into portland cement was reduced from more than one week to only one day. It was now possible to produce 1,200–1,500 barrels a day as against a unit production of about 200 barrels in from 10 to 14 days in the old-style vertical kilns. The price of a barrel of cement declined from $3 in 1880 to a record low of 81 cents in 1912. From peak imports in 1893 of 456,300 metric tons, imports had all but disappeared by 1908.

In the early days of the industry, many of the customers were dissatisfied with portland cement because its quality differed slightly from one mill to another and sometimes from one batch to another within the same mill. Until 1904 the manufacturer established his own standards. In that year the American Society for Testing Materials established standards so that all cement would be of the same quality. Thus cement became a highly noncompetitive product. There was also no advantage to purchase cement from a distant producer when a local producer provided the same quality at a lower cost. As a result cement plants developed in areas where a market would support the industry.

Once portland cement was produced cheaply in large quantities and its superior qualities were recognized, the natural cement industry declined rapidly. Although in 1900 the production of natural cement was still greater than that of portland cement, the industry had almost vanished by 1915.

The last factor—and one of great importance in the decentralization and expansion of the portland cement industry—was the rapidly expanding market after 1900. However, the region for marketing cement from a single plant has always been highly restricted. As stated in a recent report, "The marketing territory of a cement plant is extremely limited because cement is a bulky commodity of relatively low value and the cost of transporting it is high compared with its selling price. As a result there is no nationwide cement market. Instead there are a large number of relatively independent local markets, each subjected to its particular set of conditions."⁹ Because markets for cement are regional or local in nature, and the demand is national in scope, there are major forces influencing decentralization.

Until about 1915 the greatest market for cement was for public and commercial buildings, bridges, levees, and specialty uses such as sidewalks and monuments. The concrete highway was developed between 1910 and 1920. This single use soon became the most important market. As early as 1921, 4,380 miles of concrete highways had been built, consuming 4,266,200 metric tons of cement—about one-quarter of the country's total output. Because highways were being built throughout the country, cement plants were widely dispersed to reduce transportation costs.

LOCALIZATION DURING THE PERIOD OF INSTABILITY, 1928–1946. Between 1928 and 1946 production not only declined from 176,300,000 to 162,287,000 barrels of cement, but output fluctuated greatly. The year of lowest production was 1933, when only 63,473,000 barrels of cement were produced. During this long period, in only one year, 1942 (when 182,781,000 barrels of cement were produced) did the output exceed the 1928 level. In 1946 cement production was only 92 percent that of 1928.

There were some significant shifts in production during this period of stagnation (Fig. 3.5). Eight districts experienced a comparative loss, and ten districts experienced a comparative gain. The areas with a comparative loss were concentrated in the Northeast. Eastern Pennsylvania experienced about 48 percent of the total comparative loss. Other large areas of comparative loss included the districts of Indiana, Kentucky, and Wisconsin, Michigan and western Pennsylvania, and West Virginia. The areas of comparative growth were concentrated in the South and on the West Coast. California experienced the largest comparative growth, followed by Texas. These two districts had about 55 percent of the total comparative gain.

CEMENT INDUSTRY AND THE BASING-POINT SYSTEM. As a result of the geographic expansion of the industry, portland cement manufacturers in 1902 began to use the multiple-basing-point pricing method of quoting delivered prices for cement. The early, simple method of soliciting business and quoting f.o.b. mill prices (the purchaser paying the freight) used in the Lehigh District before 1900 was considered inadequate to meet conditions created by the extension of producing areas from coast to coast. Because cement is a heavy, low-priced commodity of standard quality, transportation charges—if the distance is great—constitute a large proportion of the total cost to the purchaser. As mills were built in new areas, bringing production closer to many consumers, the older mills were forced to absorb a part of the freight costs or withdraw from the market near the new mills. This led manufacturers to adopt the practice of adding the freight costs to the mill price and quoting an f.o.b. destination price. This practice, with few exceptions, was adopted by all cement manufacturers and

⁹*Prospectus* prepared by Blythe & Co. (November 1957) relating to the consolidation of Riverside Cement Co., Peerless Cement Corp., and Hercules Cement Co.

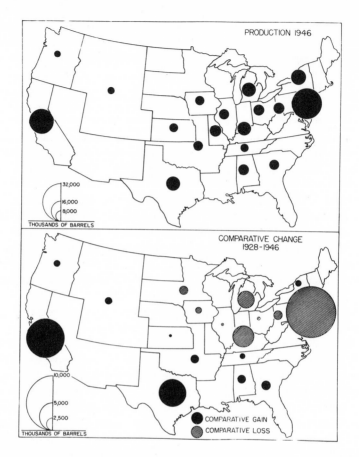

Figure 3.5. U.S. Portland Cement. *Above:* Production, 1946. *Below:* Comparative change, 1928–1946.

became a convenient and accurate means of achieving uniform quotations by all manufacturers at any point of consumption. The basing-point system enabled a distant mill to quote a delivered price equal to that of a competitor located nearer the buyer.

Serious questions concerning the legality of all geographic pricing formulas—except f.o.b. mill—were raised as early as 1921 by the Federal Trade Commission. The issue of basing-point selling was brought into sharp focus by the decision of the U.S. Supreme Court on April 26, 1948, in the "Cement Case." The decision declared that the maintenance of a basing-point-delivered-price system was an unfair method of competition and, as such, was prohibited by the Federal Trade Commission Act.

Since 1949 all portland-cement-producing companies have abandoned the basing-point system of determining transportation freight rates. This marketing change appears to have had little influence on the location of the industry, largely because most plants were originally market oriented. A few plants located farthest from their market have disappeared, and the plants nearest the largest markets have increased in size.

MODERN GEOGRAPHIC STRUCTURE.   Since 1946 production has experienced a generally upward curve from an output of 164,064,000 barrels in 1946 to 411,573,000 barrels in 1972. The growth was particularly rapid from 1946 to 1955, when production rose by 133,389,000 barrels, or about 8.1 percent, annually. Since then the rate of growth has been slower, averaging about 2.3 percent annually.

Locational changes continued during the period of rapid growth from 1946 to 1955 (Fig. 3.6). Of the 20 districts, 11 experienced comparative declines and 9 experienced comparative growth. Northeastern United States continued its trend in comparative losses, with eastern Pennsylvania experiencing nearly 40 percent of the total. The areas of comparative gain continued to be concentrated in the South and interior West.

In the period between 1961 and 1972, 15 districts experienced comparative gains and 11 districts experienced comparative losses (Fig. 3.7). In contrast to previous periods, when one or two districts experienced a large proportion of the total gain or loss, the gains and losses were more widely distributed. A number of districts continued their traditional decline, but at a lower rate. These included eastern Pennsylvania, Ohio, Illinois, Tennessee, Alabama, and the Indiana, Kentucky, and Wisconsin districts. Some areas that had long experienced a comparative growth were now experiencing a comparative decline. Notable in this group were northern California and the western mountain states. In contrast, districts that were experiencing comparative losses were now experiencing comparative growth. These included New York, western Pennsylvania, and Missouri. Finally, comparative growth continued in Texas, Michigan and in the South.

Today no district dominates cement production in the United States. The leading districts, with 6–9 percent of output, include eastern Pennsylvania, Texas, southern California, and Michigan. Cement production is closely correlated with industrial output and markets. Distributional changes in the future will most likely occur in the dynamic regions of economic growth.

UTILIZATION OF CAPACITY.   The utilization of the cement capacity of the nation has fluctuated greatly in recent times. In 1944, 37.8 percent of the cement industry's capacity was utilized. This percentage utilization increased steadily to a peak of 94 percent in 1955. Utilization then declined to 78 percent in 1957, but since then utilization of existing capacity has varied from about 71 percent in 1962 to 90 percent in 1972.

From 1928 to 1946, the number of cement plants operating annually varied from 150 to 160. Between 1946 and 1955, during the period of rapid rise in production, there was no overall increase in the number of plants operating— only in the greater utilization of capacity. However, since 1955, although pro-

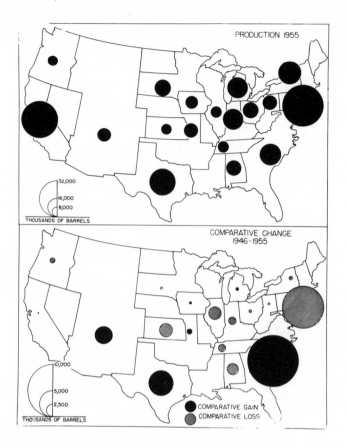

Figure 3.6. U.S. Portland Cement. *Above:* Production, 1955. *Below:* Comparative change, 1946–1955.

duction has increased only moderately, the number of plants increased from 157 to a peak of 188 in 1967; but the number declined to 175 in 1975.

FACTORS AFFECTING GROWTH TRENDS.   A basic question is why new plants are being built and old plants modernized when the cement industry is utilizing only about three-quarters of its capacity. There is a series of complex factors that have influenced the growth trends in recent years.

Production Technology and Plant Cost.   Until 1955 there had been few technical advances in cement production for decades. Since then there have been significant engineering advances. Most important of these has been the development of the larger plants. In 1944 the average-sized plant had a 1,600,000-barrel annual capacity. This increased to 2,000,000 barrels by 1955. Between 1955 and 1975, the average plant increased by more than 40 percent, to about 2,750,000 barrels annual capacity. Most of the new plants exceed 3,000,000 barrels annual capacity.

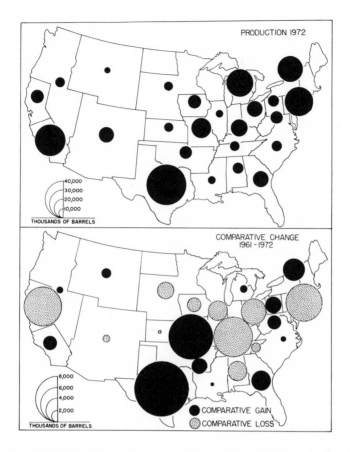

Figure 3.7. U.S. Portland Cement. *Above:* Production, 1972. *Below:* Comparative change, 1961–1972.

Efforts to reduce not only the initial plant costs per barrel of capacity, but also the cost per barrel of production, have brought dramatic changes in technology. The basic change has been to replace the numerous parallel production units of kilns and mills with one or two large units to centralize the control of most plant-operating departments. A typical old plant with a capacity of 2,200,000 barrels per year would have 8 kilns and 15 mills. A modern plant of the same size has 1 kiln and 3 mills. As a result of the reduction of units, the cost per barrel of capacity has been reduced by about one-half. Capital costs have also continued to be reduced.

There have also been considerable cost reductions in the operation of the modern plant. These include savings in labor, fuel requirements, overhead costs, and by-volume purchase of supplies. Automatic plant control by closed-loop computer installations linked with X-ray analyzers to control raw material blending, nuclear sensors in kiln control, and temperature pressure gauges afford efficiencies in processing systems not economical in older units. Computer control not only gives improved quality and increased output, but also reduces costs. According to one firm, computer control has reduced operating costs by at least 7 percent.

As a result many companies have found it advantageous to build new plants in a region rather than enlarge existing plants. At the same time the older plants, although not producing at the same cost advantages, have managed to survive. Market demands have not kept pace with plant capacities. Therefore many of the plants are built on the expectation of future growth potentials.

Economies of Scale.   There are appreciable economies of scale in current production methods that favor the development of large plants (Table 3.3). Labor is the most important single cost factor. In the typical old 2,000,000-barrel plant, labor costs are nearly double the next most important cost factor, depreciation. By contrast, in the modern 4,000,000-barrel plant, the labor costs are nearly four time lower than in the 2,000,000-barrel plant. In a recent study by Capriola, it was found that an old 2,000,000-barrel plant required 250 men, or 0.25 man-hours per barrel of cement; in a modern 2,000,000-barrel plant, only 100 men are required, or 0.10 man-hours per barrel of production; and in a 4,000,000-barrel plant, only 135 men are required, or 0.068 man-hours per barrel of cement (8–72). Thus a 4,000,000-barrel plant will have a labor cost that is nearly 72 percent lower than that of a 2,000,000-barrel old plant.

There are also economies of scale in fuel costs. In a 2,000,000-barrel plant, there is an average requirement of 1,350,000 Btu per barrel; in a 2,000,000-barrel new plant about 950,000 Btu are required per barrel; and about 800,000 Btu per barrel are required in a modern 4,000,000-barrel plant. There is thus a savings of about 30 percent in fuel in the larger, modern plant, reducing the cost from 40 to 24 cents per barrel.

Maintenance and materials costs are reduced about 40 percent in a modern 4,000,000-barrel plant because of the decrease in number of units operating. Supervision and overhead costs are reduced because of the reduction in the labor force and the more compact plant and service operations. Depreciation costs are reduced because of the lower initial costs per barrel of capacity. In an old plant of 2,000,000-barrel capacity, the investment cost per barrel of capacity was about twice that of a modern 4,000,000-barrel-capacity plant. Evidence indicates that economies of scale are not important in miscellaneous supplies and maintenance and raw materials costs.

As markets develop in new regions, economies of scale in cement production are highly influential in encouraging the construction of the larger plants, even if not all of the capacity is utilized at the time of initial construction.

Integration in the Cement Industry.   There was limited integration in the cement industry prior to 1960. Since then there has been a noticeable trend in both vertical and horizontal integrations.

Vertical integration has become a rather common practice between cement companies and ready-mixed concrete companies. This has been accomplished by a number of procedures. Several ready-mixed concrete companies have de-

Table 3.3

Operating Costs of Cement Plants

	Typical Old 2,000,000-Barrel Plant Cost Per Barrel	Typical Modern 2,000,000-Barrel Plant Cost Per Barrel	Typical Modern 4,000,000-Barrel Plant Cost Per Barrel
Labor	$0.99	$0.39	$0.27
Fuel	0.40	0.28	0.24
Power	0.21	0.21	0.21
Miscellaneous supplies	0.20	0.20	0.20
Maintenance and materials	0.20	0.12	0.12
Supervision and overhead	0.21	0.10	0.10
Depreciation expense	0.50	0.35	0.25
Total	$2.71	$1.65	$1.39

Source: R. S. Harwell, "For the Cement Industry, a Time of Crisis," *Rock Products,* 71 (May 1968), 110.

veloped their own cement production through backward integration. Likewise, a number of cement-producing companies have entered the ready-mixed concrete industry by forward integration. Finally, there have been mergers of existing cement and ready-mixed concrete companies. Vertical integrations have occurred in the largest market areas—those of New York, Texas, and California.

Several factors have encouraged the different forms of vertical integration. There are anticipated economies as a result of combining cement production and concrete marketing under a single management. Even if the physical operations are separated, there is better coordination in order to reduce costs, particularly freight charges. With the increase in competition, there is also a desire to achieve a higher degree of economic security. Through backward integration the ready-mixed concrete companies guarantee their source of cement; through forward integration, companies protect their market for potential customers. Vertical integration may also occur when profits at one level of activity differ significantly from those attained at another producing or consuming level of activity. When capital is available, firms in adjacent market areas will attempt to develop the most effective competition.[10]

Vertical integration is an attempt by the portland cement companies to improve their economic situation at a time of increasing excess capacity and declining prices and profits through selective acquistions of large ready-mixed concrete companies. The portland cement companies guarantee their market outlets. Competition has been greatly reduced in the areas where vertical integra-

[10]*On Mergers and Vertical Integration in the Cement Industry* (Washington, D.C.: Federal Trade Commission, 1966), pp. 95–104.

tion has occurred. These mergers tend to eliminate other suppliers within a given market area. There has been a tendency for high-cost producers to develop defensive mergers. As a result the net effort is to decrease the size of the open market for cement. Furthermore, the smaller, unintegrated cement consumers may find suppliers less willing to engage in aggressive competition in serving their needs. Vertical integration also has the effect of eliminating the entrance of new cement companies into a region.

Because of the large number of vertical integrations, the Federal Trade Commission indicated on June 3, 1967, that all mergers of cement and ready-mixed concrete companies would be challenged if they involved a ready-mixed concrete company that (1) is one of the four largest nonintegrated producers in the market area or (2) annually purchases 50,000 barrels or more of cement. Vertical mergers and acquisitions are considered today to be the most significant, critical and important problems faced by the cement and ready-mixed concrete industries. The commission believes that mergers can have a substantial adverse effect on competition in a particular market area.

Horizontal integrations have also occurred with increasing frequency. The most common type of horizontal integration has been for cement companies to become associated with companies producing natural and manufactured aggregates for construction. Cement companies have also become associated with petroleum refining companies in order to produce materials for road construction. There have also been mergers between cement and swimming pool companies, and even between cement and aircraft companies. These mergers have tended to diversify the market and give greater stability. They have also favored the increase in capacity of the cement industry.

Markets of Cement Companies. No cement company has been able to attain a national market. The cement industry is, however, increasingly dominated by companies that are extending their market area. Because the market area is limited by transportation costs, companies have enlarged their market areas by constructing new plants or merging with companies in new market areas. Today the 4 largest companies produce about 30 percent of the nation's cement; the 8 largest, about 50 percent; and the 20 largest, over 80 percent.

Although no firm has a national market, several firms market cement in large sections of the country. The Ideal Cement Company, the largest cement firm, operates 18 plants and markets cement in the southeastern, south central, and western states. The second largest company, the Lone Star Cement Corporation, has 15 plants and sells cement in the northeastern, south central, and western states. The third largest company, Universal Atlas, has 10 plants in the East and Midwest. Lehigh Cement, with 12 plants, has its market in the East, Midwest, and Northwest.

COTTON TEXTILE INDUSTRY

The mechanized cotton textile industry was one of the first industries to be stimulated by the Industrial Revolution. The United Kingdom had inaugurated the revolution, which launched the migration of cotton manufacturing from the handloom centers of India to the North Atlantic countries of western Europe and the United States. During the nineteenth century, the United Kingdom and the United States dominated the production of cotton textiles. There were lesser centers in Germany, France, Belgium, Switzerland, and Russia.

At the beginning of the twentieth century, new forces in the localization of cotton textiles were appearing, which caused a shift in the distribution of production. The rise of the industry in the Orient and the migration of mills from New England to the Piedmont of the southern United States were outstanding locational changes. India was the first nation in the Far East to adopt mechanization of cotton textile production; Japan followed.

After World War I, another change in the location of world cotton manufacturing began and is still in progress. The growth of cotton textile manufacturing has been taking place in most of the developing countries and especially in the cotton-producing countries of South America, Africa, and Asia. This trend has been encouraged by the efforts of most countries to develop national self-sufficiency in such basic commodities as textiles. Because the cotton textile industry requires a minimum of skilled labor, it is one of the first industries to be established in a country just starting its industrialization. Also, the low cost of domestic raw cotton in comparison with the high prices of imported textiles has promoted the growth of the textile industry in underdeveloped nations.

As a response to decentralization, most of the older producing nations have lost a portion of their international market and their output has declined. Most important in this group has been the United Kingdom, where textile production has declined from about 3,000,000,000 m in the early 1930s to about 670,000,000 m in recent years. Other nations in which production has stabilized or declined are the United States, France, Belgium, Japan, West Germany, and Italy. In the socialist nations, where emphasis was originally placed on heavy industrial development, the output of textiles has been increasing. The Soviet Union exemplifies this trend; textile production rose from 4,004,000,000 m in 1953 to 6,200,000,000 m in recent years. Although the cotton textile industry has been established in most countries of the world, it is still concentrated in relatively few nations. Using production of cotton yarn as the criterion, the seven leading nations are the United States, with 18 percent of the world's total; the Soviet Union, 13 percent; India, 9 percent; Japan, 5 percent; and France, West Germany, and Pakistan, each about 2.5 percent. There is no uniform method for compiling textile production statistics by country. The three measures used by countries are meters, square meters, and metric tons. It is therefore impossible to have an accurate figure for the cotton textile production of the world.

Theoretical Framework

The cotton textile industry has traditionally sought a least cost point of production. The single factor of low-cost labor long remained the dominant factor of localization. When a single factor dominates, it is easier to determine empirically areas of economic advantage. The traditional search for the least cost site has been a major factor in the massive migrations of this industry. The movement of the industry from New England to the Piedmont in the United States and the migration from Lancashire, England, to the Far East were primarily motivated by the search for least cost regions.

The Weberian framework of localization prevailed when the cost of labor was the dominant factor in localizing the industry. As the industry becomes capital rather than labor intensive, it appears that the attempt to seek the lowest-cost area is being abandoned. There is growing evidence that a series of factors now enter the locational decision process, with maximum profit playing a greater role. As a consequence market potential will play a more significant role in the future localization of the industry.

Factors of Localization

The factors affecting the localization of the cotton textile industry are complex (3). Because this industry is old, each region has undergone a different set of experiences in its evolution. In many instances the older areas continue to grow even when the original causes for the establishment of the industry have disappeared. In other instances textile centers that were once important have declined and are of little significance today.

RAW MATERIALS. The earliest cotton textile centers, prior to the Industrial Revolution, were usually localized by the availability of raw material. The production of cotton in India is considered the historical base for the ancient industries of spinning and weaving cloth in the Indian home. However, the textile industry has been able to detach itself from its raw material base. The development of the industry in Lancashire in England and in southern New England, where no cotton is produced, illustrates that factors other than raw materials became dominant. The diminishing importance of raw cotton as a localizing factor was due to the ease in transporting not only the raw material but also the finished product to its ultimate market. When economic factors in the cotton-producing regions did not favor the growth of a textile industry, cotton could be easily transported great distances.

ENERGY REQUIREMENTS. The importance of power has varied, depending on the existing state of technology. In the beginning there was human labor, which permitted a degree of mobility in locating the industry. With the introduction of waterpower, the textile industry became precisely localized. Watercourses were the first places where mechanical equipment could be utilized; this occurred, for example, in the valleys of the Vosges mountains in France, at the mouth of the valleys of the Prealps in Switzerland and Italy, in the foothills of the Pennine range in England, and in the valleys of southeastern New England. This localization factor persisted from the middle of the eighteenth to the middle of the nineteenth century. Because of technological limitations, only small dams could be constructed. As a result only the smaller rivers and streams could be utilized to provide waterpower. Consequently the textile industry frequently developed in relatively isolated hill regions. The major river valleys were not able to be harnessed for waterpower.

Coal gradually replaced waterpower as the primary source of power. Steam power is utilized most easily in the vicinity of the coal basins, and coal has been a major element in localizing the cotton textile industry in such areas as Lancashire, northern France, the Ruhr, and Saxony. The use of coal in providing motive power did, however, give a greater flexibility in the localization of the industry. Textile factories located at some distance from coal sources are concentrated at places where coal can easily be transported at relatively low costs. For example, its excellent railroad facilities give Mulhouse in Alsace a decided advantage over the isolated textile centers in the uplands of interior Alsace, and the low cost of shipping coal to Flanders and Brabant gives this area a vast advantage in their power requirements.

In the twentieth century, the use of electricity to power textile factories has made possible an even wider distribution of the industry. For example, availability of electricity encouraged the migration of the industry from the waterpower sites in the mountains of northern Italy to the northern Po plain, where there is a greater availability of labor and better transportation, providing accessibility to raw materials and markets.

The availability of power continues to play a role in the localization of textiles, but its influence has changed with each increase in power mobility.

MARKET. Because the textile industry serves a basic need, there is a universal market. Also, because it can be developed in technically underdeveloped countries, most countries of the world have developed the cotton textile industry to serve the domestic market. In many of the tropical and subtropical countries, a domestic cotton industry provides the necessary raw material. The domestic industry has frequently been developed to conserve foreign exchange.

Many of the small producing countries of the world have developed a limited export market. However, their entrance into the production of cotton cloth has frequently influenced the geographic structure of the industry. Many of the older producing areas, such as Lancashire in England and Bombay in India, which depended on an export market for their welfare, were adversely affected by the decentralization of production.

LABOR. The cotton textile industry is frequently the first industry established in an area because it requires an absolute minimum of technically trained personnel for its implementation. An unskilled worker can learn the essential processes of spinning or weaving in a few weeks. Thus the textile industry is one of the first types of manufacturing to evolve in a developing country. In more technically advanced nations, the textile industry is frequently established to provide work in regions that possess an excess supply of low-skilled labor.

The labor force comes not only from the adult male population, but also from women, children, and older people of both sexes. Because of the minimum training needed and the resulting low wages, textiles frequently are localized in those areas of a nation where the lowest wage rates prevail. The industry has exhibited migratory tendencies in seeking the lowest-wage regions. Thus the number of workers is not the only consideration. The cost of labor is also important in the industry's localization.

The trend toward mechanization and automation of the industry has had a profound effect on the quantity and quality of labor. In 1945 the industry's workers were 20 percent unskilled, 57 percent semi-skilled, and only 20 percent skilled. There has been a growing requirement for higher skilled workers with the introduction of more sophisticated equipment. To meet this demand, on-the-job training programs have been instituted, as has vocational training in high schools. Further, mechanization has reduced the number of workers required in the textile industry.

Conversion from a Labor Intensive to a Capital Intensive Industry

The cotton textile industry has traditionally been the supreme example of a labor intensive industry. A modern trend is to have a declining labor force coupled with a rising capital investment amounting to more than $20,000 per employee. This transformation is essentially complete in the United States and Japan, and it is proceeding rapidly in most other countries. When economic structural reforms began in the 1950s in certain countries, such as Sweden and the Netherlands, investment in cotton appeared to be higher than in gross fixed capital formation of other industries.

The cotton textile sector has one of the highest rates of new capital investment per worker of all manufacturing industries. Only in iron and steel, oil, and chemicals is investment per worker possibly higher. The high rate of investment is due to the rapid technological progress in the industry. It is now estimated that modern equipment is outdated in about ten years. This does not mean that equipment wears out, but rather that technological progress, rising wages, and the development of shift work accelerates the rate that equipment must be replaced. For example, in the spinning industry, the number of carding machines required to perform an operation was reduced by 80 percent between 1950 and 1964, while the number of operatives needed was reduced by about 75 percent. In general, for the same production, nearly three times as many workers were required in the 1945–1950 period than in 1963 in the spinning industry, and progress in weaving has been at the same level. In 1968 a modern mill of 10,000 spindles would normally have produced 200 kg of yarn per hour as against 120 kg per hour in 1935.

As a result of progressive mechanization, the cost of building a new mill and the modernization of existing mills has continually risen. In 1962 a 10,000-

spindle mill was estimated to cost approximately $1,250,000, by 1970 the cost of this mill had risen to over $2,000,000. But with the use of such highly productive equipment, labor costs have been reduced as a proportion of general production costs.

The increase in efficiency of production has created a problem of excess productive capacity in the industry. As an example, suppose that a spinning mill consisting of ten production units, each with 10,000 spindles, modernizes one of its units each year. This type unit would have an average output of 1,600 kg per hour, with the output of the oldest unit being 1,200 kg per hour and that of the most modern unit being 2,000 kg per hour. Suppose also that market demand increases at 2 percent annually. If the lowest-unit output is increased to the level of the highest unit, the total production will rise from 1,600 kg to 1,680 kg, or an increase of 5 percent. In reality, demand is increasing slowly while productivity is increasing rapidly.

As a result instability has developed in the industry. There is a constant pressure to replace old mills. At what point is this procedure justified? In theory the replacement of an old mill by a modern mill is desirable when the savings in variable costs as a result of new investments are sufficient to provide an adequate income on invested capital. In reality the risk involved due to the high investment in a modern firm is such that a firm becomes more vulnerable to a fall in demand and to market fluctuations. As a consequence there remain wide variations in output among firms in the modern industry. The establishment of a new mill does not necessarily entail the closing of an older mill if the old mill is completely amortized and is still earning a margin of profit. Nevertheless, in the long run an inadequately used productive capacity and obsolete plants in an area constitute a serious hazard to the continued prosperity of that area.

STRUCTURE OF THE INDUSTRY. Traditionally, integration played a small role in the structure and organization of the textile industry. As a result the industry has been characterized by a large number of small plants. This has encouraged a dispersal of the industry, with plants being built in a number of locations.

Horizontal and vertical integration are now evolving in an attempt to control major cyclical fluctuations and encourage rationalization. However, integration varies considerably from country to country. It is only moderately advanced in the United States. For example, Burlington Industries, the biggest textile firm in the world (having annual sales of over $1.8 billion), has only 8 percent of the American market. Integration is possibly most advanced in Japan. The five largest Japanese corporations control 80 percent of the nation's textile output. The Canadian cotton textile industry also displays a high degree of horizontal and vertical integration, having three companies that produce about 77 percent of the value added in textiles.

An age-old tradition of having numerous small firms exists in Europe. As a response to cyclical problems of production since 1960, there has been a strong incentive to integrate production from spinning to the finishing stage. Each country has evolved a different procedure to encourage integration. In West

Germany vertical integration has been encouraged by a turnover tax that involves cumulative taxation at each stage of production and marketing. Horizontal integration is fostered in France by rationalization policies that force marginal firms to close.

The increase in the integration of the cotton textile industry is largely a response to structural changes. As long as the industry was labor intensive, many companies could remain small. However, with technical improvements and more capital investment, the optimum size of the firm tended to increase. Integration has provided an effective means of reducing not only the number of companies but also the number of plant locations. The location of a single plant must now conform to the economic goals of a company having plant sites at numerous locations.

United States

The modern cotton textile industry of the United States had its origin in the last decade of the eighteenth century. The first cotton mill was built in 1790 in Pawtucket, Rhode Island. For several decades the industry grew slowly. But beginning with the War of 1812, when British imports were eliminated, the stimulus to expand was strong. To protect the growing but still infant industry, protective tariffs were enacted. By 1840 cotton textiles were the leading American industry, having approximately 75,000 workers.

EARLY LOCALIZATION OF THE INDUSTRY. The early cotton textile industry was located predominantly in the northeastern states. The greatest concentration was in New England, where the industry was centered in the southeast from New Hampshire's Merrimack River to New Bedford and Fall River, Massachusetts, and Providence, Rhode Island. The earliest mills developed at waterpower sites, so they all had river or stream locations. With the change to steam power beginning in the 1830s, the mills were freed from having to locate on waterpower sites. Many of the mills were then located on the coast, such as at Fall River and New Bedford, where they had a tidewater advantage for importing coal and cotton.

FACTORS IN NEW ENGLAND LOCALIZATION. New England possessed a number of favorable factors that encouraged the development of the cotton textile industry. The availability of waterpower was of greatest importance. New England is a relatively small area, and its rivers and streams are also small. Because of the limitations of dam-building materials and technical know-how in the nineteenth century, only smaller streams could be dammed for waterpower utilization. The New England streams were of an almost ideal size for harnessing waterpower. They also possessed other desirable qualities. New England is a humid, glaciated region; thus there is generally an even flow of water throughout the year. The glacial lakes released the water from the headwater areas slowly, thereby regulating the flow of the streams.

The coastal position of southeastern New England, with its good harbors, was also favorable. Since the raw cotton and coal had to be imported for the textile industry, and distant overland transportation was costly, a tidewater location made possible the assembly of fuel and raw material at a low cost. The shipbuilding industry developed partly as a response to the demands for raw material and fuel in the textile industry. And because New England merchants invested their capital locally, some of the profits from the ocean shipping trade were used to expand the textile industry.

The earliest New England settlers were skilled artisans, and thus spinning and weaving developed as a traditional domestic industry in New England. When the factory system was developed, skilled labor was available from among the farmers and the wives and daughters of seafaring men. The introduction of the factory system made home manufacturing unprofitable; so from the earliest days of the textile industry, a supply of trained labor that expanded as the industry grew was available.

The cool, humid New England climate also aided the industry. Before artificial humidifiers were used to regulate the atmospheric moisture, the damp area of southern New England favored the textile industry. Coastal New England possessed early optimum climatic conditions for spinning cotton yarn. The industry also found it advantageous to be near the textile machinery industry in order to have machinery repairs completed quickly and to take advantage of new designs as soon as possible. Improvements in spinning and weaving machinery were continuous throughout the nineteenth century.

MIGRATION OF THE INDUSTRY.   During much of the nineteenth century New England held a dominant position in the production of cotton textiles. As late as 1890, about 80 percent of the nation's spindles were located in New England. Because the country's population was expanding, there was a continuously rising market for cotton fabrics. The number of spindles in New England rose from over 5,000,000 in 1850 to a peak of nearly 19,000,000 in 1925. During the nineteenth century the industry assumed an increasingly important role in the New England economy; many one-industry towns devoted entirely to textiles developed.

Although the South produced the raw cotton for the New England industry, the cotton textile industry was slow to develop there. The invention of the cotton gin and subsequent rise in the use of cotton made cotton growing so profitable that the incentive for manufacturing cotton cloth was largely lacking in the South. The larger rivers of the South were also more difficult to harness by the relatively simple technology of the early nineteenth century.

The economic plight of the South after the Civil War convinced southern business leaders that industry was needed to revitalize the region. The cotton textile industry was the first modern industry to develop in the South. However, as late as 1880 there were but 561,000 spindles in the area in constrast to 8,632,000 in the Northeast. Rapid growth occurred after 1890, and by 1925 the South surpassed New England in number of spindles. In 1927 the value of cotton goods from a single southern state for the first time exceeded the value of goods from the leading northern state. In that year North Carolina produced about 20 percent of the nation's cotton goods, followed by Massachusetts with 18.7 percent, South Carolina with nearly 15 percent, and Georgia with about 12 percent.

Because of the growing number of spindles in both New England and the South during the early part of the twentieth century, overcapacity became a problem in the cotton textile industry. But during the period of readjustment after 1925, the number of spindles in the nation declined; the decrease occurred almost wholly in New England. Although the number of spindles in the South has remained nearly stable at about 18,000,000 since 1925, the spindles in New England decreased from a maximum of 19,000,000 to fewer than 3,000,000. Plant relocation reached a peak in the 1930s, but relocation has continued to the present. Between 1923 and 1948, for example, 90 cotton textile mills that had employed 74,350 workers either liquidated or migrated from Massachusetts, removing an investment of $112,258,000. Census data on establishments in selected areas indicate that between 1880 and 1972 New England's proportion of cotton textile plants decreased by more than 50 percent, while there was a more than fivefold increase in the number of mills in the Piedmont states of North and South Carolina, Virginia, and Georgia.

REASONS FOR MIGRATION.   Many reasons have been given for the migration and growth of the cotton textile industry in the Piedmont. One of the most commonly cited factors is that the industry was seeking the source of its raw material. This explanation is only partially adequate. In the early development of the industry, the localization in the Piedmont was undoubtedly stimulated by accessibility to raw materials. One estimate is that in the 1890s the Carolina Piedmont mills had an advantage in the transport cost of cotton of between 0.8 and 1.5 cents per pound of coarse products over mills in eastern Massachusetts. An even more significant transportation cost advantage was provided in the 1890s when southern railways offered special low shipping rates on finished cotton products to offset their competitive disadvantage in terms of distance to the northern market. These two advantages were important as an impetus to the early industry, but they did not last long.

As the industry grew, local sources of cotton were no longer adequate. A large percentage of the raw cotton is now imported into the Piedmont from the Mississippi lowlands and from as far away as the Black Waxy Prairie of Texas. Also, as the industry grew the railroads reverted to the normally higher rates for finished goods, so southern plants actually operated at a cost disadvantage in shipping to northern markets. Transportation cost differentials on either raw materials or finished goods do not, therefore, provide a sound reason for the continued growth of cotton textiles in the Piedmont during recent decades.

The South probably had little advantage over the North in regard to the cost of constructing and equipping factories. Although materials and labor are somewhat less expensive in the South, thus reducing construction costs, the cost of equipping factories is greater because textile machinery must be secured from New England and Pennsylvania.

A more significant factor in explaining the growth of the southern textile industry was the sizable differential in labor cost between the northern and southern mills. Thus the migration to the Piedmont illustrates the application of the Weberian principle of an industry seeking the least cost area by substituting a low-cost labor location for an area of lower transport costs. In the textile industry wages and salaries represent the largest share of mill costs, averaging about 25 percent of the value of the product. Lesser costs include raw materials, depreciation, fuel and power, taxes, marketing, and administration.

Because of the high proportion of labor costs to value of products and, even more significantly, because these costs constitute the major share of the mill margin, the industry was labor oriented. The favorable differential in labor costs for the South has been and is the result of both lower wages and higher productivity of textile workers. In the 1920s it was estimated that the wages of textile workers in the Carolinas were 20–30 percent lower than in Massachusetts. Although the differential in wages has declined, it still persists. By 1945 the average hourly earnings in northern mills was still 14 percent higher than in Southern mills. In 1972 the average hourly earnings for cotton textile workers was $2.62 in North Carolina, as contrasted with $3.10 in Massachusetts.[11] Because New England specializes in combed-yarn products and southern plants are engaged primarily in cording yarn, general comparisons are difficult; but individual companies verify that differentials do persist. The differentials have narrowed because of the influence of unions, government legislation pertaining to minimum wages, and the general increase in the level of the southern economy.

Even if wages were comparable in the two regions, the South would still have an advantage because of higher productivity (5). The work assignments have traditionally been larger for southern textile workers. This is due partly to greater adaptability and in some instances to more modern machinery and plants, as well as a general lack of early union development. Southern workers are less conscious of delegated work loads and have been more amenable to scientifically designed job assignments. In addition the tempo of technological change has been more rapid in southern plants, and management has been more willing to experiment with new fabrics and techniques. A plan recently created by an engineering firm for a 450-loom mill indicated that 118 workers would be needed for such a plant in the South; but in New England 158 workers would be needed for the same plant.

The Piedmont possesses certain other economic advantages. The differential cost of fringe labor benefits results in a disadvantage of the textile industry in the North. With the growth of unionism, the passage of such liberal legislation as unemployment insurance and workmen's compensation benefits in the northern states, and the increase in fringe benefits (e.g., group insurance, paid holidays, and unemployment compensation), the costs to mill operators in the North are considerably greater than to those in the South. It has been estimated that the

[11]*Employment and Earnings, States and Areas 1939–72*, U.S. Department of Labor, Bureau of Labor Statistics, Bulletin No. 1370-10 (Washington, D.C.: U.S. Government Printing Office).

difference amounts to about one-half of the wage differential. The conclusion is evident that differences in labor costs have constituted the fundamental economic basis for the movement of cotton textiles from New England to the South.

Other factors have encouraged this migration. The agricultural economy of the Piedmont had an excess supply of labor that was readily attracted to the higher-paying textile industry. Power and fuel costs are substantially lower in the South than in New England, partly because of the climate and partly because of production and transportation costs. Southern plants need less fuel because of the milder climate, and transportation costs of fuel are less because major coalfields are nearby. Power costs are lower partly because of the dependence on hydroelectric power and partly because coal is cheaper for steam-generated electric power.

Also, the southern states have provided inducements to attract the textile industry. These include lower taxes, capital at low interest rates, and free plant sites and buildings. These factors individually would not have caused a shift in location; but collectively they are factors to be considered carefully when new locations were sought.

SELECTED REFERENCES

1. Alexandersson, Gunnar, "Changes in the Location Pattern of the Anglo-American Steel Industry: 1948–1959," *Economic Geography*, 37 (1961), 95–114.
2. Allen, Bruce T., "Vertical Integration and Market Foreclosure: The Case of Cement and Concrete," *Journal of Law and Economics*, 14 (April 1971), 251–275.
3. Allix, André and André Gibert, *Geographie des Textiles*, Paris: Librairie de Medicis, 1956.
4. Barber, C.L., "The Farm Machinery Industry: Reconciling the Interests of the Farmer, the Industry, and the General Public," *American Journal of Agricultural Economics*, 55 (December 1973), 820–828.
5. Barkin, Solomon, "The Effect of Increased Productivity on the Labor Force and Its Development in the United States Cotton Textile Industry," *Productivity Measurement Review*, November 1964, pp. 39–57.
6. Birdsall, Stephen S., "The Development and Cost of Location Stability: The Case of Oldsmobile in Lansing, Michigan," *Tijdschrift voor Economische en Sociale Geografie*, 62 (1971), 35–44.
7. Branyan, Robert L., "From Monopoly to Oligopoly: The Aluminum Industry after World War II," *Southwestern Social Science Quarterly*, 43 (December 1962), 242–252.
8. Capriola, R.L., "Insure Your Future by Modernizing," *Rock Products*, 69 (April 1966), 71–74.
9. Craig, P., "Location Factors in the Development of Steel Centers," *Papers and Proceedings of the Regional Science Association*, 3 (1957), 249–265.
10. Ebert, R.R., "Economies of Scale in the Automobile Industry: A Case Study of Studebaker," *Ohio State University Bulletin of Business Research*, 47 (July 1972), 4–8.
11. Fogel, R.W. and S.L. Engerman, "Model for the Explanation of Industrial Expansion During the Nineteenth Century; With an Application to the American Iron Industry," *Journal of Political Economy*, 77 (May 1969), 306–328.
12. Hale, Rosemary D., "Cement Mergers-Market Dispersion and Conglomerate Entry," *Marquette Business Review*, 15 (Summer 1973), 98–108.
13. Huffmire, Donald W., "Strategies of the United States Textile Industry in the Post World War II Period," *Journal of Business Policy*, 3 (Autumn 1972), 31–36.
14. Hurley, Neil P., "The Automobile Industry: A Study in Industrial Location," *Land Economics*, 35 (1959), 1–14.
15. Hutchinson, W.T., *Cyrus Hall McCormick: Seed-time, 1809–1856*. New York: Century, 1930.
16. Isard, Peter, "Employment Impacts of Textile Inputs and Investment: A Vintage-Capital Model," *American Economic Review*, 63 (June 1973), 402–416.
17. Isard, Walter and John H. Cumberland, "New England as a Possible Location for an Integrated Iron and Steel Works," *Economic Geography*, 26 (1950), 245–259.
18. Karim, Alexander, "Economics and Directional Growth in Aluminum Industry," *Proceedings of the Council of Economics of the American Institute of Mining, Metallurgical and Petroleum Engineers*, 3 (1968), 256–297.
19. Krutilla, J.V., "Aluminum—A Dilemma for Antitrust Aims?," *Southern Economic Journal*, 22 (October 1955), 164–177.
20. Lindsay, J.R., "Regional Advantage in Oil Refining," *Papers and Proceedings of the Regional Science Association*, 2 (1956), 304–317.
21. Livingston, S.M., "Economics of Refinery Location in the United States," *Proceedings Fifth World Petroleum Congress*. New York: Fifth World Petroleum Congress (1959), Vol. 9, 75–84.
22. Manners, Gerald, *The Geography of Energy*. London: Hutchinson University Library, 1964.
23. McCormick, C.H., *The Century of the Reaper*. Cambridge: Harvard University Press, 1931.
24. Miller, Roger LeRoy, "A Short-Term Econometric Model of Textile Industries," *American Economic Review*, 61 (1971), 279–289.
25. Nelson, Paul E., Jr., *The Farm Machinery and Equipment Industry: Its Changing Structure and*

Performance. Washington, D.C.: U.S. Department of Agriculture, Marketing Research Report No. 892, 1970.

26. Odell, Peter R., *An Economic Geography of Oil.* London: Bell, 1963.
27. Phillips, W.G., *The Agricultural Implement Industry of Canada.* Toronto: University of Toronto Press, 1958.
28. Pratten, C.F., "Economies of Scale for Machine Tool Production," *Journal of Industrial Economics,* 19 (1971), 148–165.
29. Scully, Gerald W., "The North-South Manufacturing Wage Differential, 1869–1919," *Journal of Regional Science,* 11 (1971), 235–252.
30. Selander, S.E., "Is Annual Style Change in the Automobile Industry an Unfair Method of Competition?," *Yale Law Journal,* 82 (March 1973), 691–710.

PERSPECTIVE

From a broad perspective, the material of this volume was designed to provide a fuller understanding of industrial location. In a stricter sense, the objective has been to provide fluoroscopic views of strategic aspects of the localization processes by focusing on some of the critical theories and empirical factors of localization. Because a primary goal has been to understand the localization of manufacturing in the real world, special attention has been given to the spatial analysis of selected industries.

The disciplines of economics and geography have made the greatest contributions to the study of industrial location. However, each has approached the subject from a different perspective. The contributions of the economists have been primarily in the area of location theory, but rarely have their studies achieved an understanding of the real world. By contrast, the contributions of the geographers have been made largely through empirical analysis of industrial location; but these efforts have essentially lacked a conceptual framework that would ultimately provide location principles. The disciplinary approaches of the economists and geographers have, at best, provided only partial answers to understanding the forces that influence industrial location. Thus a major question still must be resolved: How can theory and empirical analysis be reconciled in order to achieve a better understanding of the real world?

Some general areas of study that appear promising in advancing an understanding of industrial location are the following:

1. The continued evolution of industrial location theory with the ultimate goal of developing a comprehensive theory that structures reality.
2. The testing of theory through more penetrating empirical studies of the factors of localization.
3. The development of new and improved quantitative methods for the analysis of industrial location.
4. The evolution of the dynamics of spatial patterns as influenced by temporal changes.
5. The study of the interrelationship of manufacturing with other economic development in a region.

The understanding of the industrial location processes lies at the core of some of the major problems of modern society. Since the beginning of the Industrial Revolution a primary goal for the peoples of the world has been to create an industrial society. Although some areas have achieved this goal and may even be approaching the postindustrial era, other areas have barely evolved a pioneer industrial economy. The basic question thus remains: Why has it been so difficult to implement industrial societies in some countries after more than two centuries of modern industrial evolution? And there is a corollary to this question: Can a comprehensive theory explaining real-world spatial patterns be achieved?

INDEX